THE WINGS OF THE SUN

*Traditional Jewish Healing
in Theory and Practice*

THE WINGS OF THE SUN

Traditional Jewish Healing in Theory and Practice

by Avraham Greenbaum

BRESLOV RESEARCH INSTITUTE

Jerusalem / New York

Published by
Breslov Research Institute

Israel: POB 5370, Jerusalem, Israel
USA: POB 587, Monsey, NY 10952-0587

ISBN 0-930213-53-X

In loving memory of our dear father

ר' משה אברהם בן עקיבא ז"ל

Moshe Avraham Weber ז"ל

נלב"ע ו' באב תשנ"ד

.ת.נ.צ.ב.ה.

who taught us that joy is the key to
life, health and healing

David Paul and Paula Judith Weber

In memory of our beloved son

ר' שלום שמחה ז"ל בן לייב נ"י

Shalom Simchah (Steven) Steinlauf ז"ל

נלב"ע י"ג באייר תשנ"ה

.ת.נ.צ.ב.ה.

Uniquely attuned to the harmony of creation,
he spread peace and joy among all he knew
and fought valiantly to reveal
the healing power of Torah and Prayer

Leonard and Geraldine Steinlauf

Guide to this book

Guide to this book

This book is an exploration of the Jewish healing tradition as taught in the Bible, Talmud, Midrash and Kabbalah, and especially in the writings of the outstanding Chassidic luminary, Rebbe Nachman of Breslov (1772-1810).

The Title

The title of the book, "The Wings of the Sun," is based on the words of the biblical verse, "And for you who revere My Name a *sun* of righteousness will arise with healing in its *wings*" (Malachi 3:20).

Theory and Practice

The book is divided into two main parts. Part I, "The Wings of the Sun," focusses mainly on "theory," examining Jewish teachings on healing from all periods, especially those of Rebbe Nachman. Part II, "In Practice," offers practical guidance concerning general healthcare, common medical problems, serious illness and care of the sick. Any suggestions made in this book are not intended to replace medical treatment where this is necessary. Those with medical problems should consult their physicians about following the ideas in this book.

How to use this book

Those wishing to investigate the Jewish healing tradition in depth are advised to read through the book in sequence. Those seeking information on specific topics may use the Table of Contents (pp. xi-xiv), Index of Rebbe Nachman's teachings (pp. 453-55) or the General Index (pp.457-67) to locate the relevant sections of the book. Where the subject-matter in one part of the book relates to material discussed elsewhere, full cross-references are given in the text. Those facing illness or other medical problems may wish to turn directly to the relevant chapters in Part II, "In Practice" (pp. 305-411). These may be read without having first studied the earlier sections of the book.

Newcomers to Chassidut and Kabbalah

A wealth of original source material is presented in this work, but the text has as far as possible been written to be comprehensible with a minimum of background knowledge. Nevertheless, certain parts of the text may prove difficult for newcomers to Chassidut and Kabbalah. This applies especially to the kabbalistic teachings in Chapter 12, and to Rebbe Nachman's Torah discourses in Chapters 18-19. If you encounter passages that you find difficult or confusing, do not hesitate to skip them and move to material that is more comprehensible.

Structure of the Book:

Part I: The Wings of the Sun

Part I is divided into seven sections, most of which contain several chapters.

Section 1: Refa'einu — Heal Us! (Chapter 1, pp. 1-14): General introduction to the book.

Section 2: The Jewish Healing Tradition (Chapters 2-5, pp. 17- 47): Traces the Jewish healing tradition to its roots in the Bible and rabbinic teachings in the Talmud and Midrashim. The Rambam (Maimonides) and Baal Shem Tov are discussed as outstanding exemplars of two divergent trends in Jewish healing.

Section 3: Rebbe Nachman (Chapters 6-9, pp. 51- 102): As an introduction to the detailed examination of Rebbe Nachman's teachings in later sections of the book, this section provides an overview of the Rebbe's life and career, and surveys the development of his teachings on healing.

Section 4: Simchah for Health and Healing (Chapters 10-13, pp. 105-173): For Rebbe Nachman, *simchah*, joy, is the key to true healing. Discussions about the Torah conception of health (Chapter 10) and simchah (Chapter 11) are followed by depth examination of the kabbalistic understanding of the soul-body connection, leading into a presentation of kabbalistic teachings on the ten kinds of pulse patterns (Chapter 12). This provides the background for understanding Rebbe Nachman's teachings on joy and the Ten Kinds of Melody as the foundation of spiritual healing (Chapter 13).

Section 5: Rebbe Nachman and the Doctors (Chapters 14-17, pp. 177-230): Rebbe Nachman's opposition to doctors and medicine must be understood in the context of his teachings about the spiritual dimension of physical illness (Chapter 14) and also in relation to a trend of opposition to medicine among important rabbinic precursors, as well as against the backdrop of the state of medicine in Rebbe Nachman's time (Chapter 15). To what extent have Rebbe Nachman's chassidim followed his warnings against doctors (Chapter 16)? How does his spiritual approach to illness and healing apply to us today (Chapter 17)?

Section 6: Sound the Shofar: Rebbe Nachman's Pathway of Healing (Chapters 18-19, pp. 233-289): Rebbe Nachman gave fullest expression to the Torah tradition of healing in his Torah discourse, *"Sound the Shofar — Dominion"* (*Likutey Moharan* II, 1). The first English translation of this discourse is presented with full explanation and commentary (Chapter 18), followed by excerpts from another major discourse of Rebbe Nachman on faith and healing (Chapter 19).

Section 7: The Wings of the Sun (Chapter 20, pp. 293-301): With the coming of Mashiach, a new world order of miracles and wonders will come into being, and the "sun" of Godly revelation will shine forth, with healing in its wings.

Part II: In Practice

Chapter 21 (pp. 305-20): Keeping Healthy. Diet, exercise, relaxation and breathing. Preventive medicine. Spiritual aspects of healthcare.

Chapter 22 (pp. 321-49): Common problems. Minor upsets, infections, injuries, etc. Spiritual healing strategies. The spiritual meaning of symptoms. Getting out of a rut.

Chapter 23 (pp. 351-95): Facing serious illness. Medical treatment. Faith. Redemption of the soul. Overcoming fear. Coping with pain. Meditation and visualization. Prayer.

Chapter 24 (pp. 396-411): Visiting the sick. Care of the sick. How those involved in sick care (whether as doctors, nurses, etc. or in a private capacity) can enhance the healing process through a warm, open, personal connection with the sick. Children's illness.

Prayers (pp. 415-23)

A selection of prayers for healing composed by Rebbe Nachman's leading disciple, Reb Noson of Breslov.

Supplementary Readings (pp. 427-37)

Additional teachings of Rebbe Nachman on healing.

Sources (pp. 441-49)

Full bibliography of works cited in the text.

Indices (pp. 453-67)

Index of teachings discussed in the text (pp.453-5). General Index (pp.457-67).

Contents

Contents

Section 4: Simchah for Health and Healing

Section 5: Rebbe Nachman and the Doctors

Section 6: Sound the Shofar: Rebbe Nachman's Pathway of Healing

Section 7: The Wings of the Sun

Part II: In Practice

<h2 style="text-align:center">Prayers</h2>

<h2 style="text-align:center">Supplementary Readings</h2>

<h2 style="text-align:center">Sources and Further Reading</h2>

<h2 style="text-align:center">Indices</h2>

Thanks

Thanks

"I will exalt You, O God, for You have lifted me up and have not let my enemies rejoice over me. HaShem my God, I cried out to You and You healed me... Sing to God, His devoted ones, and give thanks to His holy Name" (Psalms 30:2-5).

I thank God for all His goodness and kindness to me, for bringing me close to the holy Tzaddik, Rebbe Nachman, and for the tremendous privilege of working on this book.

I had always been perplexed by Rebbe Nachman's uncompromising opposition to doctors and medicine, but only a few years ago did I begin to notice how important a theme healing is in so many of his major Torah discourses. I started to realize that Rebbe Nachman was teaching a unique pathway of healing, and the more I studied it, the more convinced I became of its vital importance to this generation.

Throughout the world, medicine and healing are high on the social agenda. We face a terrible proliferation of old and new diseases at a time when the medical establishment is in a state of deep crisis. There has been a burgeoning of interest in all sorts of alternative technique and tradition. The medical marketplace is bustling with practitioners of every kind, and there is a flood of information about virtually every healing approach — except that of Judaism.

"I moan when I see every city built on its hilltop, while the City of God is degraded to the lowest pit of hell" (Selichot). It is true that there is extensive literature on Torah law relating to medical issues, bioethics and so on. But when it comes to Torah teachings about actual healing, hardly anything has been written.

Practical healing is precisely what Rebbe Nachman is talking about, even though his approach is radically different from that of conventional medicine, and indeed from that of almost any other known healing tradition. I believe Rebbe Nachman was expressing the authentic healing tradition of the Torah as taught in the book of Exodus (15:26) and championed by King Hezekiah (Berakhot 10b; Pesachim 56a).

I have had no formal training in either conventional medicine or any other branch of healing. Moreover, having begun to appreciate the awesome depth of Rebbe Nachman's teachings on healing, I realize how poorly qualified I am to discuss them. It would have been fairly easy to translate the relevant texts and present them by themselves with no suggestions as to how to interpret them or how to apply them in practice. This would have spared me from exposing my own ignorance and lack of experience. But I think it would have been unfair to the many who are searching for guidance in this area and need urgent answers to what are often life-and-death questions.

I can only hope that in spite of all its inadequacies, this book will provide some basic information and suggestions, and that it will spur scholars and experts greater than myself to investigate the Torah healing tradition with the care it deserves, in order to bring about its revival as a living pathway of health and healing, spiritual and physical.

I have discussed the ideas in this book with many people, including leading members of the Breslover Chassidic movement, especially Rabbi Yaakov Meir Shechter and Rabbi Michel Dorfman, for whose guidance I am most thankful. However, the responsibility for everything I have written, and of course for any errors, is mine alone.

I am deeply grateful to all the many friends who have helped in so many different ways to enable this work to come to fruition. First and foremost I must mention the late Moshe Avraham Weber ז"ל, who gave the lion's share of support to the project, and who was a living example of the power of simchah, inspiring all around him with the vitality and courage that he showed until the very end.

שילחטו"א, Michah Taubman gave the prompting needed to start this work in the first place, and he sustained it generously through some of its hardest moments. My heartfelt thanks to Trevor Bell, Ira & Marilyn Feldman, Nachman and Miriam Futterman, David & Betsy Heller, Eliahu Reiter, Raphael Rosen, Leonard and Geraldine Steinlauf and Avraham Shtaygrud. Not only have you all given substantial support and persistent encouragement; you have also touched me deeply with the tremendous personal kindness you have always shown. Special thanks to Herzel ben Moshe, Bezad Cohen and Joel Tartell. Your munificence made it possible to purchase the computer equipment that has made every stage of this complex work so much easier.

It would be impossible to mention by name all the many other friends who have had a part in this project. But I must single out Yaakov Abrams, Yitzchak Attias, Ezra Berg, Howard Epstein, Shraga Fisher, Seth Glass, Len & Robbie Goodman, Josh Goodman, Michael Gross, Reuven Halevy, Shlomo Lipsey, Meir Maimoni, Mrs. Miriam Meisel, Asher Morvay, Michael Perlman, Adam Perlman, Dr. Sarah Perry, Sholom Boruch Rothbart, Dovid Moshe Segal, Isaac Shamah,

Benzion Solomon, Larry Spiro, Gary Sternberg and Mervyn Waldman. Each of you has a unique share in this work — and a place in my heart. I must also record the special debt I owe to all who have participated in my seminars and workshops on healing, and whose contributions and questions have been of inestimable value in helping this book take shape.

Many thanks to Mrs. Sara Chava Mizrahi and Ms. Chaya Raphael for your superb editing and proofreading work. I am grateful to Feldheim Publishers for permission to quote from *The Way of God* by R. Moshe Chayim Luzatto, translated by R. Aryeh Kaplan.

Reb Chaim — Rabbi Chaim Kramer, Director of the Breslov Research Institute: Nothing I can say could do justice to the unfailing help and support you have always given. May you have the greatest *nachas* from the fruits of all your work in spreading Rebbe Nachman's Torah.

My dear parents: Words alone are simply inadequate to express what I owe you for the unstinting love and support you have shown throughout the years.

And finally my dear, precious wife: You have accompanied me on every step of the way through this work, bearing all the many growing pains with your unfaltering patience, understanding and support. In the merit of this work, may you and I together with our children, family and friends and all of Klal Yisrael enjoy good health and strength to serve God joyously with all our hearts, and may we quickly see complete redemption, the coming of Mashiach and the rebuilding of the Holy Temple in our lifetime. Amen.

A.G.

יום א' לחודש א'נ'י ל'דודי ו'דודי ל'י ה'תשנ"ה 1 Elul 5755

August 27, '95

PART I

THE WINGS OF THE SUN

SECTION 1

Refa'einu

Chapter 1

Refa'einu — "Heal Us!"

> "Heal us, and we will be healed."
>
> (from the blessing for healing, cf. Jeremiah 17:14)

The last hundred years have witnessed a revolution in medicine unparalleled in the history of the world. Smallpox and plague have been virtually eradicated the world over. Diphtheria, tetanus, polio and other scourges have been brought under control in countries with reasonable standards of hygiene and healthcare. Immunization prevents millions of childhood deaths a year. In advanced countries, infant mortality has dropped from about a quarter of live births to less than 1.3 percent, while life expectancy has risen from 45 to 75 years.

Techniques that were once unimaginable are now routine: organ transplants, video surgery, laser operations, molecular therapy, tissue regeneration.... Far from abating, the medical revolution continues to expand exponentially. As you read these words, intensive research in molecular biology, biotechnology and a host of other specialities makes it conceivable that within the foreseeable future, ninety percent of cancer could be prevented or cured, coronary disease might be largely eliminated, mysteries like Alzheimer's disease could be unravelled, and cures found for dozens of conditions, including allergies, migraines and other afflictions.

The medical establishment

Western medicine's many successes and the hope it offers have given it a highly prestigious place in contemporary society. Healthcare is a multibillion-dollar business, consuming double-digit percentages of the gross national products of some of the world's most advanced countries. The medical establishment consists of armies of doctors, specialists, nurses, paramedics, laboratory technicians, research workers, secretaries, maintenance and other personnel serving in public and private sector hospitals and clinics, special care centers, the pharmaceutical industry, the armed services, education, industry, business, international organizations, and so on.

It is taken for granted by governments, public agencies, the mass media and the overwhelming majority of the general public that the medical profession is the appropriate authority in all issues concerning the health of the human body. Many also assume that M.D.'s are the proper experts when it comes to the health of the mind. With their white vestments, scientific rites and terminological arcana, the doctors are like a priestly hierarchy, seemingly holding the keys to health, freedom from pain and illness, and the bestowal of life itself. Many people would give more weight to the pronouncements of a medical authority on matters of life and death than they would to those of a tzaddik. Gruelling, costly medical treatments offering a slender hope of ameliorating a person's earthly existence are often tolerated with greater willingness than the mild efforts involved in carrying out simple religious precepts which carry with them a guarantee of infinite rewards.

The strength of our belief in the efficacy of medicine is hardly surprising. In some shape or form, medical care and guidance are ever-present factors in our lives from before birth until the day we die. After months of prenatal monitoring, the newborn baby comes straight from the womb into the hands of a reception party of nurses and doctors. Growing children soon learn that ointments and bandaids make little sores, cuts and grazes disappear, while sickly-sweet syrups banish colds and coughs. Doctors and nurses are familiar figures in the worlds of most children, among whom even the healthiest receive medical and dental treatment of some kind quite regularly.

Even when everyone at home is feeling fine, health awareness penetrates our daily lives to a degree we are hardly conscious of. Every food packet we glance at has exhaustive details about its carbohydrate, fat, cholesterol, protein, vitamin and mineral content. We are bombarded on all sides with information about the healthfulness or otherwise of exercise, cigarette smoking, alcohol, sunbathing, insect repellants, computer screens and thousands of other things. Everyone has his own stock of medical wisdom culled from upbringing, general education, TV, magazines, home health guides and the like. Every household has a cache of assorted pills, ointments, lotions, sprays, etc., etc.

And if anything goes seriously wrong, God forbid, most people's immediate thought is to call a doctor. Urgently. Yes, we pray, we recite psalms, give charity, make resolutions. But is it our religious faith and trust that give us confidence that everything will turn out for the best? Or is it the arrival of medical assistance, the injections and medicines, and the look on the doctor's face that says the situation is under control?

Rebbe Nachman of Breslov

It comes as something of a shock to find that Rebbe Nachman of Breslov (1772-1810), the outstanding sage, mystic and chassidic teacher, "denounced doctors and medicine in the strongest terms. He advised anyone who cares about his life and that of his family to avoid them, even in the case of serious illness. One should depend only on God.... The art of healing involves many very fine intricacies, but they are hidden from the doctors, who are not able to take account of all the subtle details without error.... It takes only the slightest mistake by the doctor to destroy a person's life and actually kill him, as we see so often, for many people die because of doctors.... The majority of doctors are agents of the Angel of Death" (*Rabbi Nachman's Wisdom* #50).

Are these the words of the same Rebbe Nachman who told delightful stories and taught us to be happy always, to look at the better side of things and judge everyone positively? Calling the doctors murderers may be good for a laugh — haven't we all heard stories about arrogant doctors and medical incompetence, faulty diagnoses and people who received altogether the wrong treatment? Castigating the doctors could be a way of venting our resentment at feeling so dependent upon them.

But when it comes to the crunch? What would we do in a real crisis, God forbid? A child is having convulsions.... An accident victim is bleeding heavily.... Someone is experiencing severe chest pain and is vomiting and sweating profusely.... Haven't we seen miracles — cases of people who might not be alive and well today were it not for the intensive care, the miraculous operations, the extraordinary drugs, the new technologies? So we explain Rebbe Nachman away: "He was talking about *then*, the medicine of two hundred years ago, before all the amazing scientific discoveries of the modern age." Or we dismiss his ideas: "Faith healing? Surely all contemporary rabbinic authorities would agree that 'you are not permitted to rely on miracles' (*Pesachim* 64b). 'The Torah gave the doctor license to heal' (*Berakhot* 60a). You *must* go to the doctor!"

And in many cases the answer would be "Yes!" Rebbe Nachman himself insisted that people have their children vaccinated against smallpox (*Avanehah Barzel* p.31 #34). Vaccination was then a new medical technique but one that had proved itself. The same could be said to apply to countless routine medical procedures today. Rebbe Nachman also understood that many people would feel their faith was not strong enough to carry them through a serious illness. He said, "You know I don't hold by doctors. But if you're going to go, make sure you choose the very best!" (*Siach Sarfey Kodesh* I:8).

Illness can be very frightening, and some people avoid consulting a doctor — even when they have serious symptoms — for fear of what they might hear. *No one should use any of the comments regarding doctors and medicine in this book as an excuse not to see a physician when necessary or to terminate medical treatment.* Those who have questions or doubts about medical advice they have received or treatment they are undergoing should ask the opinion of other experts in the field. Religious or spiritual matters should be discussed with a competent rabbi. It must be remembered that Rebbe Nachman was addressing chassidim who devoted their lives to following his spiritual path. It would be extremely dangerous to use Rebbe Nachman's comments on doctors as a rationalization for avoiding necessary medical treatment while failing to carry out his other teachings.

But the subject does not end here. Rebbe Nachman's statements about doctors are only one facet of an entire corpus of teachings on healing that are unique in the whole of rabbinic literature. Throughout the ages many leading rabbis have been well versed in medicine. Some, notably the RaMBaM (Rabbi Moshe ben Maimon, Maimonides, 1135-1204), wrote extensively on conventional medicine. The legal and ethical implications of various aspects of medical practice have exercised rabbinic authorities throughout the generations. With the new horizons opened up by modern medical science there has recently been a great proliferation of such literature. Yet in all of it, the primary focus is on the treatment of physical disorders by physical means. Practically nowhere do we find a detailed discussion of the spiritual dimensions of health, illness and healing except in the writings of Rebbe Nachman.

> "All the illness that afflicts people comes only because of a lack of joy... And joy is the great healer" (*Likutey Moharan* II, 24).

References to healing are to be found throughout Rabbi Nachman's teachings. But in the last three years of his life, when he himself was seriously ill with tuberculosis, healing became a central theme in every one of his major discourses. Rebbe Nachman was expressing and explaining a distinctive Jewish approach to health and healing that has its roots in the Bible and is implicit in countless passages in the Talmud, Midrash, Kabbalah and

Chassidut, as well as in innumerable stories and anecdotes from all periods and all parts of the Jewish world.

Rebbe Nachman distilled the wisdom of thousands of years and turned it into a unique healing pathway. The primary focus is not the body but the soul. The gauge of spiritual health is joy. Rebbe Nachman's teachings on healing are summed up in one statement: "All the illness that afflicts people comes only because of a lack of joy.... And joy is the great healer" (*Likutey Moharan* II, 24).

Paradigms of healing

It takes considerable courage and honesty to open ourselves to unfamiliar ways of thinking. People are usually strongly committed to ideas imbibed from their social, cultural and educational milieu. Healing can be a matter of life and death. It is a subject that may be surrounded by stronger barrages of emotion than we perhaps realize. To those brought up to think of healthcare exclusively in terms of white coats, masked faces, blood tests, dials, meters, intravenous drips and the like, some of the basic concepts of Rebbe Nachman's healing pathway — faith, joy, repentance, confession, charity, song and dance — may seem irrelevant, even disturbing. To grasp the true meaning of an unfamiliar paradigm we must have the humility to look beyond our own inbred ways of viewing things and explore its concepts in their authentic breadth and depth.

The conventional medical paradigm of healing concentrates almost exclusively on the human body and its ailments. Until quite recently the majority of orthodox practitioners paid little or no attention to the owner of the body — the *person*, his or her mental and spiritual life, outlook, feelings and emotions, moral choices, lifestyle and activities — any more than a car mechanic would show other than polite interest in the lives of the owners of the cars he repairs. The body is seen as a machine. Complex, amazing, awesome, yes; but still a machine that is essentially the sum of its components and can be dissected, tested, analyzed, and adjusted to perform better.

When something goes wrong, the standard medical approach is first to probe the patient's physical symptoms in an effort to identify pathological changes and their causes. Diagnosis is followed by treatment with an ever more sophisticated array of drugs, surgery and other techniques. Many of these techniques certainly utilize the body's own amazing self-regulating mechanisms, but the tendency is for doctors not to rely on these but to intervene, sometimes quite aggressively, to reverse or stabilize the problem. If this can be done before some sort of permanent and irreparable damage has been done, the patient is said to be "cured." Through all this the patient remains for the most part passive. This is actually implicit in the very word "patient," which means someone to whom something happens. First the illness "happens" to the patient, and then the treatment. In the eyes of many doctors the patient's chief responsibility is to show up for examinations and take the medicine.

Rebbe Nachman is asking us to explore a totally different perspective on health, sickness and healing. What is happening in a person's body is seen as an inseparable part of his or her life as a whole. Physical symptoms are viewed not only as problems in and of themselves. They are also seen as a *language* that expresses what may be a far deeper disorder, one that pervades the outlook, behavior, personality and indeed the very soul of the individual. In the words of Rabbi Dov Ber, the Mezritcher Magid (1704-1772): "A small hole in the body — a big hole in the soul."

What is illness? Suppose someone is feeling generally weak, tired, strained, run down, faint and disoriented. Vitamins, tonics, a vacation haven't helped. He or she goes to a doctor (conventional or alternative). The doctor asks various questions and carries out tests. If the doctor arrives at a plausible diagnosis — hypoglycemia, post-viral fatigue syndrome, diabetes, cardiovascular disease or whatever else — the suffering individual usually accepts that this *is* the problem and starts with the recommended physical strategies for dealing with it.

But *is* this the problem? Is it the *whole* problem? Is it the *root* of the problem? Perhaps the physical symptoms are one important dimension of a far deeper, existential malady. Here is a *soul* that is tired. Why? What is it in this person's life situation, current environment, past history, conscious and unconscious thoughts and attitudes, habits and activities that may be blocking true fulfilment and happiness? A doctor may suggest that the fatigue is caused by systematic indulgence in the wrong foods. But can this be isolated from deep frustration, depression and other factors that may be driving this person to overindulge? Without confronting these problems, will any of the physical strategies bring about more than a superficial change?

The same point could be made about a multitude of other physical complaints. Is someone's heart condition or cancerous growth his essential problem? Or is it just the tip of the iceberg of a far more extensive life crisis? Medical authorities in many different times and cultures have pointed to the destructive influence of mental states such as melancholy, grief and despair on one's physical health. But such factors are hard to measure scientifically and have been largely neglected by mainstream modern medicine. Yet numerous studies conducted in recent years have demonstrated the influence of stress, inner conflict, frustration, depression and so on in a wide variety of different conditions.

Is it valid to make a hard and fast distinction between physical illness and maladies of the soul? Adherents to the conventional western medical paradigm might agree that negative traits and negative outlook could be described as "unhealthy," "diseased" and so on. Yet they would consider this use of such terms as metaphorical and secondary to their "primary" use to describe tangible physical conditions. But just because frustration, bitterness, anger and other traits are hard to quantify, does that make them any less real? Where emotional and spiritual problems are intimately bound up with physical disease, does it make any sense to treat the latter without guiding the patient to resolve the former?

And where emotional and spiritual problems have so far caused no discernible bodily ailment, does that make them any less pathological than heavy smoking, drinking, drug abuse and the like? Is there any wisdom in waiting for physical damage to set in before seeking to heal them? And what about the other kinds of secret pain so many of us hide behind our public facades?

Prevention and health

The Rambam wrote: "The ability of a physician to prevent illness is a greater proof of his skill than his ability to cure someone who is already ill" (*Yalkut Lekach Tov, Beshalach*). Rebbe Nachman's pathway of healing is first and foremost one of keeping healthy — "preventive medicine" — because true healing must begin long before physical illness strikes. Guarding our

> "The ability of a physician to prevent illness is a greater proof of his skill than his ability to cure someone who is already ill" (Rambam, *Yalkut Lekach Tov, Beshalach*).

health is a *mitzvah*, a positive duty. "Take care of yourself, and guard your soul diligently" (Deuteronomy 4:9). Good health is vital to the fulfilment of our mission in this world: obviously, physical weakness interferes with our ability to pray, study, perform acts of kindness and carry out the other mitzvot.

Guarding our health clearly involves taking the utmost care of our bodies: observing the rules of hygiene, eating wisely and moderately, exercising, not smoking, avoiding substance abuse and other hazards. But it is no accident that when the Torah asks us to take care of our health, the expression it uses is: "Guard your *soul* diligently." Spiritual healthcare is not merely an extra. It is the very foundation of sound physical health. Taking care of physical health frequently involves sacrificing immediate gratification for the sake of long-term benefit. What incentive is there to forgo the tempting pleasures of the moment unless one is firm in the belief that life in this world has a higher purpose? Factors like a sense of mission, courage in the face of obstacles and general optimism are fundamental to good health. "A joyous heart is good medicine, whereas a broken spirit dries the bones" (Proverbs 17:22).

Today preventive medicine is high on the public agenda. The sheer cost of conventional medical care has turned it into a crushing burden in even the wealthiest countries. Diagnostic testing, medications, operations and hospital care have all become so expensive that not only the poor but even the more prosperous are often simply unable to afford them. Health insurance costs have soared. People who have paid insurance all their lives discover that once they become sick they may not be covered anymore. The luxury of state-of-the art medical treatment may be affordable by the very wealthy, but for innumerable health-conscious ordinary citizens it is preferable to do everything possible to avoid the need for medical treatment through taking the best possible care of their health. The Jewish spiritual pathways of faith, joy, prayer, meditation, charity, love and kindness may yet prove to be among the world's most valuable assets in attaining the ultimate goal of freedom from illness.

Sickness and healing

Disease can be a terrible thing. But viewing it as a purely physical phenomenon makes it even more terrible, turning it into a meaningless torment, providing no comfort to those who are suffering. Medical science can often (though not always) trace the physical causes of disease. But it is silent on the deeper question of why a certain illness becomes a part of someone's destiny at a particular point in his or her life. To say that the individual had a genetic predisposition still does not answer the question of "why."

Why should a baby be born deformed? Why should a little child or a young man or woman in the prime of life suddenly be struck down with a crippling disease? The faith that God guides and controls every detail of the entire universe with unfathomable love does not in itself provide snug answers. "There is no wisdom, understanding or counsel relative to God" (Proverbs 21:30). However, faith does give us a pointer to the way in which we can eventually come to terms with suffering. Ultimately God does only good. The faith that every situation must contain good *somewhere* is what actually helps us search until we find it.

While accepting what we cannot alter, we must also take responsibility for that which we have the power to change. Conventional medicine tends to encourage patients to rely on the doctor to repair the physical damage to their bodies — "Cure me!" — allowing them to avoid confronting deep-seated problems of lifestyle and personality that may lie at the root of their illnesses. But merely attacking manifest physical symptoms can be dangerously counterproductive. The underlying disorder remains untreated and may give rise to a far more destructive disturbance later on.

The Torah view is that injury and illness may often be sent to prompt us to look carefully at ourselves and our lives. They can also help us come to a greater appreciation of the preciousness of life and health. How have we been using our bodies? What have we been doing with our lives? What is our true mission in this world? Deepening our self-understanding is itself a vital part of the healing process. This is what helps us take control of our lives and let go of unnecessary baggage — bad habits, outworn complexes, anger, bitterness and the like. It becomes easier to repair relationships with spouses, parents, children, friends and enemies, with ourselves and with God.

"Turning to God" does not mean simply replacing one kind of fatalism with another, trading belief in the ultimacy of blind physical forces for intellectual acceptance of some vague, unknowable, implacable spiritual force "out there." Cultivating faith in God involves a profound shift on every level of our being. We must learn to perceive ourselves and the world in fresh ways. We must redirect our faculties of thought and emotion, explore our ability to make decisions, embark on unfamiliar paths of action. The key to bringing Godly power into our actual lives is prayer. This means much more than simply repeating ancient formulae and hoping for God's blessings in return. We must learn a new way of using words — our *own* words — to define the blessing we seek and to channel it into the real situations we face within ourselves and in the world around us.

New directions in medicine

Today many mainstream medical practitioners are becoming increasingly open to alternative paradigms of healing. Over the last two decades an increasing body of scientific evidence and clinical experience has begun to convince not only psychologists but numerous doctors as well of the importance of emotional and spiritual factors in physical healing. The very success of western medicine in combatting infectious diseases has resulted in their replacement by heart disease, cancer and other degenerative diseases as the chief causes of death in our society. It is certainly true that lives are saved every day through sophisticated coronary care, advanced methods of cancer treatment and other medical techniques. These can help patients survive immediate crises. But more and more mainstream practitioners now realize that the long-term health of such patients depends on radical changes in lifestyle, general outlook and attitudes.

There are now thousands of documented cases of patients who have recovered "spontaneously" from extremely serious conditions, to the complete amazement of their doctors. These are miracles, though not necessarily in the sense that the patients involved suddenly stood up as if raised from the dead. Many of them put a lot of hard work — spiritual work — into their recovery. They understood their illness as a signal to take a hard look at themselves and to institute far-reaching changes in their fundamental beliefs, their view of themselves and their intimate human relationships.

More and more medical research is now focussing on the complex and subtle relationship between the mind, both conscious and unconscious, the nervous, endocrine and immune systems, and the functioning of the rest of the body. Major hospitals have established clinics for people with problems ranging from headaches, high blood pressure and back pain to heart disease, cancer and AIDS, teaching relaxation, meditation, visualization and other techniques that harness the powers of the mind to control pain and promote healing. Increasing numbers of patients are supplementing their medical treatment with psychotherapy, music therapy, creative writing and the like in order to grapple with the psychological and spiritual dimensions of their illnesses.

There is also growing awareness that these approaches may be of major importance in relieving the suffering of some of the many patients whom conventional medicine is unable to help because their complaints simply defy all diagnostic tests. The doctors can find nothing definite — though this does not make the patients' fatigue, incapacitating headaches, visual dysfunctioning, digestive troubles, chronic pain and other symptoms any less real. Many doctors are inclined to dismiss these sufferers as neurotics or malingerers. Some drift from one specialist to the next, while countless others despair of ever improving and are ready prey for downward spirals of anxiety, depression and despair.

Those in this category are by no means an insignificant minority. Studies of the patients treated by group medical practices in one major European city showed that between *thirty and forty percent* were classified as suffering from "neurotic" complaints! Another fifty percent of the patients were classified as chronically ill. That leaves a mere ten to twenty percent of patients whose illnesses responded to the standard medical procedures! (Arthur Jores, *Medicine in the Crisis of our Time* p.54).

The limited effectiveness of conventional medicine is even more striking when we remember that by no means do all sick people become "patients." Studies indicate that between a half and two-thirds of physical complaints do not result in a visit to a doctor's office — and these complaints are not necessarily trivial in nature, as proven by the statistics on untreated illnesses and the early stages of chronic diseases. Surveys of job holders — people in the prime of life — have revealed that *fewer than ten percent* of respondents consider themselves really healthy, whereas about sixty percent feel themselves to be in need of some kind of medical attention (*ibid.*).

That such enormous numbers of people in the prime of their lives feel less than healthy is a sad comment on healthcare in a society where the majority suffer no lack of food, housing and other amenities. Is the root of the problem purely physical or does it have more to do with the emptiness and lack of meaning in so many lives? Is it not tragic that some people have to wait until they become seriously ill before they realize the central role of faith and joy in good health and healing, while countless others never discover it at all? What effect would it have on the health and well-being of millions and millions the world over if not only diet and exercise, but also the basics of faith, prayer, meditation, charity, kindness, love and joy were taught as a matter of course in schools, colleges and the mass media, not to mention medical schools, hospitals, clinics and doctors' offices?

Where do we put our faith?

Rebbe Nachman's warning of two centuries ago against using doctors must be considered with the utmost caution. There is no comparison between the medicine of 1800 and that of today. No doubt, in fifty to a hundred years time posterity will view some of our most sophisticated contemporary medical techniques as being just as primitive as we think many of the methods used fifty years ago to have been. Even so, it would be absurd and irresponsible to reject contemporary medicine out of hand and throw away skills and expertise that save lives every day and can alleviate so much human misery.

For us, the main significance of Rebbe Nachman's critique of doctors is as a challenge, to force us to examine some of our assumptions about healing and how to go about it, even as we continue to take advantage of what medicine has to offer. The sleek, super-sophisticated world of modern medicine often seems to work so well that we can easily fall into thinking it's the doctors who give life and heal the body — until a grave-looking doctor eventually comes along and says solemnly, "I'm sorry but it's terminal and there's nothing we can do. You'd better pray."

Rebbe Nachman said, "What people do at the end I want you to do at the beginning!" (*Siach Sarfey Kodesh* I:293). People resort to passionate prayers when they see that all other ways of saving the situation have failed. But Rebbe Nachman wanted us to turn to God for help at the very beginning of the trouble.

The main target of Rebbe Nachman's criticisms is not so much the doctors as it is the patients who put all their faith in them. "People put all the emphasis on the *means* through which healing comes about — the medicine — as if without medicine God does not have the power to heal. That is not so. The Holy One, blessed be He, is the Cause of all causes. There is no absolute need for any one particular means. *Even while resorting to a given means of trying to bring something about, we must believe only in God, and not put our faith in the means*" (*Likutey Moharan* I, 62).

Even as we wonder at the miraculous skills and expertise of the doctors, let us thank God for opening up the gates of knowledge and giving of His wisdom to human beings. As we marvel at the amazing powers of modern drugs, let us bless God for creating the stupendous variety of plants, trees and other healing substances. Let us never forget that even as the drugs and other treatments work on the body, it is the body's own phenomenal self-regulating mechanisms that actually make it heal. It is not the suture that causes body tissues to knit together but the genius God has planted within the cells themselves.

What could be more amazing than that an instrument as subtle and intricate as the body, even when abused, battered, damaged and malfunctioning, can repair itself and often become as good as new? And what could be more wonderful than the normal functioning of the body — growth, renewal, respiration, circulation, digestion, excretion of wastes, vision, hearing, smell, taste, touch, movement, coordination, etc. etc. — every second, every minute, every day for seventy, eighty, a hundred and more years! It is for this that we bless God every day: "Blessed are You, HaShem, our God, King of the universe, Who designed man with wisdom and created within him many openings and many cavities. It is revealed and known before Your Throne of Glory that if just one of them were to be ruptured or one of them blocked it would be impossible to survive and stand before You even for a brief moment. Blessed are You, HaShem, Who heals all flesh and acts wondrously" (blessing after relieving oneself).

Refu'ah Shelemah

Healing is more than a matter of curing people's bodies. It is about healing their lives. The essential sickness, whether of an individual, a social group, a nation or indeed the whole world, is to be turned away from God and His wisdom, unfulfilled in our purpose in this world, bitter and unhappy. All other illnesses, social, psychological and physical, are ultimately rooted in this. If we would only take this essential sickness seriously and make at least as much effort to cure it as we do to try to solve our other problems, we could attain true happiness.

"Heal us, and we will be healed, save us and we will be saved, for You are our praise. Send complete healing for all our ailments, for You are God, King, the faithful and compassionate Healer. Blessed are You, HaShem, Who heals the sick of His people Israel" (from the blessing for healing, cf. Jeremiah 17:14).

Faith in God can bring healing even to those for whom medicine offers no hope because it cannot cure their bodies: the disabled, the chronically sick and those who are preparing to leave this world. The body may not be able to be healed, but the soul can always be healed. The worst suffering can be sweetened when we have faith that it comes from the loving God. Terminal illness and death have meaning when they are seen as the gateway to the higher life.

Refa'einu veneirafei. Heal us and we will be healed. Heal us — for if *You* heal us, we will certainly be healed. The Hebrew root for healing, רפא (*RePh'A*) is a rearrangement of the letters of the word פרא (*PeR'E*), meaning "wild." So long as there is no healing, the elements within one are wild and out of joint. The body, the mind, the soul, the very world are "desolate and formless" — like the earth before the revelation of God's light (Genesis 1:2). It is the light of spirituality that brings order to the elements. True healing, רפואה (*RePhu'Ah*), turns פרא (*PeR'E*), wildness, into פאר (*Pe'ER*), which means beauty and harmony, the true beauty of Godly revelation.

The traditional Jewish prayer for healing asks for complete, perfect healing: רפואה שלמה רפואת הנפש ורפואת הגוף (*refu'ah shelemah, refu'at hanefesh urefu'at ha-guf*). Complete healing: healing of the soul and healing of the body. First healing of the soul, then healing of the body. Perfect healing.

"And for you who revere My Name a sun of righteousness will arise with healing in its wings" (Malachi 3:20). At the end of the very last prophecy given to the Jewish People, the prophet Malachi reveals that in time to come a new light will shine into the world: not a physical light, but the spiritual light of *tzedakah*, the true justice, charity and love that come to right the wrongs that cause strife and disorder in countries, nations, communities, families, in individual souls and physical bodies.

Let us search for God through our studies, prayers and meditation, our mitzvot and our acts of love and kindness. Let us draw down this healing light. "Heal us and we will be healed; save us and we will be saved, for You are our praise!"

SECTION 2

The Jewish Healing Tradition

Chapter 2

Hezekiah and the Book of Remedies

$\mathbf{A}$t one of the most critical junctures of Jewish history, with Assyrian King Sennacherib's vast army closing in on Jerusalem, Hezekiah King of Judah suddenly fell mortally ill. His entire body was covered with horrible sores. The prophet Isaiah came to him and said, "Thus says the Lord: Set your house in order, for you will die and not live" (Isaiah 38:1; Kings II, 20:1).

With God's prophet telling him to make his will and prepare to die, a lesser man might have given up the fight. Not Hezekiah. He had a tradition from his ancestor, King David: "Even if a sharp sword is pressing on your neck, don't despair of pleading for God's mercy" (Berakhot 10a). Hezekiah turned his face to the wall and prayed: "Remember now, O God, I beseech You, how I've walked before You in truth and with a whole heart: I did what is good in Your eyes." Hezekiah wept bitterly.

Hezekiah's turning his face to the wall was more than a physical movement. It was a movement inwards.

> "Even if a sharp sword is pressing on your neck, don't despair of pleading for God's mercy" (Berakhot 10a).

The "face" he turned was his inner awareness. He focussed his mind on the walls of his heart in order to break through his inner armory, the rationalizations, the accumulated insensitivity (Rabbi Nachman's Wisdom #39). The sick Hezekiah turned to God with all his heart, pleading for life. That didn't mean mere chest-thumping. Hezekiah searched within himself not so much for his guilt as for his merit. Just as he had walked before God and done good in the past, so now he begged to be allowed to continue. And his prayer found favor.

God told Isaiah to return to Hezekiah and inform him that not only would he be healed, but he would have another fifteen years added to his life. Isaiah ordered figs to be laid on Hezekiah's boils — a miracle within a miracle, because normally figs cause raw flesh to become putrid — and the king was healed. On the third day Hezekiah went up to the Holy Temple, while an angel passed through the Assyrian camp, killing one hundred and eighty-five thousand men. Sennacherib retreated to Nineveh, and was murdered by his own sons as he worshipped in his idolatrous temple.

The Book of Remedies

The Midrash throws light on the meaning of Hezekiah's illness. "Rabbi Levi said: Hezekiah mused, 'It isn't good for people to enjoy constant good health until the day they die. This way they'll never think of repentance. But if they fall sick and then recover, they'll come to repent their sins.' God said to Hezekiah, 'This is a good idea. And I'll start with *you!*'" (*Bereshit Rabbah* 65:9). Hezekiah saw that illness can have a positive side if it prompts us to examine ourselves. What have we been doing with our lives? How have we been using our bodies? What is our true purpose in this world? How can we attain it?

As Hezekiah lay in mortal danger, he asked the prophet where he had gone astray. Isaiah explained that he had failed to carry out the first commandment of the Torah, to be fruitful and multiply. Hezekiah said this was because he had seen with holy spirit that his offspring would be unworthy. But Isaiah said this was not his business: he had an obligation to have children. Hezekiah understood his mistake and undertook to marry and have children.

That sickness is a prompt from God to examine ourselves was a lesson Hezekiah, spiritual leader of his people, had long wanted to teach. The point is brought out in a rabbinic comment on Hezekiah's prayer as he lay sick: "I did what is good in Your eyes." Enumerating Hezekiah's achievements during his reign, the Rabbis said he was alluding in his prayer to two major innovations: he "joined Redemption to Prayer, and he put away the Book of Remedies" (*Berakhot* 10b; *Pesachim* 56a).

"Joining Redemption to Prayer" literally refers to Hezekiah's institution of the rule that during the daily prayer services no interruption may be made between recital of the blessing of Redemption that follows the *Shema* and commencement of the silent *Amidah* prayer. But what about the Book of Remedies? What was it, and why did Hezekiah ban it?

Extant clay tablets and papyruses indicate that the ancient civilizations of Mesopotamia and Egypt possessed a vast body of medical knowledge. Hundreds of therapeutic plant, mineral and animal substances were in use, as well as a wide variety of surgical and other treatments. It would be easy to speculate that the Book of Remedies included medical techniques borrowed from other cultures with which the Jews had contact. On the other hand, Rabbi Shimon bar Tzemach (the TaShBaTz, 1361-1444) states that the source of the book was supernatural: when Noah was in the ark during the flood, destructive spirits injured his sons, but an angel took one of them to the Garden of Eden and taught him all the remedies in the world (*Seder HaDorot* #1657). The Ramban (Rabbi Moshe ben Nachman of Girondi, 1194-1270) opines that the Book of Remedies was composed by Hezekiah's ancestor, King Solomon, whose God-given wisdom enabled him to deduce the healing properties of the various trees and plants from allusions buried in the Torah (Ramban, Commentary on the Torah, Introduction).

By any account, the Book of Remedies contained the accumulated healing wisdom of the Jewish People. Why then did Hezekiah put it away? It was not that the remedies were ineffective. On the contrary, in Hezekiah's view they were too effective! "When a person became sick, he would follow what was written in the book and be healed, and as a result people's hearts were not humbled before Heaven because of illness" (Rashi on *Pesachim* 56a). In the words of the Rambam (*ad loc.*): "They did not have trust that it is the Holy One, blessed be He, Who heals and binds up wounds."

Resort to the Book of Remedies turned sickness and healing into nothing but a mechanical process. Hezekiah was not seeking to withhold medical expertise because of some morbid desire to make people suffer their sicknesses to the full so as to somehow expiate their sins. Far from wanting them to be sick, Hezekiah saw that reliance on the Book of Remedies actually prevented people from being truly healed. While the remedies it contained might alleviate their bodily ailments, the very effectiveness of these physical cures allowed those who used them to avoid confronting the underlying spiritual flaws to which their bodily ailments pointed.

King Hezekiah wanted the people to understand that illness, terrible as it may be, is sent by God for a purpose. It is to prompt us to examine ourselves and our lives, to ask ourselves where we have strayed from our mission and what steps we must take in the future in order to attain genuine self-fulfilment. Concealing the Book of Remedies would encourage people to take their lives in hand and actualize their latent spiritual powers, playing an active role in their own healing process.

Putting away the Book of Remedies was thus intimately bound up with King Hezekiah's second innovation, "joining Redemption to Prayer." This was more than a technical rule of religious ritual. Hezekiah redeemed prayer itself! He taught people how to pray again. Prayer brings us to the ultimate connection with God. And precisely because prayer is so exalted, it is surrounded by endless obstacles. For many people it seems like a meaningless, tiresome burden: prayer is in exile. Hezekiah sought to tear down the barriers and reveal the new-old pathway of prayer in its true splendor. Prayer is not just a matter of asking God for favors. It is our way to channel divine power and blessing into ourselves, our lives and the whole world. Through prayer the soul rises to God and is healed, and in turn sends healing power into the body. By truly redeeming prayer Hezekiah was able to put away the Book of Remedies. There was simply no more need for it.

Chapter 3

Healing in the Bible

"I kill and I make alive, I wound and I heal, and there is no one that can deliver out of My hand."

(Deuteronomy 32:39)

King Hezekiah wanted to bring the Jewish People back to the original Jewish pathway of healing through faith and prayer, Torah and mitzvot. The Torah *is* the Jewish path of health and healing. Directly after the Exodus from Egypt, as the Jews made their way from the Red Sea to Mount Sinai to receive the Torah, God gave them the first injunctions of the Torah code. "And He said, If you will listen carefully to the voice of HaShem your God and do what is right in His eyes and give ear to His commandments and keep all His statutes, I will put none of the diseases upon you that I have put on the Egyptians, for I, God, am your Healer" (Exodus 15:26).

The Egyptians, among whom the Jews had been exiled for over two hundred years, were afflicted with all kinds of ailments. Papyruses, paintings, inscriptions and mummies provide evidence of plague, smallpox, poliomyelitis, arteriosclerosis, cancer, arthritis, cirrhosis of the liver, trachoma and many other diseases. Besides seeing all this, the Jews who left Egypt had also witnessed the plagues that came upon the Egyptians because of their refusal to submit to God, including lice, pestilence and boils.

God was now inviting the Children of Israel to follow a whole new way. They were to *listen carefully to God's voice*, His call to man to elevate himself spiritually, step by step, through carrying out the divine will at

> "When a human being prescribes a medicine it may be good for one person but harmful to another. Not so the Holy One, blessed be He. The Torah He gave to the Jewish People is an elixir of life for the whole body, as it is said (Proverbs 4:22): 'and health to all his flesh'" (*Eruvin* 54a).

every juncture in life. They were to *give ear to His commandments*, to observe them carefully and precisely, including even the statutes that seem to make no sense to the rational human mind. For the Torah code is a pathway of perfect harmony, protecting those who sincerely embrace it from illness: "I will put none of the diseases upon you." True, we are only human. We are often neglectful and easily lay ourselves open to sickness. Even so, "I, God, am your Healer" — "I am teaching you Torah and mitzvot in order that you may be saved from these diseases, like a doctor who says to a person, 'Don't eat such and such because it will make you ill.' And so it is written (Proverbs 3:8): '[The Torah] will be health to your navel and marrow to your bones'" (*Rashi* on Exodus 15:26).

In the words of one of the classic Bible commentators, "At first this pathway may be unfamiliar and its meaning and purpose unclear. It may be difficult and even bitter. But in the end it is very sweet. It is like the medicines given by an expert doctor. The patient may not understand their purpose or enjoy taking them. Some of them may be very bitter. But if the patient has faith in the doctor and follows his prescriptions faithfully, he will be cured and have his health restored" (*Kli Yakar* on Exodus 15:26).

The injunctions of the Torah are not, of course, mere health guidelines. The purpose of the dietary and other prohibitions goes far beyond protection from physical health hazards, though careful observance of the letter and spirit of the Torah code does in fact keep people from the avarice, immoderate physical gratification, sexual licentiousness and other abuses that are among the major causes of physical disease in our society. But the path of Torah and mitzvot leads beyond the physical world to the ultimate joy of genuine connection with God. It is this spiritual fulfilment that is the true guarantor of health, giving immunity against the physical excesses, the lack of balance, the loss of meaning and purpose, the depression and despair that lie at the root of so many diseases.

Avimelech's dream

For the idolators of antiquity, the vagaries of illness were thought to be in the hands of a pantheon of capricious deities who had to be placated in order for healing to come about. The human was merely their helpless plaything, just as he felt himself to be the passive victim of his own inner urges. But the Torah teaches us that we are free. We have the power to rise above the dictates of our physical natures and choose our own destiny. The Torah reveals a pathway of true fulfilment and happiness, and warns that straying from it will lead to pain and suffering in the end. It is up to us to decide which way we will go, and we must therefore take responsibility for the consequences of our actions. Illness is not a quirk of fate or chance, but rather a heaven-sent response to free human choices.

The moral dimension of physical illness is evident in the first direct reference to sickness and healing in the Bible (Genesis 20:1-18). Abraham and Sarah had come to sojourn in the land of the Philistines. Avimelech, king of the Philistines, instead of concerning himself with the welfare of this caravan of visitors, immediately enquired after Sarah. Informed that she was Abraham's sister, he seized her for himself, whereupon he and his entire court were smitten with a mysterious plague. All the orifices of their bodies were closed up, making it impossible for them to pass water, ease themselves, cohabit or even clear the mucus from their noses and wax from their ears (see Rashi on Genesis 20:9). Avimelech and his court were in mortal danger.

The key to the mystery was revealed to Avimelech that night, when God came to him in a dream. In the dream Avimelech protested that he had acted innocently and had not touched Sarah. But God sees into the heart and replied that this was because God Himself had held him back. Although Avimelech had not carried out a criminal act, his intentions had not been pure and innocent. Only by making amends would Avimelech and his court be healed. "And now return the man's wife. He is a prophet and will pray for you, and you will live" (Genesis 20:7). Avimelech restored Sarah to Abraham, who prayed to God, and Avimelech, his wife and maidservants were healed.

Consciously Avimelech rationalized his action by telling himself that, as far as he knew, Sarah was Abraham's sister. But the truth was that if he had known she was Abraham's wife he would have had no qualms about killing him. Abraham realized this, which was why he concealed the truth about his relationship to Sarah in the first place. Avimelech saw nothing wrong with kidnapping a visitor to his kingdom. This was because he let his lower urges blunt his moral sensibility, and instead of taking responsibility for his choice he covered it over with a specious excuse.

The plague was not just a punitive visitation. It was an invitation to Avimelech to be more honest and search beneath his conscious rationalizations. What he most needed to release himself and his court from illness was *insight*, and this was sent to him in a dream. In the ancient world sick people would often go to sleep in cult temples in the hope of being sent a dream that would reveal the cause of their illness. For the Torah, idolatrous cults are abhorrent, but the dream state is accepted as one that can open us to levels of understanding that are presently beyond us, as can prayer and meditation *(Sha'arey Kedushah 3; Derekh HaShem 3:1:6)*. Avimelech was forced to realize that he was in the wrong. Healing came not through physicians and medicines but by Avimelech's rectification of his own error and through Abraham's intercession with God.

Leprosy

Physicians were known figures in the world of the Bible: for example, Joseph called in Egyptian doctors — though not in this case to heal the living, but to embalm Jacob's body (Genesis 50:2). Yet significantly, there is no mention whatever of either doctors or medical treatment of any kind in connection with the illness that receives the most attention in the Bible: צרעת *(tzara'at)* (Leviticus chapters 13-15). This is usually translated as leprosy for want of a better word, but the detailed typology given in the Bible includes not only what we today would call leprosy but also a variety of other skin disorders seemingly akin to ulceration, eczema, psoriasis, impetigo, melanomas, carcinomas and alopecia (hair loss). The biblical section dealing with the laws of *tzara'at* is followed by a section on זיבה *(ziva)* — genital discharges in men, sometimes identified with gonorrhea, and abnormal genital bleeding in women — to which many of the same rules apply.

Someone displaying symptoms of *tzara'at* is called a מצורע *(metzora)*. The *metzora* had to be examined not by a doctor but by a priest. The priest's task was to give not a physical but what might be termed a "moral" diagnosis. What the priest had to determine was whether the visible symptoms put this affliction into the category of a "pure" or "impure" affliction according to strict criteria handed down in the written and oral law. If the priest declared it impure, the sufferer had to go into isolation outside the city until he was healed. He was effectively in a state of mourning. He was not allowed to shave, launder his clothes or greet anyone. He had to cover his head like a mourner and inform passers-by that he was ritually impure. A drop of his saliva or urine was enough to render others impure. Any food, clothes or utensils he touched became impure, as did a chair or a bed he sat or lay on. If he entered a house, everything inside it became impure.

Throughout the biblical passages on *tzara'at* not a word is said regarding how the *metzora* was actually healed. Before he could return to normal community life, he had to undergo an elaborate procedure of purification and atonement involving ritual sprinkling, shaving of the body, immersion, sacrifices and anointment with oil. But none of this had anything to do with healing. It all took place only *after* the affliction was healed.

The fact that any person or object the *metzora* touched became ritually impure must certainly have discouraged people from having any contact with him, which doubtless served to prevent contagion. But the main purpose of forcing the *metzora* into complete isolation and mourning was to encourage him to "turn his face to the wall," as did King Hezekiah, to contemplate the spiritual meaning of his affliction. And this itself was what caused him to heal.

The Bible teaches that although *tzara'at* is unquestionably a physical disease, it is sent because of a spiritual flaw in the *metzora*. The slanderer becomes a מצורע (*metzora*) because of being מוציא רע (*motzi ra*) — "bringing out evil" about others, while turning a blind eye to his own shortcomings, until the conspicuous blemish on his own body forces him to confront it. Moses' sister Miriam was a saint and a prophetess, but she was not spared when she spoke disparagingly of her brother (Numbers 12:1-16). As in the case of Avimelech, it was through prayer that Miriam's healing came about. Moses intervened and said, "God, I beseech You, heal her now" (Numbers 12:13). Another celebrated case of *tzara'at* was that of King Uziah, who usurped the priestly functions and sought to burn incense in the sanctuary. *Tzara'at* broke out on his forehead and afflicted him until his death (Chronicles II, 26:18-21). The Rabbis enumerate various other transgressions for which leprosy might be sent, including atheism, blasphemy, idolatry, murder, incest, immorality, robbery, perjury, jealousy and arrogance (*Erkhin* 16a and *Yalkut* #563).

Yet *tzara'at* should not be seen merely as a penalty for sin. When a human being inflicts punishment the intention is often simply to make the offending party "pay" for his offence. But God sends suffering "as a man chastens his son" (Deuteronomy 8:5), "out of hidden love" (Proverbs 27:5). God wants *us* to take the initiative and do the necessary work to cleanse ourselves of the traits and behavior that keep us from experiencing His goodness. Long before He inflicts actual suffering He sends us hints indicating that all is not in order and that we need to make changes. Sometimes we are given a sudden shock, or we lose something that is precious to us. If we are willing to stir ourselves and take responsibility, well and good. But to those who remain obtuse to such promptings, it may be necessary to send a sharper, clearer message.

A physical ailment is something the sufferer cannot deny or ignore. It is not merely a punishment. It is a call to the sufferer to use his God-given faculty of self-judgment and ask what has gone wrong in his life. How has he strayed from the path of spiritual striving, kindness, charity and love taught by the Torah? What traits or actions may have caused this visitation? What changes must he make in order to erase the offending traits and behavior and return to his soul-path?

King Asa and the doctors

Even the most spiritual of people are sometimes unwilling to hear the message. We must be prepared to scrutinize ourselves with the utmost honesty, even if the truth is painful, as when we see things that contradict our image of who we like to think we are.

Ten generations before Hezekiah, his ancestor, the saintly King Asa, fell sick with excruciating pain in his feet. The swelling spread upwards to his whole body until he was misshapen and disfigured from head to toe. The Rabbis said Asa's sickness was a punishment for causing Torah scholars to neglect their studies by forcing them to take part in the work of dismantling the stone barriers erected by the rulers of the Northern Kingdom as part of their blockade on the Kingdom of Judah (*Sotah* 10a and see *Likutey Moharan* II, 2:3).

However, King Asa himself was reluctant to accept that his affliction was divine chastisement. "Even in his sickness he did not seek out God, but he turned to the doctors" (Chronicles II, 16:13). The saintly Asa had made it his life's work to teach the inhabitants of the Kingdom of Judah to search out God — but he was unable to see his own fault. His affliction should have moved him to repent, which might have saved his life. But he saw it as a natural phenomenon and sought to have it cured by physicians — and died. Asa was criticized because a man on his level was expected to understand that if he becomes sick it is not a chance occurrence but a providential visitation.

The mysteries of providence

Is the Bible teaching that *all* illness is caused by sin? This would be a gross oversimplification. What about illness in little children and babies? What about the terrible diseases that afflict some of the most saintly and spiritually-fulfilled individuals, while others who have perpetrated the worst evils often enjoy robust good health for years and years?

Why do the righteous suffer? This profoundest of all questions is the subject of the book of Job, about whom God Himself testifies, "There is none like him on earth, a pure and upright man, who fears God and shuns evil" (Job

1:8). The book graphically portrays the excruciating agony of Job, smitten with boils from the soles of his feet to the crown of his head, longing for death. His words heart-rendingly evoke the torment of protracted pain and illness.

Three of Job's friends, Eliphaz the Temanite, Bildad the Shuhite and Tzophar the Na'amatite, come to comfort him. They argue eloquently that God is righteous in all His ways and deals justly and truly with all mankind. "Whoever perished, being innocent, or where were the upright cut off? ... Those who plough iniquity and sow mischief reap them back...." *(ibid.* 4:7-8). If God sends a person suffering, it is because he has transgressed, and he must repent. If Job is sick it must be because of something he has done.

The three friends' powerful assertion of faith in God's justice are the basis for some of the fundamental tenets of Judaism. Yet their lofty moralizing is no salve for the anguished Job. For him these friends are "physicians of no value" *(ibid.* 13:4). Again and again Job protests that he is not guilty of any of the transgressions his friends are talking about. He refuses to accept that his trial can be explained through a simple schema in which all suffering is sent because of sin. That Job is right is confirmed in the prologue to the book, where the reader is taken beyond the confines of normal human perception and is allowed a glimpse of the inner workings of Providence. When God praises Job in the heavenly court, Satan objects, saying that he has not been tested. God challenges Satan to torment Job in every way short of killing him in order to prove that he will remain unshakable in his faith. This is the reason for Job's suffering.

Why the test? Why the agony and torture? For what purpose? These are questions we cannot help but ask in the face of apparently meaningless suffering, children's illness, the diseases that suddenly strike at those in their very prime, cases of protracted pain and torment, disability, debilitation, helplessness and degradation, where smug moralizing is offensive.

After all the eloquence and wisdom of Job and his friends we are still left only with questions. This indeed is the lesson of the whole book: ultimately God is utterly inscrutable. Puny man cannot hope to comprehend the secrets of providence. In the end God Himself answers Job out of the whirlwind: "Where were you when I laid the foundations of the earth? Declare if you have the understanding" *(ibid.* 38:4). In one of the most awesome passages in the entire Bible we are reminded of the staggering grandeur and unfathomable mystery of Creation — the mountains, deserts, seas, planets, stars and constellations, the wondrous variety of life-forms and their weird and amazing ways *(ibid.*

chapters 38-41). "Who is able to stand before Me? Who has given Me anything beforehand that I should repay him? Whatever is under the whole heaven is Mine..." (*ibid.* 41:2-3).

At last Job confesses his insignificance and ignorance. "I know that You can do everything and that no purpose can be withheld from You.... I spoke, but I did not understand, things too wonderful for me, which I did not know..." (*ibid.* 42:3).

God is infinite, supreme in majesty, beyond all the worlds. Yet in His lovingkindness He willed to create the worlds and reveal Himself to us. Our very existence is a mystery. "Against your will you were created; against your will you were born; against your will you live; against your will you die, and against your will you are destined to give an account before the King Who rules over kings, the Holy One, blessed be He" (*Avot* 4:29). Who can understand the mysteries of souls and their incarnations, the repairs they have to make, the suffering they must go through and the supreme goodness they will eventually come to?

Now that we have been created, our purpose is to find God in all the different situations and circumstances He sends us. "Know Him in all your ways" (Proverbs 3:6). King Asa was criticized not so much for going to doctors as for failing to seek out God in his time of distress. This was what King Hezekiah sought to correct when he put away the Book of Remedies. When illness strikes and all is rush and panic, Hezekiah asks us to take a moment to turn our faces to the wall, cry out to God and take a careful look at ourselves. "Where is God? And where am I?" Illness is sent to make us cry out to God and search for Him. "For I, God, am your Healer."

Chapter 4

The Rabbinic Tradition

The Talmud reports that the Sages of Israel endorsed King Hezekiah's action in concealing the Book of Remedies (*Pesachim* 56a). Hezekiah had sought to instill trust in God and faith in the Torah and mitzvot as the *exclusive* Jewish pathway of healing. To what extent did this remain at the center of the healing lore of the Rabbis of the Talmud and Midrash?

Many rabbinic sayings attest to the superiority of the Torah's healing power over that of natural medicine. "Rav Yehudah the son of Rabbi Chiya said, Come and see the difference between God and human beings. When a human being prescribes a medicine it may be good for one person but harmful to another. Not so the Holy One, blessed be He. The Torah He gave to the Jewish People is an elixir of life for the whole body, as it is said (Proverbs 4:22): 'and health to all his flesh'" (*Eruvin* 54a).

"Rabbi Yehoshua ben Levi said, Someone with a headache should busy himself with Torah, as it is said, 'For they shall be a diadem of grace for your *head*' (Proverbs 1:9). Someone with a sore throat should busy himself with Torah, as it is said, 'and chains about your *neck*' (*ibid.*). Someone with stomach pains should busy himself with Torah, as it is said, 'it shall be health to your *navel*' (*ibid.* 3:8). Someone with aching bones should busy himself with Torah, as it is said, 'and marrow to your *bones*' (*ibid.*). And if his whole body is aching, he should busy himself with Torah, as it is said (*ibid.* 4:22), 'and health to *all* his flesh'" (*Eruvin ibid.*).

Not only does the Torah heal: it prevents illness in the first place. The point is brought out in the following midrash: "Is a Jew who is suffering from an ear-ache allowed to have medical treatment on Shabbat? Yes: the Sages taught, Wherever there is a possibility of danger to life one may violate Shabbat. Thus an earache, which can be a threat to life, may be treated on Shabbat. But do you want to avoid getting an earache, or indeed any other pain, in the first place? Then turn your ear to the Torah and you'll inherit life, as it is written, 'Incline your ear and come to Me, hear and your soul shall *live*' (Isaiah 55:3). For as Rabbi Levi said, Man is made up of two hundred and forty-eight limbs, and all of them receive vitality from the ear" (*Devarim Rabbah* 10:1).

The biblical teaching that injury and illness are sent from God is reflected in many rabbinic sayings. "Nobody bruises so much as a finger here on earth unless it was decreed against him in Heaven" (*Chullin* 7b). "A snake only bites a person when a command from Heaven forces it to do so" (*Yerushalmi Peah* 1, 16a). And just as God sends the blow, so God alone can heal. "R. Alexandri said in the name of R. Chiya bar Abba: Recovery from illness is a greater miracle than Chananiah, Mishael and Azariah's being saved from Nebuchadnezzar's furnace (Daniel 3). Anyone can put out a man-made furnace, but the furnace of sickness is made by Heaven — who can put it out?" (*Nedarim* 41a).

"If you see a Jew who has symptoms of one of the four kinds of leprosy mentioned in the Torah, it comes only to heal him of all his sins, and through his suffering he merits the World to Come" (*Tanna de-vei Eliahu* 5).

Since it is God Who heals, the sick person's first step must be to turn to Him sincerely. "When a person sees that suffering has come upon him he should carefully examine his behavior" (*Berakhot* 5a). "R. Alexandri said in the name of R. Chiya bar Abba, One who is sick cannot be healed unless he is first forgiven for all his sins" (*Nedarim* 41a). "Rabbi Meir used to say, Two people take to their beds with the same illness. One recovers while the other does not. One prays and is answered, the other prays and is not. Why is one answered and the other not? Because this one prayed with true sincerity while the other did not" (*Rosh HaShanah* 18a).

Besides the prayers of the invalid himself, those of others can also help. "If a person is sick for more than a day, he should let people know so that they will pray for him" (*Berakhot* 55b). Especially effective are the prayers of the saintly. "Someone who has a sick person in his house should go to a Sage and ask him to pray for him" (*Bava Batra* 116a). Thus Rabbi Chaninah ben Dosa would pray for the sick, and if his prayers flowed forth without hesitation or error he knew that the patient would recover (*Berakhot* 34b). Some of the tzaddikim had other ways of channeling the healing power of the Torah. When R. Chiya bar Abba was sick, Rabbi Yochanan stretched out his hand to him and healed him. Rabbi Yochanan did the same to R. Eliezer. Yet when R. Yochanan himself became ill he could not heal himself because "a prisoner can't release himself from prison." But R. Chaninah came to him, stretched out his hand and healed him (*ibid.* 5b and see below pp. 138 and 149ff.).

Sanction to heal?

These teachings show clearly that the talmudic Sages viewed physical illness as a manifestation of what is at root a spiritual problem. It follows that true healing can come about only when the spiritual flaw is repaired by the sick person himself with the help of a Tzaddik who prays for him and guides him in his repentance. But does this mean that as long as we attend to our spiritual health we can leave our physical health to take care of itself?

"Take care of yourself and guard your soul diligently" (Deuteronomy 4:9). The Rabbis were emphatic that we have a duty to take all reasonable precautions to guard our physical health and avoid becoming sick in the first place. When they said that "everything is in the hands of Heaven except chills and colds" (*Bava Batra* 144b), they were not implying that the power of Heaven is anything but total. What they meant is that we must use our common sense and take responsibility for our physical welfare. The world we live in contains good and evil on every level, physical as well as spiritual. Having been created with the freedom to choose between them, we have an obligation to avoid not only cold drafts but all other obvious health hazards as well. The Talmud therefore offers practical advice about general hygiene, healthy elimination, washing and bathing, exercise, and especially diet, since "more people are killed by the cooking pot than suffer from starvation" (*Shabbat* 33a).

So much for preventive medicine. What about when illness strikes? While taking the biblical viewpoint that the roots of illness are spiritual, did the talmudic Sages follow King Hezekiah in his rejection of all physical strategies of healing?

In fact the Talmud itself contains a wealth of practical medical advice including detailed herbal and other remedies for all kinds of problems from toothache and stomach pains to fever and heart complaints (see *Gittin* 67b-70b, *Avodah Zarah* 28a-29a, etc. and Julius Preuss, *Biblical and Talmudic Medicine*). Moreover, throughout the Talmud and Midrashim there are innumerable references to the רופא (*rophé*) or אסיא (*asya*), "healer" or "physician," who treated ailments ranging from eye infections, bone fractures and snakebites to gangrene and consumption. Another familiar figure in the world of the Talmud was the אומן (*uman*), the "blood-letter." Some physicians are referred to as רופא מומחה (*rophé mumcheh*), an "expert healer." There were also scholars who, although they did not practice as professional doctors, were considered authoritative in medical matters, such as Mar Shmuel (*c.* 200 C.E.), head of the rabbinical academy of Nehardea.

Where the opinions of physicians might have a bearing on questions of ritual, civil and criminal law, they were sought and respected by the Rabbis. But what was the Rabbis' attitude to actual medical treatment? As with any detail of life, before asking if it is desirable, the first question a Jew asks is whether it is permissible. If King Asa was criticized for going to doctors, did that mean that nobody should go to a doctor? In hiding the Book of Remedies was Hezekiah seeking to forbid resort to medicine for all time?

On the general question of the permissibility of medicine, nowhere is there any suggestion that the use of physical therapies is actually forbidden. While the Rabbis unquestionably saw faith, prayer, Torah and mitzvot as the essential elements of the Jewish path of healing, unlike King Hezekiah they made no efforts to prevent resort to medical remedies as long as they did not involve transgression of the prohibitions against idolatry, sexual immorality and murder (Pesachim 25a). Doctors were consulted on all kinds of medical problems without opposition from the Rabbis, some of whom themselves received treatment on occasion, such as Rabbi Yehudah HaNasi, who was treated by Mar Shmuel for an eye ailment (Bava Metzia 85b). The Talmud itself advises against living in a city that does not have a doctor (Sanhedrin 17b).

In the centuries following the destruction of the Second Temple the talmudic Sages faced very different conditions from those that had existed in Hezekiah's time, when there was no division between state and religion. Hezekiah was at once a spiritual and a political leader, and had sufficient influence to "put away the Book of Remedies" as part of a more general religious revival. But in talmudic times the Jews were already in exile and living side by side with adherents of all kinds of other religions and cults. The medicine of the non-Jews was a mix of physical therapies and idolatrous rites. While the talmudic Sages made every effort to lead the people in the traditional Jewish path of faith, their primary concern in their halakhic deliberations was to clarify what Torah law explicitly forbids and what it permits. The Talmud and later halakhic literature therefore discuss an enormous range of medical questions, such as receiving treatment from a doctor who worships idols, the permissibility of various medical procedures on Shabbat and festivals, abortion when the life of the mother is at risk, the obligation of sick people, new mothers, etc. to fast, the extent of liability in cases of injury, etc.

Whether the talmudic Sages *favored* the use of medical remedies or not is another question altogether. There is a revealing passage in the Talmud (Berakhot 60a) on the subject of blood-letting, in those days a common procedure used for a variety of conditions. "Rav Acha said: Someone going in for blood-letting should say, 'May it be Your will, HaShem my God, that this operation should be beneficial to my health. Heal me, for You, God, are the faithful Healer and Yours is the true healing, *because it is not the way of human beings to bring about a cure, but this is the practice."*

Commenting on the last part of the prayer, "it is not the way of human beings to bring about a cure," Rashi (*ad loc.*) explains: "That is to say, people ought not to have recourse to medical treatments but should rather pray for mercy." "But this is the practice" — i.e., despite this, people *do* resort to medicine because they fear their merit may not be sufficient to allow them to expect to be healed through a miracle. The last part of the prayer is effectively an apology by the supplicant for using a physical strategy of healing instead of relying on God alone (see *Turey Zahav* on *Shulchan Arukh, Yoreh Deah* 336:1). The feeling that resort to medicine betrays a lack of faith is clearly an echo of King Hezekiah's tradition.

However, in a rejoinder to this way of thinking, the Talmud (*Berakhot ibid.*) immediately quotes Abaye: "A person should not say this [last part of the prayer], because the Academy of Rabbi Yishmael deduced from the words 'he shall cause him to be thoroughly healed' (*Exodus* 21:19) that the physician has sanction to heal." According to this second view, there is no question that God is the Healer, but He may grant the physician the power to heal as His agent. This is derived from the biblical passage decreeing that one who causes injury to another has an obligation to "cause him to be thoroughly healed." According to the Oral Law, this means that he must cover the injured party's medical expenses (*Bava Kama* 83b), implying that medicine is effective. (See below, pp.186ff. for Rebbe Nachman's discussion of the saying that "the physician has sanction to heal.")

This latter viewpoint is vividly expressed in a midrash telling of a sick man who approached Rabbi Yishmael and Rabbi Akiva as they were walking in Jerusalem one day. The sick man asked the two rabbis what he should do to be cured. They gave him a number of recommendations, upon hearing which a farmer who had been listening said to them, "You're interfering in something that's none of your business! God afflicted him with illness and you want to heal him?" "But don't you as a farmer do the same?" they replied. "God created the earth, but you have to plow, till, fertilize and weed if you want the land to yield produce. 'As for man, his days are as grass' (*Psalms* 103:15). The human body is the tree, the medicine is the fertilizer and the physician is the tiller of the earth" (*Midrash Shmuel* 52a #4).

Judaism rejects the fatalistic view that if God sends illness it must be borne with complete resignation without making any efforts to overcome it. It is up to us to take the initiative to seek healing. The question is: what kinds of steps are we to take? The tradition of Rabbi Yishmael, as reflected by Abaye, accepted the use of medical strategies of healing. Certainly we must know that illness is sent from Heaven. We must direct ourselves to repentance and prayer even as we turn to doctors and undergo treatment. We must know that ultimately God is the Healer even when the cure is channeled through the agency of a person, a substance or an operation. But we may resort to doctors and medicine without qualms since "the physician has sanction to heal."

On the other hand, the tradition of King Hezekiah, while certainly rejecting fatalistic resignation, holds that action in the spiritual realm alone has the power to bring complete healing without resort to physicians and medicines. It is up to us to take the initiative, but the very essence of what we have to do is to cry out to God, search our hearts and seek healing through the redemptive joy of the Torah and mitzvot. This view finds an echo in the sentiments expressed at the end of Rav Acha's prayer before blood-letting as Rashi explains them: "People ought not to have recourse to medical treatments but should rather pray for mercy." The same view is expressed even more directly in the rabbinic statements quoted earlier about the power of the Torah to heal the entire body (see p. 29).

These divergent tendencies are reflected in the views of later rabbinic authorities. Many of them took the statement that the doctor has sanction to heal at face value as giving us complete license to resort to medicine. This is accepted by virtually all contemporary rabbis. On the other hand, some of the most outstanding authorities of all times, including the Ramban and Rabbi Eliahu, the Gaon of Vilna, championed King Hezekiah's path of faith (see pp. 194ff.). While not disputing that the physician may have sanction to cure, they argued that this does not mean that a Jew has sanction to resort to doctors and medicines when he can achieve complete healing through faith and Torah.

From this point of view exclusive dependence upon physical strategies of healing can be seen as diverting the sick person from the path of true healing. This was why King Asa was criticized for turning to physicians. It may also be among the considerations underlying the much-discussed mishnaic dictum, "The best of physicians are destined to go to hell" (*Kiddushin* 82a). One of the reasons given for this is that the physician is not afraid of illness and therefore does not turn to God with all his heart (*Rashi ad loc.*). It could be added that if the physician allows the patient to believe that illness can be conquered by physical means alone he is allowing him to avoid turning to God with all *his* heart, causing him to evade the very spiritual issues his illness was sent to make him confront.

The question remains, if the Sages of Israel endorsed King Hezekiah's concealment of the Book of Remedies, why does the Talmud itself give explicit details of so many medicines and treatments? This question is addressed by the Maharsha (Rabbi Shmuel Eliezer Aideles 1555-1632) in his commentary on the Talmud:

"Certainly sanction to heal and to know the remedies for all illnesses has been granted. But it is not proper that they should be revealed to everyone because of the unworthy people who will trust not in God but in the doctors. Originally it was forbidden to write down the Talmud itself, but because later generations became so forgetful, permission was given to put the oral traditions into writing (*Gittin* 60a). For the very same reason, the Sages were permitted to write down these remedies and reveal them publicly. It was impossible to remember them by heart and they were in danger of being completely forgotten. From their inclusion in the Talmud you can see that no branch of wisdom is lacking from it. Those who understand the language of the Sages will find a true and complete remedy for every illness, and no scoffer will be able to say that the Sages of the Talmud lacked healing wisdom" (*Maharsha* on *Gittin* 68a).

Two Outstanding Healers

From the talmudic period until today many outstanding rabbinic scholars have pursued the art of healing with the greatest devotion. The study of philosophy, speculative science and other branches of secular learning was often discouraged by the Rabbis: not only could it lead to neglect of Torah study, but many of the axioms and values of secular thinkers are contrary to Torah teaching.

Medicine, however, was an exception. Healing the sick is an act of kindness and can save lives. In addition, anatomical and medical knowledge have a bearing on many areas of Torah law, such as *niddah* (menstrual uncleanness), *trefot* (defects rendering animals unfit to eat), the laws of damages, *mumim* (disqualifying blemishes of priests and sacrificial animals), *tzara'at* (leprosy), etc. The RaShBA (Rabbi Shlomo ben Avraham ben Aderet 1235-1310) and his rabbinical court placed a ban on the study of natural sciences and philosophy by those under the age of twenty-five. However, they explicitly excluded medicine from the decree, "even though it is based on natural science, because the Torah has given the doctor sanction to heal" (Responsa of the Rashba I:415).

As we saw in the last chapter, two divergent approaches to healing can be discerned in the Talmud. One of them accepted the use of medicines and other forms of physical treatment, while the second remained faithful to King Hezekiah's rejection of all but spiritual methods of healing. These two tendencies are also discernible in the approaches to healing taken by later Rabbis. In order to provide a broader perspective on Rebbe Nachman's teachings on healing, let us consider two towering Rabbis who can be seen as representative of these divergent approaches and who must be counted among the outstanding healers of all time: the Rambam, and Rebbe Nachman's own great-grandfather, Rabbi Yisrael, the Baal Shem Tov.

The Rambam

Not only was the RaMBaM (Rabbi Moshe ben Maimon, Maimonides, 1135-1204) the major codifier of Torah law and one of the most influential of all the Jewish philosophers. He is also universally acknowledged as one of the greatest medical authorities that has ever lived. The Rambam expressed his attitude to the use of medicine clearly and simply. He saw no difference between a hungry person who eats bread "to heal himself of the illness of hunger" and a sick person who takes a certain herb to cure himself of *his* illness. "Just as when I eat I thank God for providing me with food to satisfy me and remove my hunger so that I may live, so too will I thank Him for providing me with the medicine that can heal my illness" (Commentary on the *Mishneh, Pesachim* 4:9).

The Rambam probably first learned medicine from his father, R. Maimon, himself a renowned scholar and *dayan* (rabbinic judge) of Cordoba, where the Rambam was born. The family was forced to leave Cordoba around 1154 because of religious persecution by the Moslem rulers. After several years of wandering they arrived in Fez, Morocco in 1160, and spent several years there. At the same time as he was preparing material for his Commentary on the Mishnah, the Rambam studied medicine with a variety of physicians, both Jewish and non-Jewish. In his medical writings he often refers to the knowledge and experience he gained among the Moslems of North Africa. He also studied Arabic translations of the writings of the ancient Greek physicians, especially Hippocrates and Galen, whose views on physiology and healthcare are reflected in the Rambam's own writings.

To avoid forced conversion to Islam, the Rambam and his family fled Fez in about 1165, and after a few months' stay in the Holy Land went to Egypt, where they eventually settled in Cairo. For several years the Rambam was supported by his brother David, a gem merchant, and spent the time preparing his works for publication while also serving as religious and lay leader of the Jewish community. But in 1169 his brother drowned at sea during a business trip. The Rambam rejected the thought of earning his living from the Torah and decided to support himself by practicing medicine. In 1185 he was appointed as one of the physicians of Al Afdhal, eldest son of Saladin the Great and vizier of Egypt.

The Rambam described his day in a famous letter to R. Shmuel ben Yehudah ibn Tibbon, who translated his philosophical writings into Hebrew:

> "I dwell at Fostat, while the Sultan resides in Cairo [a distance of 2-3 km. away]. My duties to the Sultan are very heavy. I am obliged to visit him every morning, and when he or any of his children or the inmates of his harem are indisposed I dare not quit Cairo but must remain in the palace for most of the day. It also often happens that one or two royal

officers fall sick and I have to treat them.... Even if nothing unusual happens I do not return to Fostat until the afternoon.

"By then I am dying of hunger. I find the ante-chamber filled with people, Jews and gentiles, nobles and common people, judges and bailiffs, friends and foes — a mixed multitude awaiting my return. I beg my patients to bear with me while I take some light refreshment, the only meal I eat in twenty-four hours. I then go forth to attend to my patients and write prescriptions and directions for their various ailments. Patients come in and out until nightfall, and sometimes, I solemnly assure you, for another two hours or more into the night. I converse with them and make prescriptions while lying down from sheer fatigue, and by nighttime I am so exhausted that I can barely speak."

The Rambam prized the pursuit of medicine as one that can deepen a person's faith, knowledge and love of God through witnessing the amazing wisdom and intricacy of His creation as manifest in the human body and in the incredible diversity of healing plants and other natural wonders. Seeking to ease the suffering of the sick inculcates precious traits of kindness and patience. "The acquisition of medical skill is one of the great gateways to intellectual expansion, the development of a noble character and the knowledge of God. When a person reaches true proficiency, his quest is a great act of service" (*Shmonah Perakim* 5).

"The physician should make every effort to see that everyone, sick and healthy alike, should always be cheerful, and he should seek to relieve them of the spiritual and psychological forces that cause anxiety. This is the first principle in curing any patient" (Rambam, *Hanhagat HaBri'ut* 3:13-14).

The Rambam's voluminous medical writings include a compendium of about three hundred and fifty herbal and other remedies, works on asthma and hemorrhoids, and a study of poisons and their antidotes that is still used in medical research today. Far more relevant to the lay student are a number of other works exemplifying the Rambam's conviction that the most important task of the physician is not so much to cure the sick as to prevent illness in the first place (see p. 7). His "Aphorisms of Moses" is a collection of advice on healthcare with quotations from Galen, Hippocrates and various Arabic medical authorities. His classic *Hanhagat HaBri'ut* ("Guide to Good Health") (see *Sources and Further Reading*) was written in 1198 in response to a request for medical advice by the Egyptian Sultan, who suffered from depression and a variety of physical complaints. This concise and highly practical treatise outlines the main

(continued on p.42)

Insights from the Rambam on the Art of Healing

(from the Rambam's *Hanhagat HaBri'ut*)

1. If a person cared for himself the way he cares for his horse he would avoid many serious illnesses. You won't find anyone who gives his horse too much fodder. He measures out only as much as the horse can tolerate. But he himself eats to excess. He makes sure his animal gets proper exercise to keep it healthy. But when it comes to himself he neglects exercise even though this is a fundamental principle in health maintenance and the prevention of most illnesses (1:3).

2. Even with the utmost care and caution it is impossible to avoid constant minor fluctuations in our physical functioning. Sometimes the stools become a little soft, sometimes a little dry. One day a person may find a change in his digestion or feel a mild headache or a slight pain in some other part of his body, and so on. Don't be in a hurry to take medications for these kinds of minor problems. Nature will take care of them without any need for medicines. Follow your normal health regime. If you try to treat these minor ailments, either you will do the wrong thing and cause harm or, if you do the right thing, while you may succeed in restoring the normal balance, you have also taught your body to become lazy and it will no longer function properly without outside assistance (4:3).

3. If the illness is stronger than the patient there is no hope of saving him and the physician is of no benefit at all. If the patient is stronger than the illness he has no need for a physician because nature will cure him. It is only when the strength of the patient and the illness are equal that medicine is needed to strengthen the patient... Most doctors are greatly mistaken in this and think they are strengthening the patient's natural vitality when in fact they are weakening it. On this subject Aristotle in his *Perception and the Perceptible* said that the cause of most patient deaths is the treatment they receive from physicians who are ignorant of nature (2:4).

4. If the patient can be treated through diet alone he should not be treated with medicines. If it is impossible to control the illness without medications, the first choice should be medicines that are nourishing and foods that have medicinal properties. When using medicines one should begin with mild ones. If these are sufficient, well and good. Only if they are insufficient should

(Rambam on the Art of Healing, cont.)

one use stronger medicines. Wherever a single, simple drug can be used one should not use a compound. If the illness cannot be controlled without a compound, one should use the least number of ingredients. Medicines consisting of many ingredients should only be used when absolutely necessary (2:21-22).

5. One should never forget to strengthen the patient's physical vitality with nourishing food and to strengthen his spiritual powers with fragrant odors, with music, by telling him happy stories that expand the heart, and by distracting his mind with things that make him and his friends laugh. The people chosen to take care of him should be those who know how to cheer him up (2:20).

6. The physician should make every effort to see that everyone, sick and healthy alike, should always be cheerful, and he should seek to relieve them of the spiritual and psychological forces that cause anxiety. This is the first principle in curing any patient, especially if his illness is bound up with his mind and emotions, as in the case of those who are gloomy and depressed. In all such cases the physician should do nothing before improving their state of mind.... The physician should not think that he can alter these emotions through his medical knowledge and expertise. This can be achieved only through moral guidance and the religious teachings we have received from the prophets (3:13-14).

7. Sometimes doctors make a serious mistake but the patient survives. Other times they make what they think to be a minor mistake, and the patient also thinks it to be of little consequence, but it becomes the cause of the patient's death. Every thinking person should bear this in mind. Any intelligent person can study medical literature and understand when or when not to use various treatments. What is so difficult, even for a skilled physician, is to apply this knowledge in individual cases. For those who know nothing about the fundamentals of healing and treat it casually and talk a lot, nothing seems difficult. They don't think there is any illness that requires careful deliberation. The common run of people think medicine can be learned quite easily, whereas it is really extremely difficult to master even for a conscientious physician (4:7-8).

principles of diet, exercise, hygiene and general healthcare, the key to which, says the Rambam, is emotional balance.

Most accessible of all is the chapter on healthcare in the Rambam's all-encompassing code of Jewish law, the *Mishneh Torah* (*Hilkhot De'ot* 4), the opening words of which are: "Bodily health and well-being are part of the path to God, since it is virtually impossible to know or understand anything of the Creator if one is sick. One must therefore avoid anything that may harm the body, and cultivate healthful habits" (*ibid.* 1). The Rambam then proceeds to give practical guidance about how, when and what to eat, physical exercise, sleep, hygiene, healthy elimination, bathing and sexual life (see pp. 108-9). Much of the Rambam's advice is based on passages in the Talmud and elsewhere. The *Mishneh Torah* runs to a thousand chapters covering every aspect of Jewish law, and is printed with lengthy commentary material and dissenting opinions by later Sages. Interestingly, the chapter on healthcare is one of the only chapters in the entire work that appears with no questions or dissenting opinions.

The Rambam's writings on healthcare are one of the main sources of later rabbinic guides to healthcare, such as Chapter 32 of the *Kitzur Shulchan Arukh* ("Concise Code of Jewish Law") and the *Tav Yehoshua* (see *Sources and Further Reading*). Although the Rambam gave detailed advice about which foods are healthful and which are to be avoided, he was aware that his specific recommendations did not necessarily apply in cultures other than his own (see *Hanhagat HaBri'ut* 1:6 and 13). With the tremendous innovations in food production, supply, refrigeration, etc. since the time of the Rambam, his advice on diet cannot be applied today without modification. But his guidance on moderate living, how and when to eat, the importance of exercise and especially of positive attitudes anticipates accepted contemporary healthcare wisdom by eight hundred years.

The Baal Shem Tov

To move from the Rambam to Rabbi Yisrael Baal Shem Tov (1698-1760) is to make not only a five hundred year journey through time, but also to journey into another world. To the modern, western-educated mind, the rationalistic world of the Rambam, notwithstanding the dust and teeming crowds of Cairo, may seem closer than the mystical world of the Baal Shem Tov. Besides the feudal lords, the furious priests, the uncouth peasants and the Jewish scholars, merchants, innkeepers and their wives and children peopling its towns and villages, the Baal Shem Tov's was a world in which the open hills, vast plains and forests seem to have had their own population of werewolves, witches, demons and spirits.

While some of what is told about the Baal Shem Tov may be legendary, the reliability of our main biographical source, *Shevachey HaBaal Shem Tov (Praises of the Baal Shem Tov)* by R. Dov Ber of Linetz, was endorsed by Rebbe Nachman (*Avanehah Barzel* p.29 #30), and in almost all cases it gives full details of those from whom the author heard the stories. But much of what is recounted there involves kabbalistic devotions, holy spirit, visions of higher worlds, miracles and other supra-rational phenomena that must be accepted simply on trust.

It is difficult to glean more than the most general information about how the Baal Shem Tov acquired his Torah knowledge, let alone his healing powers. Orphaned at a young age, he was for a while taken under the wing of the residents of his native town and seemed to be a promising student. But he would disappear to the forests for days at a time and before long went his own way, working on occasion as a teacher's assistant, study-house attendant or in other capacities while pursuing his devotions. When the hidden tzaddik Rabbi Adam Baal Shem was on his deathbed, he instructed his son to seek out this young R. Yisrael and entrust him with his secret kabbalistic writings, which evidently gave directions for attaining holy spirit and also, very probably, for invoking holy names in order to achieve practical results.

In the years that followed, the Baal Shem Tov spent most of his time in the hills and forests in study, prayer and devotion. The extent of his talmudic and halakhic knowledge is impossible to gauge, though it is unimaginable that outstanding scholars like the Mezritcher Magid and R. Yaakov Yosef of Polonnoye would have submitted themselves unreservedly to his leadership had his learning not been of the highest order. The Baal Shem Tov himself said that he reached his spiritual levels primarily through his efforts in prayer and devotion. Many stories attest to his exalted wisdom and holy spirit, his power to communicate with the souls of the living and the dead, with angels, spirits and demons, and his ability to understand the languages of birds, animals, trees and plants.

Such levels give one access to sources of information that are concealed from most people. For example, Rebbe Nachman said of the Baal Shem Tov that "he learned the names of all the different remedies in each of the seventy languages from the biblical section (Leviticus 11:13-21) enumerating the twenty-four impure birds" (*Tzaddik* #557). Perhaps it is knowledge of this kind that the Baal Shem Tov had in mind when he answered a prominent doctor who had asked him where he learned medicine, "God taught me!" (*Shevachey HaBaal Shem Tov* #15 and #206 and see below.*)

In his early life the Baal Shem Tov hid himself completely, posing as an ignoramus. It was only in 1734, when he reached the age of thirty-six, that he started to show his phenomenal capacity to fire scholars and simple folk alike and inspire them to rise to the heights of fervent devotion and selfless love of others. Over the next twenty-six years he attracted the following that was to spread his message of spiritual revival throughout Eastern Europe. But even after his revelation he was known initially to many people primarily as a healer, and in later years was also involved in numerous healings.

The Baal Shem Tov treated Jews, and sometimes non-Jews as well, both in the Ukrainian town of Medzeboz, where he made his home, and when he went traveling, as he did very frequently. Besides their requests for blessings for children and livelihood, etc., people turned to him with all kinds of problems, from somatic illnesses, paralysis and blindness to cases of psychotic behavior and "possession." The Baal Shem Tov often took money for healing and sometimes went out to the villages to heal when in need of money for some purpose (*Shevachey HaBaal Shem Tov* #73 & #143). However, his primary intent was not to make a living but to sanctify the Name

> The Baal Shem Tov said: "When a person's body is sick his soul is also weakened and he is unable to pray properly despite the fact that he may be clean of sin. *Therefore a person must take the utmost care of his physical health*" (*Keter Shem Tov* #231).

of God and reveal His power and glory. He certainly prescribed herbal remedies, but he also gave amulets and used prayer and kabbalistic formulae known only to himself.

The Baal Shem Tov's view of the relative effectiveness of spiritual and natural remedies can be seen from one of the versions of his first meeting with Rabbi Dov Ber, the Mezritcher Magid, who became his closest disciple and the main leader of the Chassidic movement after his death. The Magid was lame and very sick. Although the Baal Shem Tov had long wanted to bring him under his wing, when the Magid first arrived the Baal Shem Tov made a show of rejecting him. The Magid pleaded with the Baal Shem Tov to heal him, but the latter retorted, "My horses don't eat matzos" (as if to say, Do you think I'm such a great tzaddik that even my horses keep the mitzvot and I'm therefore on a level where I can heal you right away?) The Magid began sweating profusely and felt so poorly that he had to leave the room. He called one of the young followers of the Baal Shem Tov and requested that he go in and ask him why he did not fulfil the commandment to "love the stranger" (Deuteronomy 10:19).

In the words of the *Shevachey HaBaal Shem Tov*:

"The Baal Shem Tov came out and appeased him, and wanted to heal him with words. He went to him regularly for a period of two weeks and would sit by his side reciting psalms. However the Magid asked him to give him a more immediate cure using medicines. Later the Baal Shem Tov said to him, 'I wanted to heal you with words, because this brings lasting healing. But seeing that you want to be cured quickly I have no option but to use medicines.' The Baal Shem Tov did so, and provided him with a place to live nearby. At first the Magid was unable to go to the Baal Shem Tov because he was too weak, but after a little while he began to improve and would go to him" (ibid. #41).

The Baal Shem Tov was evidently quite familiar with "orthodox medicine." The saintly Rabbi Chaim, Chief Rabbi of Byela Cherkov (Sadeh Lavan), who was chronically ill, called for the Baal Shem Tov to heal him.

"He spent an extended period with him trying various treatments, but when the Rav's sons saw that their father was not improving they sent for a well-known doctor. This doctor had already sworn that if he were to so much as catch sight of the Baal Shem Tov he would take a pistol and shoot him. The Baal Shem Tov hurriedly took his leave of the Rav and departed. When the Rav's sons brought the doctor to him, the doctor prescribed a variety of treatments. Whatever the doctor said, they replied, 'The Baal Shem Tov already did that and it didn't help.' The doctor left under a cloud. The Rav then thundered at his sons, 'What have you done? Even though I didn't get a cure from the Baal Shem Tov, I knew that the Shekhinah (Divine Presence) came with him. But when the doctor entered it was as if a *galach* (a gentile priest) came in'" (ibid. #15).

Another story tells of a prominent doctor who had come to visit the wife of the local lord.

"The countess lavishly praised the Baal Shem Tov as a great man and an expert healer. The doctor asked the countess to send for him. When he came, the doctor asked him if it was true that he was an expert healer. 'True,' replied the Baal Shem Tov. 'Where did you learn? Who was your professor?' asked the doctor. 'God taught me,' replied the Baal Shem Tov. The doctor laughed heartily and asked him if he knew how to take someone's pulse. The Baal Shem Tov said, 'I myself suffer from a certain problem. You take my pulse and see if you can find what it is, and I'll take your pulse and see what it reveals.'

"The doctor took the Baal Shem Tov's pulse and could tell that he had some kind of problem but he did not know what it was, because the truth was that the Baal Shem Tov was sick — he was love-sick for God (cf. Song of Songs 2:5), but this was beyond the doctor's level of understanding. After this the Baal Shem Tov took the doctor's hand and examined his pulse. The Baal Shem Tov turned to the countess and asked, 'Have you had a burglary here?' The Baal Shem Tov listed a number of precious items. 'Yes!' replied the countess, 'It's some years since they were stolen and I have no idea where they are.' 'Send to the doctor's lodgings,' said the Baal Shem Tov, 'and open his chest. You'll find everything there, because I can feel this theft in the doctor's pulse.' The countess sent to search the doctor's lodgings and found the stolen goods, as the holy Baal Shem Tov had said, and the doctor left in disgrace" (*ibid.* #206. On pulse diagnosis in the Kabbalah, see pp. 138-47).

An episode during the Baal Shem Tov's abortive attempt to journey to the Holy Land gives a few hints about some of his spiritual healing methods as well as shedding light on his aim of sanctifying the Name of God. While he was in Istanbul he was approached by an extremely wealthy man whose only son had suddenly become blind in both eyes. The doctors had tried all kinds of cures but none of them was of any avail, and they had given up hope of curing him.

"The Baal Shem Tov told the man he could cure his son completely. The man was overjoyed and brought him to his house with great honor. However, when the man's wife saw the Baal Shem Tov (whose clothes were somewhat the worse for wear as he had been traveling for such a long time) she looked at him contemptuously and said angrily to her husband, 'Why did you bring him to me? None of the doctors could help. What can this man achieve with incantations?' Her lack of faith in the power of God's Holy Names aroused the wrath of the Baal Shem Tov, who said, 'Where is the blind boy. Bring him to me and I'll heal him right away and he'll be able to see normally.' These words shook the man's wife, because a fraud normally avoids being tested.

"They brought him the sick boy, whereupon the Baal Shem Tov whispered something in his ears and immediately asked them to bring a volume of Talmud and told him to read. The boy read quite normally, and everyone in the house was overjoyed. Immediately afterwards the Baal Shem Tov passed his hand over the boy's eyes and he became blind as before, bringing the whole household to tears. They pleaded with the Baal Shem Tov and offered him an enormous sum of money, but the Baal Shem Tov said, 'You wicked woman! You mocked God's Holy Names! On no account may you benefit from them. When I cured him it was not for my own honor, God forbid, or for money, but only to sanctify God's Holy Name. That is why I showed you the great power of the Holy Name in front of your eyes. But you will not benefit from it!' And with that he left" (*ibid.* #192).

The healing wisdom of the Baal Shem Tov was never recorded systematically and most of what we know of it has come down to us only through such stories. The underlying philosophy is revealed in the following:

"There was a certain sick man whom a great and famous Jewish doctor had given up all hope of curing. The man was unable to speak. The Baal Shem Tov was visiting his town and was asked to come to see him. The Baal Shem Tov told them to prepare the invalid a meat soup and said that as soon as he ate it he would start to speak. They gave him the soup and he recovered. The doctor said to the Baal Shem Tov, 'How did you cure him? I know that his blood vessels were irreparably damaged.'

"The Baal Shem Tov replied, 'Your approach to his sickness was physical but mine was spiritual. A person has two hundred and forty-eight limbs and three hundred and sixty-five veins and arteries corresponding to the two hundred and forty-eight positive precepts of the Torah and its three hundred and sixty-five prohibitions. When a person fails to carry out a positive mitzvah the corresponding limb is damaged, and when he contravenes a prohibition the corresponding blood vessel is damaged. If he contravenes many prohibitions many blood vessels become damaged. The blood does not flow and the person is in danger. But I spoke to his soul and persuaded her to repent, and she undertook to do so. This way all his limbs and blood vessels were repaired and I could heal him'" (*ibid.* #125).

SECTION 3

Rebbe Nachman

Chapter 6

A new path which is really the old path

Besides the brief statements of the talmudic Sages about the Torah path of spiritual healing, we find little more than a few oblique hints in the Zohar and other kabbalistic texts, scattered references in later biblical and talmudic commentaries, and a variety of stories and other folklore material from different parts of the Jewish world. It was left to Rebbe Nachman of Breslov to explore this pathway fully and explain its meaning for our times.

Rebbe Nachman was born in 1772. His brief life of thirty-eight years spanned the era of the American Declaration of Independence, the French Revolution, the Napoleonic Wars and the beginnings of the Industrial Revolution — convulsive events and processes that inititiated waves of political, social, economic and ideological changes that have since spread throughout the world.

The collapse of faith

As the ancient regimes of kings and feudal lords began to crumble all over Europe, so did the entire framework of beliefs and values upon which people had hitherto based their lives. Until the late 18th century the validity of religious belief was still largely unquestioned by the vast majority of people. It is true that philosophers and scientists of the "Age of Reason" had long espoused views that flew in the face of traditional faith. It was well over a century since René Descartes had proposed that the entire universe could be explained mechanistically and that all natural objects were nothing but machines, including the human organism. If everything is held to be causally determined, what place is there for human freedom and morality? Such ideas were already common currency among the lettered elite of France, but it was only towards the end of the 18th century, amidst the social ferment set off by the French Revolution, that they began to penetrate the consciousness of a wider public.

How was the new thinking going to affect the Jews? Attacks on the basic tenets of Judaism were nothing new. The Greeks, Romans, Christians, Moslems and others had repeatedly challenged the authority of Torah law, the uniqueness of God's Covenant with the Jewish People, the promise of future redemption, and so on. But their main intent was to induce Jews to abandon their own religion in favor of another. Throughout the ages there were those who succumbed to the pressures to convert, but the great majority of Jews remained loyal to their own ancestral faith.

What was unique in the challenge posed by the new philosophical outlook was that it was an assault on religious belief as such. If man is merely a machine why should he seek to curtail his natural urges? What meaning is there in his efforts to "elevate himself" to a "spiritual" plane that, according to this view, does not exist? Unlike the Christians and Moslems, the apostles of the new philosophy were not trying to force the Jews to embrace an alien religion. They were inviting them to divest themselves of religious obligation as such and become "free." The invitation was made all the more attractive by the promise that, if the Jews were to discard the practices that separated them from others, they would be able to enter the mainstream of society on equal terms with everyone else and escape the discrimination, humiliation and persecution that had been their usual lot in exile.

By the end of the 18th century assimilation was already making inroads among the Jews of France, Holland, Germany, Britain and America. But in Eastern Europe and Russia, where the overwhelming mass of Ashkenazic Jewry was concentrated, tradition was still very strong. Rumors emanating from St. Petersburg had it that the Russian rulers of the million or so Jews living in the Pale of Settlement not only wanted to encourage them to adopt gentile clothing, language and customs but also intended to force them to send their children to secular schools. However, many Jews found it hard to see this as a serious threat. It seemed unimaginable that anything could induce the bearded, ringlet-adorned Jews of the towns and villages of the Pale to abandon the traditions of their fathers.

But Rebbe Nachman knew otherwise. Again and again he said to his followers, "Great atheism is coming into the world" (*Rabbi Nachman's Wisdom* #35 & 220). The figure of the Sophisticate in his story of the "Sophisticate and the Simpleton" (*Rabbi Nachman's Stories* pp. 160-196) typified the growing number of young Jewish intellectuals who would increasingly set the tone for their fellow Jews. They felt constricted by the traditional culture of the small towns in which they had grown up. They wanted to travel the world — to Germany, Italy, France, Spain — and explore the new horizons that seemed to be opening up in science, philosophy, literature, art, music.... Having tasted the fruit of the "tree of knowledge," they could no longer accept the simple religious faith they had been fed in their childhood. "There is no King!" they declared.

Nor were they content simply to adopt this new outlook for themselves. They felt compelled to try to "open the eyes" of their fellow Jews as well and "free" them from the "shackles of tradition." Thus intellectuals like the clique of three atheistic *maskilim* (literally, "enlightened") whom Rebbe Nachman befriended in the town of Uman supported and encouraged the efforts of the authorities to introduce compulsory secular education among the Jews. Rebbe Nachman saw that this would cause vast numbers of Jews to become cut off from their religious heritage for generations to come.

For Judaism, the notion that the world is entirely governed by natural law and that humans are merely complex machines is a terrible affront to the dignity of man, in praise of whose creation the Psalmist says to God, "You have made him but a little less than the angels and You have adorned him with glory and splendor" (Psalms 8:6). Our physical nature puts us beneath the angels, but the souls that are our glory are *beyond* nature and higher than the angels, giving us dominion over them. Our souls are "a part of God above" (Job 31:2), and every one of our practical mitzvot and good deeds, each word of our prayers and every one of our noble thoughts set off chains of effects in the higher worlds, channeling blessing and goodness into the entire creation. To have faith in God is to have faith in ourselves and in the exaltedness of our mission. To lose faith in God is to lose faith in ourselves and in our purpose. Life becomes meaningless, absurd.

> "The main thing is faith! Every person must search within himself and strengthen himself in faith. For there are people suffering from the most terrible afflictions, and the only reason they are ill is because of the collapse of faith" (*Likutey Moharan* II, 5:1).

Rebbe Nachman saw the collapse of faith as the essential sickness of the age and indeed the cause of some of the most pernicious physical diseases afflicting our societies. "The main thing is faith!" he cried. "Every person must search within himself and strengthen himself in faith. For there are people suffering from the most terrible afflictions, and the only reason they are ill is because of the collapse of faith. The Torah says, 'God will send you wondrous plagues, great and faithful plagues and great and faithful sicknesses' (Deuteronomy 28:59). The plagues and sicknesses are called 'faithful' because they come on account of a lack of faith" (*Likutey Moharan* II, 5:1).

The true healer is therefore the Tzaddik, the doctor of the soul, who comes to show us how to leave our doubts, confusion, darkness and despair behind and rise to ever higher levels of connection with God. The Tzaddik seeks people's good in all the worlds and wants them to enjoy the good of this world too (*Tzaddik* #471), which includes bodily health. A Jewish body is very precious since it is necessary for the performance of the practical mitzvot, upon which the rectification of the entire world depends. "Every person must take great care of his physical body" (*Likutey Moharan* I, 22:5). But the key to the health of the body is that of the soul, for it is the soul which gives the body life.

"I set God before me constantly"

It was just twelve years after the Baal Shem Tov's passing that his great-grandson, Rebbe Nachman, came into the world in 1772. He was born in Medzeboz in the very house where his great-grandfather had lived. Rebbe Nachman's father was R. Simchah, son of R. Nachman Horodenker, one of the Baal Shem Tov's closest disciples. R. Nachman's mother was Feiga, whose mother, Adil, was the Baal Shem Tov's only daughter.

From his earliest childhood R. Nachman was thus surrounded by the influence of the Baal Shem Tov. The latter's followers would regularly visit Medzeboz to pray at his graveside and used to stay in the house of R. Nachman's parents, so that the young R. Nachman saw many of the outstanding luminaries of the Chassidic movement and imbibed the tradition from them. The stories he heard inspired him to devote himself completely to the service of God. As a young child R. Nachman wanted to fulfil the verse, "I set God before me constantly" (Psalms 16:8). He would try to depict God's name before his eyes even while studying with his tutor, and was often so preoccupied that he did not know his lessons, causing his teacher great anger.

As a child R. Nachman wanted to detach himself completely from the material world. At the age of six he decided that his first step would be to stop having any pleasure from eating. Realizing that he was still growing and could not give up regular meals, he used to swallow his food without chewing it so as not to derive any pleasure from it. He continued doing this until his throat became completely swollen. Already at this age he would constantly visit the Baal Shem Tov's grave, asking him to help him draw closer to God. He would go there at night even during the great winter frosts. After leaving the grave, instead of immersing in the indoors *mikveh* (ritual bath), he would do so in the outside *mikveh* even though he was thoroughly chilled from his trip. He forced himself to do this so as to gain total self-mastery (*Praise of Rabbi Nachman* #1-2, #19).

At the age of thirteen R. Nachman married Sashia, daughter of Rabbi Ephraim of Ossatin, and for the next five years lived in his father-in-law's house in Ossatin in the Eastern Ukraine, where he continued with his studies and devotions. He spent long periods in the hills and forests. He engaged in lengthy fasts, often from Shabbat to Shabbat, persisting in spite of extreme weakness. At the age of eighteen he moved out of his father-in-law's house and went to the nearby town of Medvedevka, where he lived for the next ten years. He soon attracted a substantial following, including men who were leaders in their own right, such as Rabbi Yudel of Dashev, a great kabbalist, and the renowned Rabbi Yekusiel, Magid of Terhovitza, who had been one of the foremost disciples of the Mezritcher Magid and who was now an old man with authority over a region of more than eighty towns and villages.

It was from Medvedevka that Rebbe Nachman set out on his pilgrimage to the Holy Land (1798-9). Not long after his return he moved to the nearby town of Zlatipolia, where he spent what he described as "two years of hell," because shortly after his arrival there, Rabbi Aryeh Leib, the "Shpola Zeida" (1725-1812), who was by that time the oldest surviving chassidic leader, began his relentless persecution of Rebbe Nachman. In the fall of 1802 Rebbe Nachman, then aged thirty, moved further west to the town of Breslov and was immediately joined there by the twenty-two year old Reb Noson Sternhartz (1780-1844), who became his closest disciple and recorded almost all of his extant teachings. Rebbe Nachman spent most of the next eight years in Breslov, before finally moving to the town of Uman, where he died on 18 Tishri 5571, October 16, 1810.

Asceticism and beyond

Many people will find Rebbe Nachman's self-mortifying practices quite shocking. Eating without chewing, immersing in the freezing cold and lengthy fasts are hardly practices most people today would consider conducive to sound, robust health even in an adult, let alone in a child of six! Not surprisingly, Rebbe Nachman was very thin, and one of the doctors who saw him during his last illness commented that by nature he had a strong, healthy body, but that he had broken it by his devotions (*Siach Sarfey Kodesh* III-162; *Avanehah Barzel* p.67 #44). Are these examples of the pathway of health Rebbe Nachman is recommending?

The only way to begin to understand such practices is in the context of the Jewish tradition of asceticism as expressed in the devotional literature in which Rebbe Nachman immersed himself from his boyhood onwards. Works like the *Reishit Chokhmah* of R. Eliahu de Vidas, which he read and reread, teach that while the body is the means through which the soul achieves its purpose in this world, bodily cravings for gratification over and above what is necessary for normal functioning are an obstacle to spiritual growth and must be conquered.

But what is normal functioning? How far is one supposed to go in denying one's bodily appetites? Strictly speaking a Jew is obliged to abstain only from what is forbidden by Torah law. For the rest, he may indulge himself in all permitted pleasures. But the spiritual seeker soon comes to understand that the pursuit of physical gratification interferes with the quest for spirituality. The higher the levels of spiritual perception and holy spirit one aspires to, the greater the mastery of the body that is required. Rebbe Nachman sought to follow the kabbalistic path of devotion to the ultimate degree, even to the point of self-sacrifice.

To those who are strongly attached to their physical pleasures, fasting and other forms of self-denial seem like nothing but a recipe for misery. However that is not necessarily the way they are experienced by spiritual adepts. In his story of the "Master of Prayer," Rebbe Nachman tells us that the Prayer Master's band of disciples spent their time engaged only in prayer, song and praise to God. For them, "fasting and self-mortification were better and more precious than all worldly enjoyment. They would have greater pleasure from fasting or self-mortification than from all worldly pleasures" (*Rabbi Nachman's Stories* p.283).

Nevertheless, it is true that for most people such practices would only lead to depression. Rebbe Nachman understood this, and recognized that, although asceticism had been an integral part of the classic kabbalistic path of devotion, it was no longer appropriate in his time, as people lacked the power of endurance possessed by earlier generations. Did that mean that henceforth the heights of devotion would be inaccessible to all but a minute number of spiritual supermen? Rebbe Nachman was determined to find a new pathway that could lead people to the most exalted spiritual levels without the misery of onerous penances, fasting and the like. This indeed was why he demanded so much of himself, like an explorer who stretches himself to the limit in order to benefit others. He said:

> "I am constantly working to open up a path in places that were previously desolate wilderness. I have to cut down all the obstacles blocking the road. There are gigantic trees that have been growing there for thousands of years. They have to be cut down. I have to go back and

forth again and again, cutting and cutting, in order to prepare a public way for everyone to go on" (*Tzaddik #235*).

The path Rebbe Nachman found was that of simplicity and joy. He told his followers: "I will lead you on a new path which no man has ever traveled before. It is really a very old path and yet it is completely new" (*Tzaddik #264*). Rebbe Nachman's pathway does not veer from a single detail of the Code of Jewish Law. The point is to live this code as a vital, joyous pathway of spiritual growth and ever deeper connection with God. The foundation of this connection is simple, direct communication with God in our own words, cries, shouts and songs. The Hebrew word for this is התבודדות (*hisbodedus*), which literally means "making oneself alone." It signifies separating oneself from other people and activities for regular periods of meditation, introspection and private prayer.

"Hisbodedus is the highest level of all. It is greater than everything else. You must fix an hour or more to go off by yourself to some room or meadow and express your thoughts and feelings to God. Appeal to God with every kind of argument and endearment. Plead with Him to bring you to serve Him truly. This conversation should be in your own native language. Pour out your whole heart to God, including your regrets and contrition about the past and your yearning to come closer in the future, each person according to his level. Make sure you get into the habit of practicing this regularly for an hour every day. Then be happy for the rest of the day.

> "You must fix an hour or more to go off by yourself to some room or meadow and express your thoughts and feelings to God. Plead with Him to bring you to serve Him truly. Pour out your whole heart to God. Practice this regularly for an hour every day. Then be happy for the rest of the day" (*Likutey Moharan* II, 25).

"This is the best way of coming close to God because it includes everything else. No matter what is lacking in your spiritual life, even if you feel totally remote from God, talk it out and ask God to help you. Many well-known great tzaddikim have said that they achieved their levels only through this practice. Any intelligent person can see the supreme value of hisbodedus. It is something that everyone can practice, from the smallest to the greatest. Everyone can talk to God and thereby reach the highest levels" (*Likutey Moharan* II, 25).

Rebbe Nachman told his followers not to fast. True, the body is gross, strong and forceful, and a formidable obstacle to spirituality. But instead of wearing it down with fasting and self-mortification, they were to master it with holy words (*Tzaddik* #443). Rebbe Nachman himself said, "If I had understood the power of hisbodedus earlier in life I would never have wasted my body through fasting. The body is too important a tool for serving God to have been subjected to such a strenuous discipline" (*Hishtapkhut HaNefesh*, Introduction).

Taking responsibility

Chassidism had restored to the forefront of Judaism the concept of the Tzaddik as a spiritual leader who guides people in healing the maladies of their souls and fires them to serve God. It was an ancient idea: after the exodus from Egypt the Jewish People "believed in God *and* in Moses His servant" (Exodus 14:31). Since that time every age had its leaders. When the Rabbis taught that one must submit oneself to a teacher (*Avot* 1:6) it is clear that this meant more than just a professor from whom one would gain information, but rather a saintly individual whose conduct and bearing would serve as an inspiring example of living Torah even in his most intimate personal activities (*cf. Berakhot* 62a).

The Baal Shem Tov and his disciples were charismatic figures who galvanized whole communities into new religious fervor. But by Rebbe Nachman's time the passion of the chassidic movement had cooled somewhat. The outstanding leaders of the first and second generations were often succeeded by children and grandchildren of lesser calibre who tended to institutionalize chassidic practice. Whereas the original adherents of the Baal Shem Tov had turned to him for inspiration to lead them to greater heights of spiritual achievement, more and more people now looked to their rebbes for quick, miraculous solutions to financial, health and other problems.

While deeply respectful of the outstanding chassidic leaders of the time, Rebbe Nachman was scathingly critical of mere wonder-rebbes, or "false leaders," as he called them. He himself was highly unconventional. He rejected the outer trappings of a chassidic court. He went without a large entourage and often traveled incognito. People did come to him to intercede on their behalf for children, healing, livelihood, etc. and he certainly had the power to bring about miracles. However for Rebbe Nachman, the true miracle is when a person wakes up spiritually and works to develop his own latent powers.

Rebbe Nachman once said to his followers: "The only thing that gives me any pleasure is when I see one of you showing his attachment to the Torah and serving God. I could have been a famous leader just like all the other rebbes whose chassidim come to them without knowing what they've come for. They come and go and have no idea why. But I never wanted any of this. My only concern is to get you to come closer to God. If you want to know what's precious to me, it's when I see the poorest beggar going about with a torn hat, torn clothes and torn shoes, serving God. I beg of you: be good Jews!" (*Tzaddik* #335).

If Rebbe Nachman emphasized the importance of attaching oneself to a Tzaddik, it was not as a "mediator" who could somehow free us of our responsibility to do our own spiritual work. The role of the Tzaddik is to teach us what to do and how, leaving *us* to actually do it. Attachment to the Tzaddik means setting aside preconceived ideas about how to find God and surrendering oneself to the Tzaddik's teachings, immersing oneself in them, pondering them and, most important, *practicing* them, even when unable to see where they are leading — much like a patient who persists in following a trusted doctor's prescriptions to the letter even if the treatment is sometimes bitter and protracted.

"The tongue of the wise brings healing"

Rebbe Nachman never wrote a systematic presentation of chassidic thought. He taught a pathway, but his way of communicating it was by speaking face-to-face with his followers. He would chat with them, discourse, throw out pithy aphorisms and tell parables and stories about princesses, giants, beggars, demons, magic stones, exotic sea voyages, conversations between the sun and the moon.... His informal discussions — filled with sharp images, brilliant turns of phrase, novel perspectives on familiar ideas and a devastating honesty — focus especially on the practical "how to" of prayer, meditation, faith, joy, celebration of Shabbat and the festivals and a host of other topics (see *Rabbi Nachman's Wisdom* & *Tzaddik*).

Five or six times a year all the Rebbe's followers gathered at his side, especially on Rosh Hashanah (the Jewish New Year). He would then discourse to them more formally, often for several hours. His Torah discourses, which were transcribed by Reb Noson, are collected in *Likutey Moharan*. Each one stands by itself as a separate teaching exploring in depth a particular facet of the spiritual journey. What should we do to make our prayers acceptable?

What is the way to come to perfect repentance? How can one accept that everything that happens is for good? How can one taste the inner light of the Torah? What is the pathway to inner peace and universal peace? These are but a few of the themes of his teachings.

In each discourse Rebbe Nachman elucidates the practical steps that lead to the spiritual goal under discussion. With the utmost subtlety he builds the discourse brick by brick, explaining an idea, introducing a second and showing its connection with the first, then bringing in a third, then a fourth, and so on — until a breathtaking edifice is revealed: a complete spiritual pathway. At every turn in the argument Rebbe Nachman brings supporting texts drawn from all over the Bible, Talmud, Midrashim, Codes, Zohar and the Lurianic kabbalah. His use of his sources is as novel as it is brilliant, yet his purpose is not to make a display of Torah acrobatics, but rather to elucidate the foundations of what are first and foremost practical spiritual pathways.

Explaining the craft of the Torah sage, Rebbe Nachman says:

"All medicines are made by combining specific quantities of various medicinal herbs which are then steeped or boiled together. Each herb has its own unique properties, and several herbs must be mixed together to produce a compound that has the power to cure the illness. In other words, the power of a given medicine derives from the way it is compounded. This gives it a new power over and above the properties of the individual herbs of which it is composed. Only through the power of the compound is the illness cured. For this reason the doctor has to be an expert who knows how to produce the right compound. Someone who is not an expert might take herbs with curative powers and still not achieve anything because he does not understand how to combine them.

"In the same way, the Torah has a cure for everything, as it is written, 'It is health to all his flesh' (Proverbs 4:22). But only the Sages of the generation understand the Torah, because they are entrusted with the key to its interpretation, i.e. the thirteen rules by which the Torah is expounded. From the Torah itself it is impossible to understand anything without the guidance of the Sages of the generation, who explain the true meaning. For the Torah is 'poor in one place and rich in another.' The Sages select, mix and combine Torah teachings, using what is said in one place to throw light on the meaning of something said elsewhere, in accordance with the thirteen rules. They subtract from one place and add somewhere else in order to discover the true meaning (Bava Batra 111b). Even though the Torah writes such and such, they subtract a letter or a word here and add it somewhere else, thereby interpreting the Torah in accordance with what they know from tradition.

"This is the reason why someone who despises a Torah sage has no cure for his wound (*Shabbat* 119b), because the cure that comes from the Torah can be received only through the Sages of the generation, who have been entrusted with the power to interpret the Torah. They know how to combine the letters of the Torah — and as explained above, the power of any medicine depends upon how the ingredients are combined.... Therefore the healing power of the Torah depends on the Sages of the generation: it is through their knowledge of how to interpret the Torah and combine its letters that all the compounds of medicinal herbs that depend upon the Torah receive their power.

"The main thing is to have faith in the Sages and to take care to give them due respect, honor and reverence. Even if a person considers something they teach to be incompatible with what appears to him to be explicitly stated in the Torah, and he thinks them to be contradicting the Torah, God forbid, he must nevertheless have faith that they are certainly correct and that their teaching is in full accord with the Torah, because the Torah has been entrusted to them. For example, the Torah seems to state explicitly that 'he must give [the sinner] *forty* lashes' (Deuteronomy 25:3). Yet the Sages teach that the penalty consists of thirty-nine lashes and no more (*Makkot* 22b). For the Sages knew — according to the rules of interpretation which they received by tradition — that the required number of lashes is thirty-nine. One must therefore have faith in the Sages and put aside one's own opinions. One must rely only on the Sages, because the interpretation of the Torah has been entrusted to them" (*Likutey Moharan* I, 57 end).

Chapter 7

Rebbe Nachman's Book of Remedies

The watershed in the development of Rebbe Nachman's pathway of healing came with his mysterious and dramatic eight-month trip to Lemberg in 1807-8 (see next chapter). By then he was already seriously ill with the lung disease that was to take his life three years later. From that time on until his death the topic of healing took a central place in practically every one of his major teachings. Never was he more outspoken in his rejection of resort to medicine than in that last period of his life. But in the healing approach he took in the earlier part of his life — which is the subject of the current chapter — although he certainly put his main emphasis on the spiritual aspect, his rejection of physical strategies as a part of healing was somewhat less absolute.

In the course of Rebbe Nachman's upbringing in his parents' home he must have heard much about the healing lore of his great-grandfather, the Baal Shem Tov. We have seen that the Baal Shem Tov made use of medicines as well as spiritual healing. Although he told the Mezritcher Magid that only the healing that comes about "through words" is really lasting, some of the stories that have come down to us about his healing activities indicate that he was fully expert in herbal remedies (see pp. 43ff.). And so too Rebbe Nachman also showed an interest in physical as well as in purely spiritual remedies, at least in his earlier years.

We have no information about the sources of Rebbe Nachman's healing wisdom, any more than we have about the identity of those from whom he learned Torah. Unquestionably he was a prodigious student. His Torah knowledge encompassed the entire range of biblical, talmudic, midrashic, halakhic and kabbalistic literature, which contain a wealth of healing wisdom. But whether Rebbe Nachman ever read any of the secular medical literature that was available in his time is impossible to tell. He strictly forbade his followers to study works of חקירות (chakirut), philosophy and speculative science, on the grounds that they undermine people's faith in God. This prohibition included even Jewish philosophical works like the Rambam's *Guide for the Perplexed*, not to speak of non-Jewish works. On the other hand, Rebbe Nachman taught that the outstanding Tzaddik is obliged to delve into this realm in order to elevate Jewish souls that have become entrapped there (*Likutey Moharan* I, 64). There seems little doubt that Rebbe Nachman's own reading extended to this area, but as to whether it included any medical works we can only speculate.

In one place Rebbe Nachman states that "all the medical authorities have spoken at length about how all illness is rooted in depression" (*Likutey Moharan* II, 24). This could be construed as a hint that Rebbe Nachman had some familiarity with medical literature, but it is hardly conclusive evidence. We know that he discussed medicine with many great doctors (*Rabbi Nachman's Wisdom* #50), and he could equally well have gained this information from them. Most of the medical literature at that time was written in Latin, but we have no clear evidence as to whether Rebbe Nachman read other languages besides Hebrew and Yiddish. Whether any of the Rambam's medical writings were available to Rebbe Nachman is an open question. The Rambam's technical writings were all in Arabic. Moshe Ibn Tibbon's Hebrew translation of the Rambam's *Hanhagat HaBri'ut* had been in existence since 1244, but while many manuscript copies have survived until today, the work was not actually printed until 1838, twenty-eight years after Rebbe Nachman's death.

One work that Rebbe Nachman may well have seen is the *Sefer HaBrit* of R. Pinchas Eliahu of Vilna (see *Sources and Further Reading*), a comprehensive survey of what was then known in the fields of astronomy, geography, physics, chemistry and biology. It includes a lengthy section on human anatomy with various references to medical knowledge of the time. The *Sefer HaBrit* was first printed in 1797, when Rebbe Nachman was twenty-five, and it quickly spread to Jewish communities throughout Europe, including Greater Poland and the Ukraine.

However, speculation about Rebbe Nachman's involvement in secular studies is probably gratuitous. For it is clear that in the main, his understanding of the workings of the human body and his healing wisdom came, like the rest of his wisdom, from his study of the Torah. Rebbe Nachman himself stated that he learned all the remedies in the world from the section of the book of Joshua detailing the boundaries of the Land of Israel (Joshua 15-19). He explained that the names of all the cities in each tribe's portion are ciphers denoting the names of all the remedies in the world in all languages. The reason is that the Land of Israel corresponds to the human form and the division of the land corresponds to the divisions of the body. One tribe's portion is the "head," another's the right arm, etc. The Rebbe said that the biblical passage describing each tribe's portion contains the remedies relating to the corresponding body-part (Reb Noson's Introduction to the *Aleph-Bet Book* p.3).

The *Aleph-Bet* Book

Unlike the Baal Shem Tov, there is no evidence that Rebbe Nachman ever went about as a healer. But from his early years he collected remedies of all kinds. By the time he was in his early thirties he had assembled an entire file of material. This was originally part of his *Aleph-Bet Book*, a collection of brief aphorisms in which he presented the distilled wisdom of the Torah on all kinds of topics, from dreams, memory and music to children, money, eating, clothing and many others. The Rebbe began compiling the *Aleph-Bet Book* in his youth in order to direct and encourage himself in his spiritual quest, but he kept its existence a secret until after his arrival in Breslov in 1802. He then began dictating the work to Reb Noson at intervals, until the transcription was finally complete in 1805.

The chapter on healing, however, was an exception. Rebbe Nachman never revealed its contents. Reb Noson tells us that the Rebbe said he had as many as two hundred pages of material on healing (*ibid.*). This could well be more than the length of the entire *Aleph-Bet Book* as we have it today. The chapter on healing that we have contains only four items, whereas some of the other chapters in the book have well over a hundred, and the chapter on the Tzaddik has over two hundred. Reb Noson, in his biographical portrait of Rebbe Nachman, *Tzaddik*, states:

> "On the subject of healing and medicine, the Rebbe said that the chapter on Healing in the *Aleph-Bet Book* originally contained all the cures in the world: there was not a single illness whose cure was not included. But he did not want this copied, and burned it" (*Tzaddik* #200 and cf. #380).

Like so many aspects of Rebbe Nachman's life, this "Book of Remedies" remains shrouded in mystery. We have no information whatever about the kind of remedies it contained. We know that on occasion Rebbe Nachman prescribed herbal remedies, such as an antidote to seasickness that was prepared by steeping a bitter herb known as *polin* in boiled wine. This was actually used by certain Breslover Chassidim in later generations when travelling at sea (*Siach Sarfey Kodesh* I-104), but we have no way of knowing if it is an example of the kind of remedies that were contained in the burned chapter on healing from the *Aleph-Bet Book*.

It seems unlikely that the few items on healing that Rebbe Nachman did give over to Reb Noson are in any way representative of the material he destroyed. The first item in the chapter on healing as we have it is typical of many throughout the *Aleph-Bet Book* that state very concisely an idea that is explored at length in one or another of the discourses in *Likutey Moharan*.

> "Know that each herb has a unique power to heal a particular illness. But all this is only for the person who has failed to guard his faith and morality and has not been careful to avoid transgressing the prohibition against despising other people (*Avot* 4:3). But when someone has perfect faith, guards himself morally, and lives by the principle of not looking down on anyone at all, his healing does not depend on the specific herbs that have the power to cure his illness. He can be healed through any food and any drink, as it is written, 'And He will bless your bread and your water, and I will remove sickness from you' (*Exodus* 23:25). Such a person does not have to wait until the specific remedy for his illness is available" (*Aleph-Bet Book, Healing* #1).

Here we have the essence of the healing pathway that Rebbe Nachman taught in the last years of his life. These few lines are a concise statement of ideas that are explained in depth in five pages of intricate text in his discourse, *"Sound the Shofar — Dominion"* (*Likutey Moharan* II, 1, see Chapter 18, pp. 237-77).

The other three items in the chapter on healing in the *Aleph-Bet Book* as we have it are:

> "Through deep contemplation of the mystical secrets of the Torah one can bring barren women to give birth and cure severe illness" (#2).

> "Salty foods are harmful for *tzara'at* (leprosy), the remedy for which is living waters...." (#3).

> "Gazing at an *etrog* (the citron fruit taken as one of the "four species" on the festival of Succot) is a remedy for eye pain" (#4).

We find a few more items on healing scattered in some of the other chapters of the *Aleph-Bet Book* (see Inset on facing page). Unlike the remedy for seasickness, none of them could be called herbal. Eating small fish for fertility and avoiding garlic and onions during pregnancy and nursing are dietary recommendations, while the use of feathers by those with lung disease could possibly be regarded as a physical remedy. But all the other remedies are in the realm of סגולות, *segulot*. A *segulah* is a strategy or practice designed to bring about a desired effect (in this case, physical healing) though it may not be susceptible to any rational explanation, as it operates on a plane beyond nature (*cf. Likutey Moharan* I, 21:9).

The surviving teachings on healing in the *Aleph-Bet Book* are a tiny fraction of the original material. Why did Rebbe Nachman decide to destroy all the rest, especially if, as he said, it "contained all the cures in the world"? Was it because he feared that people lacking true faith would try out the remedies, and if they saw no results they would blame the remedies and despise Torah wisdom, while if they were healed it would encourage them to apply these remedies mechanically without having faith that God is the Healer? If this was the reason, Rebbe Nachman's burning of his earlier teachings on healing was similar to Hezekiah's concealment of the Book of Remedies! Hezekiah did not want people to rely on the particular means through which healing is channeled, but rather to turn to God in faith, prayer and teshuvah. This is in

---

Remedies from the *Aleph-Bet Book*

"Small fish are conducive to fertility" (*Conception #3*).

"Pregnant and nursing women should not eat garlic and onions" (*ibid. #4*).

"A woman whose children die in childbirth should place an apple on her head" (*Children #32*).

"It is helpful for a woman who has suffered miscarriages to go about with a magnet and also a piece of wood from a tree growing over the grave of the Tzaddik. She should also give charity" (*Miscarriage #2*).

"Feathers of wild birds are helpful for those with lung disease and are conducive to strengthening the life force" (*Segulah #1*).

"Where somebody has suddenly been struck dumb, a kosher slaughtering-knife should be passed over his mouth" (*ibid. #9*).

"For someone suffering neck pain, it helps to weep over the destruction of the Holy Temple" (*ibid. #9*).

"Blessing the New Moon helps heal those with weak vision" (*Vision #3*).

"The Midnight Lament over the destruction of the Temple helps those with weak vision" (*ibid. #4*).

fact the essence of Rebbe Nachman's healing pathway as expressed in the later teachings that he left for posterity, having "put away" his own "Book of Remedies."

The power of words

Rather than prescribing specific cures for people, Rebbe Nachman wanted them to awaken their own spiritual healing powers. This was true even on occasions when he did offer a *segulah*. We see this in the way he dealt with a nine-year-old boy who had a slight fever. Eventually Rebbe Nachman gave him a remedy, but not before speaking to him at length.

The boy was a very fearful child. The Rebbe said to him, "Why are you afraid *now*? Think how afraid you'll be when they take you out to the cemetery and leave you there alone! Everyone will go off and leave you there lying among the dead. Today you're afraid to go out alone at night. What will you do *then*?" Rebbe Nachman continued along the same lines, and then asked, "Who in the world wants to burn himself with his own hands? When you sin it is as if you burn yourself with your very own hands, because eventually you will receive the hard, bitter punishment for sin. Surely you care enough about yourself not to burn yourself with your own hands?"

Only after this talk did the Rebbe give the boy a *segulah* for his fever. It was to take dust that had been trodden into the threshold and place it in a pot on the fire until it became bleached. The dust was to be put on the boy's side, and then he would be healed (*Tzaddik #490*). Reb Noson writes: "When this boy grew up, the words the Rebbe spoke to him remained inscribed on his heart.... From this we can see the way the Rebbe would look at even a young child and seek to imbue him with heavenly awe in order that he should begin to learn how to serve God" (*ibid.*).

Clearly Rebbe Nachman saw this boy's fever as being bound up with his fearfulness, which is why he spoke to him the way he did. More than this, he thought of ailments that most people today would consider primarily physical as being essentially spiritual, and he sought to correct them at their very roots. There were times when he did this through words of Torah.

The first occasion we explicitly hear of his channeling healing through a Torah teaching was in January 1805, when he was visiting Medvedevka for Shabbat Shirah. His daughter Chayah, who was then in Medvedevka, was suffering from a stye on her eye that had left her almost blind. Rebbe Nachman was informed of this upon his arrival in the town. In the discourse he gave that Shabbat (*Likutey Moharan* I, 62) he included a discussion on a passage in the Zohar which speaks about "the beautiful maiden who has no eyes" (*Zohar* II, 95). "And through this," writes Reb Noson, "she was healed." Reb Noson continues:

> "When the Rebbe returned home, he told me this story himself, and I understood from his holy gestures that he found it wonderful that he had brought her healing through the words of his discourse. Whatever happens to people involves many mysteries, because nothing happens without a reason. The greater the person, the more far-reaching the implications of what happens to him. The level of the Rebbe's holy offspring was in the most exalted realms. Everything that happened to them involved great battles, because the implications went so far" (*Tzaddik* #152).

Evidently the Rebbe understood that his daughter's eye ailment was an expression of a flaw on the spiritual plane, and it was this that he sought to correct through his discourse.

Another occasion when Rebbe Nachman channeled healing through a Torah teaching was almost a year and a half later, on the festival of Shavuot 1806. Shavuot was one of the fixed times for Rebbe Nachman's followers to gather at his side. One man came with his daughter, who was epileptic. Her fits came at regular intervals. In Rebbe Nachman's Torah discourse that Shavuot (*Likutey Moharan* I, 29) he included a discussion of epilepsy, in the course of which he quoted the verse, "She has fallen but will no more; rise, O virgin of Israel" (Amos 5:2 according to the talmudic interpretation in *Berachot* 4b). The expected time for the girl to have a fit passed without incident, and from then on she was cured (*Tzaddik* #146 and Rabbi Gedaliah Koenig).

We also hear that while Reb Noson was in Breslov for Rosh Hashanah 1807, news came that his wife, who had stayed in Mohilev, was dangerously ill with no one to take care of her. Reb Noson told Rebbe Nachman, who gave a lesson the following morning that included healing as one of its themes and also discussed the concept of Shabbat as the "wife of all Israel" (*Likutey Moharan* I, 277). Reb Noson's wife recovered. People in Mohilev criticized Reb Noson for having left his wife alone in order to be with Rebbe Nachman, but Reb Noson saw things differently: "If my wife remained alive, it was all through the prayers and holy Torah of the Rebbe" (*Yemey Moharnat* I, 26). Reb Noson writes: "Countless times we saw before our eyes how things which were happening in the world, and especially to the Rebbe's followers, were all included in his discourses. Through his Torah teachings he drew sweet, salutary influences into all aspects of the world, both in general and in particular, spiritually and physically" ((*Tzaddik* #390).

Besides Torah teachings, Rebbe Nachman's main weapon in the fight against illness was prayer. Essentially he saw illness as a heavenly decree (see below, pp. 188ff.), but "repentance, prayer and charity remove the evil of the decree" (from the High Holiday liturgy).

Rebbe Nachman's earliest follower was Reb Shimon. Once Reb Shimon's son was critically ill and he asked Rebbe Nachman to use his special abilities to pray for the child. Rebbe Nachman did not respond. Reb Shimon understood this to mean that the situation was very desperate. When he came home he told his wife, "If you want a live child, don't go to sleep tonight." The whole night Reb Shimon's wife stood over the child's cot weeping and crying for her son. When Reb Shimon went to the Rebbe the next morning the Rebbe said, "Until now I did not fully appreciate the power of a woman's prayers. The decree that the child would die was already sealed, but she, with her simple prayers, not only won him life but long life at that! Do you see the power of prayer?!" Reb Shimon's son recovered and lived for close to a hundred years (*Siach Sarfey Kodesh* 1-100).

Heavenly decrees

Rebbe Nachman was no stranger to illness either in his own life or in the lives of his immediate family. Besides his final illness, he himself suffered a number of bouts of serious illness, including one during his trip to the Holy Land in 1798, and another in the spring of 1807 (see below). Of his eight children, four — two boys and two girls — died in infancy or early childhood. His first wife, Sashia, died of tuberculosis at the age of thirty-four in 1807. Needless to say, Rebbe Nachman did not view any of these tragedies in a medical context. He saw them all as being sent from heaven for mysterious reasons which had to do with the very intensity of his efforts to bring redemption into the world.

This is evident in comments he made when his granddaughter was stricken with smallpox in the summer of 1805, shortly after two of the greatest spiritual triumphs of his life: his revelation of the *Tikkun HaKlali*, the General Remedy (see below pp. 153ff.), and his handing over of the manuscript of his major Torah discourses to date for binding. He poured out his anguish over his granddaughter's illness to Reb Noson, who writes:

"The Rebbe then spoke of how God's ways cannot be understood. Once the holy Ari (Rabbi Yitzchak Luria, 1534-72) lost a son. The Ari said this happened because of a secret teaching he himself had revealed to Rabbi Chaim Vital (see *Shevachey HaAri*, Warsaw 1875 p.11b f.). In fact the Ari had no other choice: Rabbi Chaim Vital had pressed him greatly and the Ari was therefore compelled to reveal the secret, because he himself had said that the only reason he came into this world was to rectify Rabbi Chaim Vital's soul. He was therefore compelled from on high to reveal this mystery at Rabbi Chaim's request. But despite having been compelled, the Ari was still punished for what he did. These are ways of God that cannot possibly be grasped by the human intellect.

"From what the Rebbe said we could understand that the same was true of him. Both he and his children had suffered greatly, and this all happened because he was involved in bringing us closer to God. God certainly desired this, and the Rebbe had no other choice. It is written, 'He thinks thoughts that the outcast not be banished' (Samuel II, 14:14). God wanted the Rebbe to bring the 'outcasts' back to Him, but still, the Rebbe had to suffer because of this. This is God's incomprehensible way" (*Rabbi Nachman's Wisdom #189*).

In the spring of 1805 Rebbe Nachman's first son, Shlomo Ephraim, was born. Rebbe Nachman had tremendous hopes for his son, but some time during the first year of his life Shlomo Ephraim contracted tuberculosis. This happened soon after Rebbe Nachman had handed over the manuscript of his "Burned Book" (see next chapter) to two of his closest followers with instructions to travel from town to town reading a little section in each one. Rebbe Nachman asked Reb Noson to pray for his baby son, saying, "I knew when I handed the book over to those two that *they* [the accusing forces] would brace themselves for an attack on this little baby...." (*Tzaddik #74*).

In the summer of 1806 Rebbe Nachman himself traveled to the Baal Shem Tov's grave in Medzeboz to pray for his son. He remained at the graveside for a very long time, but he knew that his prayers were fruitless. Shlomo Ephraim died while Rebbe Nachman was on the road from Medzeboz to Breslov. He later spoke of the greatness the child could one day have achieved, and likened his death to that of the Ari's son, who died because of the secret his father had revealed. Rebbe Nachman said to his followers, "I am suffering because of you. The holy Ari was punished for revealing one secret mystery. How much more is this true of me, seeing that I have revealed so many secrets like these" (*Rabbi Nachman's Wisdom ibid.*).

The following winter Rebbe Nachman's second son, Yaakov, was born, but died not long afterwards. By then the Rebbe's wife, Sashia, had already been sick with tuberculosis for some time. At the end of that same winter, in March 1807, Rebbe Nachman went on a mysterious journey to Novorich, Ostrog and a number of other cities in the area northwest of Kiev. While traveling, he sent his attendant, Reb Shmuel of Teplik, back to Breslov to bring his wife to Ostrog, where he intended to have her examined by a doctor. In a letter to his followers in Breslov he wrote, "Encourage my wife to come to me, for the wife of one's youth is impossible to replace" (*Alim LiTerufah* #1).

It is something of a mystery why Rebbe Nachman was willing to have his wife go to a doctor, seeing as he had already expressed his opposition to doctors and medicine, though not as vociferously as he was to do after his trip to Lemberg (*Rabbi Nachman's Wisdom* #50). In Jewish law one of a husband's obligations to his wife is to heal her (*Shulchan Arukh, Even Ha'Ezer* 79:1). Was it that Rebbe Nachman felt that even though he had no faith in medicine himself, he should still leave no possibility untried? Or could it be that his wife was the one who wanted to consult a doctor, and that Rebbe Nachman had no desire to oppose her wishes in a matter that concerned her very life?

Even so, it is highly doubtful whether Rebbe Nachman saw any hope in consulting a doctor. Before despatching Reb Shmuel of Teplik to Breslov, Rebbe Nachman made some cryptic remarks to him that are barely comprehensible in themselves but do nevertheless give some indication of his attitude: "Tonight I have been busy with a book of remedies, even though medicines are nothing. But the wife of my youth is not here. From *meizar* [the Aramaic word for medicine] will be made Mezritch. From there go to Ostrog and from there to Breslov for my wife in order to bring her there to be treated" (*Tzaddik* #60).

In any event, Rebbe Nachman tried to remain faithful to his own saying, "I don't hold by doctors. But if you're going to go, make sure you choose the very best!" (*Siach Sarfey Kodesh* I:8). He wanted his wife to be seen by the renowned Dr. Guardia (or Gordon), Rabbi Aharon ben Shimon Rofey (see Inset on facing page), who having been physician to the Mezritcher Magid was held in high esteem in chassidic circles. But for reasons unknown, his wife did not want treatment from Dr. Guardia and asked to travel to Zaslov, where she had family. In Zaslov she at first showed signs of improvement, but soon afterwards she began to languish and died on the eve of Shavuot, June 11, 1807, with Rebbe Nachman at her side.

Even before his wife's death Rebbe Nachman himself had gone through a bout of illness in Zaslov (*Tzaddik #56*). We do not know what it was, but evidently it was quite serious. In a letter to his followers in Breslov he asked them to pray for him.

"I shall not write the details of my illness in order not to make my *mazal* worse. I only ask that you pray for me in each and every prayer, and don't forget all the good that I have done for each one of you until now. It is possible that God will allow me to live, and you will be able to receive even more good from me. Remember how I found each of you when I came to Breslov, and how much energy, spiritual and physical, I have

Rabbi Aharon ben Shimon Rofey (Dr. Guardia) d. 1810

Born into a Jewish family in Prussia, Dr. Guardia strayed from his religious roots, eventually becoming court physician to the King of Prussia. Once the king paid a state visit to Vilna, bringing his physician with him. It happened that a prominent member of the Vilna Jewish community, who was a follower of the Mezritcher Magid, was seriously ill. The town doctors despaired of helping him but his family asked that the visiting king's physician be brought to see him. Miraculously the man was healed. Afterwards he mentioned to Dr. Guardia that some time before he became sick, his Rebbe, the Magid, had told him something that he could only now understand: it isn't the medicines that bring healing, but each doctor is accompanied by a unique angel of healing, while the greatest of doctors is accompanied by the Angel Raphael himself. [The Angel Raphael is charged with healing the sick.]

These words of the Magid aroused the Jewish spark in Dr. Guardia, who requested a period of leave from the Prussian Court in order to visit the Magid. When he arrived, the Magid said, "I've been waiting so long for you to come. I will heal your soul, and you, my son, heal my body." The doctor decided to stay with the Magid, and from then on devoted himself with all his heart and soul to Torah and prayer, becoming a tzaddik and a Torah scholar. He was known as Rabbi Aharon ben Shimon Rofey. After the death of the Magid he settled in Ostrog, where he spent his entire day in the synagogue engaged in Torah and prayer. Anyone in the region who was in need of treatment knew where the doctor was to be found. Whenever he was called to attend the sick he removed his tallit and tefilin, paid his doctor's visit, and then returned to his Torah study (from *The Magid of Mezritch* by R.Y. Klapholtz).

expended on your behalf. It is therefore only proper that you should now likewise pray for me and ask God to 'heal me and show me the pleasure of His splendor'" (*Alim LiTerufah* #1).

In a letter to his son-in-law, R. Yoske, husband of his daughter Adil, Rebbe Nachman wrote from Zaslov:

"I should also like to inform you that I am not making use of medicine, for God has helped me and has not taken His beneficence and truth from me" (*ibid.* #2).

In a second letter to his followers, he writes:

"Let me also tell you that I am now quite healthy without having resorted to any physical cures" (*ibid.* #3).

In the same letter, he said to his followers:

"What I ask of you is that my toil and labor on behalf of each one of you should not turn out to have been in vain. For I have taken my life in my hands for the sake of your souls. God is the righteous one, it is I who did evil. It was my own deeds which caused my suffering, the death of my precious children, the opposition and the accusations. But I know full well that it was also the work which I did with you to extricate you from the teeth of Satan that caused him to sharpen his eyes upon me and grind his teeth against me" (*ibid.*).

Rebbe Nachman later told his followers that it was their prayers that had brought about his recovery from illness in Zaslov (*Tzaddik* #63) — but not for long. Satan's vice was tightening on Rebbe Nachman. In the summer of 1807 he left Zaslov and went to Brody, where he became engaged to his second wife. From there he returned to Breslov, but on the way back he started coughing, and he knew at once that this was a sign of the illness he would die of. He lived for another three years, which he said was a miracle. But from this time on he began talking about his death (*Tzaddik* #58-59).

Chapter 8

Lemberg

Prior to his last illness Rebbe Nachman had always been very vigorous and active. He said: "It was as if someone for whom the world had tremendous need was snatched away and confined to a room high up on the third or fourth floor. 'Now you sit *here!*' I used to be like a busy merchant going out to the market with any number of things to do, always snatching at business opportunities. Even if they told me I needed to take a little rest and relaxation I wouldn't hear of it. I didn't know what rest and relaxation were. All the time I had to do... do...! And now I have to be careful how I eat, I have to make sure I get my sleep and so on — all because of my illness. I used to have a beautiful body. It never made demands or pushed itself forward. But now I have to be so careful...." (*Tzaddik #77-78*).

In the days before immunization and antibacterial drugs, tuberculosis, or "consumption" (*hoost* in Yiddish), was a dreaded disease. The most usual symptoms are persistent coughing, fever, night sweats and chronic exhaustion. Tuberculosis generally starts in the lungs but can spread to the gastrointestinal and urogenital tracts, the nervous system, joints, bones and skin. Reb Noson tells of Rebbe Nachman's constant coughing and weakness throughout his illness, and in one place gives a heart-rending description of one of his worst coughing attacks, in which he brought up enormous quantities of blood and phlegm (*Tzaddik #116*).

> "Pain and suffering may sometimes be imposed on a Tzaddik for his entire generation. In atoning for them through his suffering, this Tzaddik saves them in this world and greatly benefits them in the next world" (R. Moshe Chaim Luzzatto, *Derekh HaShem* 2:3:8).

However, for Rebbe Nachman his illness was not a personal tragedy but an expression of the plight of the Jewish People as a whole. In the words of Rabbi Moshe Chaim Luzzatto, the outstanding 18th century kabbalist:

"Pain and suffering may sometimes be imposed on a Tzaddik for his entire generation. In atoning for them through his suffering, this Tzaddik saves them in this world and greatly benefits them in the next. An even

higher category of suffering is that which comes to a Tzaddik to provide
the help necessary to bring about the chain of events leading to mankind's
ultimate perfection. Man has to undergo at least some suffering before he
and the world can attain perfection. He must be punished for his wicked-
ness until the attribute of justice is satisfied. However, God arranged
matters in such a way that select perfect individuals can rectify things for
others. The only reason they suffer is because of others. The merit and
power of these Tzaddikim are increased because of such suffering, and
this gives them an even greater ability to rectify the damage of others.
They can therefore not only rectify their own generation but can also
correct all the spiritual damage from the beginning...." (R. Moshe Chaim
Luzzatto, *Derekh HaShem* 2:3:8).

In Rebbe Nachman's own words:

"Know that while sometimes forgiveness of sins comes about through
the collective merit of the community, there are times when the members
of the community are not sufficiently worthy to have their sins forgiven
in their own merit. The Tzaddik is then obliged to undertake to suffer for
the sake of the Jewish People. 'Surely he bore our diseases and carried our
pains' (Isaiah 53:4). The community in general is saved from illness but not
the Tzaddik, because he undertakes to suffer on behalf of the Jewish
People" (*Likutey Moharan* II, 8:6).

In discourse after discourse during his last illness, Rebbe Nachman spoke
about the spiritual significance of the lungs. The physical life of the entire body
depends upon the lungs, which bring oxygen from the air to the blood, which
in turn takes it to all the body's tissues, where it is needed to produce the energy
the cells require in order to function. The life of the spirit also depends upon
the lungs, whose five lobes correspond to the Five Books of Moses — the Torah
— and to the five divisions of the Book of Psalms — Prayer. Words of Torah
and prayer are the breath of life and the essential "soul food" of the Jewish
People. Rebbe Nachman saw his diseased lungs as expressing the crisis of faith
that was afflicting the nation. When the "lungs" are wasted, the entire nation
is in danger.

Death held no terrors for Rebbe Nachman. He said that for him it was "just
like going from one room to another" (*Rabbi Nachman's Wisdom* #156). He explained:
"If you grasp at this world, there is an agonizing difference between this world
and the grave. This world is spread before you, while the grave is a tight,
cramped place. But when you have purified your mind and your thoughts,

there is no difference between this world, the grave and the next world. When you desire only God and His Torah, all are the same. In all three you can grasp onto God and His Torah" (*ibid.* #51). What haunted Rebbe Nachman was not death but the need to complete his mission — to heal the fissure between God and the Jewish People through holding out a redemptive Torah of faith and joy that would speak to those alienated from their spiritual roots.

Does the fact that Rebbe Nachman succumbed to his illness at the age of only thirty-eight in any way invalidate his healing pathway? That he died young says very little in itself. In his thirty-eight years he achieved far more than most people could achieve in multiple lifetimes. But what about the fact that he did not "recover" from his tuberculosis? Is his pathway of healing through faith and joy to be judged as a failure on the grounds that he was unable to heal himself?

Was it even possible that he could have recovered from a disease that in those days was invariably fatal? Presumably Rebbe Nachman believed that it was possible, at least in principle (see *Sichot HaRan* #157). He said: "I believe that God can turn a triangle into a square, for God's ways are hidden from us. He is omnipotent and nothing is impossible for Him" (*Tzaddik* #407). It is quite unlikely that medicine as known at that time could have brought about a complete remission, and in any case Rebbe Nachman did receive medical treatment in Lemberg, as we shall presently see. But should he have been able to do better through spiritual healing?

If healing is understood to mean nothing but a complete and permanent reversal of physical illness, it is true that Rebbe Nachman was not cured, though he did survive for a full three years despite several extreme crises in which he came very close to death. But healing means more than physical recovery. True healing means living one's life to the fullest up to the very last moment. In this sense Rebbe Nachman *was* healed, because he refused to allow his physical limitations to turn him into an invalid.

He continued his spiritual quest just as he had done throughout his life, constantly moving forward as fast as he could, never standing still for a moment. He turned his very illness into a means of self-elevation. Many of the greatest treasures that he left to posterity date from this last period of his life, including all his longer stories and many of his most outstanding discourses in *Likutey Moharan*, which contain priceless, life-giving spiritual guidance and encouragement for generations to come. Since his illness was ultimately the illness of the Jewish People, it was not possible for his body to be healed. The rectification that had to be accomplished could come about only through his death. But out of his very illness and suffering Rebbe Nachman forged the healing pathway that could bring succor for the wounds of the nation.

"I will tell you the beginning of my journey"

In the late summer of 1807 Rebbe Nachman married his second wife, and soon afterwards celebrated the Days of Awe in Breslov. With all his followers gathered at his side, Rosh Hashanah was always the high point of the year for him and the occasion for some of his greatest discourses. This Rosh Hashanah Rebbe Nachman already knew that a long journey lay ahead of him. He intended to leave for Lemberg (Lvov), the capital of Galicia, directly after the conclusion of Succot.

It would be a long and difficult journey from the Russian Ukraine to an area of Poland that was then ruled by Austria. The whole of Europe was in the grip of the Napoleonic Wars. It was to be one of the most dramatic journeys of Rebbe Nachman's life, and one that was to have the utmost significance for the development of his teachings on healing. But as yet he had no idea how his journey would end. He was very sick and weak. Would he ever return to Breslov and see his followers again?

Rebbe Nachman's journey to Lemberg was a mission for the sake of the future of the Jewish People. In the words of Reb Nachman of Tcherin (1825-94), outstanding scholar of the third generation of the Breslov movement:

"Rebbe Nachman saw with his holy spirit that atheism and skepticism were destined to attack the Jewish People. In Lemberg he worked to subjugate these trends. When he returned from there he raised a bitter cry about the atheism that was spreading throughout the world. Today we can actually see how everything he predicted has come about. The cancerous disease of atheism and unbelief is everywhere. The main thrust of the attack is on the young. From their earliest years they are brought up to be skeptical about the teachings of our Rabbis. The Rebbe labored to rectify this situation, and this was the purpose of his journey to Lemberg" (*Parpara'ot LeChokhmah* on *Likutey Moharan* I, 282).

For Rebbe Nachman, his mission had already begun that Rosh Hashanah, while he was still in Breslov. The discourse he gave (*"Rabbi Shimon rejoiced," Likutey Moharan* I, 61) was a kind of last will and testament to his followers, emphasizing the importance of faith in the Tzaddik and of spreading his teachings through the printing of books. The true Tzaddik attains the supreme wisdom of the

Torah, through which all conflicts and contradictions can be resolved and sweetened. In a pointed hint to his chassidim, Rebbe Nachman quoted the saying of Rabbi Shimon bar Yochai: "For us, everything depends upon חביבותא (*chavivuta*), mutual love" (*Zohar Bemidbar* 128). Love between chassid and chassid and between Jew and Jew would be the remedy for conflict within the Jewish People and in the world as a whole, bringing unity and joy — all through faith in the Tzaddik. Three weeks later, on Shemini Atzeret — just two days before he was to leave Breslov — Rebbe Nachman gave the discourse that he saw as the most fundamental of all his teachings, and one that is also basic to his approach to health and healing: "*Azamra — I will sing!*":

> "Know that you must judge all people favorably. Even in the case of a complete sinner, you must search until you find some modicum of good by virtue of which he is *not a sinner*. By finding this small amount of good and judging him favorably, you really do elevate him to the scale of merit, and you can then bring him back to God.

> "And so too you must seek out the good in yourself. It is a known principle that one must take care to be happy at all times and keep well away from depression. Maybe when you start looking at yourself, it seems as if you have nothing good in you at all. Even so, you must not allow yourself to become discouraged. Search until you find a little bit of good within yourself. You may start to examine it, only to see that it is full of blemishes and devoid of purity. Even so, how is it possible that it contains not a modicum of good? You have to search until you find some little good point in yourself to restore your inner vitality and attain joy. In just the same way you must carry on searching until you find another good point in yourself, and then another....

> "When a person refuses to let himself fall but instead revives his spirits by searching out his positive points, collecting them together and sifting them from the impurities and evil within him, through this melodies are made. He can then pray and sing and give thanks to God" (*Likutey Moharan* I, 282).

The teaching of "*Azamra*" was a further step in Rebbe Nachman's mission. Not only is the search for the good points in others and in ourselves the basis of *chavivuta*, mutual love between Jew and Jew. It is also the foundation of genuine faith, which means not merely belief in God "out there," but faith in the Godliness within ourselves and those around us. Each one of us is God's precious creation. We are important in God's eyes. Flawed as our efforts to act right and do good in the world may often be, every one of them is cherished in God's eyes. Even the tiniest modicum of goodness can become a pregnant point of connection with God, leading to abundant joy, song, ecstatic prayer and complete *teshuvah*, return and restoration.

The teaching of the good points lies at the very heart of Rebbe Nachman's pathway of healing through joy (see pp. 159-73), and it was also the key to his remedy for the atheism he saw spreading through the world. For in the words of R. Nachman of Tcherin, "When a person first starts having doubts and atheistic ideas, in most cases it is because of the demoralization he experiences when he starts thinking about his sins. This makes it hard for him to remain firm in the Torah path and cheer himself up with the good points he still has in him. In the end he falls away completely, becomes caught up in totally bad ways, loses all faith and turns into an atheist" (*op. cit.*). Showing people the way to discover their own true value was Rebbe Nachman's medicine for the demoralization that lies at the core of the vicious cycle of sin and alienation from God.

Immediately after the conclusion of the festivals, Rebbe Nachman set off hurriedly for Lemberg. Reb Noson and his lifelong friend, Reb Naftali, went running after the Rebbe's carriage, and caught up with it as the horses labored up a hill.

> "We stood there in front of the Rebbe and he gave us a kindly look. 'Which would you prefer,' he said, 'a blessing or a Torah teaching?' 'Give us the blessing when you come home safe and well from Lemberg,' I answered. 'But for now, teach us Torah!' — for I knew that if we didn't hear it at once it would be lost forever.' He said, 'I will tell you the beginning of my journey'" (*Yemey Moharnat* 23a).

It was then that Rebbe Nachman revealed the concluding section of his teaching "*Azamra*," which speaks of the Tzaddik as the one who has the power to gather all the good points that are to be found in every Jew, even those who have rebelled against the Torah. The teaching of "*Azamra*," foundation of Rebbe Nachman's pathway of health and healing, was indeed the "beginning of his journey" — because Rebbe Nachman's trip to Lemberg was a mission of healing for the entire Jewish People. At the conclusion of the teaching, the carriage moved off, taking the sick, weak Rebbe Nachman on his way to Lemberg.

Lemberg

The largest city in Eastern Galicia, Lemberg had been a transit center for trade between the orient and the west. Jews had lived there from time immemorial. The town had been a center of Shabbatean activity, and in 1759 was the scene of a major disputation between the Rabbis and the followers of the neo-Shabbatean Jacob Frank, after which over five hundred Frankists were converted to Christianity amidst great pomp and ceremony. The partition of Poland in 1772, the year of Rebbe Nachman's birth, placed Lemberg under Austrian rule. Although this led to an artificial curtailment of its role in trade, it had important effects in other directions.

For one thing, the Austrian authorities encouraged assimilationist tendencies in their Jewish population. By the time of Rebbe Nachman's visit in 1807-8, Lemberg's Jewish community, which numbered over 18,000, already included a group of *maskilim*. Under the influence of the notorious Naftali Hertz Homberg (1749-1841), whom the Austrian authorities had appointed as superintendent of the Jewish schools in Galicia, Lemberg had four boys' schools, three girls' schools and a teachers' seminary run according to his principles, which included a prohibition against the use of the Hebrew language and the censorship of traditional texts. Lemberg later became one of the major battlefields in the conflict between observant Jews and the proponents of assimilation.

Another effect of Lemberg's annexation to Austria was that it became a major center for Jewish doctors. Until the end of the eighteenth century the medical schools of Poland and Russia were closed to Jews, and those wishing to study medicine were obliged to travel to Italy. However the Edicts of Tolerance issued by Emperor Joseph II of Austria starting in 1782 gave Jews admission to Austria's medical schools. These had become the most progressive in the whole of Europe ever since the Empress Maria Theresa had brought leading alumni of the University of Leiden to reorganize medical teaching in Vienna. Austrian doctors were among the first to popularize use of the thermometer in medicine and pioneered the procedure of percussing the chest (tapping with the fingers) to diagnose abnormalities of the thorax. Vienna's famous *Allgemeines Krankenhaus* teaching hospital became a model for all Europe.

All this encouraged intelligent young Jews who were disenchanted with the traditional Jewish occupations of trade, estate management, distilling and tax collection to enter the field of medicine. As a major Jewish population center, Lemberg boasted a large number of doctors, so many, in fact, that they were divided into two camps locked in dispute over how to treat various diseases (*Rabbi Nachman's Wisdom #50*).

Compelled from on high

Did Rebbe Nachman journey to Lemberg purely for the purpose of receiving medical treatment?

Reb Noson writes:

"The Rebbe himself underwent medical treatment in Lemberg, but this involved deep mysteries. It was not for medical treatment that he made this trip but for deep reasons known only to himself. His intentions were as hidden and mysterious as they were on his journeys to Kaminetz, Novorich and Sharograd. All the Rebbe's travels involved awesome mysteries hidden from all human eyes. Who can unravel the mystery of his travels? Everything the Rebbe did involved impalpable secrets. The same is true of his journey to Lemberg. Once he was there, he was compelled from on high to accept medicines, for reasons known only to himself" (*ibid.*).

We can perhaps gain a glimmer of insight into Rebbe Nachman's reasons for accepting treatment from a comment he himself made:

"I cannot describe the suffering I endured there — spiritual suffering, needless to say. I received medical treatment. I used to drink חינא (*hina*).* The people living where this plant grows are total unbelievers. They say, 'There's no law and no Judge.' I used to take other remedies grown in other locations where there are different kinds of heresy. When all these drugs came inside me, they turned into whatever they turned into" (*Tzaddik #78*).

---

*It seems likely that חינא (*hina*) is quinine, which at that time was used as a remedy for malaria, a disease that affected much of Europe. Quinine is derived from the bark of the *cinchona* plant, named after the Spanish Countess of Cinchona, who was said to have introduced the plant into Spain from Peru. The name quinine comes from the *quina quina* plant, which was mistaken for *cinchona*. The latter was very expensive, so many physicians continued to use the ancient arsenic salts for a multitude of external and internal conditions.

The editor of *Tzaddik* explains:

"The drugs from each location all had to come into his stomach in order for the atheism of the place to be crushed. This was true of several drugs. From this it is possible to gain a little understanding as to why the Rebbe submitted himself to medical treatment, although there were other hidden reasons, as there were behind all his actions. His advice to other people was very emphatically to keep away from doctors and medical treatment!" (*ibid.*).

It is a strange paradox that Rebbe Nachman received treatment in what must then have been one of the most progressive medical centers in Europe, only to go on to attack doctors and medicine more vociferously than ever before. We might therefore ask whether another of his reasons for taking treatment was that he wanted to penetrate to the very core of the developing medical orthodoxy, since it was destined to become the ascendant healing paradigm in the new world that was coming into being. In many ways it was the complete negation of the healing paradigm that Rebbe Nachman championed. Was it that he wanted to know what he was fighting against, even if it meant learning it on his very own flesh?

During his stay in Lemberg, Rebbe Nachman was in a very critical condition. Reb Noson writes:

"For a long period he was only able to lie on one side and he found it impossible to lie on the other. Afterwards God worked miracles and wonders, and he began to improve a little. Suddenly one night he turned onto his other side and was able to lie on it. He said this improvement owed nothing to the doctor. In fact what had happened was that someone had come that night and told him there was a decree in heaven that he should lie on his right side, and he did indeed lie on his right side as he had always done (cf. Ezekiel 4:4-8). It had been a long time since he had been able to do this. The person who came to him that night was the famed and saintly R. Aharon of Tetiev (d.1827), grandson of the Baal Shem Tov" (*Tzaddik* #65).

Rebbe Nachman said that during the time that he was unable to turn onto his other side, there was one period when he suffered continuous pain and inflammation for three days. When he related this, he said, "But then I cried out to God differently!" (*Siach Sarfey Kodesh* 1-98).

The Burned Book

One day in the early spring of 1808 the Rebbe went into a private room and there he wept and wept. He called for Reb Shimon, who was attending him.

Reb Noson relates:

"With tears running down his cheeks Rebbe Nachman sighed and said: 'I have no one to ask for advice.' The Rebbe told Reb Shimon that in his house in Breslov was a book he had written, for the sake of which he had lost his wife and children. For this book they had died, and he himself had sacrificed himself greatly. Now he did not know what to do. He saw that he would be forced to die there in Lemberg. Only if this book were to be burned could he survive. It caused him great anguish to think of burning this awesome and holy book, for which he had sacrificed himself so heavily. [This work was known to the Breslover Chassidim as *Sefer HaNisraf*, the "Burned Book," which Rebbe Nachman had dictated to Reb Noson at intervals between 1805 and 1807 and had given to two of his other followers to read extracts in various towns, see above p.71.] There is no way of communicating the exaltedness of this book. If it had survived, everyone would have seen the greatness of the Rebbe with their own eyes.

"Reb Shimon answered him: 'If there are any grounds for supposing that your life depends on this, there is no doubt that it would be better to burn the book so that you should remain alive.' The Rebbe said, 'At least my time would be extended. But even so, it would be very painful for me to burn it. You don't realize the preciousness and holiness of this book. I lost my first wife and my children for it. I have endured terrible sufferings for it.' The Rebbe wept and wept. Afterwards the doctor came to the house. Reb Shimon and the Rebbe were still talking. Reb Shimon told the doctor how worried he was about the Rebbe crying like this at a time when his condition was so serious. The doctor was shaken by the sight of the Rebbe. He spoke with him a little and left.

"After this Rebbe Nachman and Reb Shimon continued talking. The Rebbe wept even more than before. Finally he said to Reb Shimon, 'If that is the case, here is the key to my drawer. Go quickly. Hurry! Don't delay! Hire a carriage and go straight to Breslov. Don't let the rain and snow hold you up. Go as fast as you can, and when you get to Breslov take two books. One of them is lying in my drawer, the second is in my daughter Adil's chest. Take them and burn them. For God's sake be as quick as you can.'

The Rebbe warned Reb Shimon not to try to be clever and hide a part of the book instead of burning everything.

"Reb Shimon hired a carriage and left immediately. But when he came to Dashev, which is close to Breslov, Reb Shimon suddenly fell ill. He was laid up in bed and simply could not get up. He realized that this was the work of the Evil One, who wanted to prevent him from carrying out the Rebbe's instructions. We had already discovered that anything the Rebbe told us to do was attended by countless obstacles, especially something as important as this, on which the Rebbe's very life depended.

"Reb Shimon gave orders that they should carry him out to the coach, lay him down inside and press on to Breslov. He was determined to make for Breslov as long as he had any life at all. All he could think about was to get to Breslov, where at least he would be able to tell someone else to burn the books in his presence. They put him into the carriage and he hurried on towards Breslov. As soon as he arrived he recovered. He took the two books and burned them both" (*Tzaddik* #66).

When Rebbe Nachman originally dictated the *Sefer HaNisraf* to Reb Noson, he said to him, "If only you knew what you are writing." Reb Noson replied, "I really have no idea at all." Said Rebbe Nachman, "You don't even know what it is that you don't know!" (*ibid.* #67). We too are in the same position. We have no idea what was lost to the world when the *Sefer HaNisraf* was destroyed. But Rebbe Nachman himself survived, and was able to go back to Breslov. And Reb Noson writes: "After his return from Lemberg, the Rebbe found a path and spoke in such a way as to ensure that his light would never be extinguished. The Rebbe himself said, 'My fire will burn until the Mashiach comes'" (*ibid.* #126).

Chapter 9

Sound the Shofar

Rebbe Nachman left Lemberg for Breslov in mid-June of 1808. The doctors said it was dangerous for him to travel because of the gravity of his condition, and that he should travel no more than about ten kilometers a day. But the Rebbe paid no attention and pressed on at high speed, covering tens of kilometers every day, just as the busy merchants used to do (*Tzaddik #80*). He arrived in Breslov two weeks later. He was still very sick and extremely weak, but he continued to teach his followers as before. He would often ride with them to the outskirts of the town and take walks in the meadows.

Reb Noson tells us that after Rebbe Nachman's return from Lemberg he spoke out against physicians and medicine more emphatically than ever before, denouncing them in the strongest terms (*Rabbi Nachman's Wisdom #50*). Rebbe Nachman's attacks on doctors and medicine are fairly well-known, not only among his present-day followers but among students of rabbinic thought in general. Sadly, most people are far less familiar with the positive pathway of health and healing he was teaching in precisely the same period.

Dominion over the Angels

The first Rosh Hashanah after Rebbe Nachman's return from Lemberg (September 22, 1808), hundreds of people came to Breslov to be with him. However, the Rebbe was so weak that, as Reb Noson put it, "it seemed as if there was no earthly way he would be able to give a discourse" (*Tzaddik #116*). But in the end Rebbe Nachman marshaled all his strength and gave a very lengthy discourse. This is *Likutey Moharan* II, 1: "*Sound the Shofar — Dominion over the Angels*," the fullest and most extensive statement we have of his healing pathway. (For complete translation and commentary, see pp. 237-77.)

This first major teaching of Rebbe Nachman's since his return from Lemberg is a magnificent elaboration of the pathway he had set forth in the last teaching he had given before leaving on his trip, "*Azamra — I will sing!*" There he explained how to awaken our soul-powers and attain true prayer — through finding our good points (see pp. 79f.). The power of the soul of the Jew is the starting point of "*Sound the Shofar — Dominion*."

"The Jew was created to have dominion over the angels! This is the ultimate destiny of the Jewish People, as our Rabbis taught: 'In time to come, the position of the Tzaddikim will be superior to that of the ministering angels.' Each person must see that he attains his destiny and rules over the angels" (*Likutey Moharan* II, 1).

This striking affirmation of the greatness of the Jewish soul is a rebuttal of the mechanistic ideas of the natural philosophers of Rebbe Nachman's time, who argued that human beings are nothing but machines and totally subordinate to the imperatives of natural law just like everything else in the world. Rebbe Nachman wanted us to realize that although we live within nature, our souls place us above it. *Through the force of our wilful embrace of our*

Rebbe Nachman's Teachings on Healing

All of Rebbe Nachman's major discourses, together with numerous shorter teachings, are collected in *Likutey Moharan* (literally, The Collected Teachings of MoHaRaN — *Morenu* [our teacher] HaRabbi Nachman). Part I of *Likutey Moharan* contains Rebbe Nachman's teachings prior to his trip to Lemberg. It was first printed soon after his return to Breslov in the summer of 1808. Part II, which is shorter, contains his major discourses and other teachings from the time of his return from Lemberg until his death in 1810. It was first printed in 1811. Today both parts of *Likutey Moharan* are usually printed in one volume.

The teachings in Part I include various discussions of healing but no detailed analysis of the subject. The main references to healing are in discourses #14, 21, 27, 56, 57, 58, 62 and 74, and in the shorter teachings in #164, 231, 263, 267, 268 and 277. In Part II healing is the central theme of #1, 3, 5, 6, 24 and 42, and it is a major theme in #2, 4, 7 and 8.

The other main sources of Rabbi Nachman's teachings on healing are: *The Aleph-Bet Book*, Healing 1-4; *Rabbi Nachman's Wisdom* #50, 98 and 187; *Tzaddik* #194, 390, 391 and 459 and *Rabbi Nachman's Stories* pp. 410-37 and 479-80.

See pp. 453-5 for a complete index of all Rebbe Nachman's teachings on healing translated and discussed in this book.

spirituality we have the power to master and control nature. Our prayers and good deeds turn the "angels" — the vital forces of creation — into our agents. It is our holy words and deeds that channel power to them, bringing goodness and blessing into the entire creation.

This is our ultimate destiny — and we can actually attain it in this world. But first we have to be tested: incarnated in our bodies, our souls are confronted with the challenge of our physical natures. Will we pursue our spiritual mission or succumb to the temptations of the flesh?

"One must guard oneself carefully and see that one has the strength to stand firm in this position of power and not let the ministering angels cast one down out of jealousy. For the angels are very jealous of a man like this who has dominion over them" *(ibid.)*.

The jealousy of the angels finds expression in each one of us in the impulses of our *yetzer hara*, the evil inclination, which tries to distract us from our spiritual mission by focussing our attention on our material desires. And if we succumb, we do indeed fall under the power of nature.

Who is the true leader?

"*Sound the Shofar — Dominion*" comes to teach us how we can remain firm in our mission and attain our destiny, transcending our bondage to the natural order — through binding ourselves to the souls of our fellow Jews. "Together we stand!" It is through working together as a spiritual community, supporting and encouraging each other, that we become immune to the temptations and distractions that plague us as long as we remain isolated and wrapped up in ourselves. This is a further development of the theme Rebbe Nachman expressed in his discourse the previous Rosh Hashanah, just before his trip to Lemberg. "For us, everything depends upon *chavivuta*, mutual love" (*Likutey Moharan* I, 61).

But in order to bind oneself to the souls of the Jewish People it would be necessary to know the root of every single soul. Since this is practically impossible for most people, the main thing is to bind oneself to the true leaders of the generation since all the individual souls are grouped under them, and in this way one is bound to all the souls. The key question, then, is: how can we *recognize* the true leaders and distinguish them from the false leaders who have thrust themselves to prominence through sheer brazenness? Rebbe Nachman's answer to this question takes up almost the whole of the rest of this lengthy teaching. And it is in the course of his answer that Rebbe

Nachman explains in full detail the foundations of the Torah path of healing — for true healing of the soul and the body comes through attachment to the spiritual teacher who guides us to our ultimate destiny.

Rebbe Nachman tells us that our difficulties in recognizing the true leaders stem from the fact that the spiritual consciousness in our heart becomes dulled to the extent that we gratify our cravings for wealth, food and sex in excess of what we need to fulfil our mission in this world. To recover our spiritual sensitivity we have to rectify these cravings, learning to satisfy our material needs in a balanced, harmonious way as part of our overall spiritual life. The way to do this is by turning our intellectual knowledge of God's existence into an awareness of His presence that we actually *feel in our hearts* as we go about the daily business of living. "Know *this day* and put it into your *heart* that HaShem is God...." (Deuteronomy 4:39).

The healing power of prayer

The effect of developing complete awe and reverence in the heart is to release prayer from its exile.

"And when this happens, there is no more need for medicines. All medicines are derived from plants, and every single plant receives its powers from its own particular planet or star, because 'there isn't a single plant that doesn't have a planet or star that strikes it and says, "Grow!"'" (*Bereshit Rabbah* 10). Every planet and star receives its power from the stars above it, and the highest stars from the higher powers, until they receive power from the supreme angels, who in turn receive from the powers beyond them, one higher than the other, until they all receive from the root of all things, which is the 'Word of God,' as it is written, 'Through the *word* of God the heavens were made and all their hosts by the breath of His mouth' (Psalms 33:6).

"This explains why, when we attain prayer, there is no need for medicines. The reason is that prayer is the 'Word of God,' which is the root of all things. And 'He sent His word and *healed* them, and delivered them from their abominations' (Psalms 107:20). 'He sent His *word* and healed them....' The Torah says: 'And you will serve the Lord your God, and He will bless your bread and your water; and I will remove sickness from among you' (Exodus 23:25). 'And you will *serve* the Lord your God' — '*service* means prayer' (*Bava Kama* 92b). And then, 'He will bless your bread and your water, and I will remove sickness, etc.' In other words, you will be healed through bread and water, because they will receive blessing from the root of all things, namely the 'Word of God' — prayer — and then bread and water will have the same power to heal as herbs.

"For the division and allocation of the various powers, which give one plant the power to cure one kind of illness and another a different illness, are found only in the lower world. But above, at the root of all things, i.e. the 'Word of God,' everything is unity, and there is no difference between bread and water and plants and herbs. When one grasps the root — the 'Word of God,' prayer — one is able to channel curative powers into bread and water, and one can be healed through bread and water.... And this is why King Hezekiah was able to put away the book of remedies — because he redeemed prayer from its exile" (*Likutey Moharan* II, 1:6-9, and see above pp. 17-20.).

Since prayer is the foundation of spiritual healing, Rebbe Nachman continues his discourse with a detailed analysis of the negative traits that vitiate our ability to attain true prayer and must therefore be broken. Essentially there are three: lack of adequate faith, sexual immorality and the tendency to look down upon other people.

"*Sound the Shofar — Dominion*" teaches not only a path to prayer but a balanced, harmonious way of life founded on faith and free of immorality and materialistic excesses. Such a way of life is itself a guarantor of sound health and freedom from the diseases caused by self-abuse. More than anything Rebbe Nachman emphasizes the need to overcome our tendency to look down upon other people. Mutual respect is the only solid basis for good interpersonal relationships, which are in themselves a vital factor in sound health. Moreover, it is only through love and unity between Jew and Jew that we are able to resist the "jealousy of the angels" and attain a level of prayer that brings blessing and healing power into the world. The theme of mutual respect and love again connects with Rebbe Nachman's teaching of "*Azamra!*" which emphasizes judging all people favorably through searching for their good points.

The answer to the key question — how can we recognize the true leaders of the Jewish People so as to bind ourselves to the roots of all the souls — is that the true leader is the one who reaches the level of perfect prayer, the "Word of God." The "Word of God" is the supreme Source from which all the multiplicity of specific forces within creation receive their power. These forces therefore fall into the category of "debtors" in relation to this Master of Prayer, because they depend upon his prayers for their power. The true Tzaddik is the great "creditor" of all creation, and the Rabbis taught that "a person does not act impudently towards his creditor" (*Bava Metzia* 3a). The false leaders who owe their position to brazen impudence are really no more than "borrowers." In the face of the true leader they are put to shame and fall away.

To draw healing power through prayer may seem to demand a level of spiritual perfection that is beyond the average individual. But this is why Rebbe Nachman taught his pathway of healing in the context of a discussion about how to find the true leader. On our own, as isolated, individual Jews, we do not have the power to withstand the "jealousy of the angels" — the *yetzer hara* — and to attain the heights of prayer. But through attaching ourselves to the Tzaddik, studying his teachings and making a sincere effort to follow in his spiritual pathways, not only do we have immeasurably greater power to elevate ourselves; we also each have a share in the blessings the Tzaddik himself draws into the world through his prayers, and through this we can be healed. Ultimately, the true leader is the Mashiach, the Master of Prayer *par excellence*, who will bring healing to all of the Jewish People and indeed to the entire world.

The power of speech

After Rosh Hashanah, the next gathering of the Breslover Chassidimwas on the Shabbat during Chanukah, and on Shabbat Chanukah of 1808 Rebbe Nachman gave another major discourse, *"The days of Chanukah are days of thanksgiving"* — *Likutey Moharan* II, 2. Although each of the Rebbe's discourses is a separate teaching, they are by no means disconnected. The thematic connections between them are particularly apparent in the discourses he gave in the period after his return from Lemberg. Each one can be seen as a further elaboration of a unitary pathway that the Rebbe was unfolding for his followers and for posterity. Every time his followers gathered he focussed on different aspects of this pathway.

The central theme of *"The Days of Chanukah"* is our power of speech and how we can develop it to perfection. "Someone who perfects his speech can accomplish what he wants through words alone: he can change nature according to his desire through the power of perfect speech" (*Likutey Moharan* II,2:6). This is clearly linked with the idea that is at the heart of *"Sound the Shofar — Dominion,"* that when prayer is redeemed it is possible to channel healing through words alone without medicine: prayer has the power to change nature. To be able to do this requires a very high level of prayer, and the discussion in *"The Days of Chanukah"* on how to perfect one's speech can be seen as a further exploration of the method by which to achieve the necessary level.

The foundation for perfect speech is our awareness and acknowledgement of God's presence at all the different junctures of life, especially in times of trial and suffering. In this connection Rebbe Nachman mentions the rabbinic teaching that four categories of people have to bring a thanksgiving offering (*Berakhot* 54b), including those who recover from sickness. Reb Noson tells us that this discourse was Rebbe Nachman's "thanksgiving offering" for having returned home safely from Lemberg (*Tzaddik* #79).

The discussion of suffering in *"The Days of Chanukah"* includes a detailed and very vivid description of the way that extreme stress affects the heart-rate and blood circulation. This connects thematically with a later discussion about the relationship between the heart and the lungs, and lung disease. In these discussions, physical anatomy becomes a metaphor for the spiritual anatomy of the Jewish People, with the Tzaddik as the heart and lungs. There is an "oil" that heals "lung disease": this is the oil of the Chanukah lights, which radiate the truth of God's presence throughout creation.

Pidyon Nefesh: Redemption of the Soul

Following this Chanukah discourse comes *"Redemption of the Soul"* — *Likutey Moharan* II, 3, a short but very important teaching on healing. It is undated, but since all the dated discourses in this first section of *Likutey Moharan* II are printed in chronological order, we may presume that this teaching was also given in the winter of 1808-9.

In this teaching Rebbe Nachman confronts the obvious objection to his rejection of doctors and medicines. This is that the Talmud clearly states that "the Torah gave sanction to the physician to heal" (*Berakhot* 60a and see above pp. 32f.). In *"Redemption of the Soul,"* Rebbe Nachman tells us that the physician does indeed have sanction to cure the patient — but only after the heavenly decree that caused the illness in the first place has been mitigated. This is brought about through *pidyon nefesh*, "redemption of the soul" of the sick person accomplished by a Tzaddik. In many cases illness is a manifestation of a spiritual flaw and can only be healed when the spiritual flaw is dealt with. Physical healing cannot come about until steps are taken to heal the soul. Only then can medicine be of any benefit. (For a full analysis of this teaching and its implications, see below pp. 185-92.)

The true doctor is thus the Tzaddik, who is the doctor of the soul and who intervenes with his prayers on behalf of the sick. This ties in closely with *"Sound the Shofar — Dominion,"* where the central question is how to find the true leader. The Tzaddik judges all people favorably and compassionately, and this gives him the power to plead on their behalf before the heavenly tribunal. The search for the true Tzaddik is a theme Rebbe Nachman returned to again and again in his later discourses.

Beyond nature

After his return from Lemberg, Rebbe Nachman no longer traveled about the Ukraine to visit his followers as he used to in earlier years. Thus the next major gathering of his chassidim was not until they came to Breslov for Shavuot 1809. This was when he gave his discourse on *"The Ravens"* — *Likutey Moharan* II, 4, based on the verse, "I have commanded the ravens to feed you" (Kings I, 17:4). The raven is cruel by nature, yet when Elijah the Prophet was in the wilderness God made the ravens bring him food. And so we too must break our innate tendency towards selfishness and insensitivity in order to develop the traits of kindness and charity.

Our ability to control and transcend our natural instincts testifies to the power of the spirit over nature. This power is the foundation of spiritual healing, and is the main theme of *"The Ravens,"* which is an elaborate teaching about how the entire creation and all human affairs are under the direct providence of God. Our awareness of God's power brings us to revere Him, enabling us to create the spiritual vessel with which we can receive the love and kindness that God wants to bestow upon us. This discourse is an explicit rejoinder to the mechanistic philosophies that were gaining ever greater influence in Rebbe Nachman's time, and which sought to explain the entire universe exclusively in terms of natural processes and scientific laws.

> "The natural philosophers seek to show through their erroneous theories that everything goes according to nature, as if there is no Supreme Will. Even the awesome wonders that God has done for us they seek to explain away as having come about through natural causes" (*Likutey Moharan* II, 4:5).

If that were the way the world worked, there would be no place for man's struggle to elevate himself spiritually since everything would be predetermined. Nor would there be any point in trying to effect changes in the world through prayer, since nothing except actual physical intervention could ever alter the inexorable course of nature.

The implications of such a worldview for healing are clear. According to this kind of mechanistic philosophy there can be no such thing as spiritual healing, because the only way to effect any change in a person's physical condition would be through treating him physically with drugs, surgery and the like. We may presume that this was the view taken by many of the physicians who were practicing in Rebbe Nachman's time, including, no doubt, some of those he encountered in Lemberg. Among the major influences on 18th century medicine were the German Friedrich Hoffman (1660-1742), who taught an openly mechanistic system, and the French Julien de la Mettrie (1709-51), whose book *L'homme machine* ("The Man Machine") was admired by a wide audience.

Rebbe Nachman did not explicitly refer to healing until towards the end of his discourse on *"The Ravens."* However, since the entire teaching is a rebuttal of the mechanistic worldview, it is an implicit vindication of spiritual healing. The essence of Rebbe Nachman's argument is that, just as God forced the cruel ravens to go against their nature and feed Elijah, so too, when we use our free will to conquer our innate selfishness and to practice charity and kindness, we transcend the laws of nature and manifest the Will of God as the supreme power over the entire creation. God created the laws of nature, and He is beyond them. The obvious corollary is that God has the power to send healing without our having to resort to physical remedies and medicines.

Miracles

Hearing Rebbe Nachman's warnings against doctors and medicine, some of his followers must have felt as disconcerted as many of us today do when we read about them. Rebbe Nachman's teachings about the greatness of the Jewish soul and the healing power of prayer are most exalted and inspiring. But what about when it comes down to practice. Can we really do without the doctors? What about in a real crisis? Dare we rely on faith alone?

Perhaps it was to show his followers what he was talking about that Rebbe Nachman let them witness a miracle that Shavuot of 1809. Having developed a most elaborate argument in this discourse on *"The Ravens,"* he began its concluding section by saying that all the concepts he had been explaining at such length are connected with healing. He then launched into a detailed, step-by-step account of the healing of a wound. First the wound is opened, then all the pus and other infected material must be drawn out. Next the blood must be cleansed, and finally the wound must close and heal completely. In a dazzling display of Torah hermeneutics, Rebbe Nachman explains how each of these steps is bound up with the concepts discussed in the main body of the discourse (see *Supplementary Readings* pp. 433-4). Nevertheless, at first sight the connection between this concluding section and the whole of the earlier part of the discourse seems a little tenuous. Why this sudden discussion of the healing of a wound?

Prior to that Shavuot, one of the most prominent of Rebbe Nachman's followers in the town of Ladizin, Reb Getzel, had been taken ill with an extremely severe rectal abscess. He was in great pain and his condition was critical. The doctors had given up all hope of saving his life. The only conceivable treatment would have been to break open the infected area, clean it and drain all the dangerous fluids from within. But this was impossible since the infection was deep inside the rectum and the treatment would undoubtedly be fatal.

When Rebbe Nachman's other followers from Ladizin came to Breslov for Shavuot, they told the Rebbe about Reb Getzel's plight. It was during the festival that the Rebbe gave this discourse, discussing the healing of a wound step by step. A few days later, when the chassidim from Ladizin returned home, they found Reb Getzel in good health. He told them that quite suddenly, with no medical intervention whatever, his abscess had opened and quantities of pus and infected fluids had flowed out, until the wound closed and healed. According to what Reb Getzel told them, the opening of the abscess took place at the exact time that Rebbe Nachman was giving his discourse in Breslov (*Tzaddik* #390 and *Parpara'ot LeChokhmah* II, 4:9).

Another (undated) instance of a healing performed by Rebbe Nachman was of a follower who had a serious ailment in his arm and was in such pain that he was unable to move it at all. His arm was in a sling and he was totally incapable of lowering it. In the words of Reb Noson:

"The Rebbe's followers told him that this cripple was very poor and could not afford the expensive salts and other medical treatments that he needed for his arm. The man was sitting at the Rebbe's table for the Shabbat noon meal. The Rebbe remarked that this man certainly had faith, and all those sitting there agreed. The Rebbe discussed this for a while, and then repeated himself, asking again if this cripple had faith. Those present again answered, 'Yes.'

"Suddenly the Rebbe commanded the cripple: 'Lower your hand!' The cripple was amazed, as were all those present. What was the Rebbe saying? The man had been afflicted for a long time and it was absolutely impossible for him to move his arm. Why was the Rebbe telling him to do the impossible? But as soon as the Rebbe gave the order, 'he decreed, spoke, and it became fulfilled' (Job 22:28). His followers removed the man's sling, and he instantly lowered his arm. He was totally healed, and it was an obvious miracle. He regained full use of his arm, and it remained healthy for the rest of his life" (*Rabbi Nachman's Wisdom* #187).

After Reb Noson's account of this miracle, he adds: "I saw the Rebbe soon after he healed the cripple, and I spoke to him about it. It was obvious that the Rebbe was not feeling well. He said, 'Whenever I am involved in miracles, I always suffer from it. Whenever I do anything like this, I pray to God that it be forgotten'" (*ibid.*). An oral tradition among the Breslover Chassidim has it that the *misnagdim* (opponents of Chassidism) in Breslov spread a rumor that the man had not really been ill at all, and Rebbe Nachman rejoiced, because the miracle was thus concealed (*Siach Sarfey Kodesh* I-188).

Compared with the Baal Shem Tov and other chassidic luminaries, we hear of relatively few miracles performed by Rebbe Nachman. Reb Avraham b'Reb Nachman Chazan (1849-1917), leader of the third generation of Breslover Chassidim, suggests that Rebbe Nachman generally refrained from using miracles, because "the power of his sweet, pleasant words to inspire, vitalize and restore fallen souls was so great that if he had used miracles as well, people would have had no option but to believe in him, and free will would have been totally removed. Even when he performed a miracle, he would afterwards request God that the matter be forgotten" (*Kokhvey Or* p.36).

It could also be that Rebbe Nachman did not want his followers to depend upon the Tzaddik to accomplish miracles for them. Rather, he wanted them to put their main emphasis on following his Torah teachings in order that they should awaken and develop their own spiritual powers. This may help explain why, before Rebbe Nachman healed the man with the crippled arm, he repeatedly asked those present if the man had faith. It is as if the Rebbe wanted to imprint upon the minds of all who witnessed this miracle that spiritual healing cannot simply be administered by the Tzaddik. We ourselves have to forge a vessel to receive it: pure, simple faith in God, which is the channel for all goodness and blessing. And since, as Rebbe Nachman had taught long before, "faith, prayer and miracles are all one concept" (*Likutey Moharan* I, 7) every

Jew has the power to open himself to God's miracles through deepening his faith and cultivating the art of prayer.

The main thing is faith!

The issue of faith was becoming ever more urgent. In the summer of 1809 Napoleon was campaigning in central Europe, and succeeded in defeating Austria, taking control of Austria's share of Poland including the Warsaw area. Wherever Napoleon advanced, he sought the support of the Jews by holding out hopes of a new life free of the old social disabilities. Great numbers of Jews saw him as a sincere benefactor, and eagerly embraced not only the French revolutionary ideals of "liberty, equality and fraternity," but also, in many cases, the secular outlook that went with them. Even though the French were eventually forced to retreat from Eastern Europe, one of the lasting effects of Napoleon's campaigns there was to give the secular-oriented *Haskalah* ("Enlightenment") a strong foothold among the Jews. From this time on more and more began questioning their faith and abandoning their religious traditions.

Rebbe Nachman's response was to put faith at the very center of his teachings. He said, "The world considers faith a minor thing. But I consider it an extremely great thing" (*Rabbi Nachman's Wisdom* #33). Faith had a place in *"Sound the Shofar — Dominion"* as one of the three preconditions for attaining true prayer. Belief in God's providence is the underlying theme of *"The Ravens."* And faith is at the very forefront of the Rebbe's discourse on Rosh Hashanah 1809, which marked the start of the last year of his life. This was *"Sound the Shofar — Faith"* (*Likutey Moharan* II, 5, see below pp. 284-9). [Each of Rebbe Nachman's Rosh Hashanah discourses in the last three years of his life takes its main title from the verse they are all based on, "Sound the shofar" (Psalms 81:4). To distinguish the three discourses from one another, each is subtitled according to its main theme.]

Just before that Rosh Hashanah Rebbe Nachman had told his closest followers that numerous people had come to him complaining bitterly about their lack of faith, including several who were sick (*Tzaddik* #167). The first words of his Rosh Hashanah discourse are a ringing cry: "The main thing is faith!"

> "The main thing is faith! Every person must search within himself and strengthen himself in faith. For there are people suffering from the most terrible afflictions, and the only reason they are ill is because of the collapse of faith. The Torah says, 'God will send you wondrous plagues, great and

faithful plagues and great and faithful sicknesses' (Deuteronomy 28:59). The plagues and sicknesses are called 'faithful' because they come on account of a lack of faith. The collapse of faith causes 'wondrous' plagues, for which neither medicine nor prayer nor the merit of the fathers are of any avail" (*Likutey Moharan II, 5:1*).

The discourse continues with an intricate analysis of why the collapse of faith makes it impossible to be cured either by medicine, ancestral merit, prayer or even cries and screams. This analysis includes a passage on the healing properties of plants and some important statements about the causes of illness (see below pp. 284-9). All this reinforces the main point, which is that without faith there can be no true healing. Rebbe Nachman therefore continues:

"The remedy is to dig down until we find the waters which nurture faith. These are the waters of counsel — the spiritual pathways which enable us to deepen our faith. True counsel springs from the depths of the heart. When the crisis of faith is so great that even cries without words cannot help, one has to cry from the heart alone. The heart alone cries without our letting out a sound. And from the depths of the heart comes guidance, for 'like deep waters, so is counsel in the heart of man....' (Proverbs 20:5). And to draw and reveal the waters of counsel, what is needed is a man of understanding, as the verse continues: '...and a man of understanding will draw it out'" (ibid.).

The man of understanding is the true Tzaddik, who is the key figure in the healing of the individual and the whole world. Since faith is the foundation of true healing, the remainder of this lengthy discourse — the longest Rebbe Nachman ever gave — is devoted to a profound and very detailed exploration of all the *tikkunim* (rectifications) that have to be accomplished in order to bring about the complete restoration of faith within the Jewish People, and indeed in the entire world. At the climax of the discourse Rebbe Nachman again discusses the heart and lungs, explaining how their health and sound functioning symbolize the *tikkunim* examined in the main body of the teaching.

It is manifestly clear from "*Sound the Shofar — Faith*" that Rebbe Nachman's concern with healing encompassed not only the healing of the individual but that of the whole Jewish People and the world in general. He never ceased to address the needs and concerns of the individual. This is true in his tales and formal discourses, and even more so in the simpler, more intimate conversations and parables with which he reached out both to his immediate followers and to the generations to come, giving practical, down-to-earth guidance as to how to actually follow his path of faith, purity, joy and prayer. Yet at the same time many of his discourses from this period focus on his broader concern for universal rectification and healing, as do stories like the "Burgher and the Pauper," the "Exchanged Children" and the "Master of Prayer," all of which were told during the winter of 1809-10.

Rebbe Nachman's Shabbat Chanukah discourse that winter, "*Those who have compassion upon them will lead them*" (Likutey Moharan II, 7), speaks about the true leader of the Jewish People, who seeks to bring about forgiveness and atonement for their sins. This is the greatest compassion, for nothing in the world is more painful than the separation from God caused by sin. It is only towards the end of the discourse that Rebbe Nachman explicitly mentions healing, relating all the concepts discussed in it to the health of the lungs. But in fact healing is one of the underlying concerns of the entire discourse since it is all about the Tzaddik, who brings atonement for sin, and as Rebbe Nachman was to state ten months later in his last ever discourse, "Sin and illness are bound up with each other, because illness is basically caused by sin, which is a dark cloud hiding the healing light of Godliness. But when the sins are forgiven, the cloud disappears and the sun rises and shines, bringing healing" (Likutey Moharan II, 8:6).

It was in the spring of 1810 that Rebbe Nachman told the last of his tales, the "Seven Beggars," in which seven mysterious beggars come in turn to the wedding celebration of a young couple and each tells a story. Although this is the most recondite of all Rebbe Nachman's tales, the theme of healing is discernible in many places. The stories of the second, fourth and fifth beggars allude to the healing of the wounds of the nation. The third beggar's story of the "Heart and the Spring" relates to many of Rebbe Nachman's teachings about the heart and the lungs, while the story of the sixth beggar explicitly deals with the healing of the "Princess," who symbolizes the Jewish People and the Shekhinah, the Divine Presence (see below, pp. 149-52).

Uman

In May 1810, just one month after telling this story, Rebbe Nachman left Breslov and went to the town of Uman, where he knew he was to die. By the time Rosh Hashanah came, he was critically ill. In the morning of the first day of the festival, just as he should have been preparing himself to give his teaching, he had a very serious attack of coughing which became worse and worse. He began coughing up blood in great quantities. The attack was so severe that he nearly died there and then. The attack lasted several hours. Night came, and still it continued. Hundreds of people were waiting in the prayer-hall, hoping that the Rebbe would come to teach. He sent for Reb Noson: "What can I do?" It was impossible for him to give a discourse. Reb Noson tried to persuade him. "If so," the Rebbe said, "I'll give my last drop of strength and try." Reb Noson writes:

> "He started his discourse in a very low voice. When he began to speak, it was against all the laws of nature that he would be able to finish. He was so weak, he could hardly say anything at all, let alone teach a discourse as great and exalted as the one he was giving. But God helped him, and he finished the entire discourse except for the concluding explanation of the key verse, which he gave after Yom Kippur" (*Tzaddik* #116).

This last discourse, "*Sound the Shofar — Reproof*" (*Likutey Moharan* II, 8), looks forward to the future, when the world will come to the knowledge of God and all will recognize that everything is under God's providence. Through the power of the prayers of the outstanding Tzaddik, the Master of Prayer, God's glory will be revealed. Prophecy will come into the world, and through it our faith will be cleansed and purified, and we will come to see that everything around us is all miracles.

This was when Rebbe Nachman spoke about the wings of the sun:

> "The revelation of God's glory is the 'rising sun.' And with the shining of the rising sun will come healing, as it is written, 'But for you who revere My name the sun of charity will rise, with healing in its wings' (Malachi 3:20). For the prophetic spirit that will spread as God's glory is revealed is itself the healing brought by the rising sun. The revelation of God's glory comes through prayer, which causes the 'clouds' — the forces of unholiness and impurity — to disperse and disappear. The nations of the world will turn to God, and His glory will be revealed. Through abundant prayer, sin will be forgiven, and then the sun will rise and shine, bringing healing" (*Likutey Moharan* II, 8:6).

This was Rebbe Nachman's very last teaching. Just eighteen days later he finally succumbed. Reb Noson writes:

> "Shortly before his death the Rebbe was so weak and his condition so critical that he could have died at any moment. We were standing around him and he sat on the chair, suffering terribly. He was complaining how great the pain was. But suddenly he clenched his fist strongly and waved

it about, as if to say, 'Even so, I have very great strength inside.' There is no way of describing this in writing. No matter how weak he may have been physically, his spiritual strength was firm, and indeed increasing. He was quite determined to complete everything as he wanted with the help of God" (*Tzaddik* #120).

Rebbe Nachman left the world on Tuesday, 18 Tishri 5571, October 16, 1810. He was not "healed" in the physical sense, because the sickness of his body was an expression of the sickness of the whole Jewish People. They were — and still are — in exile, physically and spiritually. But Rebbe Nachman had fulfilled his mission. Out of his own illness and suffering he found the remedy for the larger sickness and revealed it for all posterity. In the tradition of King Hezekiah, he chose to put away his own "Book of Remedies." But what he left in its place is far more than a collection of medical "recipes." It is a complete pathway of health and healing, spiritual and physical, for the individual and for the whole world.

Before turning to a detailed examination of the teachings that make up Rebbe Nachman's healing pathway, let us conclude our account of his life with a parable that he told in order to explain why he revealed so many amazing ideas even though it did not yet seem possible that his words could achieve their purpose.

"Once there was a king whose only son became so ill that all the doctors despaired of curing him. Meanwhile, a doctor of outstanding wisdom came. The king begged him to try his best to cure the prince. The doctor told him truthfully that the chances of healing the prince were very remote. However, there was still a means of last resort. If they tried this, there was a very faint possibility that the prince might be cured. 'But I don't know whether I should tell you what this method is,' said the doctor, 'because it will be very hard indeed to apply.' The king pressed him to reveal what the method was.

"The doctor said: 'You should know that your son's illness is so critical that it is now quite impossible to give him even a single drop of medicine to swallow. However, there exist certain remedies which are so priceless that a single small bottle costs thousands and thousands of gold pieces. What you have to do is to fill barrels full of these precious remedies and to pour bucketsful of them over your son! Obviously all these precious remedies will go to waste, but the prince will become very slightly stronger as a result. And it may be that as you pour all this over him, a tiny drop will go into his mouth and then he may just possibly be healed.' The king immediately agreed and gave instructions to do what the doctor had said. And this was how the prince was healed" (*Tzaddik* #391).

Reb Noson writes: "The meaning is obvious. It is precisely because we are so crushed by our sickness — the sickness of the soul — that the Tzaddik, the faithful doctor, is forced to pour such priceless remedies over us, even though it would seem that virtually all of them will go to waste. Nevertheless, the sweet scent is absorbed, and in the fullness of time it may be that we will be able to let a drop penetrate our mouths and our inner being. Then there will be some hope for us to be healed, spiritually and physically" (*ibid.*).

SECTION 4

Simchah for Health and Healing

Chapter 10

What is health?

Billions are spent on healthcare and preventive medicine, not to speak of all the money paid out for doctors and medical treatment when things go wrong, God forbid. We are constantly being urged to make sure we get enough vitamins and minerals, cut our fat intake, quit smoking, reduce tension and do a thousand and one other things to guard our health. But what is the purpose of it all? What is health *for*?

At first sight the answer would seem quite obvious: health is a prerequisite for having a good life — which of course it is. As to what constitutes the good life, many would say this is not for healthcare personnel to decide. Isn't health a basic human right? One of the principles of the traditional physician's code of conduct is to provide treatment for all without discrimination. It is not for the doctor to ask what someone intends to do with his health. If the patient is sick, be he a saint or a sinner, the doctor should heal him.

The supreme value of human life is one of the cardinal principles of Judaism. For the sake of preserving life it is permissible to violate any commandment in the Torah except for the prohibitions against idolatry, sexual immorality and murder (*Pesachim* 25a). But for Judaism, health is more than a matter of being able to function normally in order to work, eat, drink and be merry. Life is God's precious gift, given to enable us to draw closer to Him. The importance of health lies in the fact that it is necessary in order to devote oneself to Torah, prayer and practice of the mitzvot without impediment. In the words of the Rambam: "Bodily health and well-being are part of the path to God, since it is virtually impossible to know or understand anything of the Creator if one is sick. One must therefore avoid anything that may harm the body, and cultivate healthful habits" (*Mishneh Torah, Hilkhot De'ot* 4:1; see above 5, p. 42).

A similar idea is expressed by Rabbi Moshe Chaim Luzzatto: "Man's use of the world for his own needs should be circumscribed by the limits imposed by God's will and should not include anything forbidden by God. It should be motivated by the need to best maintain his health and preserve his life, and not merely to satisfy his physical urges and superfluous desires. One's motivation in maintaining his body should furthermore be so that the soul should be able to use it to serve its Creator without being hampered by the body's weakness and incapability. When man makes use of the world in this way, this in itself becomes an act of perfection, and through it one can attain the same virtue as in keeping the other commandments. Indeed, one of the commandments requires that we keep our bodies fit so that we can serve God" (*Derekh HaShem* I:4:7; cf. *Shulchan Arukh, Orach Chaim* #231 and *Choshen Mishpat* #427:8).

Prevention is better than cure

It is tragic that many people never learn to value their health until it breaks down. Vast numbers of people consume excessive amounts of the wrong foods, neglect all exercise, smoke, drink and abuse themselves in other ways for years, only to come running to their doctors when their resulting health problems are so advanced that it is often impossible to reverse them. It is far more difficult to restore health to a body that has been allowed to degenerate than to maintain and enhance the health of a body that is still basically sound.

Research in the U.S. suggests that two thirds of the deaths of those under the age of sixty-five are preventible. It is the height of folly to wait until illness manifests itself in actual physical symptoms before taking the decision to cultivate healthful habits. For best results, healing should start long before the body ever gets sick! It is never too early to begin taking proper care of ourselves. And if we are among those who had to become sick in some way in order to realize the preciousness of good health, let us thank God for the warning and make up our minds to live wisely and sensibly from now on!

But what *are* the right healthcare habits? Preventive medicine receives tremendous emphasis in contemporary society, but even those who do want to take proper care of their health often find themselves thoroughly confused because of the welter of conflicting advice on all sides. Are we supposed to be vegetarian or macrobiotic, or doesn't it matter? Is proper food combining vital or irrelevant? Are nutritional supplements necessary or superfluous? Are dairy foods good or bad? And fruits? Is it OK to take a little coffee, white sugar and refined flour? Or are they deadly poisons? What about food coloring, flavor enhancers, preservatives, aluminium pots and countless other things? Is jogging beneficial, or does it put stress on the joints? What about aerobic dance? Yoga? Tai Chi? etc., etc.

Healthcare education in schools, where it exists at all, is often only partial, and receives nothing like the emphasis given to mathematics, the sciences and other academic subjects. School fitness programs have been found to be woefully inadequate. It would be hard to find a doctor who disagrees with the basic principles of healthcare and preventive medicine. Yet in practice the majority of mainstream doctors tend to wait until their patients come to them with actual medical problems before offering any suggestions as to how they might best safeguard their health. In the absence of undisputed, authoritative healthcare guidance, most people depend on a medley of ideas culled from grandmothers, hearsay, TV, books and magazines, favorite medicine men and other "experts."

The free society in which we live connives with the innate weakness of human nature to undermine people's best intentions of following a healthful lifestyle. Manufacturers are at liberty to sell all kinds of food and other products that pander to people's cravings and appetites regardless of whether they are conducive to their health or not. All the candies, pastries, refined, processed and other junk foods that people find most tempting are readily available, but it takes considerably more effort to find simple, wholesome foods. Bad habits take root early. What child is content to nibble at carrots and celery while all the others in the class are enjoying their gooey candies?

Today, anything and everything is advertised as being "natural" and "healthy," but manufacturers and suppliers of so-called "health foods" and other "health aids" have little incentive to supply sound information about the true value of their products. A lot of money can be made from selling expensive little bottles of exclusive-formula preparations, elaborate home exercise contraptions and the like — far more than from providing basic guidance about the fundamentals of good nutrition and simple exercise techniques that don't require equipment.

The fact is that many people would far rather seek health from a bottle or a machine than put in sustained efforts themselves. The prevalent consumerist culture of instant satisfaction militates against the self-discipline necessary to adhere to a wise regimen of diet and exercise and follow other genuinely healthful habits. People find it much more comfortable to swallow a few vitamin pills and eat a salad as a kind of sop to their consciences, and then carry on eating more or less what they please. Weeks of inactivity are followed by sudden crash-courses in fitness, which simply lead to sore muscles, stiff joints and further inactivity.

Ironically, the pursuit of "health" in our materialistic society often contains a built-in contradiction. The dominant philosophy of "eat, drink and be merry, for tomorrow we die!" has turned health into an obsession for all those who

(continued on p.110)

Healthcare Advice from the Rambam

Adapted from *Mishneh Torah, Hilkhot De'ot*, Chapter 4.

Eating:

Eat only when hungry. Drink only when thirsty. Don't keep eating until your stomach is full. Eat approximately a quarter less than the amount that would make you fully satisfied. In the summer eat cooling foods and don't use excessive seasoning. In the winter months eat warming foods with plenty of spices. Don't drink with your meal except for a little water mixed with wine. When the food starts to be digested, drink as much water as you need, but even then don't drink water to excess. Always sit down to eat. Don't walk about, ride, take exercise or engage in any other kind of demanding physical activity until the food is digested. Physical exertion immediately after meals can cause serious illness.

Exercise:

Before you eat, walk about to warm up your body, or engage in some other form of physical activity. Every morning you should exercise until your body is warm. Then rest a little, and after this have your meal. If you wash with warm water after your exercise, so much the better. After washing, wait a little and then eat.

Bowel movements:

When you need to relieve yourself, do so immediately. You should check to see if you need to relieve yourself before and after meals, exercise, bathing, sexual intercourse and going to sleep.

Sleep:

It is sufficient to sleep for eight hours a day. Don't sleep on your front or back but on your side: at the beginning of the night on the left side, and at the end of the night on the right side. Don't go to sleep directly after eating: wait about three or four hours after your meal.

Bathing:

Don't bathe immediately after eating, or when you are hungry, but when the food begins to be digested. Wash your entire body with water that is hot but not scalding. After this, wash your body with lukewarm water, then with tepid water, until you finally wash with cold water.

(Healthcare Advice from the Rambam, cont.)

Don't stay in the bath too long: as soon as you perspire and your body becomes supple, rinse yourself and leave the bath. Then dress and cover your head so as not to be caught in a cold draft. This applies even in the summer. After your bath, wait till you are calm, your body is rested and the warmth of the bath has dissipated. You may then eat. If you sleep a little after your bath and before eating, this is excellent. Don't drink cold water after bathing, and certainly not while in the bath. If you are thirsty after leaving the bath and cannot restrain yourself, drink water mixed with a little wine or honey.

Sexual intercourse:

The semen is the life and strength of the body and the light of the eyes. Whenever semen is emitted to excess the body becomes wasted and its life and strength fail. Someone who is sunken in sexual activity will age prematurely. His strength will wane, his eyes will weaken, and a bad odor will emit from his mouth and armpits.... All kinds of maladies will afflict him. Someone who wants to live a wholesome life should be very cautious about this. One should not cohabit unless one's body is strong and healthy and one experiences repeated involuntary erections which persist even when one diverts one's thoughts to something else. One should not cohabit when either sated or hungry but only after one's meal is digested.

General healthcare:

As long as a person exercises, takes care not to eat to the point of satiation and keeps his bowels soft, he will not fall ill and his strength will be fortified, even if he eats unhealthy foods. But the opposite is true of someone who leads a sedentary life, takes no exercise, fails to relieve himself when necessary and allows himself to remain constipated. Even if such a person eats good food and takes care of himself according to proper medical principles, all his days will be full of pain and his strength will wane. Excessive intake of food is a deadly poison to the body and one of the main causes of illness. Most of the illnesses to which man is prey are caused by eating the wrong foods or by excessive eating even of good foods.

are terrified that heart disease, cancer, AIDS and other terrors could cut short their pursuit of happiness. People everywhere are popping vitamins, working out and trying anything else that offers a hope of extending their youth. Producers of all kinds take full advantage: even cigarette ads show scenes of lusty, blooming youth wandering about in the glorious outdoors. The contradiction is that the very pursuits for which many people are desperate to prolong their lives are precisely those that can be the most destructive to their health: gastronomic excess, fast living, sexual promiscuity, drinking, drug abuse and the like.

Body, Mind, Soul

The obsession with physical health and strength for its own sake is one of the things Rebbe Nachman ridicules in his story of the "Master of Prayer," in which he caricatures the various mistaken ideas that different groups of people have about the purpose of life.

> "One group maintained that the main goal was to pamper oneself with food and drink in order to develop large muscles. They searched for a man with large muscles who exercised in order to develop them. Such a person would have large limbs, thus having a greater portion in the world. The person with the largest limbs would be closest to the goal and should be king. They went and found a very tall athlete and took him as their king. They also sought a land that was conducive to this, and went and settled there" (*Rabbi Nachman's Stories* p.321).

Rebbe Nachman was far from being opposed to physical healthcare. Quite the contrary. He warned his followers not to smoke or drink (see facing page), and told them to take good care of themselves: "Get as much sleep as you need, and eat properly. Just make sure you guard your time" (*Kokhvey Ohr* p.25). One of Rebbe Nachman's foremost interpreters, R. Avraham b'Reb Nachman (1849-1917), outstanding leader of the fourth generation of Breslover Chassidim, said: "Since Rebbe Nachman warned us against doctors and medicines, we must make every effort to eat only healthful foods" (*Siach Sarfey Kodesh* III:539). The same could be said to apply to all other aspects of preventive healthcare.

What Rebbe Nachman ridiculed was the devotion to body culture as a goal in itself: to develop large muscles in order to have "a greater portion in the world" — i.e. in *this* world. In the Torah view, this transient world is merely the ante-chamber to the World to Come (*Avot* 4:21). Even the most

(continued on p.112)

What Rebbe Nachman said about...

General healthcare:

"When a person is well, he must do and do and do (in serving God). But when he is not well, he should engage in the service of God only as required by the *Shulchan Arukh* in accordance with his state of health, and must fulfil the mitzvah of 'Guard your soul'" (*Avanehah Barzel* #64 p.44)

Eating:

"One of the marks of human dignity is to eat only what one needs. Someone who eats more than he needs is like an animal, who eats and chews the whole day. This can bring on fever, God forbid" (*Likutey Moharan* I, 263).

"Eating properly subdues the tendency towards folly, heightening one's intellectual and spiritual faculties. But when one overindulges and eats like a glutton, folly will get the upper hand and overcome one's intellectual and spiritual faculties" (*Likutey Moharan* I, 17:3).

"Be careful not to gobble your food hurriedly like a glutton. Get into the habit of eating at a moderate pace, calmly and with the same table manners as if an important guest were present" (*Tzaddik* #515).

"What is gluttony? To be picky about food and make an issue about what is good and tasty and what isn't" (*Siach Sarfey Kodesh* I-12).

Drinking:

"Never get drunk. Be careful never to drink more than your capacity. A little drink may help expand the mind, but excessive drinking and drunkenness lead to harshness, anger, impurity and evil" (*Likutey Moharan* II, 26).

Rebbe Nachman once poured a tiny drop of *schnapps* for one of his followers, who said, "*Nu*, a little is also good." Hearing this, Rebbe Nachman said, "*Schnapps? Only* a little is good!" (*Siach Sarfey Kodesh* I-151).

Smoking:

"Don't get into the habit of smoking. It is a waste of precious time that should be spent on Torah and prayer. Smoking is of no benefit whatever and can be hazardous" (*Tzaddik* #472).

A good sweat:

"Sweating over a mitzvah brings joy. Depression is caused by a build-up of impurities in the blood and spleen. The remedy is to sweat, because the illness-generating toxins in the blood are exuded in the sweat, and the blood is left pure. One then comes to joy" (*Likutey Moharan* II, 6).

well-developed body must eventually die and rot, whereas the soul goes on to eternal life. To put all the emphasis on physical healthcare while neglecting spiritual growth is to have one's priorities totally wrong. The purpose of cultivating the health of the body is, as Rabbi Moshe Chaim Luzzatto expressed it, "so that the soul should be able to *use* [the body] to serve its Creator, without being hampered by the body's weakness and incapability" (*op. cit.*).

Healthcare is a mitzvah: "Guard your soul" (Deuteronomy 4:9). But even the purely physical aspects of healthcare require *soul-power*. It takes very strong motivation to sustain a sound routine of diet, exercise and other physical healthcare practices throughout one's life. Every day there are hosts of good excuses to eat badly, put off exercising and abuse oneself in other ways. The only way to remain firm is by keeping one's eyes fixed on higher spiritual goals. But how is this possible unless one is wholeheartedly committed to these goals and finds true joy in pursuing them?

Moreover, physical health is directly influenced by our mental, emotional and spiritual states, positive or otherwise. The point is graphically illustrated by the Rambam:

"Everyone can see how emotional experiences produce marked changes in the body. You may see a well-built man with a strong, pleasant voice and shining face. But the moment he hears worrisome news, his face drops and loses its shine. His color changes, his posture droops and his voice becomes hoarse and weak. His strength fails, and he may become so weak that he starts trembling. His pulse becomes weak, his eyes change and his eyelids become too heavy to move. His skin becomes cold and he loses his appetite. The very opposite happens when a man with a weak body, pale face and soft voice hears joyous news. His whole body becomes stronger. His voice becomes firmer, his face brightens, his movements become faster, his pulse becomes stronger, his skin becomes warmer and his eyes exude happiness and joy.

"Similarly, fear, hope, security, tranquillity, despair, success and so on all have their effects on the body. Sometimes a person may become so dejected by misfortune that he literally cannot see because his faculty of vision becomes darkened. On the other hand, a successful person sees everything more brightly because the light in his eyes is increased. Because of this, the physicians have emphasized the importance of paying attention to emotional states at all times" (*Hanhagat HaBri'ut* 3:12-13).

The Rambam had full grasp of a point that was largely ignored by mainstream western medicine until quite recently. This is that our mental, emotional and spiritual states directly influence all aspects of our physical functioning both in the short- and long-term. It is now universally accepted that many cases of heart disease and other illnesses are directly related to bad diet, lack of exercise, high stress, excessive smoking and drinking, and so on. In addition, there is a growing body of scientific evidence that factors like thwarted emotion, chronic frustration and depression may play a major role in many different physical conditions, from low immunity to cancer and other diseases. But what is it that *drives* people to the compulsive overindulgence, drinking, smoking and other addictions that take such a heavy toll on their health as the years pass? What is it that prevents so many from relaxing and letting go of the worries and tension that shorten their lives? What is it that keeps people locked in the frustration, bitterness and anger that consume them?

Rebbe Nachman was looking to the very root of the patterns that destroy so many lives when he said: "All the illnesses people suffer come only because of a lack of joy" (*Likutey Moharan* II, 24). Obviously he was not talking about superficial contentment — he knew that many people's placid exteriors belie deep pain, a pain some dare not even acknowledge for fear it could engulf them. It is this profound inner unhappiness that drives people to the compulsive behavior that eats away at their health. Whether it appears as gloom, depression, despair, bitterness, anger or in other guises, we have to conquer it — with a wholehearted, joyous embrace of *life!* Without this, even the strictest physical regime can never bring genuine health and well-being.

In Rebbe Nachman's view, technically sound physical functioning is of little value in itself. He said, "Even if someone dies at the age of eighty it may still be that his life was cut short — in the sense that he failed to elevate himself, and therefore all his years were empty" (*Tzaddik* #576). "There are many different kinds of 'life.' Some people lead very troubled lives even though it may not be apparent on the surface. Within the category of 'troubled lives' there are various gradations. The various forms of life are very different. Without doubt the life of a horse bears no comparison with the life of a man. Just as there are great differences between different forms of life on the physical level, so there are differences in the quality of people's spiritual lives. The true life is to delight in God. Some people achieve this even in this world, others not at all" (*ibid.* #400).

In the words of Reb Noson:

> "Real life is the life of true wisdom, as it is written, 'Wisdom gives *life* to those who possess it' (Ecclesiastes 7:12). And the essence of wisdom is to labor and endeavor to know and acknowledge God, Who is the Life of life. The closer one comes to God, the more one's life is genuine life. The opposite is also true. This is why 'the wicked are called dead even in their lifetimes, and conversely, the righteous are called alive even after their deaths' (*Berakhot* 18a). The righteous are constantly attached to true life, as it is written: 'And you who are attached to the Lord your God, all of you are *alive* today' (Deuteronomy 2:4). This is the life for which we pray repeatedly on Rosh Hashanah and Yom Kippur: 'Remember us for *life*,' 'inscribe us for *life*,' etc. Besides this, everything else is vanity: it isn't life at all" (*Tzaddik, Author's Introduction* pp.6-7).

The life of delight in God is one of constant striving, starting afresh each time, applying oneself with ever renewed efforts. "Don't be old!" cried Rebbe Nachman. "It's no good to be an old chassid or an old tzaddik. Old is no good! You must remain young, renewing yourself each day and making a fresh start" (*Rabbi Nachman's Wisdom* #51). For Rebbe Nachman, it is this embrace of *life* that is the foundation of good health and strength, spiritual and physical. This is the essence of all his teachings on health and healing. It is summed up in a single word: *Simchah!*

Chapter 11

The Great Mitzvah

Mitzvah gedolah lihyot besimchah tamid! — מצוה גדולה להיות בשמחה תמיד — "It's a great mitzvah to be happy always!" (*Likutey Moharan* II, 24). These famous words are among the most quoted of all of Rebbe Nachman's sayings. But few are aware that they are the opening words of one of his most important teachings on healing. (For the full teaching, see below, pp. 123f.) It is a short teaching — no more than three paragraphs — but its implications are most profound and far-reaching. In the current chapter and the two that follow it, we will explore some of the worlds of thought that lie behind this teaching and seek to understand the power of שמחה, *simchah* — happiness and joy — to bring health and healing.

But first of all, what *is* simchah? Rebbe Nachman gives us a vivid picture of a truly joyous personality in the figure of the Simpleton in his story of the "Sophisticate and the Simpleton."

"The Simpleton had learned the trade of a shoemaker. Being simple, he had to study very hard to master it, and even then he was not very expert in the craft. He married and earned a living from his work. But he was simple and not expert in his craft, so his livelihood was very meager and limited. With only limited skill, he had to work constantly. He didn't even have time to eat. He would eat as he worked: he'd make a hole with his awl, draw the thick shoemakers' thread in and out, and then take a bite of bread and eat it.

"Throughout this he was always very happy. He was constantly filled with joy. He had every type of food, drink and clothing. He'd say to his wife: 'My wife, give me something to eat.' She'd give him a piece of bread, which he would eat. Then he'd say, 'Give me some soup with groats.' She'd cut him another slice of bread, which he'd eat and praise highly. 'How nice and delicious this soup is!' He'd then ask her for some meat and other good food. Each time she would give him a piece of bread. Each time he would savor it and praise the food very highly, saying how well-prepared and delicious it was. It was as if he were actually eating the food he'd asked for. And in fact, when he ate the bread, he really did taste in it any kind of food he wanted. This was because of his simplicity and great happiness.

"He'd say to his wife: 'Bring me some beer to drink.' She'd bring him some water, but he would praise it and say, 'How delicious this beer is! Now give me some honey wine.' She'd give him water, and he would speak most highly of it. 'Give me some wine...' or other beverages. Each time she'd give him water, but he would enjoy it and praise it as if he were actually drinking what he'd asked for.

"The same was true of clothing. Between them, the only overcoat he and his wife possessed was a sheepskin. Whenever he wanted to go to the market he'd say to his wife, 'Give me the sheepskin,' and she'd bring it to him. When he wanted to wear a fur coat to go visiting, he'd say, 'Give me my fur coat.' She'd give him the sheepskin, but he would enjoy it and praise it, saying, 'What a nice fur coat this is.' When he needed a caftan to go to synagogue, he'd say, 'Give me the caftan.' She'd give him the sheepskin, and he would praise it: 'What a beautiful caftan this is!' Similarly, when he needed a silk coat, she would also give him the sheepskin. He would enjoy it and praise it: 'What a gorgeous, comfortable silk coat!' This was true no matter what happened. He was always filled with happiness and joy.

"Since he had not completely mastered his trade, when he finished a shoe, it was usually triangular in shape. But he would take the shoe in his hand and admire it, deriving the utmost enjoyment from his handiwork. He'd say: 'My wife, what a beautiful, wonderful shoe this is! How sweet this shoe is! This shoe is as sweet as honey and sugar!' Sometimes she'd answer him: 'If that's true, how come other shoemakers get three *gulden* for a pair of shoes while you get only a *gulden* and a half?' 'What do I care about that?' he'd say. 'That's their work, and this is my work! Why must we think about others? Let's think about how much clear profit I make on this shoe. The leather costs such and such, the glue and the thread cost such and such.... I have a clear profit of ten *groschen*! As long as I make such a clear profit, what do I care?' He was thus always filled with joy and happiness" (*Rabbi Nachman's Stories* pp. 168-73).

Wholehearted with God

The Simpleton is the perfect example of the joy that leads to health and healing — which is why he tasted all the tastes in the world in his bread and water. Rebbe Nachman told the story of the "Sophisticate and Simpleton" in the late winter of 1808-9, just a few months after giving his teaching in *Likutey Moharan* II, 1, "*Sound the Shofar — Dominion*" (see above pp. 86-91). There he taught that someone who attains perfect prayer grasps the "Word of God," which is the root of the entire creation. There, all is unity: there is no difference between bread and water and plants and herbs, and this personcan therefore channel curative powers into simple bread and water. This clearly connects with the Simpleton's ability to taste anything he wanted in his bread and water.

It is a pity that the English word "simpleton" carries a suggestion of someone foolish and gullible, because Rebbe Nachman's hero is far from being so. In Hebrew he is called תם (*tam*), sincere and wholehearted. He is the perfect example of fulfilment of the mitzvah to "be wholehearted (תמים, *tamim*) with HaShem your God" (Deuteronomy 18:13). As the story develops, it becomes clear that the Simpleton has complete faith in God — without doubts or questions or any need for elaborate proofs and explanations. The entire Torah opens with the utmost simplicity, without any philosophizing: "In the beginning God created the heaven and the earth" (Genesis 1:1 and see *Rabbi Nachman's Wisdom* #5). The Simpleton takes this at face value. He accepts that God is the source of everything in life. And since God is perfect goodness and beneficence, everything must be for good.

It is this faith that is the foundation of the Simpleton's simchah. He *knows* that the life and circumstances God has given him are the very best possible — and he is overjoyed. To the outside world he may seem to be poor and struggling, but in fact he's the richest person on earth, because "Who is rich? The one who is satisfied with his portion" (*Avot* 4:1). Rather than lamenting what he lacks, the Simpleton looks at how much he *has* — and rejoices. He relishes his "soup," "meat" and "honey wine" as delicacies fit for a king. He luxuriates in his "silk" coat. By other people's standards his income is meager. But far from worrying about it, he makes a simple calculation, sees that he's more than surviving, and rejoices.

One of the main reasons many people are so unhappy is that they look at what they have — their mental and physical endowments, their financial and social standing, their academic, career, spiritual and other accomplishments, their domestic, family and other circumstances — and they grieve, because what they see does not match up with what they think they deserve. They compare themselves with others (or at least, with the way other people seem to *them*), and this just rubs salt into their wounds. Essentially this unhappiness is self-inflicted. It stems from their using the wrong standards to evaluate their lives, and then torturing themselves for having fallen short of them.

We are all under great pressure to adopt the prevailing cultural standards of success and failure as reflected in the approval or disapproval of those around us. But who says these "standards" apply to us? There's always a nagging voice that says, "Why do other shoemakers get three *gulden* for a pair of shoes while you only get a *gulden* and a half?" "Why is he or she so bright, good-looking, wealthy, successful, etc. etc. while I am only so so?" But the truth is that what others are or have is quite irrelevant. "That's their work, and this is my work!" Each person is totally unique. Each one of us has his or her unique role in the scheme of creation. The hallmark of God's greatness is that He creates not mass-produced, standard items but unique individuals, each one of whom is precious in His eyes — and never more so than when we quit trying to be what we aren't and concentrate on being our true selves to the very best of our abilities. And so the Simpleton would take his triangular shoe in hand and say, "What a beautiful, wonderful shoe this is! It's as sweet as honey and sugar!"

Whether our lives are good or bad depends largely on the way we look at them. Many things in this world are negative and painful. The reason is that in this world God conceals His true goodness from us in order to create an arena of challenge in which we have to *earn* our share of this goodness through our own efforts. Our task is to search for God's goodness by stripping off the veils. We have to "know this day and put it into our hearts that *HaShem* is *Elokim*...." (Deuteronomy 4:39). *Today*, at each of the different turns in life, we have to *know*, not only in our minds but in our very hearts, that "*HaShem* is *Elokim*." Even when faced with hardship and suffering, we must understand that they stem from God's justice, alluded to in His name of אלקים, *Elokim*, and this is in perfect unity with His lovingkindness, alluded to in His name of ה', *HaShem*. Seen as a preparation for the enduring goodness of the world to come, even the harshness of this world is ultimately for good.

There are many times when it's far from easy to feel wholeheartedly that our pain and suffering are good. Faith is not a magic wand that instantly turns everything into sheer delight. If it were, there'd be no challenge. Sometimes we can see it, other times it takes deep heart-searching and repeated efforts to penetrate beneath the surface in order to accept that what God has sent us is ultimately for the best. At the outset faith may be no more than a signpost pointing in the right direction in which to search for the answers. It can take years of steady work on ourselves to refine our faith, resolve our doubts and clarify our understanding of how to find God in this most confusing world. But in the end, "It is as if the believer actually sees with his very eyes the thing he believes in" (*Likutey Moharan* I, 62:5). This was the level of faith that the Simpleton attained. He *knew* not just that everything *will be* good, but that it already *is* good *now* — very good — and he was overjoyed.

We have to slough off the part of ourselves that takes a jaundiced view of our endowments and circumstances, as if somehow they do not befit us. We have to depose the cruel King Ego who spoils the look, taste and smell of everything we have in our lives by keeping us focussed on what we think we lack. Instead we must enthrone God as the King over the entire universe and everything in our lives, and search for the goodness in all He has given us. The life of faith is a joyous quest to find and know God ever more fully in every detail of life: *intellectually*, through deepening our knowledge of His Torah; *emotionally*, through setting aside our selfishness, anger, and other negative traits, opening our eyes and hearts to the loving flow of blessing all around us; and *practically*, through acts of charity and kindness and carrying out the other mitzvot, all of which come to manifest God's kingship over the world.

The Mitzvot

The mitzvot are the royal road to simchah. The Torah path consists of six hundred and thirteen mitzvot, each of which applies at one of the various junctures of life. Every mitzvah is a unique pathway that enables us to forge a connection with God at and through the particular juncture to which it applies, be it at a given point in the life cycle (e.g. circumcision, marriage, mourning, etc.), during the course of the daily, weekly and yearly cycles (*tzitzit*, *tefilin*, Shabbat and festivals, etc.), when we eat and drink or make a living (e.g. tithes, blessings, laws of honesty in business etc.), in our family and other interpersonal relations (teaching our children, kindness and charity, avoiding slander, grudge-bearing and revenge, etc.), spiritual growth (prayer, Torah study, personal sanctity, etc.) and so on.

God's purpose in the creation was to bestow His goodness upon His creatures. In order that they should truly possess it as their own, God created this world of trial in which man is placed between perfection and deficiency, with the task of earning his perfection through his own free will. Man comprises two opposites: his pure, spiritual soul and his unenlightened physical body. Each is drawn to its nature: the body inclines towards the material, while the soul leans towards the spiritual. Man's environment and everything in it are physical, and his physical nature forces him to engage in worldly pursuits. But God in His wisdom so arranged things that man should be able to attain perfection through his worldly activities in the physical realm.

God arranged and circumscribed the ways in which man should make use of the world and all it contains according to their intended purpose. When man abides by these limits and arrangements, his mundane activities themselves become acts of perfection by means of which he incorporates excellence within himself. These patterns and restraints are the 248 positive mitzvot and the 365 prohibitions. The purpose of each one is to allow man to earn and incorporate in himself a particular kind of excellence, or to remove an area of deficiency. Being God-given, the mitzvot have infinite depth and can be fulfilled on higher and higher levels, leading to ever stronger connection with God. The very word מצוה, *mitzvah*, is related to the Hebrew-Aramaic root צוות (*tzavat*) denoting "attachment." The various mitzvot have a unique meaning for each individual soul, and each person has his or her unique way to connect with God through the mitzvot.

When we carry out the mitzvot not as burdensome obligations but as joyous outreach to God on every level of our being — thought, emotion, speech and action — we give God joy and delight, as it were. This is because His whole

What is Simchah?

"At every stage in a person's spiritual growth, there is an aspect of Torah and mitzvot which is 'revealed' to him — a level he can understand and practice — and then there is a higher level that is as yet 'concealed.' Through prayer, the level that was previously 'concealed' becomes 'revealed,' leaving an even higher 'concealed' level to aspire to. *Simchah* is when one constantly advances from level to level, turning the 'concealed' into the 'revealed'" (*Likutey Moharan* I, 22:9).

purpose in creating the world is fulfilled when we, His creatures, receive the divine goodness He wants to bestow upon us. And so too our fulfilment of the mitzvot brings *us* to the greatest joy, because they are our connection with God's supreme goodness. Thus "God rejoices in His works" (Psalms 104:31) when "Israel rejoices in his Maker" (*ibid.* 149:2). This reciprocal joy of God and man is the innermost "point" — the ultimate purpose — of each and every mitzvah. The mitzvah is the interface of God's joy and man's, which are ultimately one. And thus the words of Rebbe Nachman's famous saying can be rearranged to read: "The greatest happiness is to be always engaged in a mitzvah!"

"All Your mitzvot are faith!" (*ibid.* 119:86). The basis of this whole path of connection with God is, and can only be, faith — since God cannot be grasped or fathomed by the puny human intellect. The mitzvot must be accepted and fulfilled on faith alone in order to "*taste* and see that God is good" (Psalms 34:9). It is through practice of the mitzvot that we are able to "know this day and put it into our hearts that *HaShem* is *Elokim*...." (cf. Deuteronomy 4:39) — to know that everything is for good. Faith is the foundation of our search for God's goodness, while *simchah* is actually enjoying it.

Faith and joy are what the Simpleton attained to perfection. It took him a long time to master his craft. Even then he was not an expert: he had to work constantly. But he tried his best. Things didn't always turn out right: his "shoes" were usually triangular in shape. But they were his own, his unique form of self-expression. He would look at his handiwork and derive the utmost enjoyment from it: "What a beautiful, wonderful shoe this is! How sweet this shoe is! This shoe is as sweet as honey and sugar!" Perfect joy.

Chapter 12

The Soul and the Body

1. Simchah and Healing

For Rebbe Nachman, simchah is the essential key to health and healing. He expressed this idea in his teaching on the great mitzvah of always being happy:

"It's a great mitzvah to be happy all the time, and to make every effort to avoid gloom and depression. All the illnesses people suffer come only because of a lack of joy. For there are ten basic types of melodies, and these are the foundation of true joy. Thus it is written, '[It is good to give thanks to God, and to sing to Your Name, O Most High....] With an instrument of *ten* strings.... For You have made me *joyous*, O God, through Your work' (Psalms 92:2-5). These ten types of melody enter into the ten different pulses of the human body, giving them life. For this reason, when a person is lacking in joy, which consists of the ten types of melody, his ten pulses become weakened because of the flaw in the ten types of melody, giving rise to illness. For all the different kinds of illnesses are included in the ten kinds of pulse, and all the different kinds of songs and melodies are included in the ten types of melody. The particular illness that arises corresponds directly to the flaw in the joy and the song. Eminent medical authorities have also spoken at length about how all illness is rooted in depression and gloom.

"And joy is the great healer! And in time to come there will be tremendous joy. For this reason our Rabbis said, 'The Holy One, blessed be He, will be the Head of the dance circle of the tzaddikim in time to come' (*Yerushalmi Succah, Lulav veAravah* and *Vayikra Rabbah* 11 end). That is to say, God will form a dance circle of the tzaddikim, and He will be the Head of the circle, ראש חולה, *rosh choleh*. For the Divine Presence is above the head (ראש, *rosh*) of the sick person (חולה, *choleh*), as our Rabbis learned from the verse, 'HaShem will sustain him on the bed of sickness' (Psalms 41:4, *Nedarim* 40a). For the invalid has no vitality at all: it is only the Divine Presence that gives him life. Through the joy that will reign in time to come, all sickness will be remedied. The sickness of the invalid, the חולה (*choleh*), will be turned into חולה (*choleh*), a dance circle, and then God will be the ראש חולה (*rosh choleh*), Head of the dance circle, because joy is the remedy for the invalid. This is the reason that joy and dance are called *choleh*: because they are the remedy for illness.

"The main point is that one must make every effort and put all one's strength into being happy at all times. Man's natural tendency is to let himself become depressed and discouraged because of the vicissitudes of life. Everyone has his full share of suffering. For this reason one has to force oneself to be happy at all times and to bring oneself to a state of joy in whatever way possible, even with good-natured fun and jokes. It is true that true contrition over wrongful behavior is a good thing, but only for brief periods. One should set aside time each day to examine oneself and regret any wrong one may have done and open one's heart to God (see *Outpouring of the Soul*). But one should then be happy for the whole of the rest of the day. The dangers of grieving over one's sins, which can easily lead to depression, are much greater than those of veering from joy into light-headedness. Contrition is far more likely to lead to depression. One should therefore always be happy, and only at set times feel regret for any wrongdoing" (*Likutey Moharan* II, 24. For Reb Noson's prayer based on this teaching, see *Prayers* pp. 415-7.)

*

Clearly the main thrust of this teaching on simchah is practical: we should do everything we can to keep ourselves in a joyous frame of mind at all times. But brief as the teaching is, it also mentions ideas that are at the very core of Rebbe Nachman's spiritual view of illness and healing, such as that the functioning of the human body depends upon "ten pulses," and that the vitality of these pulses depends on the "ten types of melodies," which themselves are the foundation of simchah. What exactly *are* the "ten pulses," and what are the "ten types of melody"? What does it mean to say that the ten types of melody *give life* to the ten pulses? How do the ten types of melody foster health and bring healing?

A further question is how Rebbe Nachman's statements about illness and healing in this teaching are to be reconciled with other statements of his elsewhere. Here Rebbe Nachman says that the underlying reason people become sick is because of a lack of joy. This causes the ten pulses to become weakened owing to the flaw in the ten types of melody that enliven them, resulting in illness. And therefore the great healer is joy. However, elsewhere Rebbe Nachman says that "the main cause of illness is a lack of harmony: the four basic elements making up the body are in conflict, with one element rising up against another" (*Likutey Moharan* I, 56:8 and see I, 14:13). "Healing comes about essentially through bringing harmony among the elements" (ibid. II, 5:1). What are the "four elements," and how do they relate to the "ten pulses"?

In order to elucidate these concepts we must examine them in the broader context of Torah teachings about the soul and the body and how they are bound together. In this chapter we will first consider the mystical idea that the soul is "clothed" in the body, after which we will focus on the four elements and the ten pulses. Then, in the next chapter, we will turn to the ten types of melody and the healing power of simchah.

In our search for deeper insight, let us bear in mind that the bond between the soul and the body, the spiritual and the physical, is nothing less than an amazing wonder — one for which we daily bless God, "Who heals all flesh and acts *wondrously*." Some of the material in the sections that follow may be difficult for newcomers to Kabbalah and Chassidut, who may wish to skip passages that they find confusing. As we consider some of the profoundest concepts of the kabbalah, let us remember that we are entering a realm where, when clarity eludes us, we can depend only on faith.

2. The body: garment of the soul

Man's body is not the essential person, the man himself — for man's body is called his "flesh," as in the words of Job: "You have clothed me with skin and flesh, and knitted me together with bones and sinews" (Job 10:11). The essential person is the soul, the אני (*ani*) — I (*Likutey Moharan* I, 22:5). The soul is a particular class of spiritual entity destined to enter a physical body, and this distinguishes it from angels and other purely spiritual forces in the creation, which are not associated with physical bodies.

In the previous chapter we saw that the soul attains its destiny through fulfilling the 248 positive precepts of the Torah and avoiding infringement of any of its 365 prohibitions. Each mitzvah enables the soul to earn and incorporate in itself a particular level of true excellence or remove an area of deficiency and darkness. Thus the soul is said to consist of 248 spiritual "limbs" and "organs," which are connected by 365 spiritual channels. Each of the positive mitzvot comes to bring excellence into one of these limbs, while adherence to the prohibitions ensures that none of the corresponding connecting pathways becomes damaged, which would prevent the free flow of vitality to the "limbs."

The soul comes into the physical body in order to carry out the mitzvot, all of which relate in some way to the physical world. The body is by nature drawn to the material aspects of existence, and this is what presents the soul with its challenge in this world. But the soul has the power to harness the body for its own purposes and use it as its tool or instrument to carry out the mitzvot that bring it to its destiny.

R. Chaim Vital (1542-1620), principal disciple of the Ari, explains the relationship between the soul and the body as follows:

"The body is a garment in which the spiritual soul, which is the man himself, clothes itself during his sojourn in this world. Just as a tailor makes a bodily garment to fit the limbs of the body, so the Creator fashioned man's body, which is the garment of his soul, to fit the soul's 248 'limbs' and their 365 connecting pathways. After the formation of the body, God breathed into it the living soul with its 248 spiritual limbs and 365 spiritual pathways. These are then clothed in the 248 physical limbs and organs of the body and its 365 arteries, etc. [The Hebrew גידים (*gidim*), often translated as "sinews," includes the arteries, veins, lymph vessels, and nerves.]
(For the numbers of bodily limbs and arteries etc. see *Ohalot* 1:8 and *Maccot* 23b).

"The limbs of the soul are then able to carry out their functions through their instruments, the limbs of the body, which are like a hatchet in the hands of the person using it to chop. Thus the physical eyes and ears see and hear only when the soul is in them, but the moment the soul leaves the body, the eyes are darkened and all sensation and vitality departs from its 248 limbs and organs. In the same way, the 365 spiritual channels of the soul are clothed in the 365 bodily arteries, veins and other channels of the body. These carry the physical sustenance — the blood — to the 248 limbs of the body, together with the spiritual food within it to sustain the 248 limbs of the soul. But at death the soul departs, the vitality ceases to flow, and the 365 channels of the body decay and decompose, as do its 248 limbs" (*Shaarey Kedushah* I:1).

(continued on p.128)

The Torah view of the Human Body

"This is the Torah — man..." (Numbers 19:14). Besides the wealth of esoteric teachings about man's spiritual nature contained in the Bible, Talmud, Midrash and kabbalistic literature, we also find countless references to various aspects of human anatomy and functioning. But while many of these references presuppose a broader view of the nature and workings of the body, it was not the purpose of the talmudic and kabbalistic Sages to write scientific texts. Nowhere in the classic literature do we find a systematic exposition of the underlying system of ideas or a detailed explanation of the meaning of concepts like that of the "four elements" making up the human body or their four corresponding "humors."

Until the 18th century similar ideas were common currency in Europe, as well as in North Africa and large parts of Asia. In fact, the theory of the four humors was espoused as late as the 1870's by the respected Czech medical authority, Carl Rokitansky (1804-78). But since the 18th century, the general tendency has been to reject such ideas as hopelessly primitive, and where they are not ignored completely they are often grossly misunderstood. Nevertheless, today a number of scholars seem more willing to overcome the traditional western myopia when looking at unfamiliar worldviews and to try to understand them in their own terms.

The time may thus be ripe for a re-evaluation of the true significance of Torah concepts like that of the "four elements" etc. However, to date there has been no comprehensive study of Torah teachings about the human body. Julius Preuss' *Biblical and Talmudic Medicine* gives much valuable information about biblical and talmudic ideas on anatomy and physiology but does not explain the underlying view of the four elements and four humors, and also does not encompass kabbalistic teachings in works like the *Sefer Yetzirah, Zohar* and *Tikkuney Zohar*. In these we are in a very different world from that of contemporary anatomy and physiology, not least because details of the human form and functioning are often seen as alluding to aspects of the soul and the higher worlds. Valuable Hebrew sources include *Etz Chaim, Shaar Kitzur ABYA* #10 and *Sefer HaBrit* by R. Pinchas Eliahu of Vilna. See also R. Chaim Kramer, *Anatomy of the Soul* (see *Sources and Further Reading*).

In the absence of conclusive evidence, it is meaningless to speculate whether the Torah Sages borrowed some of their ideas from Egyptian, Assyrian, Greek and other cultures or vice versa. However, there is an interesting tradition (Oxford Ms. 2134) that at the time of the destruction of the Second Temple, the Roman Emperor Titus asked Rabbi Yochanan ben Zakkai to order the Jewish Sages to set down for him in writing the Jewish healing lore. Rabban Gamliel composed the requisite work, which the Romans later attributed to Galen (129-199 C.E.), whose writings were the dominant influence in European medicine until the 17th century.

Hitlabshut

At the center of the Kabbalah teaching about the relationship between the soul and the body is the concept of התלבשות (*hitlabshut*), where one thing "clothes itself" in something else. The soul is said to "clothe itself" in the body. We can try to understand this through the analogy of a glove puppet. The hand of the puppeteer "clothes itself" in the puppet. The puppet itself moves, but only because of the movements of the puppeteer's hand inside it. If the puppeteer is very expert and we are deeply absorbed in the show, the puppet may at times seem like an independent character. But the truth is that its every movement depends on the movements of the hand inside it. Without the hand, the puppet would be "dead."

A glove puppet is a clear example of "clothing." But in the Kabbalah view, a string puppet is also a case of "clothing," even though the hand of the puppeteer is not literally inside the limbs of the puppet. Even so, the string puppet also only moves because of the puppeteer's hand, which pulls at the attached strings from above. In kabbalistic terms, the movements of the puppeteer's hands are "clothed" in the movements of the strings, and thus in the resultant movements of the puppet. To those watching the string puppet show, only the puppet is visible. The puppeteer keeps out of sight: he is in another "plane," outside the artificial world of the puppet theater. But it is only through his movements that the show can continue "down there."

Using the same terminology, we might say that a person's inner spirit — his thoughts, feelings, desires and intentions — are "clothed" in his words or actions, though it would be quite impossible to detect *where* "inside them" they are. This is because the sounds coming from his mouth and the movements of his body exist on the physical plane, while the spirit that animates them, his soul, though no less *real*, exists on a different dimension of reality, albeit one that interconnects with the physical. The link between the person's spirit or soul and his physical words or actions is the body that produces them. In kabbalah terms, the spiritual soul is "clothed" in the physical body.

The divine and animal Souls

It is important to be aware that the term "soul" is used to refer to two different aspects of man's being. One type of soul that man has is similar to that which exists in all living creatures. This is called his "animal soul." This is the animating force of our physical bodies, governing bodily growth, development and functioning, including both those aspects of our physical functioning that are under our conscious control and those that are not. On the level of consciousness, we experience the animal soul as our "worldly ego" — our basic instincts and feelings, and the faculties of will, intelligence, memory, imagination, etc. with which we satisfy our material needs and desires.

Besides this, however, there exists in man a spiritual entity that is very different from this animal soul and spiritually far more exalted. This is the "divine soul," which connects us with the highest spiritual planes of creation. Through it, our thoughts, words and actions have an effect on those planes, and conversely, the divine soul is the channel through which the influences bestowed upon us from those planes are transmitted. From the divine soul, these influences are then transmitted via the animal soul to the physical body. Thus the divine soul is "clothed" in the animal soul, and the animal soul is "clothed" in the body.

This divine soul is often referred to as a single entity, but in fact it consists of a number of parts on different levels, bound together like links in a chain. Just as all the links form a single chain, so do all these levels of the soul constitute a single entity, which is called the divine soul. Its five parts, from the highest downwards, are called: the *Yechidah* ("unique essence"), *chayah* ("living essence"), *neshamah* ("breath"), *ruach* ("spirit") and *nefesh* ("soul"). Each of these levels is bound to the one below it, until the lowest one is bound to the animal soul, and the animal soul to the body (*Derekh HaShem* III:1).

Food of the soul

Although the divine soul is higher than the animal soul and clothes itself within it, we actually experience the two of them as if they exist side by side. They express themselves in our conscious minds in the constant ebb and flow of our different and often conflicting thoughts, desires and impulses. The mission of the divine soul in this world is to harness the faculties of the animal soul and the body for its own purposes, in order to turn even their necessary material functions in this world — eating and drinking, making a living, procreation, etc. — into acts of outreach and connection with God. All the associated mitzvot (e.g. blessings, the laws governing interpersonal relationships, business activities, etc.) are "food" for the divine soul, nourishing and strengthening it.

But to provide the divine soul with its challenge in this world, the animal soul is vested with a will of its own, the "Evil Urge," which craves the material pleasures of this world and seeks to enlist the body to pursue them rather than the mitzvot. Worldly pleasures are the "food" of the animal soul. From the Torah point of view, some of these come into the category of the permissible, while others are strictly forbidden. Those that are forbidden — the "impure food" — cause actual damage to the limbs of the divine soul. But even the pursuit of the permissible can weaken it when carried to excess. In the words of Rabbi Chaim Vital:

"Each of the divine soul's 248 limbs is nourished by its corresponding mitzvah, and if a person fails to fulfil a certain mitzvah, the corresponding limb will lack the nourishment it needs from the four letters of the essential Name of God, the Tetragrammaton, of which it is said 'You give life to them all' (Nechemiah 9:6). The mitzvot themselves depend on these four letters (*Zohar* I, 24a), which are also the roots of the four elements making up the divine soul. [Thus the mitzvot are the channel through which holy vitality comes into the soul.] Therefore, by failing to fulfil a mitzvah, the corresponding limb dies, and when the holiness departs, it becomes clothed in an impure spirit from the four elements of the person's animal soul. This limb is then nourished with impure 'bread' from there, and 'dies' — for 'the wicked are called dead even in their lifetime' (*Berakhot* 18b, and see *Zohar* III, 123a). For the divine soul that comes from the living God leaves them, and death — the ultimate source of all pollution — dwells within them.

"So too when a person observes the 365 prohibitions by refraining from what is forbidden, the spiritual sustenance that comes from carrying out the positive commandments is able to flow through the 365 channels of the divine soul to vitalize her 248 limbs. But when a person transgresses one of the prohibitions, the channel corresponding to that sin becomes blocked by the filth of the impure food that becomes stuck there. And when the channel becomes dried up, the limb also dries up, even though it does not fall away completely as it would if the person failed to fulfil one of the positive commandments. But even so, it will be damaged" (*Shaarey Kedushah* I:1).

The struggle of the souls and bodily health

Rabbi Chaim Vital tells us that the outcome of the struggle between the divine and animal souls for dominion over the body can have a decisive effect on actual physical health. He explains this as follows:

"Know that after the first man sinned and ate from the tree of knowledge of good and evil, both his soul and his body became composed of good and evil. This is the concept of the 'filth of the serpent' with which the snake infected Adam and Eve, and through which he caused illness and death to their souls and their bodies. Thus it is written, 'For on the day you eat from it, מות תמות (*mot tamut*), you will surely die' (Genesis 2:17). The Hebrew expression for 'die' is doubled, indicating both the death of the soul and the death of the body. When Adam sinned by eating of the tree of knowledge of good and evil, he caused good and evil to be mixed in all the worlds: there is nothing that is not comprised of good and evil....

"Just as good and evil became mixed in all the worlds, so it was in man's soul. For the soul is hewn out of the four spiritual elements from which all spiritual beings were formed, which are rooted in the four letters of the Tetragrammaton. Of this it is said (Ezekiel 37:9): 'From the four directions come, wind (רוח *ruach*, which also means spirit).' Man's evil side consists of the four main destructive forces enumerated in *Bava Kama* (2a), stemming from the evil aspect of the four elements. From this evil side of the soul comes the evil inclination, and when this soul dominates over the good side of the soul, she becomes afflicted with destructive forces, physical maladies and diseases of the soul, and if it becomes extremely dominant it will kill her....

"Man's body is formed out of the four lower, physical elements of fire, air, water and earth, and they are each composed of good and evil. Man's body is formed out of the good in the four elements. But the bad in them causes the formation of the four bodily humors: the white, the black, the red and the green. And when the bad aspect of any of these becomes dominant and prevails over the good, illnesses and afflictions assail the person. And if the bad aspect becomes extremely powerful, it will kill his body" (*Shaarey Kedushah ibid.*).

In other words, the four constituent "elements" of the body, which we will discuss in more detail presently, have both positive and negative potential. When their positive aspect is dominant, the body functions normally and healthily. But when their negative aspect becomes dominant, bodily functioning becomes pathological, leading eventually to disease and death. Rabbi Chaim Vital's explanation of illness clearly relates to Rebbe Nachman's statement cited earlier that "the main cause of illness is a lack of harmony: the four basic elements making up the body are in conflict, with one element rising up against another." According to Rabbi Chaim Vital, whether the positive or negative aspect of the four bodily elements will become dominant depends upon which of the two souls, the divine or the animal, is allowed to take command of the body.

The divine soul is rooted in the four letters of God's Name, which are the source of creation in general and of the soul's vitality in particular, as mentioned in the passage from *Shaarey Kedushah* quoted earlier (p. 130), and as we will discuss in more detail below. The mitzvot — the divine soul's "food" — are likewise rooted in the four letters of God's Name. This is because God arranged the various mitzvot as the means through which the souls, the intended recipients of His goodness, can attain this goodness. Each mitzvah is a pathway of action in this world designed in such a way as to enable us to connect with a particular facet of Godliness. Since God is known through His Name, each mitzvah is designed to connect us with one aspect or another of the Name, as can be seen from the mystical literature on the *kavanot*, the inner intentions of the mitzvot. The various mitzvot channel vitality from the four letters of God's Name to the four spiritual elements which make up the divine soul, giving dominance to the positive aspect of the four physical elements of the body.

The animal soul, on the other hand, receives its vitality from what the Kabbalah calls the *sitra achra*, literally "the other side," the unholy side of creation that was brought into being to test man in this world by confronting him with desires and temptations that can lead him away from his spiritual destiny. The forces of the "other side" are ultimately evil and destructive, but if this were immediately obvious to all there would be no challenge. Thus the "food" of the animal soul — excessive or forbidden material pleasures, unholy art, music, literature, entertainment, etc. — has a grace and attractiveness of its own. But in the long term this "food" nurtures the destructive elements of the animal soul, which in turn give dominance to the negative aspect of the physical elements of the body, leading to physical malfunctioning, ill health, disease and death.

In order to see how these ideas relate to contemporary understanding of how the body works, let us now turn to a more detailed examination of the kabbalistic doctrine of the "four elements" of which the human body, like the whole of creation, is composed: fire, air, water and earth.

The four elements

The doctrine of the four elements is an integral part of traditional rabbinic thought, and is found both in classic Jewish philosophy and in the Kabbalah (see *Mishneh Torah, Hilkhot Yesodey HaTorah* chapters 3 & 4, *Shaarey Kedushah* III:1-2, *Etz Chaim, Shaar Kitzur ABYA* 10, etc.). It is rooted in the Bible, which tells us that "a river comes out of Eden to water the garden, and from there it divides and becomes four heads" (Genesis 2:10). The "river" alludes to the unitary creative power of God, which contains in potential all the multifarious powers that are manifest in the actual creation. Just as a single beam of white light can be refracted to reveal its constituent colors, similarly the unitary power of God is "refracted," as it were, in the finite creation, dividing into four "heads," alluded to in the four letters of the Tetragrammaton, *Yud Heh Vav Heh*. [When pronouncing the letters of the Holy Name in sequence, it is customary to say the letter *heh* as *keh* in order not even to come close to pronouncing the Holy Name as written, which is strictly forbidden.] These four "heads" are the four elements of fire, air, water and earth (*Likutey Moharan* II, 67).

It is most important to grasp that the use of the word "elements" here has nothing to do with its use in modern chemistry to refer to the various physical substances of which all natural phenomena are composed. In chemistry, the "elements" are those substances that cannot be resolved by chemical means into simpler substances. The "four elements" of Torah thought, on the other hand, which in Hebrew are called יסודות (*yesodot*), "foundations," are not necessarily physical at all, and they are certainly not to be simply identified with physical fire, air, water and earth as we know them.

The Kabbalah pictures the creation as a downward chain of spiritual "worlds" stretching from the most exalted spiritual realms of *Adam Kadmon* ("Primordial Man") and *Atzilut* ("Emanation") down to the spiritual world of *Asiyah* ("Action"), which finally generates the material world in which we live, including our physical bodies. The four "elements" might best be understood as the underlying dynamic principles that govern processes on every level of creation, spiritual and physical, holy and unholy. These "elements" interact in various ways to produce all the different processes and phenomena found in all the different worlds. None of the four elements ever appears alone, but only in combination with all the others. Each of the different natural substances in our world ultimately derives from a unique combination of these elements. Thus the physical water with which we are familiar results from a particular combination of all four elements, but out of the four it is the water element that is dominant, making physical water the appropriate symbol for the basic "water element." The same applies to physical fire, air and earth.

Discussing the four elements as manifested in the physical world in general, Rabbi Aryeh Kaplan writes:

> "In the simplest physical terms, 'water' represents matter, 'fire' is energy, and 'air' is the space that allows the two to interact.... Earth, however, is not a basic element, but a confluence of the other three. It is therefore represented by the final *heh* in the Tetragrammaton, which is actually a repetition of the first *heh* in this name.... These three elements also relate to the experiential. Fire represents the radiation of energy, while water represents the absorption of energy. These are thesis and antithesis, giving and receiving, which themselves are manifestations of cause and effect. Air, which represents the transmission of energy, is then the synthesis, linking the two" (Rabbi Aryeh Kaplan, *Sefer Yetzirah* pp. 145f).

Different kabbalistic texts bring out the interrelationship between the four elements in different ways. However, one thing that is abundantly clear from the above discussion is that the four elements of Torah thought are not to be conceived as primitive substances of some kind. The elements of water, fire and air are to be seen rather as dynamic principles governing chains of cause and effect, while the earth element is the medium through which these principles are manifested. This applies on all the different levels of creation, spiritual and physical. In the physical realm, the earth element would be physical substance in general.

The four elements in the human body

Clearly, when the Torah Sages speak of the human body as consisting of the four elements, this should not be taken to refer only to the physical composition of the different bodily tissues. Without doubt the Torah view is that bodily tissues, like all physical substances in general, are indeed the product of various combinations of the four elements. But just as the four elements exist at all levels of creation, so too they exist at all levels of bodily structure and functioning. They may thus be understood as dynamic principles governing the structure and functioning of the various body parts and systems, both in themselves and in relation to each other.

The four מרות (*marot*, "humors") mentioned in the above-quoted passage from R. Chaim Vital's *Shaarey Kedushah* are, in physical terms, four kinds of fluids or secretions involved in bodily functioning. The red humor refers to the blood, the white to the phlegm and mucus, the yellow to the yellow-green bile secreted by the liver and stored in the gall bladder, while the black refers to black bile, congealed blood from the spleen, associated both in Torah literature and in the pre-19th century world in general with "melancholy" — depression (which Rebbe Nachman frequently refers to as מרה שחורה, *marah shchorah*, "black bile.") Each of the four humors corresponds to one of the four elements. The four humors are all necessary for normal bodily functioning, but they become "bad" when something causes them to exceed their normal levels. As toxic waste which the body is unable to neutralize or eliminate, they cause pathological deviations from the normal, healthy functioning of the various bodily cells, tissues and organs.

Harmony among the elements: homoeostasis

The human body consists of a multitude of diverse substances held together in the various interrelated structures that constitute the tissues, organs and systems of the body: skeletal and muscular, skin, respiratory, cardiovascular, lymph vascular, digestive, excretory, nervous, endocrine (hormonal), immune, reproductive, etc. When all the body systems are functioning harmoniously and the tissues are growing, developing, regenerating and maintaining themselves within their proper limits, we say that the body is "healthy." But when its systems fail to function harmoniously — when they *malfunction* — and the body tissues degenerate, we say that the body is "unhealthy," "diseased" or "dying."

Physical health is essentially a function of the body's success at maintaining a stable internal environment in the face of the various external changes and provocations to which it is constantly exposed as a result of normal wear and tear, improper diet, inadequate exercise, stress, pollution, radiation, micro-organisms, injury, actual abuse (smoking, drugs, etc.) and so on. Homoeostasis is the contemporary term for the necessary stable equilibrium between the various bodily organs and systems. In Kabbalah terms, this is called "harmony among the elements." And, as we have seen, the Kabbalah view is that the key to this harmony lies ultimately in the ability of the divine soul to keep the animal soul in rein. For the "impure food" of the animal soul causes the negative aspect of one or more of the four bodily elements to become dominant, which may eventually lead to manifest physical malfunctioning and actual illness. On the other hand, the "pure food" of the divine soul channels holy vitality from the Root of all creation, strengthening the positive aspect of the four elements and thereby fostering harmony among them, bringing health to the whole body.

3. "The soul is in the blood"

How does the divine soul influence the workings of the body? We saw earlier that the divine soul is "clothed" in the body. What is the actual point of connection between the two? In the words of Rabbi Moshe Chaim Luzzatto:

> "The divine soul directs the lower animal soul, and through it performs its necessary functions.... The divine soul is bound to the animal soul, and the animal soul in turn is linked to the most ethereal element of the blood" (Derekh HaShem III:1.).

The saying that "the soul is in the blood" is found in the Bible (Genesis 9:4, Leviticus 17:11 & 14, and Deuteronomy 12:23). What does this mean? There are varying opinions among the Rabbis. One view is that the blood in question is the "last *revi'it*" (approximately 3 oz.) of blood in the body (Rabbenu Bachya on Leviticus 17:11). Another is that it is the minimal amount of blood with which a person can live (Rashi on *Sotah* 5a), while others say that this is the amount of blood in the heart (*Tosafot ibid.*).

For our purposes, the most significant explanation is that of the Ari, who explains that this "*revi'it* of blood" refers to the highest element in the blood, namely the "life of the brain," and that this in turn is the intermediary between the spiritual and the physical (Shaar Derushey ABYA 1). In the words of Rabbi Aryeh Kaplan:

> "We can understand this on the basis of other statements found in the *Etz Chaim*. The nerves, as well as the veins and arteries, are said to contain a type of 'blood,' but that in the nerves is its highest fraction (Shaar HaMochin 5, Shaar Penimuat veChitzoniut 12, Shaar HaChashmal 1). The only thing that flows through the nerves, however, is the neural impulses, and therefore these impulses must be considered the highest fraction of the 'blood.' This, of course, is the 'life of the brain,' since all mental activity depends on neurological impulses. According to this, the 'animal soul,' which is the information in man's brain as well as his ability to process it, would depend on this 'blood,' namely the neurological processes. This is the meaning of the statement that the 'soul is in the blood'" (Derekh HaShem p.347, translator's note #3).

According to this explanation, the kabbalistic view of the "blood" includes not only the proverbially thick red fluid we tend to think of as blood, but more besides. Even blood as we think of it is far from being a simple, uniform fluid. In its colorless plasma float millions of red cells, white cells and platelets. The red cells transport vital oxygen from the lungs to all the body tissues, and carbon dioxide waste back to the lungs to be exhaled. The various different kinds of white cells play a vital role in defending the body against diseases, while the platelets cause the blood to clot. In addition, blood plasma is the vehicle for transporting the body's main fuels (such as glucose and basic fats), minerals and other nutrients. Besides this, the blood transports hormones around the body: these are the chemical "messengers" that keep the various body parts and systems working harmoniously with each other, and influence our functioning in other ways that medical science is only beginning to uncover.

The red blood is thus crucial to the metabolism of all the cells of the body and to overall bodily functioning. If we then add the "life of the brain" — the neural impulses involved in sensory perception, physical movement and the regulation of a wide variety of different bodily functions — when we talk about the "blood," we are talking about the key to the life of the entire body.

The Pulse

Crucial to all physical functioning is the way the blood circulates around the body. In the words of Rebbe Nachman:

> "From the very beginning of life there is a vital spirit in the heart which causes it to contract and beat. This beat affects all the blood and fluids in the body. It beats in all the limbs of the body, and by constantly beating and churning them, it keeps them from stagnating and degenerating, just as the wind blows over the sea and beats and stirs the waters so that they do not stagnate. Most importantly, this beat pulsates in the arms and hands, which are constantly active and therefore need this beating, churning and cleansing more than anywhere else in the body. This is why the doctor can discover everything about a patient's condition by laying his hand on the patient's wrist and taking his pulse. This is because the arms are the main place where it is possible to feel the action of the heartbeat, which is responsible for the life of the whole body" (*Likutey Moharan* I, 56:9).

A pulse is a recurrent rhythm, a pattern of beats. For most of us, the bodily pulse means the rhythmic throbbing of the arteries as the blood is propelled along them through the pumping action of the heart. The pulse can be felt in a number of the arteries that lie near the surface of the body. The most easily accessible is the radial artery in the wrist, which can be felt on the inner surface of the wrist just below the thumb, but there are also various other points where the pulse can be felt.

When a western physician takes a patient's pulse, what he is mostly interested in is the pulse rate itself and the rhythm. Secondarily, he may also assess its relative strength or weakness. He may then be able to draw certain inferences about the state of the patient's heart and circulatory system. However, oriental medicine makes far more use of subtle pulse patterns as detected at various different pulse points to give precise and detailed information about the state of a wide range of bodily functions. Classical Chinese medicine differentiates between as many as twenty-eight individual pulse patterns, each with its own pathological significance (Manfred Porkert, *Chinese Medicine* pp. 186-90).

The ten pulses in the Kabbalah

When we turn to the Torah tradition, we find that the kabbalistic masters could discern not only physical pathologies from the pulse pattern, but spiritual pathologies as well. In the words of Rabbi Chaim Vital: "Know that just as physical illnesses can be diagnosed from a person's pulse by physical doctors, so my Master [the Ari], of blessed memory, could discern the maladies of the soul by feeling a person's pulse" (*Shaar Ruach HaKodesh* 3, and see above p. 30 and pp. 45f.).

In the Kabbalah view, the pulse is the interface between the spiritual and physical dimensions of our being. Rabbi Chaim Vital brings a kabbalistic teaching of the Ari explaining the matter (*Shaar Ruach HaKodesh* p. 3. See Inset pp. 142-3 for the full teaching.) The Kabbalah teaches that God brought about the creation through the ten *sefirot* — ten modes of creative power through which God's infinite light was successively "contracted" and muted in order to bring about a finite realm in which man can come to know God. The ultimate source of the entire creation is God's *will* to bring it about. This is the highest sefirah, *Keter*, "the Crown." However, the infinite vitality of Keter cannot be revealed directly within the finite creation. The vitality flowing from Keter therefore comes down to the creation through a "garb": it is "clothed" in the sefirah of *Chokhmah*, "Wisdom," also called *Abba*, "father," which could be understood as the underlying "conception" or "plan" of creation. All the sefirot below

Chokhmah are successive steps in the realization of this plan, and as such they are said to receive their vitality from Abba.

In his teaching on the pulses, the Ari says: "The vitalizing power of Abba extends into the arteries and veins of the human body in the form of the pulse patterns governing the blood circulation. And these pulse patterns are a garb for the supreme vitality of the Infinite, which is concealed and clothed within these pulse patterns. The pulse itself is Abba, while the vitality contained within it is the light and vitality of the Infinite, which gives man life." Each of our souls is ultimately rooted in Abba through the level of the soul called the *chayah*, the "living essence" (see above p. 129). From here vitality is channeled down level by level, from the divine soul to the animal soul and from there into the body. We have seen that the soul "clothes itself" in the "blood" — i.e. "the life of the brain," the neurological processes. Thus the Ari's 16th century kabbalistic explanation of the pulse would seem to mesh in well with contemporary scientific understanding of how the hypothalamus in the brain (corresponding to Abba as clothed in the body) ultimately controls the heartbeat via sympathetic and parasympathetic nerves from the cardioregulatory center in the spinal cord.

The vitality flowing into the body from Abba is expressed in the pulse, which in Hebrew is called the דפק (*dofek*). The Ari points out that the numerical value of the Hebrew letters of the word דפק — 184 — is the same* as that of the letters of the holy name associated with Abba: this is the "expansion" of the four letters of the Tetragrammaton with *yud*'s — יוד הי ויו הי (when written by the method of *achorayim* — see Inset p. 142).

As the underlying conception or plan of the creation, Abba itself contains *in potential* all the steps that are involved in the realization of this plan — the

---

*Kabbalistic letter equivalencies are far from being arbitrary. The Kabbalah teaches that the Hebrew letters are the "building blocks of creation." Various combinations of letters make up what we might call the underlying spiritual "formulae" for all the different phenomena in creation. Each of the letters of the Hebrew alphabet has infinite potential. This is expressed in the fact that a simple letter, e.g. י (*yud*), can be "filled in" with the other letters that make up its name — in this case ו (*vav*) and ד (*dalet*) — so as to be spelled out in full: יוד. All of *these* letters can then in turn be filled in with the letters making up *their* names, and so on *ad infinitum*. The name of each letter is bound up with its very essence. The "fill-in letters" were contained in the simple letter *in potential*, and now they are manifest. At the root of all creation are the four letters of God's essential name, the Tetragrammaton. Particular "expansions" of this and related holy names constitute the spiritual roots of all the particular levels and phenomena in creation. The numerical equivalence of the letters of the holy name associated with Abba to those of the word *DoFeK*, the pulse, demonstrates that Abba is the spiritual source of the vitality of the pulse.

ten sefirot. Thus Abba is alluded to in the first letter of the Tetragrammaton, *yud*, which is written with a single dot of ink, yet has the numerical value of ten, alluding to the ten sefirot.

Thus Abba has ten sefirot of its own, which are subsequently manifested on successively lower levels in the actual creation. This is why there are ten main pulse patterns. Each one is a manifestation of a particular kind of vitality flowing into the body via the soul from the ten sefirot of Abba. In the words of the Ari, "A given pulse pattern indicates from which aspect of Abba the vital energy in the pulse is coming at the particular moment this pattern appears."

During Rebbe Nachman's stay in Lemberg (see above pp. 75-85) there was one occasion when the doctor came to visit him and took his pulse. After examining the Rebbe for a few minutes, the doctor took his pulse again, and was surprised to find that it had changed dramatically. Shortly afterwards he took his pulse again, only to find that it had changed yet again. The doctor was quite perplexed, but Rebbe Nachman said, "You see, every moment I live a completely new life!" (Oral tradition)

The ten pulses and the Hebrew vowel signs

A pulse pattern is made up of a series of rhythmic beats or, in the language of the Ari, "dots," which vary in their spacing and intensity. The Ari teaches that the various patterns exhibited by the pulse at different times correspond to the forms of the Hebrew vowel signs, which are themselves made up of dots and short lines in various combinations. The Hebrew vowels, like the letters, are creative forces. In fact, Kabbalah teaches that the vowels are on a higher level than the letters. The twenty-two Hebrew letters are all consonants and cannot be pronounced without vowels. By themselves the letters are "lifeless": it is the vowels that "animate" them. If the letters are the building blocks of creation, it is the vowels that enable them to function together to form meaningful structures — words. Thus the Kabbalah speaks of the Hebrew letters as bodies and the vowels as souls. Just as the vowels "animate" the letters in different ways, so our various pulse patterns — expressions of various spiritual influences — give rise to different rhythms of bodily functioning and different kinds of vitality.

The vowels are said to be "in Abba." This means that, as creative forces, their roots lie in the ten sefirot of Abba, which as we have seen are the roots of our various pulse patterns. There are nine principal Hebrew vowels corresponding to the nine higher sefirot (see table below). The last sefirah, *Malkhut,* "Kingship," does not have its own associated vowel, but is said to receive from the nine sefirot above it. Thus Malkhut may express itself through the vowel associated with whichever of the higher sefirot is dominant at a given moment. With their roots in the ten sefirot of Abba, the Hebrew vowels as we write them actually correspond in shape to the patterns of "dots" and "lines" that make up our pulses. Thus by identifying the vowel sign formed by a particular pulse pattern and knowing the sefirah that corresponds to that vowel, it is possible to understand what is the spiritual source of the vitality coming into the individual's soul and body at this moment.

Vowel sign	Name	Sound	Sefirah
ָ	Kamatz	o (doll)	Keter (Crown)
ַ	Patach	u (cut)	Chochmah (Wisdom)
ֵ	Tzere	ay (day)	Binah (Understanding)
ֶ	Segol	e (let)	Chesed (Kindness)
ְ	Sh'va	e (the)	Gevurah (Power)
וֹ	Cholem	o (roll)	Tiferet (Harmony)
ִ	Chirik	i (sit)	Netzach (Victory)
ֻ	Shuruk	u (rule)	Hod (Splendor)
וּ	Kubutz	u (rule)	Yesod (Foundation)
(no specific sign)	-	-	Malkhut (Kingship)

The Hebrew vowels and corresponding sefirot

The Ten Pulses as explained by the Ari

from *Shaar Ruach HaKodesh* p.3

It is written: "You have made everything with חכמה (*chokhmah*), wisdom" (Psalms 104:24). *Chokhmah* is the source of the vitality of the world of *Atzilut* ("Emanation," the highest of the spiritual worlds.) When Ein Sof, the Infinite God, extends His supernal light into Atzilut, the light is first clothed and concealed within Chokhmah, which is called *Abba*, "father," and then Abba in turn is clothed in Atzilut, extending to its very end. Thus through Abba, Atzilut draws from the supreme vitality of Ein Sof, which vitalizes the entire world of Atzilut. This is the meaning of the verse, "You have made everything with wisdom."

The vitalizing power of Abba extends into the arteries and veins of the human body in the form of the pulse patterns governing the blood circulation. These pulse patterns are a garb for the supreme vitality of Ein Sof, which vitalizes the whole of Atzilut and is concealed and clothed within these pulse patterns. The pulse itself is Abba, while the vitality contained within it is the light and vitality of Ein Sof, which gives man life....

Now we know that Abba is associated with holy name of *YHVH* expanded with *yud*'s (i.e. each of the four root letters of the name is written out in full, יוד הי ויו הי). When this name is written out according to the method of *achorayim*,

יוד, יוד הי, יוד הי ויו, יוד הי ויו הי

the numerical value of all the letters together is 184, which is the same as that of the word דפק (*DoFeK*), which means "pulse."

The explanation of this is that it is not the inner essence of Abba that descends and clothes itself in the human being but a lower, external facet —his *achorayim* (lit. "hinder parts"). For it is a known principle that when a higher power influences a lower one, it does not itself descend, but only its lowest, most external facet. This is the דפק (*dofek*), the pulse [the sum

(The Ten Pulses as explained by the Ari, cont.)

of the Hebrew letters of which is the same as that of the *achorayim* of יוד
הי ויו הי, the name associated with Abba, as we have seen]. And this is
why a person's entire life depends on his pulse. All his ailments can be
felt in it, because any sin or transgression he commits results in a
corresponding lack of light and vitality in the pulse.

There are ten kinds of pulse patterns, corresponding to the Hebrew
vowels, *kamatz, patach, tzéré,* etc. *(Tikkuney Zohar #69, 108a).* The explanation
is that the Hebrew vowels originate at their root from the level of Abba.
[As a *partzuf* Abba has ten sefirot, each of which is associated with one
of the nine Hebrew vowel signs, with the exception of the last sefirah,
Malkhut, which receives from all the others.] All the pulse patterns are in
the form of dots. When you feel the pulse with your fingers you will
sometimes find it to be a single point followed by a second point at its
"side." This is the vowel sign *tzéré.* Sometimes the first point is "above"
and the second point "underneath" it. This is the vowel sign *sh'va.*
Sometimes the first beat is a longer fleck and the second beat a single
point. This is the *kamatz.* All the other vowel signs are fashioned
accordingly.

A given pulse pattern indicates from which aspect of Abba the vital
energy in the pulse is coming at the particular moment when this pattern
appears. For example, a pulse pattern like a *kamatz* indicates that the
prevalent influence originates from the level of *Keter* ("Crown") of Abba.
This is the source of the vitality radiating to all the limbs and organs of
the body at that moment. A pulse like a *patach* indicates that the source
of the vitality coming into the body is *Chokhmah* ("Wisdom") of Abba.
The same applies to all the other vowel signs. Sometimes two vowel
points are joined together, such as *sh'va-tzéré, sh'va-kamatz, sh'va-patach,
sh'va-segol* and so on...

*

4. Health, Sickness and Healing

Why should a particular pulse pattern appear at a given time, indicating the influence of a particular sefirah and giving rise to a distinctive pattern of body functioning and vitality? According to the Ari, our behavior in this world has an influence on the kind of vitality that flows into our souls and bodies through our pulses. Every act of sincere outreach to God, every mitzvah forges a channel for the flow of vitality from the aspect of Godliness — the sefirah — in which that mitzvah is rooted. On the other hand, when a person turns away from the path of connection with God, "any sin or transgression he commits results in a corresponding lack of light and vitality in the pulse" (*Shaar Ruach HaKodesh* p.3).

Each transgression impedes the flow of blessing from one or more of the sefirot, resulting in a corresponding flaw in the person's pulse. Yet the effects may be paradoxical, as Rabbi Chaim Vital tells us in the name of the Ari:

"If a person's pulse pattern is like the vowel sign *kamatz*, for example, this indicates that he has committed a sin relating to the sefirah of *Keter*, and therefore this sefirah is now dominant in order to show its strength. The flow of vitality from the sefirah in question does not simply cease as a result of the sin. On the contrary, when we see that a certain sefirah is dominant, this indicates that the problem lies in that sefirah. This is in accordance with the idea expressed in the verse, 'You add to their spirit, they expire' (*Psalms* 104:29). The verse teaches that immediately prior to death, a person's soul powers are actually enhanced: 'You *add* to their spirit.' This is because it is in the nature of the weak to marshal all their strength to fight back in order to survive. However, there are times when the dominance of a particular sefirah indicates the opposite — that the person carried out a mitzvah relating to this level. We have no one who understands how far this reaches" (*Shaar Ruach HaKodesh* p. 3).

Rabbi Chaim Vital's closing words here — "We have no one who understands how far this reaches" — are a poignant reminder that a full understanding of the spiritual significance of the different pulse patterns was granted only to select Sages of outstanding saintliness throughout the ages, such as Rabbi Shimon bar Yochai, the Ari, the Baal Shem Tov, and Rebbe Nachman himself (see next chapter). The few references to pulse diagnosis in Kabbalah literature are brief and highly allusive (*Tikkuney Zohar* #69, 108a, *Shaar Ruach HaKodesh* p.3 and *Likutey Torah, Taamey HaMitzvot, Vayera* #2). We have no details about how specific transgressions and related flaws in the pulse might be bound up with particular physical conditions of one kind or another. There is certainly not enough information to form the basis for a practical method of kabbalistic pulse diagnosis that could be used today by healers or spiritual counsellors.

Yet the general contours of the Kabbalah view are clear. It is choices made by the individual — either to embrace the mitzvot or to neglect them in favor of other pursuits — that are the key influence on the vitality of the pulse and consequently on our bodily functioning. This relates to our earlier discussion about the influence of the divine and animal souls on the body through their respective "food," holy or non-holy. We saw that the various mitzvot channel vitality from the four letters of God's Name to the four spiritual elements which make up the divine soul. Observing the mitzvot gives dominance to the positive aspects of the four physical elements of the body. We can now understand that the pulse is the channel through which the soul has an influence upon actual bodily functioning. Conversely, when the animal soul is allowed to dominate, it has a negative effect on the pulse, and this is what gives dominance to the negative aspect of the physical elements of the body, leading to physical malfunctioning, ill health, disease and death.

The ten pulses and the four elements

The ten bodily pulses are bound up with the four constituent elements of the body, just as the ten sefirot are bound up with the four elements of creation in general. We saw earlier that the ten sefirot are the ten modes of creative power through which God brought about the creation as a whole, and they are manifest in various ways on all the different levels of creation, spiritual and physical, holy and non-holy. The four elements, which are also manifest on every level, are even more primary than the ten sefirot: "water," "fire" and "air" can be seen as the underlying principles of activity, passivity and balance governing the functioning of the nine higher sefirot — three groups of three — while "earth," corresponding to the lowest sefirah, *Malkhut*, is the "vessel" or medium through which the other three elements, as manifest in the higher sefirot, are revealed. [In most kabbalistic texts, Water (which flows downwards) is associated with the right column of Chokhmah-Chesed-Netzach; Fire (which rises upwards) with the left column of Binah-Gevurah-Hod; and Air with the central column of Keter-Tiferet-Yesod.]

Since each of the different pulse patterns is rooted in one of the sefirot, it is therefore bound up with its corresponding element. The general health of the pulse is thus the key to the harmonious balance of the four bodily elements upon which good health depends. Conversely, any flaw in the pulse leads to imbalance among the elements. Thus we can reconcile Rebbe Nachman's statement that all illness involves a flaw in the ten kinds of pulse (*Likutey Moharan* II, 24) with his saying that the main cause of illness is a lack of harmony among the four elements (*ibid.* I, 56:8).

The essential flaw, as Rebbe Nachman tells us, is a lack of joy, a "flaw in the simchah," for it is simchah that enlivens the pulses. The power of simchah to enliven the pulse and bring healing will be the subject of the next chapter. But to conclude our exploration of some of the kabbalistic ideas underlying Rebbe Nachman's general view of illness and healing, let us now turn to another teaching of the Ari, "The Bed of Sickness."

The Bed of Sickness

The Ari taught:

"'God will sustain him on the bed of sickness, You have turned all his lying down in his sickness' (Psalms 41:4). The Hebrew for 'bed of sickness' is ערש דוי (*EReS DeVoY*). The basic reason a person falls sick is because the divine flow of lovingkindness has turned to strict judgment, and the יוד (*YUD*) — the *ten* animating pulses — turns into דוי (*DeVoY*), 'sickness.' The Hebrew word for ten is עשר (*ESeR*), and this *ESeR* turns into ערש דוי (*EReS DeVoY*), the bed of sickness. The Psalm says, 'You have turned all his lying down in his sickness': two things are turned around: *ESeR* and *YUD*.

"To explain: the person is sick because the light of Chokhmah — Abba — has departed from him. To sustain and strengthen him, it is therefore necessary to bring him sustenance from there. This explains the statement in the Zohar that a sick person's sustenance comes via Wisdom. The explanation is that the sefirah of Chokhmah, Wisdom, corresponds to the *yud* of the Divine Name. When a person is sick, this *YUD* is turned around and becomes *DeVoY*, causing him to be sick and heart-stricken. The numerical value of *yud* is ten, עשר (*ESeR*), and this is turned into *EReS*, his sickbed, which is called ערש דוי (*EReS DeVoY*), the 'bed of sickness.'

"For this reason he needs God to support, sustain and nourish him, and through this very support and sustenance that comes from Abba, the *yud* of the Divine Name, 'You have turned all his lying down in his sickness'; i.e. the sickbed he is lying on, the ערש (*EReS*), turns back to עשר

(*ESeR*), ten, and his sickness, דוי (*DeVoY*), turns back to being יוד (*YUD*), the ten healthy pulses. This is how he is healed, because the reason for his illness was the absence of the flow of vitality from Chokhmah" (*Likutey Torah, Taamey HaMitzvot, Vayera #2*).

The Ari is telling us here that a person becomes sick because "the light of Abba has departed from him," leading to a flaw in the ten pulses and consequent physical imbalance and malfunctioning. "To sustain and strengthen him, it is therefore necessary to bring him sustenance from there," i.e. from Abba. In other words, the way that sickness — *DeVoY* — is reversed is by restoring the flow of vitality from the *YUD* — the ten sefirot of Abba which enliven the pulses, bringing harmony and health to the body.

Now there are many times when healing from sickness comes about spontaneously. This is because "God sustains him on his bed of sickness": God's kindness and compassion reverse the *DeVoY* and turn it back into *YUD* without human intervention. But the art of the human healer is to know which steps to take in order to facilitate recovery. The question is: what is there that we ourselves can do to "turn about the sickness" — to reverse God's decree and turn it into kindness? What can we do to restore the flow of vitality from Abba and turn the *DeVoY*, sickness, back into *YUD* — the radiant shine of the ten sefirot that vitalize the pulses of the body, bringing health? Rebbe Nachman's answer to this question is to be found in his teachings on the Ten Types of Melody, and it is to these that we will now turn.

Chapter 13

The Ten Kinds of Melody

1. The Beggar who had no hands

R ebbe Nachman used his stories as the medium for some of his most exalted Torah teachings. Healing in general, and the ten pulses and ten kinds of melody in particular, are central themes in the last major story Rebbe Nachman ever told, the tale of the Beggar who had no hands in the story of the Seven Beggars. The Beggar with no hands relates:

"You think there is something wrong with my hands. Actually, there's nothing wrong with my hands. I have great power in my hands. But I do not use the power in my hands in this physical world, since I need this power for something else entirely. Regarding this I have the word of the Water Castle.

"Once a number of people were sitting together and each one boasted about the power in his hands. One boasted that he had a certain power in his hands, another boasted that he had a different power. Finally, one boasted that the power in his hands was such that if an arrow were shot, he could retrieve it. The power in his hands was so great that he could bring an arrow back even after it was shot.

"I challenged him: 'What kind of arrow can you retrieve? There are ten types of arrows. This is because there are ten types of poisons. When someone shoots an arrow, he first coats it with some type of poison. There are ten types of poison. When one coats the arrow with the first type of poison, it does a certain degree of harm. If the arrow is coated with the second type of poison, it does worse harm. Thus there are ten types of poison, each more harmful than the other. That's why there are ten types of arrows. All the arrows are actually the same, but since they are rubbed with different poisons and there are ten types of poison, it is considered as if there are ten types of arrows.'

"That's why I asked him what kind of arrow he could bring back. I also asked him if he could retrieve the arrow only before it struck its victim, or if he could bring it back even after it had struck. To the second question, he replied, 'I can retrieve an arrow even after it hits its target.' But his answer to the first question was that he could retrieve only one type of arrow. I said to him, 'If so, then you cannot heal the Queen's Daughter. If you can only turn back one type of arrow, you cannot heal her.'

"Another of those present boasted that he had such power in his hands that whenever he took or received something from someone else, he was actually giving to him. For him the very act of receiving was an act of giving. Therefore, he was a master of charity. I asked him what type of charity he gave, since there are ten types of charity. He replied that he gave a tithe. I said to him, 'If so, you cannot heal the Queen's Daughter. You cannot even approach the place where she is; you can go through only one wall in the place where she is staying. You cannot get to where she is.'

"One of those present boasted about the power in his hands, saying that there were officials in the world — highly placed people in charge of cities and nations — each of whom needs wisdom. He said that through his hands he could give them wisdom. He did this by laying his hands on them. I asked him, 'What type of wisdom can you confer with your hands? There are ten types of wisdom.' When he specified the kind of wisdom, I said to him, 'If this is the case, you cannot heal the Queen's Daughter. You cannot understand her pulse, since there are ten types of pulse. You can only confer one type of wisdom, and therefore only understand one type of pulse.'

"One of those present boasted that he had such great power in his hands that when there was a stormwind, he could hold it back with his hands. Then with his hands he could make the wind blow with the proper force so that the wind was beneficial. I asked him, 'What kind of wind can you hold with your hands? There are ten kinds of wind.' He specified the type of wind he could hold. I said, 'If that is the case, you cannot heal the Queen's Daughter. You can play only one type of melody. She can be healed only through melody, and there are ten types of melody. But you can play only one type of melody out of these ten.'

"All the people who were there asked me, 'What power do you have?' I replied, 'I can do what you cannot do. In each of the cases you discussed there are nine portions that you cannot accomplish. I can accomplish them all.'

"This is the story: Once there was a king who desired a Queen's Daughter. He made all kinds of plots to capture her, until he finally succeeded and took her captive. Then the king had a dream. The Queen's Daughter was standing over him, and she killed him. When he woke up, he took the dream to heart. He summoned all the dream interpreters, and they all said that it would come true quite literally: she would kill him.

"The king could not decide what to do with her. If he killed her, it would grieve him. If he sent her away, this would anger him, since then another man would have her. This would frustrate him terribly after having worked so hard to get her, only to see her with someone else. Furthermore, if he exiled her and she ended up with someone else, there would be all the more chance of the dream coming true. With an ally, it would be even easier for her to kill him. Still, he was afraid because of the dream, and he didn't want to keep her near him. The king simply did not know what to do with her. Because of the dream, his love for her gradually waned. As time passed, his desire for her grew less and less. The same was true of her: her love for him declined more and more, until she came to hate him. Eventually she fled.

"The king sent his men to search for her. When they returned, they reported that she was near the Water Castle. It was a castle made of water. It had ten walls, one inside the other, all made of water. The floors inside this castle were also made of water. This castle also had trees and fruit, all made of water. It goes without saying how beautiful this castle was, and how unusual. A castle of water is certainly something wonderful and unusual. It is impossible for anyone to enter the Water Castle. It is made entirely of water, and anyone entering it would drown.

"Meanwhile, the Queen's Daughter was circling the Water Castle. The king was informed of this, and took his army and set out to capture her. When the Queen's Daughter saw them coming, she decided that she would flee into the castle. She would rather drown than be captured by the king and have to stay with him. There was also the possibility that she would survive and succeed in actually entering the Water Castle. When the king saw her fleeing into the water, he said, 'If this is how it is....' He gave orders to shoot her, saying, 'If she dies, she dies.'

"The soldiers shot her and hit her with all ten types of arrows rubbed with the ten types of poison. She ran into the castle and went inside. She went through the gates in the walls of water. The walls of water have such gates. She passed through all ten walls of the Water Castle, until she came to its interior. When she reached there, she fell unconscious.

"And," said the Beggar with no hands, "I heal her. Someone who does not possess all ten types of charity cannot enter all ten walls: he will drown in the water there. The king and his army tried to pursue her, but they all drowned in the water. I, on the other hand, was able to go through all ten walls of water. These walls of water are like the waves of the sea which stand like a wall. The winds support the waves and lift them up. The ten walls are made up of waves which stand there permanently, but they are lifted up and supported by the winds. I, however, was able to enter through all ten walls.

"I was also able to draw all ten types of arrows out of the Queen's Daughter. I also know all ten types of pulses, and could detect them with my ten fingers. Each of the ten fingers has the power to detect one of the ten types of pulse. I could then heal her through the ten types of melody. And thus I heal her. Therefore I have this great power in my hands...."
(*Rabbi Nachman's Stories* pp.410-34).

The healing power of melody

Rebbe Nachman explained that the Princess in the story is the divine soul in every Jew, which is the "daughter" of the King of the Universe. The soul seeks to escape the "evil king" who holds her captive: this is the evil urge, the animal soul. But the divine soul is weary and faint because of her sins. The sins themselves are the "ten poisonous arrows," corresponding to the ten sefirot of the unholy realm, which gain sway through transgression. In the words of Rebbe Nachman: "Only a very great Tzaddik has the power to enter every place where the soul has fallen and remove all ten arrows from her. In order to heal her, he must be able to discern all ten types of pulse-beat, and he must know all ten kinds of melody, for her main cure is through melody and joy" (*Rabbi Nachman's Wisdom* #273).

As we saw in the previous chapter, the ten pulse patterns governing the circulation of the blood around the body draw their vitality from the ten sefirot of Abba, *Chokhmah* — "Wisdom." The Kabbalah view is that illness results from an impairment in the flow of vitality from Abba via the divine soul, registered a a flaw in the pulse. The remedy is to restore the flow of vitality in order to revitalize the pulse and bring physical healing. The question we were left with at the end of the previous chapter was: *how* can the flow of vitality from Abba be restored?

The story of the Beggar with no hands provides us with the vital clue: the main cure of the soul is through melody and joy. There are ten kinds of melody, and these bring vitality to the ten kinds of pulse. The "ten kinds of melody" are mentioned in the Talmud and Zohar. "Rabbi Yehoshua ben Levi said: Through ten expressions of praise the book of Psalms was composed: *Nitzuach, Nigun, Maskil, Mizmor, Shir, Ashrey, Tehilah, Tefilah, Hoda'ah* and *Haleluyah*" (*Pesachim* 117a and see Rashi on Psalms 1:1). The Zohar tells us that the ten kinds of melody correspond to the Ten Sefirot (*Zohar* III, 223b).

Nowhere in Rebbe Nachman's writings do we find a detailed typology of the various possible flaws in the pulse, the particular spiritual and physical maladies corresponding to each one, and the specific "songs" that are the remedy for each of the different kinds of flaws. Presumably, if Rebbe Nachman had thought full knowledge of all the details to be necessary in order to follow his path of health and healing, he would have revealed them. Instead, he made it one of the most important quests of his life to discover what he called the תיקון הכללי (*Tikkun HaKlali*), the General Remedy (see *Rabbi Nachman's Tikkun*). Rebbe Nachman first began to talk about this in 1805, five years before he passed away, and he discussed it in a number of his teachings.

The General Remedy consists of all the ten kinds of melody together. Initially, Rebbe Nachman taught that any ten psalms contain the ten kinds of melody (*Likutey Moharan* I, 205). Then in the spring of 1810, shortly before he left Breslov for Uman, Rebbe Nachman revealed ten specific psalms that contain all the ten kinds of melody and are the General Remedy *par excellence*. The psalms are: 16, 32, 41, 42, 59, 77, 90, 105, 137 and 150. Rebbe Nachman's revelation of the Ten Psalms came just a week before he began telling the story of the Seven Beggars (see *Rabbi Nachman's Wisdom* #141, note 468).

Rebbe Nachman saw in the General Remedy a complete remedy for all spiritual flaws. And since these, in his view, are at the root of physical maladies, the General Remedy is an integral part of his healing pathway. He taught:

> "There are places that are so fine and narrow that no remedy has the power to penetrate them except through the General Remedy, which injects healing into even the narrowest, finest places. First it is necessary to apply the General Remedy, and through this all the individual flaws

will automatically be rectified. It is true that the General Remedy is higher and more exalted than all the individual remedies. But all the different remedies depend on the mind and brain: it is necessary to draw purity from the mind and brain. And the only way to elevate the mind is through the General Remedy. This is why it is first necessary to go to the higher level — the General Remedy — in order to rectify the mind and brain, and through this everything else is automatically rectified" (*Likutey Moharan* I, 29:4 & 10).

According to this teaching, the healing power of the General Remedy lies in the fact that it "draws purity from the mind and brain" down into the body. We saw in the previous chapter that the life of the body depends on the vitalizing power of Abba, which is clothed in the "life of the brain," and extends into the body through the pulses. If the flow of vitality from Abba is impaired, it is necessary to reach up to this high level in order to restore the flow. It is through the ten kinds of melody making up the General Remedy that this is accomplished. But before we examine the healing power of melody in greater depth, let us first look more closely at what it comes to rectify: flawed simchah.

2. The Number One Destroyer

"All the illnesses people suffer come only because of a lack of joy" (*Likutey Moharan* II, 24). At first sight Rebbe Nachman's statement is quite surprising. Does he really mean that *all* illness is caused only by a lack of joy? The human body is amazingly complex. It is enough to look at any medical guide to see the enormous number of conditions and illnesses that can afflict the various body parts and systems. Surely they have all kinds of different causes.

There are bacterial and viral infections — 'flu, diarrhea, measles, chickenpox and many more. Do all these strike only because the people who contract them, many of them children, suffer from a lack of simchah? According to medical authorities, genetic predisposition is an important factor in conditions ranging from Tay-Sachs to cancer, heart and other diseases. How can we say that these too are caused by a lack of simchah? What about the deterioration and degeneration of bodily tissues that comes with age, leading to arthritis, diabetes, heart disease and so on? What about the many medical problems related to people's occupations or the climates they live in? Are these too to be blamed on a lack of simchah? And what about the growing incidence of cancer, leukemia, asthma and other diseases related to the millions of tons of toxic chemicals being poured into the atmosphere as a result of industrial processes, automobile exhaust and so on? Can environmentally caused diseases also be connected with a lack of simchah?

It is not too difficult to name various medical problems that are seeming exceptions to Rebbe Nachman's general statement. But it would be a pity to allow this to obscure the main point Rebbe Nachman is making. Conventional medicine is skeptical about anything that cannot be measured in the blood or seen under a microscope. Western doctors tend to focus on detectible physical changes in the bones, muscles, tendons, organs, skin, nerves, veins, arteries, blood, hormones, etc., etc. Disorders are attributed to the physical intervention of bacteria, viruses, parasites, organic or chemical toxins, excessive intake of fat, inadequate vitamins, and so on. But Rebbe Nachman is not talking about the physical course of disease. He is asking us to pay attention to something even more primary. What is the *root cause* of the physical problem? What are the underlying mental and spiritual factors that cause the body to become susceptible to illness in the first place?

Atzvut and *marah shchorah*: depression

In fact, Rebbe Nachman's statement, made almost two hundred years ago, predates much contemporary thinking about the non-physical roots of many kinds of bodily illness. In order to gain a fuller understanding of what Rebbe Nachman is saying, let us first take a look at the terms he uses when talking about the flaw in simchah. In the main, he uses two terms: *marah shchorah* and *atzvut*.

The Hebrew term מרה שחורה (*marah shchorah*) literally means "black bile." The word מרה (*MaRaH*) comes from the biblical root מר (*MaR*), meaning bitter. *Marah* appears in the Talmud to refer both to the physical bile (*Bava Metzia* 107b) and to the kind of irritable, aggressive behavior that was thought to result from an excess of bile (*Ketuvot* 103b). In Zoharitic, kabbalistic and later rabbinic literature, *marah shchorah* refers simply to sadness, depression and similar states. It corresponds to the word "melancholy," which derives from two Greek words meaning black bile, congealed blood from the spleen thought to be the cause of sorrow, hopelessness, apathy and withdrawal.

The word עצבות (*atzvut*) is a noun formed from the biblical root עצב (*ATzaV*), meaning to be grieved or pained (as in Genesis 3:16, Proverbs 10:22, etc.). But *atzvut* does not refer only to what is classified as "clinical depression" in the narrower sense of the term. It also covers a wide variety of other negative states, such as frustration, worry, anxiety, impatience, irritability, fear, aggressiveness and hostility.

In essence, *atzvut* and *marah shchorah* are the states we fall into when we fail to find satisfaction and joy in what *is* (or was in the past, or seems likely to be in the future). They are terms that apply to the various complexes of disappointment, sorrow, sadness, anger, bitterness, aggressiveness, pessimism, withdrawal and the like that may arise when we look at ourselves, our lives and our circumstances, and judge them to have fallen short of the criteria we set for ourselves.

For Rebbe Nachman, the root of *atzvut* lies in a person's inability to accept the way God is dealing with him or her. "*Atzvut* is like someone who is angry and enraged, as if he is fulminating against God and complaining against Him for not arranging things the way *he* wants them to be" (*Rabbi Nachman's Wisdom* #42). This is a sign of arrogance. It is as if one is saying, "I want to be in complete control! I want to have everything *my* way" — instead of accepting that God governs all things, that He is good and beneficent, and that everything He sends is for the best.

True health involves more than normal bodily functioning. It is to be vital and *alive*, not to let our lives go to waste on negativity, frustration and depression. When Rebbe Nachman says that "*all the illnesses people suffer from come only because of a lack of joy*," he is not necessarily referring only to the kinds of complaints that would be recognized as illnesses by today's medical practitioners. His statement includes *all* the maladies — mental, psychological and spiritual as well as physical — that shorten and destroy people's lives.

Atzvut and the body

Yet Rebbe Nachman is not speaking only of spiritual maladies, but also of actual physical illnesses. It is obvious that *atzvut* and the confusion, irritability, rash impulsiveness and carelessness that may accompany it lie behind many of the tragic fatalities and injuries caused by all kinds of accidents. In addition, as the underlying reason for many people's excessive eating, smoking and drinking, etc., *atzvut* is the root cause of much of the heart disease, cancer and other health problems ravaging our societies.

But *atzvut* can have an even more direct effect upon the body. Significantly, the very word *atzvut* has definite physical connotations, as in the verse, "He binds up their *wounds* (*atzvoteyhem*)" (Psalms 147:3). The first time the Hebrew root appears in the Bible is when God said to Eve, "I will greatly multiply your *pain* and travail: in *pain* shall you bring forth children" (Genesis 3:16). Pain is felt through the nerves, and thus עצבות (*ATzVut*) is connected with the Hebrew word עצב (*ETzeV*), which means a "nerve."

The nerves are the communication system between the mind and brain on the one hand and the rest of the body on the other. Not only does the nervous system carry information *to* the brain from our skin, sense organs, muscles, blood vessels and internal organs. It also includes the so-called efferent neurons that carry orders away *from* the brain to influence specific body parts and systems in particular ways. The somatic nervous system transmits motor signals to the skeletal muscles, initiating movement. The autonomic nervous system controls involuntary, unconscious functions such as our breathing rate and blood circulation, digestion and the secretions of hormones that govern critical bodily processes. There are two divisions of the autonomic nervous system: the sympathetic and parasympathetic. In the simplest terms, the work of the sympathetic could be said to be involved with "arousal," while that of the parasympathetic is involved with "calming."

The sympathetic nervous system is perhaps the most direct link between our minds and our bodies, translating emotional states almost instantaneously into physical changes in the body. The sympathetic nervous system responds especially to anxiety, fear and anger. The effect of these is to send nerve impulses causing the release of stimulatory hormones that influence bodily functioning in a variety of ways. The heart rate speeds up, the lungs move more rapidly, the entire digestive system is inhibited, from the salivary glands (causing the dry mouth associated with anxiety) to the entire twenty-five feet of the intestines. The liver releases large quantities of stored sugar into the blood stream, making more glucose available to the skeletal muscles, increasing their contraction, while the entire body tends to be drawn into a defensive half-crouch, with the shoulders and head thrust forward, the abdomen tightly drawn in, the knees bent, hands tense, and the eyes moving rapidly.

In face of a real threat, this so-called "fight or flight response" is entirely appropriate. It gears the body for a burst of action either to confront the danger head on, or physically run away to escape it. The problems arise when our everyday fears and anxieties lead to the same response without our having any direct outlet for energetic action. Our blood remains flooded with sugar and arousing hormones, leaving us with a shaky, overstimulated feeling. Our muscles stay tensed and our heart rate and blood pressure remain unnecessarily high long after the initial stimulus. This is where mental anxiety turns into chronic physical tension.

Stress and illness

The role of stress in many cases of cardiovascular disease — the chief cause of premature death in the industrialized world — has now been established beyond all doubt. Adrenaline (or epinephrine), the hormone produced by stimulation of the sympathetic nervous system, releases fats into the blood that may end up in the plaque that blocks the coronary arteries. Another hormone, noradrenaline, causes blood platelets to clump together, increasing the chances of a blood clot that could precipitate a heart attack. When released in large quantities, as in the case of hostile encounters, noradrenaline can lead to heart rhythm disturbances that can sometimes be fatal.

The part played by anxiety and tension in many other physical conditions is also well documented. Medical authorities acknowledge that some eighty percent of digestive disorders, from nervous indigestion and stomach ulcers to colon cancer, have no obvious physical cause. Stress can be a factor in diabetes, thyroid failure and many other disorders. Doctors point to worry, frustration, financial insecurity and marital discord as the most usual conditions that bring on arthritis. Excessive muscular tension can distort the body in innumerable ways, giving rise to chronic fatigue, all kinds of back pain, neuralgia, migraine and a host of other problems.

The physiological effects of the various manifestations of *atzvut* — from "frayed nerves," negativity and aggressiveness to chronic depression and despair — are the subject of the new science of psychoneuroimmunology, which investigates the influence of mental factors on the functioning of the body's immune system. The advent of AIDS has highlighted the importance of a healthy immune system in fending off disease by showing what happens when immunity is weakened. A growing body of evidence points to the decisive role of mental states and attitudes in ailments ranging from colds and 'flu to cancer.

No one today disputes the damaging effects on health of habitual overindulgence, heavy smoking, drinking and other forms of abuse, all of which are clearly rooted in *atzvut*. But while the more subtle long-term effects of demoralization, despondency and other forms of conscious and unconscious *atzvut* may be far more difficult to measure, this does not make them any less significant. They may be precisely the factors that explain why one member of a family with a "genetic predisposition" to a particular illness succumbs while other members of the same family do not, or why some people in a toxic environment develop certain diseases while others remain healthy.

The environment

Looking more globally, the growing menace of environment-related diseases may seem less bound up with any special lack of simchah in the innocent victims than with the overall contamination of the atmosphere by the thousands of chemicals used in contemporary industrial processes and everyday life. Scientific understanding of how many of these substances affect human beings is still elementary. Even so, there is little doubt that pollution is the main factor behind the steady increases in industrialized countries in the incidence of all kinds of cancers, asthma, birth defects and a variety of insidious problems of the nervous system (fatigue, faulty memory, inability to concentrate, irritability, etc.).

Yet if we look beyond the manifest problem of degradation of the environment to the mechanisms that drive it — the appetite for ever greater consumption, and especially the mindless thirst for maximum profits regardless of the long-term consequences — we see that their roots lie in the profound lack of simchah that pervades our society and culture as a whole. It is the absence of true simchah that fuels the insatiable craving for wealth, resources and territory that is the cause not only of environmental despoliation but also of most of the conflict within and between nations in our tortured world. Thus the stricken Princess in Rebbe Nachman's story of the Beggar with no hands symbolizes not only the individual Jewish soul but the Divine Presence itself, which has been all but driven from the world by the arrows of global *atzvut*, manifest in the rampant materialism, nihilism, hatred, violence and other ills afflicting our societies.

3. Holding back the stormwind

In the story of the Beggar with no hands, the Beggar relates: "One of those present boasted that he had such great power in his hands that when there was a *stormwind*, he could *hold it back with his hands*. Then he could make the wind *blow with the proper force*, so that the wind was beneficial." The person with this power in his hands specifies which type of wind he could hold, but the Beggar replies, 'If so, you cannot heal the Queen's Daughter. She can be healed only through melody, and there are ten types of melody. But you can play only one type of melody out of these ten."

The "stormwind" is a graphic symbol for *atzvut*, the ravaging force that shortens and destroys so many lives, upsetting and distorting the vital pulse, causing weakness, illness and death. In the words of the *Tikkuney Zohar*:

"There is a pulse pattern that stems from the Tree of Knowledge of Good and Evil, which is the root of the good and evil inclinations — 'the blade of the sword that was constantly turning' (Genesis 3:24), changing from a staff into a serpent and from a serpent into a staff (cf. Exodus 4:2-4). The beat of the good inclination brings health and healing to all the limbs and organs of the body, while the beat of the evil inclination causes sickness. Whichever is stronger dominates. If a person's merits are greater, the beat changes from a serpent to a staff, kindness prevails, and his whole body is healed. But if his sins are greater, the beat changes from a staff to a serpent and bites his limbs all over, causing pain and disease....

"But there is a pulse from the Evil Tree which has no good in it at all. From here comes forth a *stormwind that ravages the human body* — 'a mighty wind that shatters mountains and breaks the rocks' (Kings I, 19:11). The 'mountains' are the bones of the body while the 'rocks' are the flanks. This stormwind comes forth recklessly without measure or limit, 'and the ship was likely to be broken' (Jonah 1:4). The 'ship' is the body. This ship tosses and turns on the waves of the sea. The waves are the ten lower crowns [the ten sefirot of the side of unholiness]..." (*Tikkuney Zohar* #69, 108b).

What we learn from the words of the Beggar in Rebbe Nachman's story is that the key to healing lies in taking this "stormwind" of *atzvut* — the source of the flaw of the pulse — and "holding it back with one's hands" in order to "make the wind blow with the proper force, so that the wind will be beneficial." The "stormwind" itself is turned into a "melody" which enlivens and restores the pulse, bringing healing.

What does all this really mean? *How* is the "stormwind" of *atzvut* held back with one's *hand* and turned into a "melody"? And how does this relate to healing in terms that we can understand?

Rhythm and melody

Let us begin by considering music. We are all familiar with the amazing power of music to sweep us up into its mood and rhythm. We may be in no particular mood to start with, or even depressed and full of negativity. But when we suddenly hear a catch of lively music or a song, the beat begins to take over, and before we know it, we are tapping and moving to the music. Our whole energy is transformed and our low spirits forgotten. Our mood is now the mood of the music. Lovers of all kinds of music can attest to its power to mold their deepest sensibilities and become a part of their very selves.

Even without a melody line, a forceful rhythm soon draws people under its spell and can hold them enthralled for long periods, as can be seen with native African and South American drummers. But rhythm alone soon becomes boring. Music's power to move and entrance lies primarily in the melody. The melody line itself calls for an appropriate rhythm. The rhythm plays a vital role in establishing the mood and energy of the music. But it is the melody that really speaks to the heart and soul. In Torah terms, the melody is "higher" than the rhythm. Holy music is far more than incidental entertainment. A holy melody contains exalted wisdom. In the words of Rebbe Nachman: "Know that every wisdom in the world has its own unique song and melody, and it is from this song that this wisdom is actually derived. And so from level to level, for a higher wisdom has an even more exalted song and melody" (*Likutey Moharan* I, 64:5).

The relationship between rhythm and melody corresponds to the relationship between the Hebrew vowels on the one hand, and the טעמים (*taamim*), the tunes or chants to which the Torah text is traditionally sung, on the other. In the previous chapter we saw that the Hebrew letters are like bodies that come to life only when animated by the vowels, which give them "soul," enabling them to function together to form meaningful structures. The vitality that the vowels breathe into the letters parallels the vitality that the pulse gives to the human body. Indeed, as we saw, the pulse patterns themselves exhibit the same forms as the Hebrew vowel signs. The vowels correspond to the "rhythm."

However, the vowels are considered to be merely a low level of soul. This means that they enable the letters to function together to form whole words, but no more. Individual, isolated words possess only a limited power to communicate. Fuller, more subtle communication depends upon the arrangement of words into the meaningful structures we call sentences. In the

Torah text, the patterns of words in each verse and the way they work together to communicate whole ideas is governed by the *taamim* — melodies — which are seen as a higher level of soul.

In the words of the *Tikkuney Zohar*:

> "The letters are the *nefesh* (the lowest part of the soul). They are the vessel for the vowels (which are the *ruach*, "wind" or "spirit," a higher part of the soul). But above them is the *neshamah* (the "breath," a yet higher part of the soul), which is a crown over all the letters and vowels. And from this crown come all the individual crowns of all the letters and vowels: these are the *taamim*, the chants that give movement to the letters and vowels." [The "crowns" mentioned here are not to be confused with the *tagin* — "crowns" — over certain letters, which are on a lower level than the vowels.] (*Tikkuney Zohar* #69, 108a).

The vowels that animate the letters correspond to the rhythm of a piece of music, which is what makes the difference between a meaningless succession of sounds — the individual notes — and an expressive progression of beats. Similarly, in the human body, it is the rhythm of the pulse that governs the metabolic rate and harmonious functioning of all the different limbs and organs. However, in the Torah text, the *taamim*, the tunes or melodies, are on an even higher level than the vowels. It is the *taamim* that determine the overall sense of the text and what it communicates, just as in music it is the melody line that conveys the essential message. Similarly, in the human being, the *neshamah* level of the soul — which expresses itself through and is influenced by melody — is higher than the *ruach*, which corresponds to rhythm and expresses itself in the pulse. Since melody is on a higher level, it has the power to influence and alter the pulse. This is the meaning of Rebbe Nachman's statement that the various types of melody "enter into the ten different pulses of the human body, giving them *life*" (*Likutey Moharan* II, 24).

We saw in the previous chapter that the human pulse, which governs all our vital processes, is a garb for the wisdom of Abba, which channels vitality into all the worlds. A flaw in the pulse is a flaw in the flow of wisdom: *YUD*, the ten sefirot of Abba, are turned away, causing *DeVoY*, illness. It is because holy melody contains exalted wisdom on the level of *neshamah* that it is the remedy for a flaw in the pulse, which is on a lower level, that of *ruach*. As Rebbe Nachman said in explaining the General Remedy: "It is first necessary to go to the higher level in order to rectify the mind and brain, and through this everything else is automatically rectified" (*Likutey Moharan* I, 29, see above pp. 153-4).

The flawed pulse is rectified by "drawing purity from the mind and brain," and this is accomplished through the power of holy melody.

The pulse is a *ruach*, the "wind" or "spirit" that gives life to the human body. When the pulse is flawed, it is because this *ruach* has turned into a *ruach se'arah*, a "stormwind," because of *atzvut*. The art of healing is to "hold back the stormwind with one's hands" in order to "make the wind blow with the proper force, so that the wind will be beneficial." The "stormwind" — the negative spirit of *atzvut* — must be transformed into a holy melody that will enliven and restore the pulse, bringing healing. But how is this done? What is the power in the hands that is needed to accomplish this — the power that the Beggar in the story possessed to perfection?

How songs are made

In the following passage, Rebbe Nachman speaks about how a musician makes melodies — by picking out the "good notes." The player's ability to create inspiring melodies depends on the skill in his *hand*, because it is with his hand that he chooses the right notes:

"It was through music that a spirit of prophecy would rest upon the prophets (as in Kings II, 3:15). A musical instrument is a vessel containing air (*ruach*, spirit). The air in the instrument is a mixture of good and bad. On the one hand there is the anxious, depressed spirit — a bad spirit, as we find in the case of King Saul: 'and an *evil spirit* terrified him' (Samuel I, 16:14). On the other hand, there is a good spirit, as it is written, 'Let Your *good spirit* lead me in an even land' (Psalms 143:10). This is the spirit of prophecy, holy spirit. But when good and bad are mixed up, it is impossible to receive true prophecy.

"The person playing a musical instrument gathers together the good spirit, the spirit of prophecy, and separates it from the anxious, depressed spirit. He must understand music in order to know how to sift out and gather up the parts of the spirit and put them together in order to construct the melody, namely the joy, so as to build the good spirit, the spirit of prophecy, which is the opposite of the depressed spirit. He has to move his hand up and down on the instrument in order to channel the joy and bring it to perfection. And when the prophet hears a melody from an expert musician, he receives a spirit of prophecy, the very spirit that the musician gathered in his hand and separated from the depressed spirit. Thus the attendants of the depressed King Saul said to him of the young

David: 'And he will play with his *hand* and it will be *good* for you' (Samuel I, 16:16).

"Thus by playing the musical instrument with one's hand, one sifts out, purifies and elevates the good spirit and separates it from the bad. This is the way to overcome the evil spirit of folly that seeks to spoil and upset the good, prophetic spirit. The bad spirit is dissipated through the joy which comes through the hand of the player. For the root of the power of the spirit of folly lies in anxiety and depression. Therefore the only way to receive a holy spirit of prophecy is through joy — the joy created by the hand of the player, as it is written: 'And it was when the musician played that the *hand* of God was upon him' (Kings II, 3:15); 'and he will play with his *hand* and it will be good for you.' The player who has the power of the hand can sift out the good spirit from the bad, and can thereby subdue the evil spirit" (*Likutey Moharan I, 54:6*).

Clearly this passage is more than an analysis of the art of the instrumentalist in the literal sense. The musical instrument is a metaphor for ourselves and our lives. We ourselves are the players. The question is: how do we play ourselves? How do we play our lives? For the way we play governs the spirit that fills our minds and hearts, putting its stamp on every facet of our experience in this world.

A musical instrument, a guitar for example, is essentially a soundbox. Plucking or strumming the strings sets the air vibrating. Potentially, the air can vibrate in an infinite variety of ways. The sounds that come out may be sweet, harmonious and pregnant with meaning, or raucous, dissonant and senseless, depending on the player. The art of playing lies in knowing how to move one's hands up and down the instrument in order to tense the strings exactly the right amount, neither more nor less, and to pick out just the right notes in the right combinations.

Similarly, our lives and personalities are full of potential. The "air" we set vibrating with our various thoughts, words and actions is both our own inner consciousness and the atmosphere that surrounds us in our various relationships and in all the different situations we face as we go through life. The vital question is: which notes do we play? Which thoughts and feelings do we choose to dwell on? What attitudes do we take towards situations and events? How do we talk about things? About ourselves? About others? What initiatives do we take? What responses do we make?

Every one of our thoughts, words and deeds is a note in the far greater symphony of life. As long as we play with a little care and good sense, we have the power to fill ourselves and the world around us with vibrations of grace, beauty and holiness. But the fact is, there are few born players. Many people carry on playing regardless of how the sounds come out, blithely unaware of the ugly din they may be creating. Some of us have uneasy feelings about the way we are playing. We start listening more carefully — only to discover a disturbing cacophony within ourselves and all around us. We take a hard look at ourselves, and wonder if we ever played a right note in our lives.

Searching for the good points

It was precisely to remedy the *atzvut* caused by this sense of inadequacy and failure that Rebbe Nachman taught his pathway of searching for the good points, *"Azamra — I will sing!"* (see pp. 79f.).

> "It is a well-known fact that when a person becomes depressed over his gross physicality and evil deeds and sees how distant he really is from holiness, it generally makes him completely incapable of praying. He cannot even open his mouth. This is because of the depression and heaviness that come over him when he sees the overwhelming distance separating him from God. But through searching for your good points you can give yourself new life. Even if you know you have caused much damage and sinned time after time, you must still search until you find the good points that remain in you" (*Likutey Moharan* I, 282).

The essence of the search for the good points is to salvage goodness even out of the worst darkness:

> "When you start examining yourself, it may seem as if you have nothing good in you at all. You see that you are full of sin, and the Evil One wants to push you into depression and sadness as a result. Even so, you must not allow yourself to fall — not on any account. Search until you find a little bit of good in yourself. For how could it be that you never carried out a single mitzvah or did anything good in your entire life? You may start to examine this good deed, only to see that it is full of blemishes and devoid of purity. Even so, how is it possible that it contains not even a modicum of good? You have to search until you find some little good point in yourself to restore your inner vitality and attain joy.

> "And in just the same way, you must carry on searching until you find yet another good point. Even if this good point is also full of blemishes,

still, you must extract some positive point from here too. And so you must go on, searching and collecting additional good points. *And this is how melodies are made*" (ibid.).

The search for the good points is itself the art of "music-making" as explained in Rebbe Nachman's earlier-quoted teaching about the music-player. Each of the "notes" which the musician plays as he "sifts the good air from the bad" is a good point. And through joining the notes together — collecting more and more good points — a "melody" is formed that dissipates the "bad spirit" of *atzvut* and causes a holy spirit of joy, prophecy and Godly connection to dwell in us.

The key to finding the good in ourselves, in others and in all the various situations we face in life lies in how we *judge* things. This is why Rebbe Nachman begins his teaching of "*Azamra!*" with the rabbinic dictum about judging positively: "Judge all people in the scale of merit" (*Avot* I:6). The Hebrew word for "scale" is כף (*kaph*), which literally means the palm of the hand. It is the *hand* that "sifts" and selects. In the same way, we have to train ourselves to use our faculty of judgment to sift through and find the good, not to accuse and condemn. People and situations are always multifaceted. There are usually many ways of viewing and evaluating the same person or situation, both positively and negatively. What aspects do we choose to focus on? What do we "harp" on?

Some people will always go for the negative, castigating themselves, other people, and life in general. But Rebbe Nachman is teaching us a different way: to use our "hand of judgment" to pick out the good at all times. It was the power of positive judgment that the Beggar in the story possessed to perfection, and with this power he was able to hold back the stormwind of *atzvut* and make it blow with the proper force so as to be beneficial. This was the power with which he healed the Princess.

Ten kinds of song

Our greatest task in life is to become expert "players," to turn this mode of positive judgment into an habitual orientation, so that we are always going from good point to good point. Every single one that we find is a spark of Godliness shining into the world, and a source of true joy. As we saw earlier (pp. 119ff.), every mitzvah we do gives us a connection with God's supreme goodness, and then God "rejoices," as it were, because His purpose in creating the world — to bestow good upon His creatures — has been fulfilled. This reciprocal joy of God and man is the innermost "point" and purpose of all the mitzvot. This is why each mitzvah is called a "good *point*": it is our point of connection with God's eternal goodness.

Each good point is a new note in the melody of life. In this world of trial we are constantly faced with "air that is a mixture of good and bad" — ups and downs, ambiguous and difficult situations, new problems. Even our most prized achievements are often followed by relapses into darkness and depression. Our inner worlds, like the outside world, are in a constant state of flux and change. Each day brings its own unique challenges. Each new situation calls for a different way of reaching out to God. All the various ways of connecting to God are included in the ten kinds of melody.

Holy song is the paradigm of devotion to God. The entire creation is a downward emanation from God to man, designed with the purpose of bringing man to connect with God. The climax of creation is when man attains his purpose and sings out joyously to God in recognition and thanksgiving. The ten kinds of melody correspond to the ten sefirot. In one aspect, the ten sefirot are *or yashar*, "direct light," creative energy that emanates from God in order to bring the universe into being and orchestrate all its workings. But the purpose of creation is that God's creatures should come to know Him and reach out to attain His goodness. Thus in another aspect, the sefirot are *or chozer*, "returning" or "reflected light." The downward chain through which God reveals Himself to the creation turns into an upward ladder of ascent on which we, His creatures, rise step by step beyond the bounds of the finite until we become totally merged within His unity.

Each of the mitzvot is rooted in the ten sefirot, and thus every mitzvah, each good point, is a "note" in the symphony of man's ascent to God. Each of the different junctures of life calls for a different mode of outreach to God. Sometimes we overflow with thankfulness, sometimes we must acknowledge God's strict justice and superior wisdom. There are times when we cannot see God's goodness at all, and we must search. Sometimes we must look deeply into ourselves in introspection, confession and contrition. There are times when we must work on ourselves without any sense of being assisted. At other times we must cry out for help — or scream in pain. Sometimes we must make requests, at other times express our gratitude. Each of the different modes of outreach is an aspect of the ten kinds of melody. All of them together make up a symphony of joy: "God rejoices in His works" (Psalms 104:31), and "Israel rejoices in his Maker" (*ibid.* 149:2).

In the words of Reb Noson:

"All closeness and attachment to God comes in essence through calls and cries — our various different prayers, songs, praises, supplications, requests, confessions and appeals to God and our conversations with Him in hisbodedus. All of these are included in the ten kinds of melody. These are the ten modes of prayer that are the foundation of the Book of Psalms. For most of the Psalms are made up of King David's cries to God and his prayers and appeals to Him to help him carry out His will and escape the turbulent seas of worldy desire and vanity. In the midst of his very cries and screams, King David starts singing, offering praise and thanks to God. All these holy pathways of the Book of Psalms are aspects of the ten kinds of melody, which include all the different prayers, songs and praises offered by the Jewish People in all times and places, and are our essential means of attachment to God.

"All the different calls and cries that make up the ten kinds of melody are experienced through our sense of *hearing*, because 'you must let your ear *hear* what you are bringing out of your mouth' (Berakhot 15a). And so too, faith depends on our sense of hearing — the 'hearing' in the heart: understanding. Thus King Solomon said, 'You have given Your servant a *hearing* heart' (Kings I, 3:9). It is in the heart that we gain our main understanding of the sweetness of faith, each according to his or her unique capacity.

"For God in Himself is exalted beyond all thought or grasp. But in His great compassion, He wanted to benefit His creatures by giving them a taste of the radiance of His Godliness. He therefore 'contracted' His light, as it were, until He put Godly awareness into the hearts of the true tzaddikim in each generation. For these tzaddikim, this awareness is like hearing a voice without being able to see where it is coming from. Thus when the Torah was given, 'you *heard* the sound of words, but you did not *see* any image besides the voice' (Deuteronomy 4:12). Even Moses was told by God that 'no man can *see* Me and live' (Exodus 33:20). If this was true of Moses, how much more is it true of all the other prophets and tzaddikim. Only through 'hearing' can we gain any awareness of God. Thus the prophet says: 'God, I *heard* Your repute and I was in awe' (Habakuk 3:2).

"This certainly applies to ordinary people like ourselves today. The vitality and holiness we draw from our faith come to us because of our ability to 'hear.' We must *listen* to the voice of our forebears, who handed down the holy Torah, our holy faith, from generation to generation. We must fulfil all the words of this Torah: '*Shema Yisrael!* — Hear, Israel! God is one!' *Hear!* Because the essence of faith depends on 'hearing' — the hearing in the heart. Herein lies the greatness of the songs and melodies sung by the Jewish People in order to attach themselves to God. All of them are included in the ten kinds of melody — calls and cries that we *hear* — because the foundation of the Jewish People's attachment to God is through hearing" (*Likutey Halakhot, Piriah veRiviah* 3 #16).

4. Does simchah really heal?

Rebbe Nachman's "General Remedy" is not a standard technique that can simply be administered like a pill or injection while the patient remains passive. The Ten Psalms that Rebbe Nachman recommended can certainly be recited with benefit by anyone. But the ten kinds of melody are not so much a matter of specific songs or prayers as a general approach to living — reaching out to God in different ways at different times, and constantly seeking the good. This is an approach to life that requires active involvement on the part of the individual. It must be internalized and cultivated over time.

In the story of the Beggar with no hands, one of those boasting about the power in his hands says that even after an arrow had been shot, he could retrieve it. The Beggar asks him if he could retrieve the arrow only before it struck its victim, or if he also had the power to bring it back and undo its effects even after it had struck. For in order to heal, it is not enough to be able to prevent sickness in the first place, important as this is. The true healer must be able to *reverse* illness even after the arrows of *atzvut* have struck and caused actual physical symptoms. While Rebbe Nachman certainly saw simchah as the best possible preventive medicine, he clearly considered the ten kinds of melody to be the remedy for full-blown illness as well, spiritual and physical.

Colossal resources are constantly being poured into research on the medicinal value of all kinds of drugs and therapies. On the other hand, it is hard to imagine how a satisfactory scientific study could be made of the healing effects of deep faith, fervent prayer, joyous Shabbat and festival observance, charity, kindness and wholehearted fulfilment of the other mitzvot. These are hardly the kind of tangible, measurable phenomena that are the grist of scientific investigation. The healing power of simchah is not a scientific claim but a divine promise: "If you will listen carefully to the voice of HaShem your God and do what is right in His eyes and give ear to His commandments and keep all His statutes, I will put none of the diseases upon you that I have put on the Egyptians, for I, God, am your Healer" (Exodus 15:26).

When someone is brought into the emergency room with all the symptoms of a heart attack or some other major life-threatening illness, it would be grotesque to say, "Sing and be happy, and everything will be fine!" Contemporary medicine has an ever-expanding array of sophisticated drugs and other technologies for effective crisis intervention, saving and prolonging life, fine-tuning vital bodily functions, alleviating pain and enabling people who were in mortal danger to enjoy normal and fulfilling lives.

Yet at the same time, growing numbers of medical doctors as well as alternative healers and psychologists, etc. recognize that patients' will to live, their sense of purpose, optimism and other positive attitudes are key factors in long-term recovery from heart disease, cancer and other medical conditions, as of course they are in recovery from mental and emotional problems, addictions and so on. Heart disease is the number one killer in all the advanced industrial countries. One of the most popular contemporary manuals of recovery gives the following advice:

> "The organ most likely to affect your life and to determine the success of your recovery and ultimate return to vibrant good health is that bit of gray matter between your ears. Most of the disability patients experience comes from anxiety, depression and distress.... One must deal with psychological distress before the very things that can improve health can be effective.... There is an increasing consensus that the angry, hostile Type-A individual is more likely to have a heart attack.... One can cut one's risk of future heart attack in half by making an effort to change behavior.... If you're thinking about something that's making you angry or stressful, think about something else.... Make a conscious effort to make music daily. Hum a tune while you walk. Whistle while you work.... Go out of your way to put some humor in your life. Not once in a while, but routinely"
> (Robert E. Kowalski, *Eight Steps to a Healthy Heart*).

Today's second major killer in advanced countries is cancer. An American cancer surgeon who has championed the power of positive attitudes and a fighting spirit in the battle against disease writes:

> "We don't yet understand all the ways in which brain chemicals are related to emotions and thoughts, but the salient point is that our state of mind has an immediate and direct effect on our state of body.... The onset

and course of disease are strongly linked to a person's ability and willingness to cope with stress.... If a person deals with anger or despair when they first appear, illness need not occur.... The simple truth is, happy people generally don't get sick. One's attitude toward oneself is the single most important factor in healing or staying well. Those who are at peace with themselves and their immediate surroundings have far fewer serious illnesses than those who are not.... We can change the body by dealing with how we feel. If we ignore our despair, the body receives a 'die' message. If we deal with our pain and seek help, then the message is 'Living is difficult but desirable,' and the immune system works to keep us alive.... When a doctor cures cancer or some other disease without ensuring that the treatment addresses the patient's entire life, a new illness may appear. Since everyone is subject to external changes, truly effective treatment must get a patient to become the kind of person who can live comfortably and happily in spite of such stresses" (Bernie S. Siegel M.D., *Love Medicine & Miracles* p.28).

The simchah workshop

Rebbe Nachman once spoke at length to a group of his followers about the importance of being joyous, and then said, "Now you have something to make you depressed!" (*Rabbi Nachman's Wisdom* #155). All this talk about the ten kinds of melody and fervent devotion may well leave us feeling further away than ever from simple heartfelt joy and zest for life as we contemplate the problems we face and the negativity within us. How often do we look at ourselves and feel as if "the whole head is sick and the whole heart is faint; from the sole of the foot to the top of the head, nothing is sound — only wounds, bruises and festering sores!" (Isaiah 1:6).

Never is this more so than when illness strikes. Many people facing serious illness feel as if a sword is pointed at them. As they wonder whether they will live or die and if they will ever again be able to lead a normal life, they are often overwhelmed by feelings of helplessness, worthlessness, fear, guilt and anger. The negative aspect of everything looms so large that anything positive seems to wither away into nothingness. Often people know all the right things they should be doing to rally and fight their illnesses, yet they find it impossible to summon the motivational power to do anything! Even the most basic everyday functions seem to require far too much effort, let alone finding the good points and rejoicing in them.

Rebbe Nachman well understood the vicious cycle of heaviness and depression that weighs people down:

> "When a person's limbs are heavy with depression, this in turn weighs down on the vital spirit animating the heart, which becomes even weaker. The heartbeat becomes weaker, and then the limbs become even heavier. And because the limbs become heavier, the heartbeat becomes weaker still. And so the cycle continues, until the person's soul goes out of him, God forbid" (*Likutey Moharan* I, 56:9).

How are we to break out of this vicious cycle? Rebbe Nachman continues:

> "Through a deep, heaving sigh one can bring new life to one's spirit, restoring the heartbeat to health and saving oneself from depression. And then the pulse returns to normal in all the limbs..." (*ibid.*).

The very sigh of sorrow and yearning is itself the first step to redemption. For in the words of the Baal Shem Tov: "When a person recognizes the wounds of his heart and the sickness of his soul, this knowledge itself is his salvation, and this is what heals him, unlike when a person lacks all such awareness and does not realize that he is spiritually sick. Then there is no remedy for his mortal malady" (*Keter Shem Tov* #25).

Rebbe Nachman's idealized portrait of the joyous Simpleton (pp. 115f.) should not lead us to imagine that only someone who instantly tastes goodness in all things at all times is following the path of simchah, while those struggling with problems and difficulties, negativity and depression have failed. The "music-player" is faced with "bad air" as well as good: it is out of the darkness and evil themselves that he salvages some good. According to Rebbe Nachman, this is the very key to composing the melodies that bring joy and healing.

The point is not to deny our negativity or pretend that our problems and difficulties do not exist. Rather it is to search carefully for more positive ways of viewing them. Even while feeling the pain and constraints of one's situation, one must ask what benefits they may bring, even if those benefits seem very slender and distant. One must learn to reevaluate oneself. Instead of judging oneself primarily in terms of looks, personality, academic, social and financial achievements and the like, one must learn to value one's rock-bottom faith in God, one's yearning for connection with Him, one's basic honesty, desire to help others and so on.

The search for the positive requires time. It should be one of the main components of the hisbodedus that Rebbe Nachman urged everyone to practice regularly (p. 57). Hisbodedus could be called the workshop of simchah and healing. It is the time to search deeply into ourselves and sift through our conflicting thoughts and feelings in search of the good. We must believe that God is so great that even the lowliest of His creatures are very dear to Him. Even our faltering efforts to carry out His mitzvot are most precious. If we are beset with problems and difficulties, we must have faith that God has sent all of them only out of love, to help us make amends for wrongdoing or to challenge us to rise to our greatest spiritual heights.

Rebbe Nachman recognized how hard it is to attain true spiritual joy, and he therefore emphasized the importance of simple, practical ways of keeping ourselves happy. When he spoke about the ten kinds of melody, he meant not only an exalted pathway of spiritual devotion but also actual song. "Get into the habit of always singing an inspiring tune. Even if you can't sing well, you can still inspire yourself with a melody sung to the best of your ability. The loftiness of melody is beyond measure" (*Rabbi Nachman's Wisdom* #273). The Rebbe urged his followers to sing many *zemirot* on Shabbat and festivals, and, down to earth as ever, he added: "Even a simple family man can make himself happy with tasty food such as fish and good soup" (*ibid.* #155). From this we can learn that we need have no hesitation about using permitted physical pleasures to keep ourselves in good spirits.

Innocent jokes and light-heartedness are all part of the path of simchah. "It seems impossible to achieve happiness without some measure of foolishness. One must resort to all sorts of foolish things if this is the only way to attain happiness" (*ibid.* #20). And if all else fails: "If you are disturbed and unhappy, you can at least *put on a happy front.* Deep down you may be depressed, but if you act happy, you will eventually be worthy of true joy" (*ibid.* #74).

SECTION 5

Rebbe Nachman and the Doctors

Chapter 14

Redemption of the Soul

After having been immersed in Rebbe Nachman's profound and moving teachings about simchah and healing, his emphatic warnings against doctors may seem almost jarring. He urged his followers to avoid medicine even in cases of serious illness. He said that the majority of doctors have no understanding of the art of healing. Being far more likely to cause damage than to do any good, most doctors are nothing but agents of the Angel of Death (*Rabbi Nachman's Wisdom* #50, see below pp. 197-201).

Many people find these views shocking and disturbing. Anyone who has had some bad experience with the medical profession is liable to laugh at and complain about doctors. But when illness strikes, God forbid, how could Rebbe Nachman apparently rule out medicine altogether? Even if we accept the paramount importance of repentance, charity, prayer and joy when facing illness, doesn't the rejection of medicine contradict one of the most basic tenets of Judaism — that we must do everything possible to protect and extend human life? Failure to treat illness could cause irreparable damage and actual loss of life, not to mention untold pain and suffering, both to the sick and to those around them!

These issues involve matters of life and death, and they must be considered with the utmost care and seriousness. It is not our purpose here to determine whether people should or should not receive medical treatment. Every present-day halakhic authority would rule unequivocally that in our times a sick person is duty bound to consult a competent doctor and must not rely on being healed miraculously. In the words of the *TaZ* (Rabbi David ben Shmuel Halevi, 1586-1667), one of the most important commentators on the Shulchan Arukh: "It is a positive obligation and a mitzvah to turn to the doctor at a time of sickness, and the Torah itself accepts that healing can come about through natural means. For the Torah penetrated the innermost recesses of man's mind and knows that his merit will not be sufficient to enable him to be healed through a miracle from heaven" (*Turey Zahav* on *Yoreh Deah* #336, and see *Birkhey Yosef ad loc.*).

No one should use Rebbe Nachman's warnings against doctors, or any other comment in this book, as a rationalization for avoiding necessary medical treatment. People have all kinds of fears about doctors and medicine, and some hold back from consulting a doctor even when they really need to. Even those who do go to doctors often neglect their advice and fail to complete the full course of recommended treatment. This can be highly dangerous. Anyone who has questions or doubts about medical advice they have been given, or about treatment they are undergoing, should consult authorities in the field. Any related religious or spiritual questions should be discussed with a competent rabbi.

Our purpose here is to investigate Rebbe Nachman's various statements about doctors and medicine in order to gain deeper insight into his own healing pathway. His opposition to medicine is founded on his basic standpoint that bodily illness reflects a flaw on the spiritual dimension. Only when the spiritual flaw is rectified can physical healing come about. To try to cure bodily problems with medicines alone is to misunderstand the meaning and causes of physical illness, which is intrinsically bound up with the maladies of the soul. Spiritual healing, far from being merely an "extra," is the very essence of healing.

Rebbe Nachman's attacks on doctors are well-known. Yet he also made numerous other statements indicating that he himself saw a place for medical treatments. As we will see in the course of our study, he recognized that medicines have the power to effect changes in bodily functioning. He himself recommended vaccination as a preventive procedure, and he accepted that at times doctors are in fact able to cure sickness.

Perhaps Rebbe Nachman's warnings against doctors and medicine should be seen not so much as an attack on medicine *per se* as an attempt to shake people's blind faith in its powers. Since God is the true Healer, to put all one's trust in the doctor and his treatment is misguided. Indeed, waiting for a complete cure through passive submission to medical treatment may actually impede genuine, long-term healing, if it becomes a way of avoiding confronting the personal issues and other problems that so often lie at the roots of physical illness.

1. Why do people get sick?

The appropriate way to treat illness depends in large measure on what is deemed to be its cause. In the following brief teaching, "Why do people get sick?" Rebbe Nachman gives a general answer to the question of why people become ill.

"When a person fails to focus on the ultimate purpose — the תכלית (*takhlit*) — what is the point of his life? The soul constantly yearns to do the will of her Maker. When she sees that this person is not carrying out His will, she becomes filled with yearning to return to her Source, and she prepares to leave the body. As a result, the person becomes sick, because the power of his soul is weakened, owing to the fact that she is trying to withdraw from his body since he is not carrying out her desire. The soul's only wish is that he should carry out God's will.

"The reason a person's health returns through taking medicines is that his soul sees that he is able to control himself and to act contrary to his physical desires and habits. Perhaps he is accustomed to eating bread and other foods, but now he curbs his desires and submits to a medical regime, taking bitter medicines for the sake of his health. His soul sees that he has the power to control his impulses in order to achieve a certain goal, and she therefore comes back to him in the hope that he will curb his desires for the sake of the true purpose — which is to carry out the will of the Creator" (*Likutey Moharan* I, 268).

Underlying this teaching is the idea that the health and vitality of the body depend entirely on the soul. The soul is the vital core which animates the body. If the body is sick, it is because the soul's power to vitalize it has been weakened, leading to deterioration and malfunctioning of the physical system. Conversely, if the body recovers, it is because the soul's power is restored.

Rebbe Nachman is teaching us that the very key to health and healing lies in a driving *will to live* — a courageous embrace of life in this world as a magnificent opportunity to develop one's soul to the fullest and strive for an ever deeper connection with God. This is the purpose for which the soul is sent into this world of challenge. When we rise to the challenge and fight to elevate ourselves spiritually at all times, our souls thrive and radiate, sending us a flow of glowing health and vigor. However, when a person mistakes the meaning of this world and goes after its "false grace and vain beauty," this merely thwarts his holy soul. Every step he takes in his pursuit brings another flaw into the soul, separating her from God and taking her further from her true goal. To "cut her losses," as it were, the soul seeks to withdraw from the body and begins to pull away. And with its life-force weakened, the body deteriorates and becomes sick.

It would be wrong to look upon this brief teaching as a general theory of illness, and to question its validity on account of the numerous exceptions that might be found. Many people are obviously far from the spiritual purpose of life, yet seemingly enjoy robust good health (though the Rabbis teach that their vitality comes from the *sitra achra*, the "unholy side" of creation). As to why people become sick, this is such a broad question that there could never be a single, all-encompassing answer. The human body is so complex and finely-tuned that it is prone to a vast range of ailments and illnesses, depending on all kinds of factors, internal and external. To attribute all the different things that can go wrong in babies, children, adolescents, young adults, the middle-aged, the old and the very old to a single factor would clearly be ridiculous.

Various statements in Rebbe Nachman's writings indicate that he fully grasped that there are many different kinds of illnesses. He discusses terminal illness (*Likutey Moharan* I, 250, see below p. 436), congenital and noncongenital illnesses (*ibid.* II, 1:11, see pp. 263ff.), infectious diseases (*Tzaddik* #459, see p. 429) and conditions caused by factors such as dietary abuse, anxiety and tension (*Likutey Moharan* I, 263, see p. 428; *ibid.* 23:5). As we have seen, Rebbe Nachman faced illness and tragedy in his own life and in the lives of his immediate family, and he knew that many cases of illness and death are bound up with deep mysteries of God's providence (see above pp. 70ff. and p. 76).

Nevertheless, numerous cases of physical illness are clearly linked with what is happening in the minds and hearts of those afflicted — from the colds and infections that develop at times of particular stress, to far more serious conditions such as heart disease, certain cancers and other problems. Much has been written in recent years on the connection between a wide variety of physical conditions and important events and developments in the lives of the patients, their outlooks, attitudes and personalities (see Norman Cousins, *The Healing Heart*; Bernie S. Siegel M.D., *Love, Medicine & Miracles* and *Peace, Love & Healing*).

Rebbe Nachman's teaching on *"Why do people get sick?"* provides a powerful approach with which to penetrate to the very core of the inner crises that so often lie at the roots of such conditions. The conscious or unconscious feelings of anxiety, frustration, meaninglessness, grief and despair involved in many different illnesses are all essentially bound up with the broad loss of purpose to whichRebbe Nachman refers. The rediscovery of meaning and personal mission — the will to *live* — has time after time proven to be the single most important factor in people's long-term recovery from all manner of serious, life-threatening conditions.

Even in the case of more minor ailments — colds, 'flu, rashes, digestive upsets, allergies, etc. — Rebbe Nachman's teaching implies that sometimes people may be afflicted because the pressures in their lives have deflected them from their purpose, weakening their soul-powers and thereby disrupting their physical balance and lowering their immunity. An important element in recovery may be to take the time to recommit oneself to one's highest goals and seek more effective strategies for attaining them.

Missing the mark

The Rabbis taught that the main reason why illness strikes is because of sin. "There's no suffering without sin, as it is written (Psalms 89:33), 'I will requite their transgressions with the rod and their iniquity with *plagues*'" (Shabbat 55a).

"If you see a Jew with one of the four signs of leprosy mentioned in the Torah, its only purpose is to heal him of all his sins, and through his suffering he attains the life of the World to Come" (*Tanna devei Eliahu* 5). "Rabbi Acha said, It is up to the individual himself not to be afflicted with illness, as it is written (Deuteronomy 7:15), 'And God will remove *from you* all illness.' That is, protection from illness comes *from you* — from the individual himself. R. Abin said, What you must protect yourself from is the evil urge, which is sweet at first but bitter in the end" (*Vayikra Rabbah* 16:8).

Once a man came to the Ari and said that for two days he had been suffering intense pain in his shoulder. The Ari looked at him and said the reason for the pain was that instead of reciting the Grace after Meals directly after washing his hands at the conclusion of his meal (*mayim acharonim*), he had paused to study some Mishnah. The Rabbis said, "Recite the blessing *directly* (תכף, *teikhef*) after washing" (Berakhot 42a). תכף, *TeiKheF*, had turned into כתף (*KaTeF*), a "shoulder," and this was why he felt the pain in his shoulder (*Shaar HaMitzvot, Ekev* p. 60).

Explicit statements by our Sages must be accepted with the utmost respect. At the same time, it is a fact that some people find the suggestion that illness results from sin to be disturbing and even offensive. The distress and anxiety suffered by those confronting serious illness are painful enough. Is it not cruel and heartless to compound them by suggesting that the sick person is responsible for his own suffering and should feel guilty about it? Why should the patient be burdened with fear and guilt at a time when he most needs sympathy, kindness and support? Surely the idea that sin is the underlying cause of illness is more likely to hinder the healing process!

Rebbe Nachman well understood that many people experience nothing but negativity and depression when thinking about sin, and he knew how damaging these can be. While he leaves us in no doubt whatever that sin and evil actually do exist and that we must try our utmost to avoid them, he also recognized that when a person has already sinned, it is counterproductive for him to sink into gloom and self-recrimination. "The reason most people are far from God is that they become demoralized when they see how destructive their behavior has been, and they fall into depression and sadness. One must use one's intelligence to fight against this, because low self-esteem is worse than anything. It is true that the person actually committed the wrongdoings that cause him to experience this demoralization. But the demoralization and depression themselves are nothing but the work of the Evil One, who wants to weaken his resolve and cast him down completely" (*Likutey Moharan* I, 282).

The last thing Rebbe Nachman would have wanted is that we should let our sins drag us into depression and despair. Yet he wanted us to recognize the truth, that illness may be caused by sin. He mentions this idea in several places (e.g. *Likutey Moharan* I, 4:5; *ibid.* II, 8:6 etc.). He did not want people to allow their distaste for uncomfortable guilt feelings to blind them to the truth. On the contrary, he urged us to confront our sins and transgressions directly, to the point of taking time each day to examine our behavior and activities and feel contrition for our mistakes. This is an integral part of hisbodedus, and careful introspection and wholehearted acknowledgement of past mistakes for what they are can be a most important part of the healing process.

Rebbe Nachman's teaching on "*Why do people get sick?*" can be seen as a restatement of the rabbinic teaching that illness is bound up with sin, clarifying the essential truth the Rabbis were expressing while avoiding the clouds of negativity and depression associated with the idea of sin in the minds of many people. The Hebrew word חטא (*chet*), usually translated as "sin" or "transgression," has the root meaning of "lacking" (*cf.* Kings I, 1:21), or "missing the mark," as in archery, when a person is aiming for a certain target but misses (*cf.* Judges 20:16). The purpose of our lives in this world is to attain the ultimate good through carrying out the positive mitzvot, which bring us to ever deeper attachment to God (see above pp. 119ff). This is our *takhlit*, or "target." If we turn aside from it, we "miss."

When we do, we ourselves are the losers. Each person has his or her own individual *takhlit* — a unique pathway of connection with God — as well as the particular constellation of obstacles that constitute his or her unique challenge in this world. Perhaps the worst *chet* in life is to fail to fulfil one's personal mission. In the famous words of Reb Zusya of Anipoli (d. 1800), "On the day of reckoning, when they ask me, 'Why weren't you like Abraham,

"The sins are inscribed upon the bones"

Rebbe Nachman taught that "a person's sins are on his bones, as it is written (Ezekiel 32:27), 'And their sins were inscribed upon their bones'" (*Likutey Moharan* I, 4:5). Immediately prior to giving this teaching, Rebbe Nachman told the following story:

One of the Baal Shem Tov's followers was very sick, and sent a messenger to the Baal Shem Tov asking him to come. The Baal Shem Tov agreed. On the way, the messenger said to the Baal Shem Tov, "This sick man would seem to have repented completely and he is surely a good Jew. He's not very old yet — so why hasn't he been cured?" The Baal Shem Tov replied, "It is certainly true that this man has repented completely for all his sins. The reason he has not yet been cured is because he has not *confessed* his sins to a true Tzaddik. My purpose in going to him is to give him the opportunity to do so."

The Baal Shem Tov continued: "If he confesses he will be cured immediately. But if he refuses, his condition will immediately deteriorate. He will start screaming with agony. He'll feel pain in all his limbs, his hands and his feet, and then he'll die. It is true that in the higher worlds not a single sin or transgression will be held against him, because he has repented completely for all his sins exactly the way he should. After his death the forces of evil will have no grip on him at all, seeing that he has rectified all the damage he has done. If he confesses to me, he will be cured immediately. But if he does not, the forces of evil will still have the power to take vengeance on him in *this* world. They will attack all his limbs until he dies."

And so it was. The Baal Shem Tov came to the sick man and said, "Tell me what you know, and God knows, and I also know" — i.e. he should confess all his sins to him. The Baal Shem Tov said this to him three times. However the man was unwilling to confess. Immediately afterwards he started screaming in agony. He felt pain in each limb in turn, and he cried out bitterly. The man carried on screaming like this until he died, as the Baal Shem Tov predicted (*Tzaddik* #184).

Isaac and Jacob?' I won't be afraid. But when they ask me, 'Why weren't you like *Zusya*?' — that's when I'll be afraid." In his teaching on "*Why do people get sick?*" Rebbe Nachman is telling us that to allow ourselves to veer from our true mission in life is not only a deep spiritual flaw; it is also a direct threat to our actual physical health.

If illness strikes, God forbid, medical treatment *may* help. As Rebbe Nachman says in "*Why do people get sick?*" the self-discipline involved in following a medical regime may pave the way for the soul to shine into the body again and so bring about a cure. (The same could be said to apply to all healthful practices, such as careful diet and regular exercise, which many find to greatly enhance their spiritual as well as their physical well-being.) But even when receiving treatment, it is vital to bear in mind that the essential work of healing is not so much to take the medicine as it is to make sincere efforts to stir ourselves spiritually. We must ask ourselves: "Where in the world am I? What have I been doing with my life? What is my ultimate purpose and how can I attain it?" Many people want to leave all the work to the doctor: "Do something — anything! Just *cure* me!!!" But there can be no *true* healing without a movement to *teshuvah* on our part — a return to our own true mission.

What?

"One should ask people 'What?' People don't think about their purpose in life. What? After all the frustrations and distractions, after all the complaining and all the empty excuses you give for being far from God, when everything is over, what is going to be left of you? What are you going to do in the end? What will you answer the One who sent you? What are you if not a visitor on this earth? Life is vanity and emptiness, a passing shadow, a vanishing cloud. You know this. What do you say? Place these words on your heart. Bring them into the depths of your being. Don't ignore them. Turn them over and over and you will save your soul" (*Rabbi Nachman's Wisdom* #286).

2. License to Heal?

The essential first step in bringing about a cure is נפש פדיון (*pidyon nefesh*), "redemption of the soul." The forces that cause people to veer from their true purpose in life often lock them in more strongly than prison bars. When a person falls into some kind of *chet* (transgression), his soul-powers are taken captive, as it were, by the impure forces nurtured by the *chet*. It may be impossible for him to free himself, because "a prisoner can't release himself from prison" (*Berakhot* 5b). The sick person needs someone with sufficient spiritual power to redeem his soul from its captivity. This is the true Tzaddik, who intercedes on behalf of the suffering individual, opening the way for a cure.

Pidyon nefesh, "redemption of the soul," is the main theme of Rebbe Nachman's teaching of the same name (*Likutey Moharan* II, 3). The essential idea is that only *after pidyon nefesh* has been accomplished does the doctor have the power to cure the patient. This teaching was probably given in the winter of 1808-9 (see above p. 92). By then Rebbe Nachman was seriously ill with tuberculosis, and he may have been alluding to his own illness in the opening words of the teaching, which refer to the mishnaic Sage, Rabbi Eliezer the Great. As the towering Tzaddik of his generation, Rabbi Eliezer had the power to accomplish *pidyon nefesh* for others, yet he was unable to do so for himself when he was sick.

"Redemption of the Soul" was taught during the period when Rebbe Nachman was most outspoken against doctors. Yet the Talmud states explicitly that "the Torah gave the doctor license to heal" (*Berakhot* 60a). On the face of it, this would seem to be a clear statement that doctors have been given the power to cure illness! But according to Rebbe Nachman, the true meaning of this statement can only be understood in relation to another saying of the Rabbis, that a sick person can only be healed "by a particular drug and a particular man on a particular date" (*Avodah Zarah* 55a).*

---

*The talmudic statement that healing can come about only "on a particular date, through a particular drug and a particular doctor" (*Avodah Zarah* 55a) comes in the context of a discussion about why sick people who go to idolatrous healing shrines (which were common in Graeco-Roman times) come away cured:

"Zonin said to Rabbi Akiva, 'You and I both know in our hearts that idols are totally powerless. Yet we see that people go into idolatrous healing shrines virtually crippled by their ailments and they come out healthy! Why?' Rabbi Akiva replied, 'Let me explain it with a parable. Once there was an honest man to whom all the townspeople used to entrust their valuables for safekeeping

Redemption of the Soul

Likutey Moharan II, 3

"When Rabbi Eliezer the Great became sick, he said to Rabbi Akiva, 'There's fierce anger in the world' (*Sanhedrin* 101a) — for there was no one with the power to sweeten the harshness of the judgment. In order to sweeten the decree, a פדיון (*pidyon*), redemption, was needed, but it was not forthcoming. *After* the decree is sweetened through a redemption, the sick person can be cured with medicines, because *after* the redemption and sweetening of the judgment, 'the doctor has license to heal,' but not before.

"For how can the doctor really undertake to cure the patient with herbs and drugs? He doesn't know which drug is needed to heal this particular patient! There are many drugs which have the power to cure the illness, but unquestionably this particular patient will not be able to be cured except by the specific drug which has been designated to cure him by divine decree. For as our Rabbis taught, it is decreed in Heaven that the sick person will be healed 'by a particular drug and a particular man on a particular date' (*Avodah Zarah* 55a). If so, how can the doctor undertake to cure the patient? He doesn't know which drug was decreed in Heaven!

"But *after* the judgment has been sweetened through a redemption, the doctor has the power to effect a cure. For the reason why the patient has to be cured by a specific drug and a specific doctor is because of the

---

without witnesses. But there was one man in town who always made a point of depositing his valuables in front of witnesses. Once it happened that this man forgot, and he placed a deposit without witnesses. The wife of the man guarding the goods said to her husband, 'Let's deny that he deposited these goods and keep them for ourselves.' But her husband replied, 'Just because this fool acted improperly, does that mean we should throw away our honesty?' So it is with suffering. When suffering is sent to a person, the agents inflicting it are bound by an oath: 'Come to him only on a particular day, and don't leave him except *on a specific day at a given hour, through a particular doctor and a particular medicine.*' When the time comes for the suffering to end, the sick person goes to an idolatrous healing shrine. At first, the agents inflicting the suffering say, 'By rights we should not let go of him [because he will attribute his recovery to his idol].' But then they relent, saying, 'Just because this fool has acted improperly, does that mean we should break our oath?'" (*Avodah Zarah* 55a).

There may be a subtle humor in Rebbe Nachman's reference to this talmudic passage in his discussion of the doctors' license to heal. Rebbe Nachman saw something idolatrous about the way people put their faith in medicine, as if without medicine God does not have the power to heal (*Likutey Moharan I, 62:6*). Interestingly, even some prominent contemporary doctors also look upon modern medicine as a form of idolatry. In the words of Robert S. Mendelsohn M.D., Associate Professor in

attribute of strict justice, which decrees that the illness must last for a given length of time, ending on a particular date. This is why it is decreed that the patient can only be cured by these means — the specific drug and doctor — in order that the illness will continue until the given date. According to the required duration of the illness, so it is decreed how it is to be cured, to ensure that it will not be cured until the necessary conditions are at hand — the particular drug and doctor — so that the patient will not be cured until a particular day.

"However, when a redemption is made and the judgment is sweetened, the decree is canceled. In the interval before another decree is passed (for when one judgment is sweetened, another decree is passed), *after* the sweetening of the first judgment and *before* the imposition of a new decree, the doctor has the power to heal the sick person with drugs. For at that moment there is no judgment, and the patient can be healed by any medicine: there is no need for a particular drug, etc. since no decree is currently in force. Thus we see that it is impossible for the doctor to heal without a redemption. First a redemption must be brought about in order to sweeten the decree, and then the doctor has license to heal.

"For this reason the numerical value of the letters of the Hebrew words רפא ירפא (*RaPO YeRaPE*), 'he shall cause him to be thoroughly healed' (Exodus 21:19), with the addition of two units for the two words themselves, is 574. This is the same as the numerical value of the words פדיון נפש (*PiDYoN NeFeSh*), 'redemption of the soul' — because essentially the cure

---

the Department of Preventive Medicine and Community Health, Abraham Lincoln School of Medicine, University of Illinois:

"Modern medicine is the religion of a secular society that has rejected its traditional value systems. Modern medicine has at least ten of the essential components of a religion: (1) A belief system, modern medical science, which can no more be validated than the proofs of other churches... (2) A priestly class — the M.D.'s. (3) Temples — the hospitals. (4) Acolytes and vestal maidens — nurses, social workers and paraprofessionals. (5) Vestments reflecting hierarchical status — the color and length of M.D.'s gowns signify their rank. (6) A rich princely class supporting the church — drug companies, insurance companies and formula houses. (7) A confessional — the history must be given truthfully to the physician. (8) An absolution — the reassuring pat on the back — 'You're fine, come back next year.' (9) Selling of indulgences — the outrageous fees, likely to bring down this modern church just as it did the medieval church. (10) Similarity of language — I have confidence in my plumber but 'I have *faith* in my doctor'; the doctor-patient relationship is 'sacred.' Unfortunately, the religion of modern medicine proves to be worship of a god who fails to answer, who is powerless and who, in fact, deceives. This, of course, is the definition of idolatry..." (from Dr. Robert S. Mendelsohn's Foreword to *Natural Healing through Macrobiotics* by Michio Kushi, 1992).

comes about through the redemption, through sweetening the decree. This explains the statement of the Rabbis that 'it is from here that the Torah gave the doctor license to heal' (*Berakhot 60a*). *From here* — i.e. from this point on, *after* the redemption. For *before* the redemption the doctor has no license to heal, because the patient can only be cured by a particular drug, etc. It is only after the redemption brings about a sweetening of the decree that the doctor has license to cure."

*

Captivity and freedom

Rebbe Nachman's essential point in this teaching is that the true meaning of the rabbinic dictum that "the Torah gave the doctor license to heal" can be understood only in relation to the talmudic teaching that the sick person is healed "through a particular drug and a particular doctor on a particular date" (*Avodah Zarah 55a*). This second statement of the Rabbis defines and limits the extent of the doctor's license to heal.

Illness is seen as a heavenly decree, a "judgment." Unless the decree is mitigated through *pidyon nefesh*, redemption of the soul, the illness will run its course, and only when its required duration is complete, as laid down in the decree, will the patient recover. In order for the illness to continue until a particular day and hour, the decree governs the very means by which the patient will eventually be cured: through "a particular drug and a particular doctor." Thus if the doctor has "license to heal," it is only as Heaven's agent to release the patient from the decree of illness when its duration is complete. The doctor is like a prison warden who is given the key to open the cell only after the sentence has run its course. The only other circumstance in which the doctor has license to heal is when the decree against the patient has been revoked or mitigated through *pidyon nefesh*.

Rebbe Nachman's response to the objection that many people receive medical treatment and recover is that the treatment itself is an incidental factor. The essential reason why the patient recovers is that the decree has reached its end, and therefore a heavenly-ordained chain of events ensures that his body heals. On the other hand, as long as the heavenly decree is in force, no matter what the patient or the doctors may try, nothing will avail. This would explain the common phenomenon of patients who wander from doctor to doctor in search of a cure, but nothing seems to help — until one day, often unexpectedly, a cure comes about through some quite simple remedy, or even spontaneously.

One of the main reasons Rebbe Nachman gave for his opposition to medicine is that even the most outstanding doctors are unable to take account of all the variables involved in illness in order to determine the appropriate treatment (*Rabbi Nachman's Wisdom* #50, see below pp. 197ff.). The concept of illness as a decree may help explain this. It is as if perfect understanding of the divinely created human body and its ailments has been withheld from humanity by design in order to ensure that no one will be able to overturn God's decrees through natural means until the heavenly appointed moment arrives. This could explain why, as medical science has uncovered cures for certain diseases, other scourges have appeared to take their place (see *Rabbi Nachman's Wisdom* #291). "Many are the designs in man's heart, but God's counsel will prevail" (Proverbs 19:21).

Indeed, far from having the power to circumvent God's decrees, Rebbe Nachman said that doctors themselves are at times cast in the role of the agents sent to impose them (*Siach Sarfey Kodesh* I-655). A medical diagnosis is really nothing but a hypothesis about a person's physical condition — a hypothesis that may or may not be accurate. But not infrequently, medical diagnoses turn into self-fulfilling prophecies. Labels like "cancer," "heart disease," "multiple sclerosis" and the like naturally tend to produce panic in patients, often leading to a sense of helplessness and depression that can itself cause a deterioration in their physical condition.

For many patients, medical treatment and all it involves can turn into a harsh decree that throws a terrible shadow over the whole of life. Even the quality of the doctor's human relationship with his patient — his sensitivity, kindness, warmth or the lack of them — can have a decisive effect on the course of illness and recovery, as is recognized by many psychologists and growing numbers of doctors.

Mitigating the decree

People turn to doctors in the hope that medical intervention will effect a cure. But Rebbe Nachman is teaching us that, as long as the decree of illness is in force, the only form of intervention that can bring about a true change in the situation is *pidyon nefesh*, a redemption that mitigates the decree. What exactly *is* a "redemption"?

According to Torah law, when a person has been captured or kidnapped and his captors are demanding a ransom, it is a mitzvah for his fellow Jews to pay to release him (*Shulchan Arukh, Yoreh Deah* #252). This is known as פדיון שבוים (*pidyon shevu'im*), "redemption of captives." The concept of "redemption of the *soul*" implies that the soul is in captivity. Just as a person may literally be held in physical captivity, so there are times when he may be "imprisoned by circumstances" through a heavenly decree. There may be no actual physical bars or chains, but the troubles and difficulties people are sent in life — family, emotional, financial and many others — can be quite as painful and limiting as actual incarceration, if not more so. In the Torah view, illness is such a decree.

Rebbe Nachman said that all the suffering people go through is sent either to arouse them to repent or to cleanse them of their sins (*Likutey Moharan* I, 65:3). Just as the length and severity of prison sentences may vary according to the offense, so every heavenly decree is measured with the utmost exactness, taking all the relevant factors into account, for the ultimate benefit of the soul that is suffering — for "God is righteous in all His ways and gracious in all His deeds" (Psalms 145:17). And just as most judicial systems include a system of appeals, with specific procedures for requesting clemency in order to reduce or revoke sentences, so does the heavenly system of justice. A prisoner calls upon a respected advocate or intercessor to plead his cause. In the same way, a Jew who sees that he or his dear ones are under the sway of stern decrees turns to one whose merits in the eyes of Heaven will give added strength to his appeal — the Tzaddik.

Thus the Talmud states that "someone who has a sick person in his house should go to a Sage and ask him to pray for him" (*Bava Batra* 116a). When a Jew is sick or in some other kind of trouble, it is customary for the suffering individual or those acting on his behalf to bring a sum of money to a Tzaddik and ask him to pray in order to bring about a *pidyon nefesh*. The money — often called the *pidyon* — is like a ransom paid to free the soul from its "captivity." The Tzaddik places his hands on the money and prays, after which the money is distributed to the poor.

In any appeal system, the intercessor will either plead mitigating circumstances or show evidence that the prisoner has undertaken to reform, making further punishment unnecessary. Since illness is sent either as a prompt to repentance or to cleanse one of sin, if the sick person does indeed repent and starts to make amends for his sins, this in itself may open the way for him to be healed. The two concepts involved in *pidyon nefesh* — charity and the Tzaddik — are both bound up with repentance.

Money is something for which people are willing to sacrifice their lives and their very souls. Money can be used to gratify man's basest lusts or to realize his highest ideals. The craving for wealth drives people to some of the worst sins — dishonesty, corruption, theft, robbery, exploitation and many others. Yet honestly acquired money can be used to reveal Godliness in the world and spread kindness and goodness — through giving charity to those in need, supporting Torah institutions, financing the publication of Torah works and carrying out other mitzvot.

When a sick person takes his precious, hard-earned money and brings it to the Tzaddik, it is like a latter-day sacrifice. His material wealth is elevated and becomes spiritualized. In addition, by breaking his instinctive selfishness and insensitivity in order to practice charity, he creates a vessel in which to receive God's love and kindness. Charity has the power to reveal the Supreme Will of God, which is beyond the laws of nature and controls the entire world: God has the power to send healing through any means He chooses, even in an instant! (*Likutey Moharan* II, 4; see above pp. 93-5).

The Tzaddik is the exemplar of Godly living. The very act of turning to him for help and guidance is itself an act of repentance. Indeed the Tzaddik is the true doctor — the doctor of the soul. In the words of the Rambam: "What is the remedy for those who are sick in their souls? They should go to the Sages, who are the healers of the souls, and they will heal the sickness through the new attitudes and behavior patterns they teach them, until they return to the good pathway" (*Mishneh Torah, Hilkhot De'ot* 2:1; *cf. Likutey Moharan* I, 30:2, see below p. 227). On one level, the Tzaddik works with the sick person directly, guiding him to make any necessary changes in his life and to rectify the mistakes of the past. On another level the

A man once came to Reb Noson and asked him to pray for him, giving him a ruble as a *pidyon*. Without even waiting for an answer, the man left, but Reb Noson called him back, saying, "Do you remember such and such a time when you were in trouble and you promised God you would repent. God helped you and you were saved, but you didn't start serving Him properly." Reb Noson went on to list the times the man had been in trouble and said he would repent. "And now you're in trouble once more and you come to ask me to pray for you again? What am I — your hired help? I should pray and then you'll return to your evil ways? The main reason why all this is happening to you is so that you should truly repent!" (*Siach Sarfey Kodesh* 1-700).

Tzaddik seeks to intercede in the heavenly court in order to "release" the sick person's soul from captivity so that healing may come about.

*

Rebbe Nachman said: "I do not understand how the tzaddikim claim to make a *pidyon*, or redemption, and intercede for someone. There are twenty-four heavenly courts [corresponding to the twenty-four permutations of the letters of the name אדני (*ADoNoY*), which is associated with judgment]. When the Tzaddik presents the redemption, he must know in which court the person is being judged. If he does not know this, he may intercede and bring the redemption to one court, while the person is actually being judged in another. [The Rebbe compared this to someone being sued in the courts of Kiev and trying to defend himself in the courts of Kaminetz *(Tzaddik #181)*.] He must therefore know precisely in which court the man is being judged, and what particular intercession and redemption is required by that particular court.

"I know all twenty-four courts. I can appeal a case from one court to another through all twenty-four courts. If I do not agree with the judgment of one court, I can ask that it be rejudged in another. Going from one court to another is certainly beneficial. No matter what the final outcome, the sentence is still set aside and delayed. Owing to this delay, the sentence can be reduced because of some merit on the part of the defendant. Even if this does not help, I can still appeal directly to the King. This takes great wisdom and effort, and no one else in this generation can do it. It is a major task to frame each petition in the precise number of words and to give proper respect to the King. For it is certainly impossible to send too many cases directly to the King..." *(Rabbi Nachman's Wisdom #175)*.

*

Kabbalistic Intentions of *Pidyon Nefesh*

Rebbe Nachman taught: "Money is related to strict judgments. Thus it is written, 'and all the living substance that was at their *feet*' (Deuteronomy 11:6), on which the Rabbis commented: 'This refers to a person's money, which is what enables him to stand on his feet' (*Pesachim 119*). From this we learn that money is the 'feet.' Now it is written, 'Justice attends his *footsteps*' (Isaiah 41:2), and 'Justice is the holy kingship (*malkhut*)' (*Tikkuney Zohar*, Introduction), and *malkhut* is judgment. This indicates that money is related to judgment.

"It is necessary to sweeten the severe judgments at their root, which lies at the level of *Binah*, 'Understanding,' as it is written, 'I am understanding, power is mine' (Proverbs 8:14). This is why the Tzaddik places his hands upon the money in order to sweeten the judgments. For there are three 'hands' in Binah: the 'great hand' (Exodus 14:31) and the 'strong hand' (Deuteronomy 7:19 etc.), which together make up the 'high hand' (Exodus 14:8). When the money — i.e. the severe judgments — comes to the hands, which allude to the three hands of Binah, the judgments are sweetened at their source.

"The severe judgments have their hold in this world of *Asiyah*. They must be sweetened by means of the three hands in each of the three higher worlds, *Atzilut*, *Beriyah* and *Yetzirah*. When one sweetens the severe judgment in the world of *Asiyah* through the three hands in the world of *Yetzirah*, the judgment is sweetened through the Name of 42 letters contained in the prayer '*Ana BeKoach*': the numerical value of the Hebrew letters of the word ד׳ (*yad*), 'hand' is 14, and 14 x 3 = 42. In the world of *Beriyah* the judgment is sweetened through the Names *EHYeH* and *YHV*, the numerical value of whose letters also adds up to 42. Higher still, in the world of *Atzilut*, the judgment is sweetened through the 42 letters of the Name of *YHVH*, its expansion (*MaH*) and the expansion of the expansion — altogether 42 letters, three times *Yad* (14).

"It is most important not to be stingy in the amount of money one gives in order that no severe judgments should remain hovering over one. It takes exceptional wisdom to know exactly how much a particular person should give to make sure that no harsh judgments remain" (*Likutey Moharan* I, 180).

* * *

The Tzaddik places his two hands upon the redemption money and says:

"May it be Your will to sweeten the harsh and severe judgments against (...) the son/daughter of (...) through *Pelé Elyon*, the Supreme Wonder, where there is nothing but utter mercy and complete, simple love with no severity at all. Amen" (*Likutey Tefilot* p.105).

Chapter 15

Rabbis vs. Doctors

Rebbe Nachman was far from being the only Torah Sage who expressed opposition to medicine. As we saw earlier (p. 26), the Bible itself criticizes King Asa for turning to the doctors in his illness instead of seeking out God (Chronicles II, 16:13). King Hezekiah, on the other hand, received praise from the Sages for hiding the Book of Remedies (*Pesachim* 56a).

There is a famous talmudic statement that "the best of physicians are destined to go to hell" (*Kiddushin* 82a). In the words of the talmudic commentator, R. Menachem ben Shlomo Me'iri (1249-1316), the reason is that the doctor "does not make enough effort in his work of healing, or at times he does not know the cause of the illness and how to cure it, but he presents himself as an expert and causes the death of the patient" (*Me'iri ad loc.*). Rashi (*ad loc.*) agrees that doctors sometimes cause the death of their patients, and he adds that the doctor is unafraid of illness and does not humble himself before God, and also fails to help those who cannot afford treatment.

As we have seen, the Talmud states that "the Torah gave the physician sanction to heal" (*Berakhot* 60a). However, later rabbinic authorities point out that it does not necessarily follow from this that a Jew who is sick has license to rely on doctors to heal him. The RaMBaN (Rabbi Moshe ben Nachman of Girondi, 1194-1270), who was himself a physician, states in his classic Commentary on the Torah:

> "In the era of prophecy the tzaddikim consulted not doctors but prophets. For *what place do doctors have in the house of those who carry out the will of God*, after He promised that 'He will bless their bread and their water, and remove illness from their midst'? (Exodus 23:25) Although the Rabbis said that the physician has been given sanction to heal, this does not mean that license has been given to the sick to resort to medicine! What the Rabbis meant is that if a patient has already come to the doctor, the doctor should not refrain from treating him. But when a person's ways find favor in God's eyes, he has no business with doctors" (Ramban on Leviticus 26:11; see Inset on facing page for full text).

The Ramban on Doctors

"When the Jewish People are in a state of spiritual perfection, neither their physical bodies nor their country, nor any of their other affairs are governed by nature at all. This applies to the nation as a whole and to each individual Jew. For God 'will bless their bread and their water, and remove illness from their midst' (Exodus 23:25). They will have no need of doctors, nor will they have to follow medical procedures even as precautionary measures, 'For I, God, am your healer' (Exodus 15:26). In the era of prophecy the tzaddikim acted accordingly. Even if they happened to sin and became sick, they consulted not doctors but prophets, as did King Hezekiah when he was sick (Kings II, 20, 2-3). It is said of King Asa that 'even in his sickness he did not seek out God, but he turned to the doctors' (Chronicles II, 16:13). If it was common for them to go to doctors, why should the verse mention doctors at all? Asa's only guilt would have lain in the fact that he did not seek out God. But this phrasing is similar to saying, 'He did not eat *matzah* on Pesach but *chametz*.' Someone who seeks out God through the priest will not consult doctors.

"What place do doctors have in the house of those who carry out the will of God, after He promised that 'He will bless their bread and their water, and remove illness from their midst'? The only function of the medical profession should be to give nutritional advice — what to eat and drink and what to avoid. Thus the Rabbis said, 'For the entire twenty-two years of Rabbah's leadership, Rav Yosef did not even call a bloodletter to his house' (*Berakhot* 64a). They went by the principle that 'a door that does not open to charity will open to the doctor' (*Bemidbar Rabbah* 9:3). It is true that the Rabbis said, 'because it is not the way of human beings to bring about a cure, but this is the practice' (*Berakhot* 60a, see above p. 33). But this merely means that, had they not been in the habit of resorting to medicine, a person who became sick because of his sin could have been healed through the will of God alone. However, since they resorted to medicines, God abandoned them to the vicissitudes of nature.

"As for the rabbinic comment on the verse, 'He shall cause him to be thoroughly healed' (Exodus 21:19) — 'from here we learn that the physician has been given sanction to heal' (*Berakhot* 60a) — they did not say that license has been given to the sick to resort to medicine! What they meant is that if a doctor is approached by a patient who was in the habit of resorting to medicine and was not part of the community of God whose share is life, the doctor should not refrain from treating him, not from fear that the patient might die under his hand — seeing as the doctor is expert in his craft — nor on the grounds that God alone is the healer of all flesh — because this patient is already in the habit of resorting to medicine. It is true that if two people quarrel and one hits the other with a stone or his fist, the Torah lays down that the attacker must pay the medical expenses of the injured party (Exodus 21:18). But this is because Torah law does not rely on miracles, for God knew that 'the needy will not cease from the midst of the earth' (Deuteronomy 15:11). But when a person's ways find favor in God's eyes, he has no business with doctors" (Ramban, Commentary on the Torah, Leviticus 26:11).

The Ramban's view is that the Jewish People were intended to live on a spiritual plane beyond the law of nature and to receive all their needs — livelihood, healing and everything else — directly from the hand of God. Wholehearted devotion to the Torah pathway will itself protect against illness, which, if it occurs, is not a chance occurrence but rather a sign of a flaw in the afflicted person's attachment to God. A sick Jew should seek out not a physician but a moral teacher who will help him repent — the Tzaddik. All of these ideas can be found in Rebbe Nachman's teachings on healing.

Unlike the Ramban, the classical Bible commentator Rabbi Avraham Ibn Ezra (1089-1164) does not reject medicine outright, but he limits its permissibility to external wounds. In his comment on the phrase, "he shall cause him to be thoroughly healed" (Exodus 21:19), Ibn Ezra writes: "This is an indication that God gave license to doctors to heal wounds and injuries that are visible on the exterior. But all illnesses that are within the body are in the hand of God to heal. And thus it is written (Job 5:18), 'For He makes sore and binds up'" (Ibn Ezra on Exodus 21:19). Ibn Ezra would countenance medical treatment for external complaints, but when it comes to internal illnesses he is no less opposed to resorting to doctors than is the Ramban — this in spite of the fact that in Jewish law all internal illnesses are considered to be life-threatening (Shulchan Arukh, Orach Chaim 328:3).

Explaining Ibn Ezra's view, the Avi Ezer (Rabbi Shlomo HaKohen of Lissa) writes: "Internal illnesses are caused by dietary excesses or climatic changes, but the soul-powers of a person who is attached to God will strengthen his natural heat and bodily fluids, and he will live longer than the normal lifespan. A person can thus heal himself of internal illnesses by binding himself to his soul, which will give him life and bodily health. A person who is attached to God is also granted protection against untimely death from injuries caused by other humans, such as war wounds or a sudden blow from an attacker. But when a person fails to serve God wholeheartedly and believes that other humans are completely free agents and not under God's control, this itself puts power into the hands of his fellow man or his master to strike him, and he must then turn to a human doctor to cure him" (Avi Ezer ad loc.).

Prominent among later Rabbis who expressed their opposition to doctors was R. Eliahu, the Gaon of Vilna (1720-1797). It is told that he once went to visit his brother, R. Yissakhar Dov, who was sick. Two doctors were present. The Gaon turned to his brother and asked, "Why do you need doctors? Surely God heals the sick?" One of the doctors interjected, "Did God create doctors and medicines for nothing?" "And why did God create pigs?" retorted the

Gaon. "Not for consumption by Jews! So too with doctors: maybe the gentiles go to them, but for the Jews, God is the Healer of the sick and Creator of remedies" *(HaTzaddik R. Zundel MiSalant, Jerusalem 1927, p.115).*

Rabbi Pinchas Shapiro of Koretz (1726-91), Rabbi Barukh of Medzeboz (1757-1810) and Rabbi Yaakov Yitzchak Horovitz, the *Chozeh* (Seer) of Lublin (1745-1815) — all older contemporaries of Rebbe Nachman — are known to have been opposed to doctors and medicine. In more recent times, Rabbi Yisrael Meir Kagan of Radin, the Chafetz Chaim (1839-1933), is also said to have avoided doctors. His son writes: "My mother told me that when I was young they virtually never consulted doctors. If one of us was sick, my father's advice was to distribute bread to the poor, while he would go up to the attic and pray" *(Letters of the Chafetz Chaim Part III, p. 12).*

We have already noted that the accepted halakhic opinion today is that of the *TaZ*, that "it is a positive obligation to turn to the doctor in times of illness" (see p. 177). Nevertheless, only a couple of generations ago a leading halakhic authority, Rabbi Avraham Burnstein of Sokhatchov (1839-1910), wrote of the Ramban's viewpoint: "The correct interpretation of the words of the Ramban would seem to be that any person who does not resort to medical treatment but trusts in God is called a tzaddik in this matter, and every person is entitled and indeed commanded to do this. Since we clearly see that doctors are prone to cause harm, one may put one's trust in God in order not to expose oneself to mortal danger in practice" *(Avney Nezer on Choshen Mishpat #193).*

Death's emissaries

The main source for Rebbe Nachman's attacks on doctors is in *Rabbi Nachman's Wisdom* #50, where Reb Noson reports the main thrust of a number of separate discussions by Rebbe Nachman, mostly after his return to Breslov from Lemberg in the summer of 1808 — this was the period in which Rebbe Nachman gave most of his major discourses on healing (see pp. 86ff.).

"The Rebbe often spoke to us about physicians and medicine, denouncing them in the strongest terms. He advised anyone who cares about his life and that of his family to avoid them, even in the case of serious illness. One should 'cast his burden on God' (Psalms 55:23) and depend on Him alone (cf. Isaiah 50:10). One should not resort to medicines and doctors even in a place where there are outstanding physicians, for they are closer to death than to life (Shabbat 129b).

"Even an outstanding doctor is unable to diagnose the illness exactly or to determine the appropriate medicine, because so many variables are involved — the constitution of the individual, the nature of the illness, the time and season, etc. It is extremely difficult for the doctor to take account of all these variables without making mistakes, as they themselves acknowledge. They can easily do irreparable damage, jeopardizing the patient's life. This applies even to the greatest doctors, and certainly to the majority of doctors found in our locality, most of whom don't understand the difference between right and left and are literally murderers, killing people with their own hands. One should flee from them as from a bowshot, not risking one's life or that of the patient one puts in their hands. It is very dangerous to depend even on the greatest physicians. One who falls into their hands separates himself from the living. The Rebbe spoke at great length, but it is impossible to record everything he said regarding this.

"He told us that when he was in Lemberg, a place in which outstanding physicians were gathered, one leading doctor testified that it is best to keep as far away as possible from medicines and doctors. He said that there has already been so much research into medicine that the experts now know absolutely nothing, because after so much research they see that it is impossible to establish the truth. There are also many deep divisions among them as to how to treat various illnesses. In Lemberg there was a controversy between two groups of doctors who argued about the correct approach to a certain dangerous illness. One group recommended a bland diet, holding that strong, spicy foods were highly dangerous. The other group advised exactly the opposite, saying that only strong and spicy foods should be taken for this illness, as sweet or bland foods were very harmful. Each of the two groups put forward strong arguments in favor of their position, and each group regarded any diet other than the one they recommended as being fatally poisonous. Each of the two groups included some of the most outstanding specialists in the field, yet they were unable to determine the truth. Even with practical experience it is impossible to ascertain where the truth lies, because sometimes experience seems to confirm one view, at other times the opposite.

"Thus we see that it is impossible to depend on doctors since they themselves are extremely confused and they are unable to ascertain the truth. How can someone put his life in their hands and let it hang there

(continued on p.200)

Medicine in the time of Rebbe Nachman

Sanitation was extremely primitive and water supplies were often contaminated. Piles of garbage bred all kinds of diseases and attracted vermin who spread them. There were freqent outbreaks of plague. Smallpox, measles, scarlet fever, chicken pox, cholera and diphtheria took an especially heavy toll on the young. Childbed (puerperal) fever was fatal, with the result that there was a terribly high incidence of death in childbirth. Congenital and acquired blindness were common, as was deafness caused by ear infections. The limited diet of the poor led to malnutrition and its associated diseases.

It was to be the better part of a century before Louis Pasteur (1822-95) would establish the germ theory of disease, laying the basis for modern bacteriology and immunology. The principles of antisepsis pioneered by Joseph Lister (1827-1912) were as yet unknown. Only the most primitive painkillers were available — not until the 1840's was anesthesia first used, opening the way for surgeons to operate on the hitherto inaccessible interior of the body.

Yet although the medicine of the late 18th and early 19th centuries may today appear primitive, many physicians of the time saw themselves as advanced pioneers, having rejected medieval dogma based on the works of Galen and Avicenna in favor of the rationalist-mechanistic approach of Descartes and his followers. The development of increasingly powerful microscopes gave a boost to the study of anatomy and pathology, and the work of the Paduan professor Giovanni Battista Morgagni (1682-1771) established concepts and study methods that remain the basis of contemporary medical investigation and teaching.

However, actual medical practice tended to lag behind what are now seen as significant discoveries. Bloodletting, purging and vomiting, dietary restriction and nonspecific drugs continued to be the mainstay of therapeutics, though there was considerable interest in faddish treatments such as the use of stimulants and sedatives, while new drugs like quinine and digitalis were taken up with great enthusiasm.

Only the wealthy could be assured of the services of a trained doctor, especially in Russia, which had only one medical school compared with the dozens in Britain, France, Germany and Italy. Dispensaries were scarce. Such hospitals as existed had no organized clinics. For the wider public, the void tended to be filled by enterprising apothecaries, mountebanks and peddlars of nostrums. Barber-surgeons carried out bloodletting and tooth extractions and also dealt with fractures, dislocations and external ulcers. Untutored itinerant wound-doctors would operate for cataracts, bladder stones and hernias. The poor relied on old wives' remedies and sometimes actual sorcery (see *Tzaddik* #140).

by a single thread — because it takes only the slightest error by the doctor and he can destroy a person's life and actually kill him, as we see so often, for many people die because of doctors. The art of medicine involves many very fine intricacies, but they are hidden from the doctors 'like bones in a full stomach' (Ecclesiastes 11:5), to the point that the doctor is unable to take account of all the subtle details without error.

"One must therefore avoid them and flee from them. When someone is sick or has a sick person at home he should not say: 'If so, who should I rely on? One must do *something* to try to cure the patient by natural means! How can I leave him without making any effort to save him?' This is really foolish. Since the doctor is closer to death than to life, in the end there is no option but to depend on God alone. Surely it is better to depend on God from the outset and not put the sick person in even greater danger by handing him over to the doctor! The majority of doctors are agents of the Angel of Death! One should imagine oneself to be in the wilderness or in a forest. There one *has* to rely on God alone because there is nothing else to do. Likewise now, even though one may live in a place where doctors and medicines are available, even so, seeing that they themselves are so confused, and considering the many other dangers involved in medicines, it is probable that, far from helping, they will actually cause harm. If so, why use natural methods when the likelihood of benefit is remote and the dangers are so great?

"The Rebbe spoke at length with outstanding doctors, and he understood this matter very clearly. He gave us the strongest warnings to keep well away from them. It is impossible to record everything he discussed in this regard. He told us of a king who killed all the doctors in his kingdom because they did so much harm. He once said in jest that the Angel of Death has to oversee the entire world and it is very difficult for him to do all the killing himself. He therefore appoints agents in each locality, and these are the doctors, who are his agents to kill people, for they kill enormous numbers of people. Happy is the man who avoids them and trusts in God alone.... The Rebbe repeatedly told us to avoid them. Regardless of what happens, one must lift one's eyes to heaven and rely on God alone.

"As for the fact that the Rebbe himself traveled to Lemberg and submitted to medical treatment, this involves very deep mysteries. His reasons for travelling there had nothing to do with medical treatment, but with other matters known to him alone. His intentions were as hidden and mysterious as they were on his journeys to Kaminetz, Novorich and Sharograd. All the Rebbe's travels involved awesome mysteries hidden from all human eyes.... The same is true of his trip to Lemberg. After his arrival there he was compelled from on high to submit to medical treatment for reasons known only to him. But when he returned from there he spoke more strongly than ever about the need to avoid medicines and he gave many lessons on the subject. Even before his journey to Lemberg he used to talk about this, but afterwards he stressed more than ever the need to keep away from doctors" (*Rabbi Nachman's Wisdom* #50).

Danger!

We might have expected that, as a religious teacher, Rebbe Nachman would have founded his opposition to doctors and medicine primarily on the need to have faith and trust in God rather than relying on human intervention to cure illness. Rebbe Nachman certainly did urge his followers to lift their eyes to heaven and cast their burden on God. He taught a spiritual pathway of healing through faith, prayer and joy, and he emphasized that the first step in all healing is redemption of the *soul*. Yet it is noteworthy that in the above passage, Rebbe Nachman does not reject doctors and medicine only because dependence on them shows a lack of trust in God. His opposition is based primarily on the fact that he sees medicine as a danger to the life of the sick person.

It cannot be said that Rebbe Nachman considered medicine to be totally ineffectual. In a number of passages in his writings he mentions the power of medicinal herbs to influence the four bodily elements of fire, air, water and earth (e.g. *Likutey Moharan* I, 57 end and II, 5:1).

As we have seen, the Kabbalah view is that illness results from imbalance among these four elements (see above pp. 130-1 and 134-6). The problem is that the human body is so complex that in

> Reb Noson said: "God is so great that He can send a cure even *after* someone goes to a doctor!" (*Siach Sarfey Kodesh* I-63, etc.)

practice no doctor could ever determine the precise nature of the imbalance involved in the illness of a given individual, nor could he know the exact combination of medicines needed to correct it.

In the words of Rebbe Nachman: "It would take a great medical expert to know how to balance the elements contained in each of the different herbs in order to produce the precise remedy needed by a particular patient given the particular element that is weak and damaged in his case" (*Likutey Moharan* II, 5:1). Illness and healing involve so many variables that medicine will always be based on unproven hypotheses and guesswork. Rebbe Nachman sees evidence of this in the disputes between different groups of doctors over how to treat various illnesses. With so much potential for error, the doctor can easily prescribe inappropriate treatment, which may cause irreparable damage or death.

One of the most usual responses to Rebbe Nachman's warnings against doctors is that it could be dangerous for the patient *not* to submit to treatment. This is what makes Rebbe Nachman's opposition to medicine seem to contradict the Torah principle that everything must be done to protect human life. The assumption is that illness poses a definite threat to the patient, while medical treatment is most likely to be safe and successful. However, Rebbe Nachman's contention is that the real danger lies in resorting to medicine. This is because it is quite impossible for even the best doctor to attain a clear understanding of the nature of a particular problem. Consequently, any treatments used are a matter of guesswork, and are more likely than not to be hazardous. Sickness itself is dangerous enough, but for Rebbe Nachman, medicine is even more dangerous:

> "If a person has someone sick in his house andsomebody came and told him to give the patient a blow with a big wooden club, he would certainly be very shocked. Yet when one puts the patient in the hands of the doctor, it is literally like handing him over to a murderer. The doctor's remedies are more harmful than the blow of a murderer. Who would want to kill the patient with his own hands? Just because you have to do something to try to save the patient, does this mean that you should hand him over to a doctor? You might as well call someone to beat the patient to death" (*Tzaddik* #194).

Tried and tested remedies

Rebbe Nachman's view of doctors and their lack of understanding was shared by other contemporaries of his. Using language no less strong than Rebbe Nachman, the *Pele Yo'etz* (Rabbi Eliezer Papo, 1785-1828) writes: "Today there are multitudes of ignoramuses who take up medicine as a way to make a living without having any insight into the art of healing. Whoever chooses can practice medicine and get a name for himself as an expert doctor while actually he is like a blind man feeling his way through the darkness without understanding the difference between right and left. Such doctors are wholesale murderers!" *(Pele Yo'etz, Rofé #1).*

It is undeniable that medical knowledge and expertise have expanded explosively since the end of the 18th century, and they continue to grow. Given that Rebbe Nachman's critique of doctors is largely founded on their lack of understanding of the workings of the body, it is fair to ask whether his polemic was directed primarily against the primitive medicine of his time or whether it would still apply today.

Nowhere in Rebbe Nachman's writings is there an explicit statement indicating that his warnings against doctors were restricted to his own time and place and would not apply if medical knowledge were to advance significantly. In fact, we see that Rebbe Nachman took a skeptical view of the growth of medical knowledge: "He said that there has already been so much research into medicine that the experts now know absolutely nothing, because after so much research they see that it is impossible to establish the truth" *(Rabbi Nachman's Wisdom #50).* It is significant that although Rebbe Nachman had always advised his followers to avoid doctors, his warnings became stronger than ever after his trip to Lemberg, whose Austrian-trained doctors were then among the most advanced in Europe (see above pp. 81f.).

On the other hand, there is one statement by Rebbe Nachman that places all his warnings against doctors into a very different light — a statement that provides a basis for those who wish to argue that his warnings simply do not apply to contemporary medicine. This is his statement urging his followers to have their children vaccinated against smallpox. This disfiguring and often fatal disease was then prevalent throughout Europe and Asia. A primitive form of innoculation had been in use for some time in Turkey, and spread to the rest of Europe in the 1720's. However, it was not without its dangers, and the best that most people could do when there was an outbreak of smallpox was to flee.

It was not until the 1790's that the English country physician Edward Jenner observed that those who had been infected with cowpox did not become infected with smallpox. In 1796 he performed the first vaccination on a young boy, and found that, despite the boy's subsequent exposure to smallpox, he did not become infected. Knowledge of the new technique spread rapidly throughout Europe, and immunization against smallpox soon became a standard medical procedure. At first it was a subject of heated controversy within the Jewish communities of Eastern Europe, but in 1804 a Dr. Shimon of

Cracow printed a broadsheet entitled "A New Remedy," in which he encouraged all Jews to have their children vaccinated as a preventive measure. Within a short time, hundreds of Jewish children were being successfully vaccinated, including those of leading rabbis and Torah scholars (*Sefer HaBrit* I, 17:2).

In the midst of this controversy, Rebbe Nachman came out in favor of vaccination in the strongest terms:

> "Every parent should have his children vaccinated within the first three months of life. Failure to do so is tantamount to murder. Even if they live far from the city and have to travel during the great winter cold, they should have the child vaccinated before three months" (*Avaneha Barzel* p.31 #34).

Rebbe Nachman's championship of vaccination is clear proof that his opposition to doctors and medicine was in no way bound up with some kind of retrogressive attitude of suspicion towards modernity and innovation *per se*. Here was a newly-discovered technique with a proven power to prevent a dangerous disease, and within a matter of a few years Rebbe Nachman came out emphatically in favor — Jenner first discovered vaccination in 1796, and Rebbe Nachman's (undated) statement must have been made some time before his death in 1810.

Strictly speaking, vaccination is not so much a remedy as a preventive measure. Rebbe Nachman's powerful endorsement seems to imply that he would have been no less in favor of tried and tested measures for preventing other diseases — unlike the Ramban, who says that "when the Jewish People are in a state of spiritual perfection... they have no need of medical procedures even as precautionary measures" (see p. 195). As we will see later, Rebbe Nachman himself saw his healing pathway of faith and prayer as the most powerful form of preventive medicine (see pp. 263ff.). Nevertheless, from his endorsement of vaccination, we can infer that Rebbe Nachman would not have been opposed to actual preventive medical techniques where they had proven their effectiveness.

An open question

A far more open question is whether the tremendous advances in medical techniques since Rebbe Nachman's time would have led him to modify his rejection of medicine when it comes to remedies for actual illness as opposed to prevention. The contemporary medical armory includes a host of well-established methods of diagnosing and treating all kinds of problems, many of them with extremely high success rates. If Rebbe Nachman accepted vaccination as a "tried and tested technique," would he also have been in favor of proven modern methods of treatment?

We saw earlier that R. Avraham Ibn Ezra, while rejecting resort to doctors for internal medical problems, acknowledged that the doctor has license to heal wounds and injuries that are visible on the exterior. R. Yonatan Eybeshetz (1696-1764) explains that in the case of an external problem, "the doctor can easily ascertain the full extent of the problem with almost mathematical precision, which is not the case when the problem lies in the interior of the body, where the doctor's eye cannot penetrate. Here he is forced to rely on inference and probability. Doctors cause much damage and are responsible for many deaths, for in such cases it takes great caution and clearheaded deliberation to avoid error" (*Kraiti uFlaiti* #188). But some halakhic authorities argue that modern scientific advances have broken down the distinction between external and internal physical problems, since blood tests, biopsies, body scans and the like provide information about the interior of the body that is at least as accurate if not more so than information gained through visual examination of the exterior of the body (see *Emek Halakhah* #18).

There is some indication that a viewpoint similar to that of Ibn Ezra — that turning to doctors for treatment of "external" disorders is permissible — was accepted by some of Rebbe Nachman's later followers. Thus while R. Avraham Chazan (1849-1917), outstanding leader of the fourth generation of Breslover Chassidim, did not go to doctors, he is known to have gone to have his teeth examined on the grounds that dentistry does not come within Rebbe Nachman's prohibition against doctors (*Siach Sarfey Kodesh* III-446). Does this mean that Rebbe Nachman's warnings against doctors and medicine no longer apply today, when there appear to be so many "tried and tested remedies," and scientific advances have made it possible for doctors to gain information about the interior of the body in ways undreamed of in the times of Ibn Ezra, Rebbe Nachman or even R. Avraham Chazan?

The fact that Rebbe Nachman's critique of the doctors is based on their ignorance of the workings of the body, while he himself endorsed one proven medical technique, leaves plenty of leeway to interpret his rejection of doctors and medicine in different ways. Purists are at liberty to argue that Rebbe Nachman never explicitly favored resort to medicine to cure actual illness, and there is nothing in his writings to suggest that his warnings against doctors were restricted to his own time and place. On the other hand, many contemporary adherents of the Breslov chassidic movement use the concept of "tried and tested remedies" to justify resort to doctors and medicine on the grounds that enormous numbers of standard contemporary medical techniques have been proven effective.

Medicine today

No one can deny that contemporary medicine provides successful aids and remedies for all kinds of conditions that used to cause great misery. The effectiveness of many present-day techniques is practically beyond dispute. At the same time, there are still many other techniques that involve a greater or lesser degree of risk — angioplasty and coronary bypass surgery for heart disease, radiation and chemotherapy for cancer, and many more. Whether a given technique is "tried and tested," "reasonably safe," "experimental," "shaky," "risky" or "outright dangerous" often depends on which doctor you speak to or which reports you read.

The weaponry in use against many all-too-common illnesses often seems blunt and crude, and involves all sorts of hazardous side-effects. In chemotherapy, for example, doctors frequently experiment with formula after formula in the hope of finding one that will be effective in a particular case. The medications involved are often so nonspecific that even if they kill the cancer cells they are aimed against, they can also cause appalling damage to healthy cells. All kinds of other drugs — antibiotics, anti-inflammatory agents, antidepressants, sedatives and many others — are prescribed quite routinely today despite the fact that no one really knows what long-term effects they may have on the immune system, the nervous system and bodily functioning in general.

Even those who regard contemporary orthodox medicine as the pinnacle of scientific achievement must concede that the mere fact that a medical student is granted a license to practice does not turn him into an expert healer. We must distinguish between the accumulated body of medical knowledge on the one hand and the living human beings who actually examine, diagnose and treat patients on the other. Much of the prestige of the medical profession stems from the fact that medicine is supposedly based on scientific method. But medical practitioners are rarely able to keep abreast of the latest in scientific research, or even to employ strict scientific method when it comes to actual diagnosis and treatment. Laboratory tests may sometimes (though not always) provide definite results. But interpreting them and diagnosing exactly what is wrong with a particular patient is almost always a matter of subjective judgment, as are decisions about the best course of treatment.

With all the advances in medical science, numerous aspects of the workings of the body remain obscure. This is especially evident in the case of various "mystery conditions" that simply defy all diagnostic tests, like certain cases of chronic fatigue, strange aches and pains, certain kinds of digestive problems, and so on. Conventional medicine is at its best when dealing with readily identifiable problems that seem to call for clear, straightforward solutions. But as we have already noted, it has less to offer the chronically ill and those suffering from what are often dismissed as "neurotic complaints," even though these groups constitute a high proportion of all patients (see above p. 11). Even diagnoses that seem fairly obvious often turn out to have been partial at best, while treatment for one problem may cause a host of new ones.

Conventional western medicine tends to present itself as an impressive edifice of scientifically based knowledge that is steadily growing. Yet there are still numerous areas of dispute within the ranks of orthodox medicine, just as there were among the doctors in Rebbe Nachman's time. Theories, techniques and treatments that were sacrosanct in one generation are discredited and rejected in the next. There are also far-reaching controversies between conventional practitioners and devotees of various types of so-called "alternative" medicine, who often take a radically different view of physica functioning and therapy.

Rebbe Nachman's critique of doctors would seem to be directed not only against orthodox physicians but against all "healers" who seek to treat bodily conditions with drugs, manipulations and other physical treatments withou taking account of the mental, emotional and spiritual dimensions of illnes. As regards "spiritual healers," this is a dangerous, catch-all phrase which i applied today to a wide variety of operators. A few may be sincere an well-intentioned, but many others "have no understanding of the differenc between right and left," while some employ methods forbidden by Torah la\

A matter of faith

It would be easy to assemble a lengthy catalog of criticisms of doctors an medicine. We've all heard horrendous tales of slapdash examinations, fault and mistaken diagnoses, wrong and damaging treatments, malpractic medical arrogance, gross insensitivity to the needs and feelings of patients an their dear ones, etc., etc. Indeed, in a conversation between Reb Avraha

Chazan (see p. 205) and his father, Reb Nachman Chazan of Tulchin (1813-84), who was Reb Noson's closest disciple, Reb Avraham said that he found Rebbe Nachman's warnings against doctors perfectly understandable after seeing how they practiced medicine. But Reb Nachman replied: "You shouldn't follow the Rebbe's teachings because you find them understandable and acceptable. That's the way you find them today, but tomorrow you might not find them acceptable! When you have *faith* in the Rebbe's words without giving explanations and reasons of your own, you will always stay firm in following his guidance" (*Siach Sarfey Kodesh* III:299).

The teachings of the Tzaddik ultimately have to be accepted on *faith*, because they are based upon axioms that are themselves founded on faith. Rebbe Nachman's critique of the doctors is ultimately rooted in the belief that physical illness is more than a matter of mere physical malfunctioning. Physical illness is an expression of a deep-seated spiritual flaw, and by seeking to treat illness on the physical plane alone, the medical doctor misses the point, and may indeed cause harm. In the words of Rebbe Nachman: "Even after the treatment, the illness remains. It's like sewing a patch onto a garment. The illness remains an illness. It's just that the doctor sews a patch over it" (*Siach Sarfey Kodesh* I:9).

Chapter 16

The Breslover Chassidim and Medicine

To what extent did Rebbe Nachman's followers, the Breslover Chassidim, actually heed his warnings against medicine in practice? As we will presently see, his closest disciple, Reb Noson, took the Rebbe's warnings at face value, and followed them unwaveringly all his life. However, it appears that not all the Rebbe's followers were so firm in times of crisis, as we learn from Reb Noson's account of the final days of the Rebbe's life. In the fall of 1810 the Rebbe was lying sick in the town of Uman, where he was to die. On the second night of Rosh Hashanah (September 30) the Rebbe's condition became very critical. Reb Noson writes:

"A few people were with him, and they wanted to summon the doctor urgently. However they could not get him to come because it was the middle of the night. The Rebbe said, 'It is good to give thanks to God that the doctor didn't come.' He said that anyone who cared about his life should make sure not to let any doctor near him. 'Even if I myself later on give instructions to bring me a doctor, I still want you to see to it that you don't let any doctor come in to me.'

"The day before Sukkot the Rebbe was in a very serious condition, and a number of people started saying they should bring the doctor. The Rebbe himself told them to do so. I myself was completely against this, even though the people there thought the Rebbe himself was willing for the doctor to come. But I knew the truth — that he was completely opposed to it. It was just that he was forced to agree because everyone around him was saying they should bring a doctor. There was nothing the Rebbe could do to change their minds. This was the Rebbe's way. Even if he knew a particular thing was nc good, if people were pressing him to do it, he would not go against them. This was why I was totally opposed to their calling him. But it was impossible to prevail, especially now that the Rebbe himself seemed to be agreeing with them and his condition was so serious. Accordingly, they summoned a doctor the day before Sukkot. If only they had not, because it did not help at all. If anything, it hastened his death" (*Tzaddik* #119).

We have no information whatever as to the identity of those who were in favor of calling the doctor, though we may assume that they were probably members of Rebbe Nachman's inner circle of followers or his attendants, since presumably they alone would have had any say in the matter. They must have been aware of the Rebbe's views on doctors, but perhaps they thought his warnings did not apply at such a time of crisis, or that they should be ignored.

Reb Noson

Despite the fact that Rebbe Nachman allowed his followers to call a doctor to see him, Reb Noson was in no doubt that the Rebbe had not changed his views on doctors and medicine at all, and that his warnings applied under all circumstances. After the Rebbe's passing, Reb Noson followed his teachings to the letter until the end of his life — this in spite of the fact that he suffered from colitis for over twenty-five years.

It is told that once Reb Noson fell ill when visiting the town of Teplik. Someone called a doctor to examine him, but as soon as Reb Noson saw him, he turned his face to the wall and said, "You brought me a messenger of the Angel of Death." Another time a nail pierced Reb Noson's foot, causing him great suffering. Someone brought him a herb which was said to have healing properties, but Reb Noson refused even this, and left his foot to heal naturally (*Avanehah Barzel* p.43, #64).

Two days before his death, Reb Noson said: "The angel Dumah comes to a person after he is placed in the grave, splits open his stomach and throws the remnants found there on his face, as if to say, 'Here is what you desired' (*Masekhta Chibut HaKever* 2)." Reb Noson sighed deeply, and added, "Oy! Especially when the dead person's stomach is full of medicine, this punishment is like burning fire! Even so, Rebbe Nachman can rectify everything!" (*Alim LiTerufah* II, p.841)

Some of Reb Noson's strongest condemnations of medicine are found in his prayers on healing in his collected book of prayers, *Likutey Tefilot*, based on the teachings of Rebbe Nachman:

> "Grant that through the power of our prayers we should be able to crush, humble, smash and nullify all the medicines of the doctors. Let the truth be revealed in the world: that not a single doctor in the whole world has any understanding at all of how to cure any illness. All healing comes only through the Word of God, through the prayers and supplications of

the Tzaddikim, the masters of prayer, who pray for the Jewish People and conciliate You, drawing healing into the world" (*Likutey Tefilot* II, 1).

"Have mercy on us and save us from healers and doctors. Let us never make the mistake of putting ourselves in the hands of doctors, for they are all 'false-god physicians' (Job 13:4). The majority of doctors are brutes with no understanding of healing whatever. With a simple error they can do tremendous damage, and the harm they do is far greater than any cures they bring about. They kill and murder souls with their very hands. More people have died at the hands of healers and doctors than from natural causes, as is revealed before You, Master of All, and as the doctors themselves acknowledge. For they themselves say that it is impossible to have a clear understanding of the art of healing — they acknowledge it, yet are not ashamed — and that it is better to keep away from medicines" (*ibid.* II, 1).

Various passages in Reb Noson's collected letters in *Alim LiTerufah* give us a clear picture of how he actually followed Rebbe Nachman's teachings on healing in practice. In 1823, thirteen years after Rebbe Nachman's passing, Reb Noson wrote to his childhood friend, Reb Naftali (1780-1860), who was Rebbe Nachman's closest follower after Reb Noson:

"As regards the news that you have been suffering from pain in your eyes, I will certainly pray for you. From this you will see and understand how important it is to keep away from doctors. I have already prepared a prescription to send you. The entire prescription is: (1) Don't take any medicine; (2) Don't take any medicine; (3) Don't take any medicine. And you most certainly *should* go to the *mikveh* [ritual bath]. And God will have mercy on you and quickly send you complete healing from Heaven" (*Alim LiTerufah* #3).

It appears that Reb Naftali nevertheless decided to seek some kind of medical treatment. Perhaps he thought that Rebbe Nachman's warnings against doctors were to be understood as applying only to medical problems in the interior of the body, just as Rabbi Avraham Ibn Ezra had made a distinction between internal and external problems (see p. 196). If so, Reb Noson told Reb Naftali that this was not the case:

"I am very upset about the pain in your eyes, but I am absolutely amazed that you have been prepared to go after 'false-god physicians' and receive medical treatment in Heisin for your eye pain — and the doctors only harmed your eyes with their treatments! I am surprised you did not remember the holy words that came from the mouth of our holy Rebbe, who said that one should go to any extreme to avoid all medicines and medical treatment. I imagine you probably think the Rebbe's words do not apply to eye pain, but the truth, my beloved friend and brother, is that you are mistaken" (*ibid.* #4).

One of Reb Noson's letters to his second son, Reb Yitzchak (1808-71), gives a revealing insight into how Reb Noson sought to inculcate Rebbe Nachman's teachings on healing in those he believed he could influence, despite the fact that many of the people around them did not agree. On this occasion another of Reb Noson's sons, Reb David Zvi (c.1819-c.1855), was sick, and apparently Reb Yitzchak was taking care of him. Reb Noson writes:

> "You can imagine my anguish... but I have trust that God will send perfect healing to my son David Zvi very quickly. It could be that he needs to have a good sweat in order to get better and have life and joy (*cf. Likutey Moharan* II:6, see p. 317). You already know that you should not resort to any physical medicines, neither those prescribed by a physician nor popular remedies. Don't listen to the cries of your wife and friends, or even to the saintly Adil [Rebbe Nachman's daughter]. Just bear lovingly the suffering you have to go through because of their cries, but don't listen to them at all, though if they insist that you apply a simple hot water enema or a castor-oil suppository, you may be forced to do this if they pressure you with their cries, as you realize. And salvation and healing will come from God" (*ibid.* #239).

We see that Reb Noson had the wisdom to show flexibility when he saw that the opposition of surrounding family to Rebbe Nachman's pathway would be too strong. When Reb Yitzchak's little daughter was suffering from some kind of abscess, Reb Noson wrote:

> "You yourself can understand that even at this stage I myself would not agree to call a doctor. But in this case it will be hard to stand up to the rest of the household and avoid calling the doctor. Still, don't let this upset you, because God has the power to heal even if a doctor is called! God's ways are far beyond us. But you should make every effort to persuade the doctor to use medicines as little as possible. But if it should happen, God forbid, that the doctor wants to cut there, see that you make every effort to dissuade him, because I do not agree with this at all. Instead, ask him to see if he might not be able to soften the spot with some kind of

medication. Salvation and mercy are from God, and He will send your daughter complete healing from Heaven very soon" (*ibid.* #189).

In his own household, Reb Noson would not brook doctors or medicine at all. Once, while traveling away from home, he wrote back to his son, Reb David Zvi, who lived with him:

"I was very grieved to hear of your anguish over your wife's weakness, and I hope that God will send her complete healing from Heaven quickly and without resorting to medicines or any other tricks. Give a very strong warning to my entire household to be sure not to use any old wives' remedies on her or to give her medicines prescribed by doctors. For all of them are lies and falsehood. They won't help and they won't save. On the contrary, they are very harmful.

"One should rely on God alone, 'Who formed man in wisdom and created in him many openings and cavities... Who heals all flesh and does wonders.' He alone is the true, faithful, loving Healer. It is He who sends pain, and He who binds up wounds, He and none other. I have already spoken about this a great deal in the name of our Master and Teacher, of blessed memory, but I see that there is still a need to talk about this a great deal. Hopefully my words will help save souls. At least in my own household I am not willing to let in the medicine of any 'false-god physician.' I want to fulfil what I heard from Rebbe Nachman's holy lips. He said, 'What does one do when one is in a forest? There one *has* to rely on God alone because there is nothing else to do' (*Rabbi Nachman's Wisdom* #50). My hands are stretched out to God, and I pray that He will send help very quickly and heal her and let her recuperate very speedily. Amen. So may it be His will" (*ibid.* #391).

Reb Noson withstood awesome tests in heeding Rebbe Nachman's warnings against medicine. In 1840, Reb David Zvi was seriously ill and in constant pain. For one period of forty-eight hours he thought he was going out of his mind because of the pain and lack of sleep. Reb Noson was extremely worried about him, yet he wrote to Reb Yitzchak: "My eyes are only to God, and my hands are stretched out waiting for His abundant kindness and mercy" (*ibid.* #296). Reb Noson asked the Breslover Chassidim to pray for Reb David Zvi. Later on, when he was feeling better, Reb Noson wrote to Reb Yitzchak:

"You can understand the terrible anguish I went through from Wednesday morning before dawn up until the small hours of Friday morning — almost two full days. All the time David Zvi was lying on his sickbed screaming and crying bitterly. From time to time he would stop, and then he would start screaming again. The whole family was standing there with me, shaking and desolate. What I went through is impossible to describe. But I was unwilling to take action of any kind. I just relied on God alone. Several times I prayed to God. Even though I saw that I had still not accomplished anything, because he would start screaming with pain again, even so I made a determined effort to carry on praying. The same thing happened several times. Eventually God had mercy, and at last he fell asleep for several hours.... What can I tell you, my dear son? We must be very strong, and pray about everything in our lives. It is useless to rely on any other stratagems" (*ibid.* #297).

The later Breslover Chassidim

For Reb Noson's closest disciple, Reb Nachman Chazan of Tulchin (1814-1884), following Rebbe Nachman's teachings to the letter was a matter of pure faith, as we have seen above (p.208). Reb Nachman's son, Reb Avraham, a towering scholar, was sickly from childhood. He was most particular about avoiding unhealthy foods. He said: "Since the Rebbe warned us against doctors and medicine, we have an obligation to make every effort to eat only healthful foods" (*Siach Sarfey Kodesh* #3-539). Reb Avraham generally avoided doctors, but as we have noted (p. 205), he is known to have gone for dental examinations on the grounds that dentistry does not come within Rebbe Nachman's prohibition against doctors (*Siach Sarfey Kodesh* III-446).

Even with advances in medical knowledge, leading Breslover Chassidim in later generations still avoided doctors. One of Reb Noson's grandsons, Reb Michel (Reb Yitzchak's second son, 1837-1917) was very sick as an old man, but refused to call a doctor. His family tried to persuade him to do so, but he slammed his hand down, saying, "If we go to the Rebbe and don't carry out what he taught, why are we going to him?" (R. Levi Yitzchak Bender). Reb Avraham Sternhartz (1862-1955), a great-grandson of Reb Noson and leader of the fifth generation of Breslover Chassidim, also avoided doctors all his life. It is told that when he died in Jerusalem at the age of 93, no doctor was willing to issue a death certificate stating the cause of death, because Reb Avraham had never been under a doctor's care. Only with the intervention of Chief Rabbi Isaac Herzog, who had the highest regard for Reb Avraham, was a doctor persuaded to issue the necessary authorization for burial (R. Nachman Burstein).

Until today some Breslover Chassidim refuse to submit to medical treatment under any circumstances. However, they make no efforts to influence others to do the same, since they recognize that only those steadfastly devoted to Rebbe Nachman's spiritual pathway in all its details can rely on faith and prayer alone for healing. One of the main foundations of Rebbe Nachman's pathway is moderation and holiness in the satisfaction of material needs, which itself helps avoid many of the health problems related to excessive indulgence.

Among the majority of modern-day Breslover Chassidim, the tendency is to avoid medicine for minor problems like colds and 'flu, etc., but to consult doctors about more serious conditions. Leading elders of the movement have undergone surgery for problems ranging from hernias to cancer. When in need of a doctor, Breslover Chassidim endeavor to follow Rebbe Nachman's advice to "make sure you choose the very best!" (*Siach Sarfey Kodesh* I:8). And even when submitting to medical treatment, they try to remember constantly that any cure is in the hands of God, and prayer, charity, introspection and repentance are at the very heart of the Jewish way of healing.

A good reason to go to a doctor

R. Matis Cohen, a well-known Breslover Chassid in Uman in the early 1900's, once fell ill and went to a doctor for treatment. When someone said to him that this was against Rebbe Nachman's teachings, R. Matis replied, "It would hurt me far more to lose so much time waiting till I heal by myself without going to the doctor — not being able to study Torah would be far more painful to me than any physical suffering" (*Siach Sarfey Kodesh* V-249).

Chapter 17

Nature and Beyond

The first item in the chapter on Healing in Rebbe Nachman's *Aleph-Bet Book* sums up his healing pathway:

"Know that each herb has a unique power to heal a particular illness. However, all this is only for the person who has failed to guard his faith and morality and has not taken care to avoid transgressing the prohibition against despising others (*Avot* 4:3). But when a person has perfect faith, guards himself morally, and lives by the principle of not looking down on anyone at all, his healing does not depend on the specific herbs that have the power to cure his illness. He can be healed through any food and any drink, as it is written, 'And He will bless your bread and your water, and remove sickness from you' (*Exodus* 23:25). Such a person does not have to wait until the specific remedy for his illness is available" (*Aleph-Bet Book, Healing* #1).

The ideas expressed concisely in this teaching are explored at length in Rebbe Nachman's discourse, "*Sound the Shofar — Dominion over the Angels*" (*Likutey Moharan* II, 1), a full translation of which will be presented in the following chapter together with commentary. As we will see there, prayer is the means by which healing power is channeled into food and drink, and Rebbe Nachman discusses the three main conditions that must be satisfied in order for a person to attain true prayer.

In the above-quoted teaching from the *Aleph-Bet Book*, Rebbe Nachman summarizes these three conditions. They are: to have perfect faith in God, to guard oneself morally — which means cleansing oneself of all desire for forbidden sexual activity — and to have respect for other people. Those who lead their lives in this way can be healed without medicines: healing power can be channeled to them even through their regular food and drink. The body is a physical entity and may need to receive healing through some physical substance. But for those who lead a Godly life, this physical substance need not be actual medicine but can be even ordinary food and drink.

A two-tiered view of healing

Implicit in this teaching is a two-tiered view of healing. By saying that "each herb has a unique power to heal a particular illness," Rebbe Nachman shows that he did accept, at least in principle, that illness may be able to be cured through the use of medicines in accordance with the laws of nature. He certainly recognized that physical factors can be the *cause* of illness — for example, he discusses how excessive eating can bring on fever (*Likutey Moharan* I, 263, see p. 428). And by the same token, he acknowledged that physical factors can bring about a cure. When he said that illness is caused by disharmony among the four bodily elements of fire, air, water and earth, he clearly saw this as a physical phenomenon, even though the roots of the imbalance may lie on the spiritual level. Now each of the various medicinal herbs has a unique power to influence one or more of the elements in a particular way, and thus a skilfully blended compound of herbs may be able to restore balance and thereby effect a cure.

However, "all this is only for the person who has failed to guard his faith...." This implies that healing through medicine is for people who are on a lower spiritual level. But for those on a higher level, there is a pathway of healing that is *beyond* nature. Healing can be channeled through faith and prayer without the need for specific herbs and medicines. We would call such healing "miraculous" or "providential."

In Rebbe Nachman's view, the spiritual pathway of healing is superior for a number of reasons. For one thing, as we have seen, he regarded medicine as hazardous, since "even an outstanding doctor is unable to diagnose the illness exactly or determine the appropriate medicine, because so many variables are involved.... It is extremely difficult for the doctor to take account of all these variables without making mistakes" (*Rabbi Nachman's Wisdom* #50). But an error could easily prove harmful or even fatal. Moreover, even though illness manifests itself on the physical level, Rebbe Nachman held that at its root it is caused by a flaw on the spiritual level. Without correcting this, medical solutions alone can never be effective over the long term. As Rebbe Nachman put it, they are "like sewing on a patch" (*Siach Sarfey Kodesh* I:9).

Yet there is also another, deeper reason why Rebbe Nachman placed healing through faith and prayer on a higher level than medicine. As we have discussed earlier, it is not man's body that is the essential person, the man himself, but his soul (see Chapter 12, p. 125). The physical body is given to man as an adjunct to his soul, an instrument to serve him during his time in this world.

With its animal needs and desires, the body provides man with his challenge in this world, and it is also the instrument with which he carries out the mitzvot, through which he comes to his ultimate destiny of connection with God.

In this world the soul certainly needs the physical body, but as a spiritual entity, the soul is on a far higher level. The physical body is *within* nature and bound by its laws. But the soul has access to higher, spiritual realms that are *beyond* nature and are governed by a different law. The soul has the ability to channel power from these higher realms to affect even the natural realm. Thus, when the body is sick, the soul has the power to channel healing to it by purely spiritual means, especially through prayer. And when man draws what he needs through prayer, he attains the highest level of human dignity. In the words of Rebbe Nachman:

> "Through prayer we have the power to channel God's providence in a way that goes beyond nature. Nature may dictate one thing, but prayer has the power to change nature. This is 'greatness' — 'For what *great* nation is there that has God so near to them as HaShem our God whenever we call on Him?' (Deuteronomy 4:7). This is our greatness — that God hears our prayers and alters the course of nature through His providence" (*Likutey Moharan* I, 250, see pp. 436-7).

Knowledge and awareness of God: *Da'at*

Rebbe Nachman taught that we must pray for everything we need:

> "God may give you food and clothing and everything else you need even though you do not ask for them. But then you are like an animal. God gives every living thing its bread without being asked. He can also give it to you this way. But if you do not draw your life through prayer, then your life is like an animal's. A *man* must draw all the necessities of life from God through prayer alone" (*Rabbi Nachman's Wisdom* #233).

It is certainly possible for us to try to satisfy our material needs and desires through exclusive use of this-worldly means and strategies. However, if we do so, we are living only on the physical, "animal" plane, and we remain unaware that all our needs are ultimately provided by God. But our whole purpose in this world is to come to know and be connected with God. This is why we must turn to God for what we need — through prayer.

God created the natural order with its laws and regularities in order to provide man with the necessary environment of trial and challenge to bring him to his destiny. The natural order may seem like an independent realm that is separate from God and governed by its own rules. But in reality, הטבע (*hateva*), "nature," is the same as אלקים (*Elokim*), God. (The numerical value of the Hebrew letters of each of these two words is the same, 86.) Nature is a veil from behind which and *through which* God governs the world.

From our side of the veil, it may often seem as if God is "not there," as it were — as if it is up to us to seek to influence the material order through our own physical efforts in order to secure our needs. It is precisely this illusion that provides us with our challenge in this world. Our task is to *search* for God behind the veil. We must have faith in that which is beyond our grasp. God wants us to attain *da'at*, understanding, to *"know that HaShem is Elokim"* (Deuteronomy 4:39). We have to believe and know that even the apparently impersonal, independent, pluralistic natural order, *HaTeva* (= *Elokim*), is also under the complete control of *HaShem*, the unitary God.

In Himself, God is beyond nature, and has the power to control and change it in ways that are not necessarily comprehensible in terms of "scientific" law. The way we come to know this is through prayer, which enables us to connect with God and to channel His higher power into this world and even to change nature. The greater our knowledge and awareness of God, the more powerful our prayers become.

To say that God governs the world in ways that are not always comprehensible in terms of scientifically observable regularities does not mean that His providence is somehow irrational and capricious. It means only that the rationale of God's providence is on a higher level than the human mind is capable of grasping. For this reason a "supernatural" event that seems to defy the laws of nature is called a נס (*ness*), a "miracle." The word *ness* signifies something elevated. Literally, it means a "flag." Just as a national flag flying over a certain territory signifies who has control over it, so an event that seemingly defies nature, a *ness*, is a "banner" pointing to the fact that "God is the King over all the earth": God is in control.

With our this-worldly, material intelligence it is not possible to make sense of the higher law through which God governs the universe. But the Torah was given to us to reveal the secrets of the divine system of providence and its rules. The deeper our understanding of the Torah, the more we can begin to grasp some of the ways in which God conducts the world. Moreover, the Torah gives us a pivotal role in this providence through our fulfilment of the mitzvot in general and especially through our prayers. These give us the power to influence the system of angels and other celestial forces through which God conducts the universe. The deeper our attachment to the Torah and the mitzvot, the greater our power.

The Torah is the Covenant between God and the Jewish People. It is a "contract," under which the Jewish People is privy to a special providence that is beyond nature, above the angels, stars and other forces through which God governs the rest of creation. The sign of this Covenant is the circumcision. The stripping off of the foreskin alludes to the way in which the Torah and mitzvot enable us to strip off the veil of the natural order so as to reveal the Godly providence that lies beyond it.

Moses told the Jewish People, "You are children to HaShem your God" (Deuteronomy 14:1). A king governs his kingdom through the agency of an hierarchical apparatus of ministers and officials. But the king's own children enjoy special favor. They have easy access to their father in person, and receive everything they need directly from him. So it is with us — as long as we observe our side of the Covenant and adhere to the Torah with all our hearts.

God's kindness

Most people find it impossible to sustain such an exalted level of spirituality for very long. Rebbe Nachman tells us that it is to their advantage that God also governs the world through nature:

"God shows us great kindness in governing the world both with personal providence and through the laws of nature. When people do good, God deals with them providentially in a way that goes beyond nature. However, when someone is not good, if God were to oversee his life providentially, no good could ever reach him [as he is not deserving. However, out of kindness,] God abandons this person to the laws of nature, and this means that things may then go well for him through the law of averages. If God's only way of running the world were through providence — rewarding good deeds and punishing sin — this could lead to a total breakdown of providence, since if God were to see someone acting im- properly and dealt with him in anger, He might cast him out completely. Instead, God abandons him to nature, and when he improves his ways, He deals with him providentially.

"But actually, we are really unable to understand what is 'nature' and what is 'providence.' The truth is that even the laws of nature are really God's providence. However, the human mind is unable to grasp the paradox that what appears to be the law of nature is really God's providence" (*Likutey Moharan* II, 17).

The two tiers of God's way of running the world — providentially and through nature — correspond to the two tiers of healing: through faith and prayer on the one hand, and by medicine on the other. Those who fulfil the Covenant are privy to God's special providence and can be healed through faith and prayer alone without medicine. This is the point of the Ramban (see p. 194-5): "When the Jewish People are in a state of spiritual perfection, their physical bodies are not governed by nature at all. This applies to the nation as a whole and to each individual Jew. For God 'will bless their bread and their water, and remove illness from their midst' (Exodus 23:25). They will have no need for doctors, nor will they have to follow medical procedures even as precautionary measures, 'for I, God, am your healer' (Exodus 15:26)" (Ramban on Leviticus 26:11).

On the other hand, those who are not on such a level of spiritual development are likely to view bodily illness as essentially a physical phenomenon, and they will seek to be cured through medicine. This view of illness is rooted in a lack of *da'at* — an absence of true awareness that physical symptoms express a spiritual flaw, and that genuine healing can come about only through correcting the flaw by turning to God in prayer and repentance. Since they lead their lives as if the things that happen to them fall under the laws of nature, measure for measure God "abandons them to the laws of nature" — to the vicissitudes of illness and of the medical services.

Yet even this is in fact a mark of God's kindness, because then "things may go well for them through the law of averages," and they may indeed be cured "by a particular drug and a particular doctor." If so, they may well bless the wonders of medicine. But these too are really God's miracles, because "the truth is that even the laws of nature are really God's providence." Their illness and medical treatment may well cause them deep distress and suffering. Yet this too is sent from God for their ultimate good, because it comes to cleanse them of their sins. Their distress and suffering are aspects of the "decree" of sickness, which will necessarily run its course unless sweetened by a "redemption" carried out by a Tzaddik.

Know your level

Without a doubt Rebbe Nachman would have wanted every Jew to attain such a level of closeness to God that he could be healed of any illness through faith and prayer alone. But the Rebbe surely understood that — at least until the time of Mashiach — the overwhelming majority will continue using medicine. This is probably one of his reasons for saying, "You know I don't hold by doctors, but if you're going to go, make sure you choose the very best!" (*Siach Sarfey Kodesh* I:8)

Many people will be happy to see Rebbe Nachman's warnings against doctors as having been primarily directed against the primitive medicine of his time, and they will have no scruples about taking advantage of the many benefits contemporary medicine seems to offer. Even those who have the deepest reverence for Rebbe Nachman, and who accept that illness has a spiritual dimension, may still feel that to depend on faith and prayer alone for healing would be beyond their capabilities. But for those who look to Rebbe Nachman as their main source of spiritual guidance and seek to follow his teachings to the very end, the question may not be whether his warnings against doctors apply to the world in general, but rather: "Do they apply to *me*? If I turn to doctors and medicine in times of illness, does that show a lack of faith?"

No one has the right to seek to prevent anyone else — even their own spouse or children — from receiving medical attention unless there are clear grounds for believing that a given treatment could be harmful or dangerous, in which case other medical opinions should be sought and a rabbi consulted. However, there are times when a person who is sincerely trying to follow Rebbe Nachman's spiritual pathway is faced with his own illness, and questions whether he should submit to medical treatment or try to rely on faith and prayer alone for healing.

The answer depends upon that person's spiritual level (Rabbi Yaakov Meir Shechter). What this means is brought out in a discussion by Rabbi Eliahu Eliezer Dessler (1891-1954) about the apparent contradiction between the view of the Ramban that "those who seek out God will not turn to the doctors" (Ramban on Leviticus 26:11; see above pp. 194-5) and the opinion of the Rambam that failure to go to a doctor in times of need is irresponsible. For in the Rambam's opinion, "just as a hungry person can and must eat and shows no lack of faith by doing so, similarly a sick person can and must turn to doctors and medicines, and should thank God for including medical remedies in His creation" (Rambam, Commentary on *Mishneh, Pesachim* 4:9; see p. 38).

In the words of Rabbi Dessler:

"A deeper examination will reveal that the approaches of the Ramban and the Rambam are not contradictory at all, but that each applies to people on different levels. The highest level is when a person recognizes the hand of God in all the different things that happen to him and understands that God governs his life directly. Such a person turns to God alone for whatever he needs, for He is the source of all things. If a person on this level becomes ill, he will go to the prophet for insight into the spiritual cause of his illness and to find out what God wants of him in order to correct his mistakes. For such a person to turn to a doctor for a medical remedy would amount to a defection from God, as if it is possible to flout God's will and be cured without rectifying the spiritual flaw that is the root cause of the sickness. Such a person is certainly a sinner, and this is the prophet's complaint against King Asa, who 'even in his sickness did not seek out God, but turned to the doctors' (Chronicles II, 16:13). In such a case, the Rambam would agree.

"On a lower level is the person who takes account of natural causes, and therefore God too hides His providence from this person and governs his life through natural causes. In the words of the Ramban, 'God abandons him to the vicissitudes of nature.' Such a person certainly has an obligation to pray to God to heal him, but he must use medicine and thank God for creating the remedy for his illness (*cf. Shulchan Arukh, Orach Chaim* 230:4), and thereby recognize God's providence and His kindness to him, and learn to improve his ways. The Ramban would also accept this.

"If a person on this level refuses to take medicine because of scruples about resorting to physical means of being cured, the Rambam considers this to be foolish and irresponsible, because each person must serve God according to his level. A person who seeks to act in accordance with a level that is in fact beyond his true capacity because he is still on a lower level is simply deceiving himself, and this is what the Rambam considers foolish and irresponsible" (R. Eliahu Eliezer Dessler, *Mikhtav MeEliahu* III, p.170-3).

To have the honesty and humility to acknowledge one's true level shows far greater spiritual maturity than to make a pretense of being on a higher level than one really is. In the words of Rebbe Nachman: "A person should look upon himself as if he were less than he really is: that is true humility. And at the very least, he should not look upon himself as if he is more than he really is" (*Likutey Moharan* I, 79). Such arrogance is all too often the prelude to a great fall (*ibid.* I, 168).

A person who is considering depending on faith and prayer alone for healing must ask himself searching questions about his true spiritual level and his real motives. How much faith does he really have? Does he turn to God alone for his livelihood and everything else he needs in life? Or does he use worldly means of attaining them? Is his sole motive for relying on God alone for healing to sanctify and glorify the Name of God? Or is this a rationalization that comes to cover over other motives, such as fears of what a doctor might tell him about his condition, apprehension about possible pain or the disruptive effects treatment may have on his life, or feelings of resentment at having to submit himself to the doctor's authority?

These and similar motives have nothing to do with pure faith in God, and have no validity at all as reasons for avoiding necessary medical treatment. As Rebbe Nachman said, "Sometimes when people don't want to suffer a little, they end up suffering a lot!" (*Siach Sarfey Kodesh* 1-6) It is far preferable to have a medical problem treated promptly in its early stages than to allow it to develop into what may turn out to be catastrophic proportions.

"What people do at the end I want you to do at the beginning!"

Rebbe Nachman said, "What people do at the end I want you to do at the beginning!" People resort to passionate prayers when they see that all other ways of saving the situation have failed. But Rebbe Nachman wanted us to implore God for help at the very beginning of the trouble (*Siach Sarfey Kodesh* I:293).

One can submit to medical treatment when necessary and still take a spiritual view of health and sickness *at the same time*, striving to follow all of Rebbe Nachman's teachings on health and healing through faith, prayer and joy. If there is any lack of faith involved in turning to doctors and medicine, it is when one pins all one's hopes of a cure on the means rather than on God. In the words of Rebbe Nachman, "Even while busying ourselves with these means, it is necessary to believe in God alone and not to make the mere means into the essence" (*ibid.* 62:6).

The late Lubavitcher Rebbe, Rabbi Menachem Mendel Shneerson (1902-94), wrote to a person undergoing medical treatment:

"When a Jew, man or woman, is unwell and is obliged to consult a doctor, the idea is not that the doctor has the power to do whatever he wants, but that the Holy One, blessed be He, has chosen the doctor to be His agent to execute the mission He has sent him on. And when one trusts in God and has complete faith that He governs the entire world, one can merit to see with one's own physical eyes how at every single step the Holy One takes each of us by the hand and leads us to good, physically and spiritually" (*Refuah Shelemah* p.33).

In another letter, the Lubavitcher Rebbe wrote:

"We know that our Torah, the Torah of *life*, teaches us in the verse 'and he will surely heal' (Exodus 21:19) that the doctor has been given sanction to heal, and it automatically follows that it is necessary to follow the instructions of a competent doctor. Yet at the same time, one must clearly know that God is the Healer of all flesh and the Worker of wonders, and 'a particular man and a particular drug' are merely His agents and means. It follows that first and foremost one must work to improve and strengthen one's spiritual health, because this strengthens one's attachment to God, and then 'you are all alive this day' (Deuteronomy 4:4) with actual physical vitality and in all one's limbs" (*ibid.* p.23).

Even when receiving medical treatment, one must follow the spiritual pathway of healing not as a mere "extra" but as the very foundation of true healing. Many people put all the emphasis on medical treatment not so much because they are committed to using every possible physical strategy to bring about a cure — if they truly had such a commitment, they would reform their diets, take up exercise and make all the other changes in their lifestyle that would be conducive to better health. Rather their reason is because passive submission to treatment involves much less effort than active steps to change one's life.

This may explain some of the antagonism people have to the idea that physical illness is often rooted in a spiritual flaw. The implication is that true healing can only come about when the patient has the courage to examine himself honestly and take responsibility for his life. For many people this is simply too uncomfortable. It is easier to believe that illness "just happens" to people, and to run to the doctor and say "Cure me! You do the work!"

Likewise, to depend on God for healing does not mean passively waiting for miracles. We have to do our part, not only by going to the doctor and receiving the necessary treatment, but by actively turning to God in every phase of illness and recovery. At times we may have to literally cry and scream out to God for help, or make heroic efforts to recite our prayers and carry out basic mitzvot despite severe pain and disability. Turning to God may involve giving charity or asking a Tzaddik to make a *pidyon*. At other times, turning to God means meditating, thinking and pondering carefully, asking what this illness means and what it comes to teach. What is our purpose in this world? How have we been leading our lives? What practical steps do we need to take to bring our lives to a higher level? And how can we take the immediate next step?

The True Doctor

"Everyone has to search very hard to find a true teacher who can help him understand the heights of wisdom and attain Godly perception. This requires an outstandingly great teacher who has the power to explain this great wisdom in terms that are comprehensible to the simplest people. The lower a person's level and the further away from God he is, the greater the teacher he needs. Thus we find that when the Jewish People were on the lowliest of levels in Egypt, sunken in the forty-nine gates of impurity, they needed the greatest, most awesome rabbi and teacher: Moshe Rabbenu. For the lowlier and further away from God a person is, the greater the teacher he needs. He needs an expert craftsman who has the ability to bring the supreme wisdom of Godly perception within the grasp of someone as lowly and far away from God as he is. The sicker the patient, the greater the doctor he needs.

"One should therefore never say, 'It is enough for me if I attach myself to someone respectable and God-fearing, even though he may not be on an outstanding level. First let me just be like him!' This is a mistaken attitude. On the contrary, the more a person understands his own lowliness and his great distance from God, the more he should search for the greatest, most outstanding doctor for his soul and aim to draw close to the greatest possible Rabbi. For the lowlier the person, the greater the teacher he needs" (*Likutey Moharan* 1, 30:2).

A word to doctors

Some doctors may be amused by Rebbe Nachman's scathing attacks on doctors, and in fact may even agree. Others, however, may be deeply upset when they hear that in spite of their years of training, hard-earned expertise and dedication to relieving people's misery, they are nothing but "emissaries of the Angel of Death."

Without doubt the great majority of doctors are sincere and well-intentioned. However, every doctor should be sobered by the disturbing present-day trend for doctors to become not only the preservers of life but takers of life as well. Not only has abortion become virtually a standard medical routine despite the fact that Torah law prohibits the killing of an unborn fetus when the mother's life is not at stake. Even more horrifying is the increasingly widespread acceptance of active medical euthanasia, which in Torah law is considered plain murder. Rebbe Nachman's accusation that doctors are "literally murderers, killing people with their own hands" certainly applies to any doctor involved in abortion or euthanasia in contravention of Torah law.

An honest healer will take his responsibility with the utmost seriousness and keep at the forefront of his mind the words of the Me'iri explaining why "the best of physicians are destined to go to hell" — because the doctor "does not make enough effort in his work of healing, or at times he does not know the cause of the illness and how to cure it but he presents himself as if he is expert and causes the death of the patient" (Me'iri on *Kiddushin* 82a, see p. 194). The Maharsha (Rabbi Shmuel Eliezer Aideles) says (*ad loc.*): "The best of doctors means a doctor who considers himself the best. He relies only on his own wisdom, and there are times when his haughtiness and conceit cause him to diagnose an illness incorrectly, and as a result, his patient dies. He should make it a habit always to consult another physician, because a life has been placed in his hands."

The awesomeness of the doctor's responsibility should not, however, deter him from practicing his craft. On the contrary, healing "is a mitzvah, and it is included in the category of saving life; and if the doctor withholds his services, it is considered as shedding blood" (*Shulchan Arukh, Yoreh Deah* 336:1). As we have seen, even for the Ramban, who asked what place doctors have in the house of those who carry out the will of God, the issue is not whether doctors have sanction to heal but rather, whether the sick have license to turn to the doctor

However, "if a patient has already come to the doctor, the doctor should not refrain from treating him" (Ramban on Leviticus 26:11, see p. 195).

Despite the severity of Rebbe Nachman's language against doctors, his main thrust is not so much against the doctors themselves as against those who put all their faith and trust in them and look to medicines to cure them instead of lifting their eyes and hearts to God. The doctor is in a unique position to help his patients put the medical aspects of their healing in the correct perspective and to influence them to deepen their faith in God. Thus the Lubavitcher Rebbe wrote to a doctor:

> "When patients consult you about their physical problems, I trust that, like many God-fearing doctors, you too take the opportunity to inspire and encourage them to work to heal their souls as well, which everyone in this orphaned generation needs, since 'no one on earth is so righteous that he does only good and does not sin' (Ecclesiastes 7:20). Moreover, we see clearly that an improvement in a person's spiritual health also brings an improvement in his or her physical health — quite literally..." (*Refuah Shelemah* p. 21).

Writing to another doctor, the Lubavitcher Rebbe recommends that he should

> "...decisively negate the theory of the dominion of the material, by paying attention to the extent to which the health of the body is dependent upon the health of the soul. If the traditional medical maxim emphasized 'a healthy mind in a healthy body,' in our days it has become manifestly clear how a small blemish in the soul leads to major damage in the body, and the healthier the soul, the greater its power over the body and its ability to rectify deficiencies in the body, to the point that many physical treatments are far more effective in healing the body when combined with the willpower and other spiritual powers of the patient" (*ibid.* p.21).

"It's not the doctor who heals, but the angel who goes with him"

Let us leave the final word on the subject of doctors to Dr. Guardia — Rabbi Aharon ben Shimon Rofey — to whom Rebbe Nachman himself was willing to take his wife (see pp. 72-3). Once a poverty-stricken woman came running to Dr. Guardia. She pounded on his door, crying "Doctor! Help! Have pity! You must save my husband! He's the father of eight children! We're totally impoverished! He struggles to give us a living, and now he's stretched out on his bed like a stone. Have pity on our children! Do what you can, Doctor!" After hearing the woman out, Dr. Guardia casually went back into his house.

"It's urgent!" cried the woman, "It's a matter of moments! Help!" "Yes," replied Dr. Guardia, patiently brushing his coat, "I'm on my way." He picked up his hat and started brushing it. More and more distraught, the woman cried out: "Is your heart made of stone? You have the power to save his life — how can you carry on like this?" Unperturbed, Dr. Guardia carried on brushing his hat. Finally, in disgust, the woman cried, "Enough! It's impossible to trust this doctor. Only You, Master of the World, You alone can help!" As she turned to leave, Doctor Guardia leapt out of the house and went running on ahead to her house. By the time she arrived, the doctor was already giving her husband medicine, and in due course he recovered.

Afterwards the man's wife asked Doctor Guardia why he had taken so long to leave his house. "Don't you understand?" he replied. "It's not the doctor who heals, but the angel who goes with him. When you unthinkingly said that only the doctor can help, I knew very well that no angel would be willing to come with me, because the angels do not attach themselves to those who forget their Creator. I therefore had to do everything I could to get you to understand that only God can help. When you finally ran out trusting only in God, I was able to come to your house and attend to your husband" (*The Magid of Mezritch*, by R.Y. Klapholtz).

SECTION 6

Sound the Shofar!
Rebbe Nachman's Pathway
of Healing

Chapter 18

Takhlis!

In the same period that he was warning his followers against medicine, Rebbe Nachman was teaching a complete pathway of health and healing through faith, prayer and joy. He gave fullest expression to this healing pathway in his first major Torah discourse after his return to Breslov from Lemberg, "*Sound the Shofar — Dominion over the Angels*" (*Likutey Moharan* II, 1). This was given on Rosh Hashanah (September 22) 1808 (see pp. 86ff.). A complete translation of this discourse together with a full commentary will be given in the current chapter.

Prayer

As we have seen, for Rebbe Nachman, the key to healing is *simchah*, joy, which is expressed through the ten kinds of melody (see pp. 149-73). In essence, the ten kinds of melody are ten different basic modes of connection with God through prayer. Prayer is the central theme of "*Sound the Shofar — Dominion.*" Rebbe Nachman tells us that prayer can bring healing without the need for medicines. Through prayer we can channel healing energy into bread and water — our regular food and drink.

This is not to say that the sick person and those around him need merely offer a few prayers — "Please heal x, the son/daughter of y" — and healing will come automatically. For Rebbe Nachman, prayer is a complete pathway of service that must be the central pillar of our lives. Prayer includes not only the fixed daily blessings and prayer services instituted by the Sages, but also our personal outreach to God through the private prayers we offer in our own words and unique style in hisbodedus. We must turn to God for everything we need, major or minor, spiritual or physical. For "prayer is the main way to relate to God and to become attached to Him. Prayer is the gate through which we enter into God's presence and come to know Him" (*Likutey Moharan* II, 84). "We receive our very *life* from prayer, as it is written, 'Prayer to the God of my *life*' (Psalms 42:9)" (*Likutey Moharan* I, 9:1).

Earlier we discussed Rebbe Nachman's teaching on "*Why do people get sick?*" (*Likutey Moharan* I, 268, see pp. 179ff.). The main idea there is that a person becomes sick because his soul-powers have become weakened through straying from his mission in life. But prayer has the power to restore the soul, which is why it brings healing. Rebbe Nachman teaches that the main work of prayer, especially our private prayers in hisbodedus, is to put our *longing* and *yearning* to come closer to God into *words* — to articulate our desires and good intentions with our lips, speaking about our inadequacies and shortcomings and how we yearn for God to help us overcome them.

> "The soul of the Jew is actually formed through the yearning and desire he feels for God and his good intentions to serve Him. Regardless of his level, each individual has a desire to reach a higher level. It is through this yearning that his holy soul is formed. The yearning and longing for something holy are themselves very precious. They are the means by which the soul is brought into being, and it reaches completion through speech" (*Likutey Moharan* I, 31).

The holy yearnings each Jew has deep in his heart are themselves the "good points" that we must search for in hisbodedus in order to "make melodies" and come to simchah (see pp. 163ff.).

Since prayer in this broad sense is the main avenue to genuine healing, a large part of "*Sound the Shofar — Dominion*" is taken up with the preconditions for prayer. First and foremost we must strive to know God in our very hearts. Mere intellectual knowledge of God's existence is not enough: we must bring our understanding from our heads down into our hearts and *feel* God's awesome presence, directing our day-to-day lives accordingly.

Our material cravings for wealth, food and sex tend to obscure our awareness of God. We must therefore bring balance into our lives, taking only what we really need from this world. In addition, to attain true prayer, we must cleanse ourselves of all flaws in our faith, purify ourselves of illicit sexual desire, and cultivate respect for other people. Thus for Rebbe Nachman, the path of prayer is a complete way of life, and as such it offers immunity from illness as well as healing if illness strikes.

For Rebbe Nachman, the essential prerequisite for success in the path of prayer is to "bind oneself to the Tzaddik" — to "get oneself a teacher" (*Avot* 1:6) and to make every effort to put his guidance and teachings into practice. Thus Rebbe Nachman's exploration of prayer as the pathway of healing in "*Sound the Shofar — Dominion*" comes in the context of a lengthy answer to the question of how we can distinguish the true leaders and teachers of the Jewish People from the false figures who owe their influence to brash self-assertiveness. The search for the true leader is itself a vital part of the quest for healing, since this can only come after *pidyon nefesh*, redemption of the soul by the Tzaddik.

Dominion over the angels

The essential reason why we need to recognize the true leaders is that we must bind ourselves to them in order to attain our ultimate destiny as Jews. The Jewish People has a central role in the scheme of creation, having been entrusted with the keys to drawing Godly blessing down into all the worlds — through prayer, Torah and mitzvot. Thus Rebbe Nachman opens this discourse with the statement that the ultimate destiny of the Jewish People is to "rule over the angels" — for they are the forces that channel God's blessing to the various parts of creation.

However, "the angels are very jealous of a man who has dominion over them." This jealousy expresses itself in the powerful internal and external obstacles people encounter when trying to serve God. To overcome them, says Rebbe Nachman, one must bind oneself to the roots of the souls of the Jewish People — "Together we stand!" But the only way most people can achieve this is through binding themselves to the leaders of the Jewish People, each of whom has a certain number of souls under his sway.

In *"Why do people get sick"* Rebbe Nachman teaches that a person may become sick when he strays from his mission in this world, his תכלית (*takhlit*), while healing comes when he takes the first steps to direct himself to a higher goal. Our *takhlit* (or "takhlis" in the Ashkenazic pronunciation) is our ultimate goal or purpose in life. An individual's destiny certainly includes the unique mission he or she has in his or her particular life. But as Jews, our ultimate mission is to play our part as members of "a kingdom of priests and a holy nation" (Exodus 19:6), ruling over the angels through our prayers, Torah and mitzvot. When we rise to this mission we become true *b'ney Adam*, children of Adam, the pinnacle of creation. This is the ultimate healing. The *takhlit* of the Jewish People is the starting point of *"Sound the Shofar — Dominion."*

How to study this teaching

Newcomers to the study of Rebbe Nachman's discourses in *Likutey Moharan* should be aware that in most cases they are highly elaborate structures, replete with references from the entire spectrum of biblical, talmudic, midrashic, halakhic and kabbalistic literature. As Rebbe Nachman lays each brick in his structure, introducing the concepts of the discourse one by one, he cites a dazzling variety of proof texts in order to explain the meaning of these concepts and their connection with the other concepts in the discourse. The assumption is that the entire corpus of Torah literature is ultimately a single, unitary divine revelation, and it is therefore valid to cite verses or sayings from one place in order to throw light on the meaning of words and ideas in another.

The freshness, grace and brilliance of Rebbe Nachman's hermeneutics are breathtaking for those with a background in Torah scholarship. However, the breadth of his references, the unfamiliarity of many of his concepts and the subtlety of his arguments can be confusing to new students. In order to clarify the structure of the discourse and throw light on the meaning of central concepts, explanatory material has been inserted throughout the text of the discourse. This material is not part of the original text. To enable readers to distinguish between the two, *the explanatory material is printed in THIS typeface*. In addition to this explanatory material, more detailed commentary is provided in the footnotes printed beneath the text of the discourse. The commentary is largely based on three major commentaries on *Likutey Moharan*: *Parpara'ot LeChokhmah*, *Biur HaLikutim* and *Torat Nathan*. For details of these works, see *Sources and Further Reading*.

It is suggested that readers wishing to make a serious study of this discourse might start by reading it through fairly rapidly a number of times together with the explanatory material, but without as yet studying the notes or making undue efforts to understand points that seem obscure. Having gained a grasp of the main drift of the discourse as a whole, one might then embark on a more detailed study, section by section, referring to the notes for pointers to interpretation and connections with other teachings of Rebbe Nachman. The main focus of this commentary is on healing, but the implications of this discourse are obviously very much broader and deeper. (For a summary of the discourse, see above pp. 86-91. For Reb Noson's prayer in *Likutey Tefilot* based on this discourse, see pp. 418ff.)

Sound the Shofar — Dominion

Likutey Moharan II, 1

"Sound the shofar on the new moon, at the time appointed for our festive day" (Psalms 81:4).

The discourse takes its title from the key verse, "Sound the shofar...". In the concluding section of the discourse, after having explained all the concepts in detail and having built them into an entire structure, Rebbe Nachman will show that all of them are alluded to in the key verse. The Rebbe took the same verse as his key verse in each of the Rosh Hashanah discourses he gave in the last three years of his life. In the printed text of Likutey Moharan *all three have the phrase "Sound the shofar" as their title. In order to distinguish the three discourses from one another, their titles in each case also include one word expressing the main theme of the discourse in question. In this case the main theme of the discourse is "dominion over the angels," and accordingly the discourse is subtitled "Dominion."*

Dominion

#1. The Jew was created to have power over the angels.[1] This is the ultimate destiny of the Jewish People, as our Rabbis taught (*Yerushalmi Shabbat* 2): "In time to come, the position of the tzaddikim will be superior to that of the ministering

---

1. **power over the angels** It is obviously a mistake to envisage angels as the winged figures portrayed in western art. The Hebrew word for angel is *malakh*, literally a messenger or agent. The angels are the spiritual forces that translate the divine will into action in the lower worlds. As such they are the agents channeling divine blessing into the world. According to the Kabbalah, the place of the angels is in the world of *Yetzirah* ("Formation"). Although man in this world is on a lower plane than the angels, his soul is rooted in the world of *Beriyah* ("Creation"), also called the World of the Throne. Thus man is potentially on a higher level than the angels, and through his prayers, mitzvot and good deeds, can bring them to channel greater blessing into the world. However, man's ability to do this depends upon his actualizing his spiritual powers.

"The key to having power over the angels is therefore to have power over *oneself* — to be in control of one's cravings and desires so as to steer oneself to the path of Torah and mitzvot. This explains why one of the central ideas in this discourse is that of bringing da'at, knowledge and awareness of God, from the mind down into the heart, which is the seat of our passions" (*Biur HaLikutim* #37).

angels, as it is written (Numbers 23:23): 'At such a time Jacob will be asked, What has God done?'" That is, when the angels want to know "What has God done?" they will have to ask the Jews. Each person must see that he attains his destiny[2] and rules over the angels. But one must guard oneself carefully and see that one has the strength to stand firm in this position of power and not let the ministering angels throw one down out of jealousy. For the angels are very jealous[3] of a man like this who has dominion over them. Our Rabbis thus mentioned several great tzaddikim whom the angels tried to cast out (*Chagigah* 15b).

The jealousy of the angels finds expression in the promptings of a person's evil urge and the external obstacles confronting him. These tend to pull him down from his level and divert him from his exalted spiritual mission. Rebbe Nachman now goes on to explain how to withstand the "jealousy of the angels" — by binding oneself to the souls of the Jewish People.

Binding oneself to the souls of Israel

#2. The way to stand firm is by binding oneself to the souls of Israel.[4] Through this bond one is saved from the angels. This is the idea of "grasping

---

2. **destiny** The concept of our ultimate destiny provides a link between this discourse and Rebbe Nachman's teaching about "Why do people get sick" (see pp.179ff), where he says that illness is caused by straying from one's ultimate purpose. When man attains his destiny and rules benevolently over God's creation, he is at the peak of his powers and this is the ultimate in health and healing. Another link is with the concept of the ultimate destiny of the soul as discussed in Rebbe Nachman's teaching of the "Garden of the Souls" (*Likutey Moharan I, 65*), where he teaches that the great Tzaddik, whose task is to guide souls to their fulfilment, examines each person's *speech* to see how near or far he is from his goal (*Garden of the Souls p.40*). This is because only through speech and prayer can we attain our destiny and rule over the angels.

3. **the angels are very jealous** "The jealousy of the angels finds expression in our own materialistic cravings and desires, and the obstacles and difficulties standing in the way of anything holy, especially prayer" (*Torat Nathan #1*). "When the angels attack a Jewish soul, they inject it with their own jealousy, so that that person too becomes jealous of others, including those superior to himself. This may lead to a flaw in his faith in the One who Himself sits upon the throne" (*Biur HaLikutim #19*). Yet there is a positive aspect to the jealousy of the angels, in that it may spur people to reach out to "take hold of the throne" and follow the pathway outlined in this discourse (*ibid. #8*).

4. **binding oneself to the souls of Israel** "Since all the six hundred thousand Jewish souls were created only for this dominion, it is clear that only when bound together can

the face of the throne"[5] (Job 26:9): one must attach oneself to the roots of the souls, which were hewn out from beneath the Throne of Glory, which is called "the mother of all living" (Genesis 3:20). Thus the Rabbis said, "When Moses ascended on high, the ministering angels said, 'What is a mortal doing among us?' God said, 'He has come to receive the Torah.' The angels protested, 'But Your glory is praised above the heavens [so how can the Torah be taken down to earth?]' (Psalms 8:2). The Holy One said to Moses, 'Give them an answer.' Moses said, 'I'm afraid they'll burn me with the breath of their mouths.' God said to him, 'Hold onto my Throne of Glory...'" (Shabbat 88b). In other words, the advice God gave Moses was to grasp and bind himself to the roots of the souls, which are the "Throne of Glory," the "mother of all living," in order to be saved from the jealousy of the angels.

In the next paragraph, Rebbe Nachman explores in greater depth why attaching oneself to the "Throne of Glory," the "mother of all living," gives one

---

they stand in this position of power over the entire host of heaven. For when the souls are in conflict with one another and even a single soul is missing, the corresponding limb of the 'body' made up by all the souls collectively is flawed" (*Biur HaLikutim* #1).

It is through the mitzvah of loving every Jew that the souls become united. This explains why it is customary to reaffirm our commitment to fulfil this mitzvah as we begin each of the daily prayer services, because unity among the souls is essential in order for us to "rule over the angels" with our prayers. Likewise, it is necessary to pray with a minyan, as our prayers are most effective when we all pray together.

5. **"grasping the face of the throne"** Reb Noson writes: "It is difficult to understand the advice given in this discourse to 'hold on to the Throne of Glory' in order to withstand the jealousy of the angels, because this in itself is something that is extremely hard for us to do. In order to achieve it, we need to follow the entire pathway explained here of honoring the three festivals so as to attain prophetic spirit and prayer, but all of this is extremely difficult.... The truth is, we have no one to lean upon except our Father in Heaven and the power of the true Tzaddik, whose Torah teachings can inspire us to action. For the true Tzaddik is one who has won the battle against his desires and overcome the jealousy of the angels, taking hold of the Throne of Glory so as to snatch the Torah from Heaven and bring it down to the Jewish People. The Tzaddik has the power to save every single Jew who is willing to draw close to him from the jealousy of the angels. This is because the Tzaddik knows how to celebrate Rosh Hashanah — i.e. he judges each person positively through his knowledge of the place of each one. He genuinely lifts each person into the scale of merit by finding good points in every aspect of his life and soul, and then even the lowliest of people can follow the pathway explained in this discourse, each according to his level, and take hold of the Throne of Glory..." (*Torat Nathan* #1).

the strength to withstand the jealousy of the angels. Essentially, this is because the spiritual force that was involved in the creation of the "mother of all living," (i.e. Eve, the first woman, mother of all the souls), came from the "Supernal Man" (= Ze'ir Anpin), who sits upon the Throne of Glory: this is God Himself, in Whose image man was made.

Of the creation of Eve, the "mother of all living," it is written, "And the Lord God built the flank which he took from the man and he brought her to the man" (Genesis 3:22). The letters of the Hebrew word for "built," ויבן (*VaYiVeN*) are the initial letters of the words in the verse, ותקעתיו י'תד ב'מקום נ'אמן (*Utekativ Yated Bemakom Ne'eman*), "And I will fasten him as a peg in a sure place" (Isaiah 22:23). [In this prophecy, God promised that he would raise Eliakim ben Chilkiah[6] to a position of authority over the whole Kingdom of Judah.] The concept is one of power, as indicated by the translation of this verse in the Aramaic Targum of Yonatan, "And I will appoint him as a faithful officer serving in a position that will endure." In other words, his power will be firm and enduring. It is through the "flank," Eve, the mother of all living, the Throne of Glory, root of the souls, that one has the power to stand in this dominion over the angels. And thus the account of the creation of Eve speaks of the flank "which He took *from the man*" — this alludes to the Supernal Man, as it is written, "And on the throne was a likeness with the appearance of a *man*" (Ezekiel 1:26). "...And he brought her *to the man*" — this refers to man down below in this world.[7] It is his connection with the root of the souls that gives man in this world the power to stand in this position of dominion.

---

6. **Eliakim ben Chilkiah** Eliakim ben Chilkiah lived in the time of King Hezekiah. He was appointed trustee over the Temple in place of Shevna, whom God rejected as a self-seeking traitor (Isaiah 22:15-19). Shevna's rejection in favor of Eliakim exemplifies many of the themes Rebbe Nachman develops in this discourse. Eliakim and Shevna were both officers in the Holy Temple. Eliakim was a true Tzaddik while Shevna was out for himself. Eliakim was a supporter of King Hezekiah, who redeemed prayer from its exile, while Shevna opposed Hezekiah and was willing to hand him over to the Assyrian invaders (*Sanhedrin* 26a).

7. **man down below in this world** Although in this life man's place is in the material world, he is far more than a physical being. The essence of man is his soul, which derives from the Supernal Man, and it is this spark of Godliness in man that gives him the power to use his speech — the faculty that distinguishes him from the animals — to attain the Word of God, prayer, and to rule over the angels.

This explains the words of Rav Amram the Chassid to the angel who was tempting him[8]: "I am flesh, (בשרא, *BiSRA*), and you are fire, and I am better than you" (*Kiddushin* 81a). The letters of the word בשרא are the initial letters of the words ש'שים ר'בוא ב'כרס א'חד (*Shishim Ribo Be-chares Echad*), "six hundred thousand in one womb," i.e. the womb of Yochebed, the mother of Moses, because Moses possessed a general soul[9] containing the roots of all the six hundred thousand souls of the Jewish People (*Midrash Shir HaShirim* on Songs 1:15). Thus the *BiSRA*[10] of which Rav Amram boasted to the angel was his connection with the roots of the souls. This is what gave him the strength to stand up in his dominion over the angels, so that he could say, "I am better than you."

Binding oneself to the Tzaddikim

Binding oneself to the roots of all the Jewish souls requires levels of spiritual insight and attainment that are beyond the capacity of most people. A simpler course is to bind oneself to the spiritual leaders of the Jewish People, in whom all the individual souls are rooted. But this raises the question of how to distinguish the true leaders from the false figures who owe their prominence to self-assertiveness.

---

8. **the angel who was tempting him** Rav Amram was sorely tempted by a freed captive girl who was staying in his house. To overcome his desires, he cried out that his house was on fire so that his neighbors would come running and he would be too ashamed to do anything in front of them (*Kiddushin* 81a). Rebbe Nachman's reference to this episode makes it clear that the "jealousy of the angels" expresses itself primarily in our material cravings.

9. **Moses possessed a general soul** Moses is the paradigm of the true Tzaddik, and all the tzaddikim in all the generations have a spark of the soul of Moses (cf. *Likutey Moharan* I, 4:5 etc.). Moses appears repeatedly throughout this discourse. Moses was the true Master of Prayer. He prayed for the Jewish People after the sins of the golden calf (Exodus 32:11) and the spies (Numbers 14:13). He also prayed for the healing of Miriam from leprosy (*ibid.* 12:13) and of the Jewish People from snakebites (*ibid.* 21:7). When a Jew binds himself to the true Tzaddik of the generation, he can be healed through the Tzaddik's prayers.

10. *BiSRA* *BaSaR* is literally flesh, but when Rav Amram said he was *BiSRA* he was also alluding to holy, spiritual "flesh" (cf. *Likutey Moharan* II, 83) — i.e. the souls of the Jewish People, all of which make up the "limbs" of the Supernal Man. This helps illumine the meaning of the phrase לב בשר (*LeV BaSaR*), a "heart of flesh," as in the verse, "I will remove your heart of stone and give you a heart of flesh" (Ezekiel 36:26). Such a heart is open and responsive to the needs and feelings of all people (see below pp. 399-407).

#3. In order to bind oneself to the roots of the souls of the Jewish People, one needs to know the source of all the souls[11] and the source of the vitality of every single soul. The main thing is to recognize all the known leaders of the generation. For if one is unable to know and bind oneself to each soul individually, one must bind oneself to all the known leaders of the generation, since all the souls are grouped under them. Each of the leaders of the generation has responsibility for a given number of individual souls. When a person binds himself to the known leaders, he is bound to all the individual Jewish souls. But one has to know who the true leaders are, because there are many famous figures who are in fact false leaders[12] who owe their position to brash self-assertiveness, as the Rabbis said, "Impudence is kingship without a crown" (*Sanhedrin* 105a).

Rebbe Nachman now embarks on his lengthy explanation of how to recognize the false leaders for what they are. This explanation extends from section #4 of the discourse up until section #13, where the question is finally answered as follows: The "Word of God" is the source from which all the forces within creation receive their power. A person who attains true prayer attains the "Word of God," and then all the forces in creation owe their power to this

---

11. **source of all the souls** "To know the source of all the souls entails understanding the secrets of *ma'aseh merkavah*, the kabbalistic lore of the 'chariot,' which *is* the Throne of Glory, because it is in the 'throne' that the souls are rooted" (*Biur HaLikutim* #2). "To grasp on to the Throne of Glory is thus to seek and know the glory of God" (*ibid.* end). Rebbe Nachman said that he knew the roots of every Jewish soul (*Rabbi Nachman's Wisdom* #185, and see #90 and #176).

12. **false leaders** A false leader is anyone whose guidance and leadership, spiritual or otherwise, not only cannot bring a Jew to his or her true spiritual fulfilment through Torah and mitzvot but may distance them from it. Reb Noson writes: "Certainly every false leader must have some good in him, otherwise he would not have the power to attract Jewish souls, because Jewish souls are by nature attracted only to good. Thus 'every lie that is not based on some truth at the start cannot endure' (Rashi on Numbers 13:27). It is just that the falsehood and evil outweigh the good" (*Torat Nathan* #3).

In this discourse, the themes of leadership and healing are closely interwoven. Just as Rebbe Nachman associated the pathway of prayer taught by the true Tzaddik with genuine healing, so he grouped false leaders together with doctors as two categories of people who fail to provide the benefits they promise. "The Angel of Death has the job of killing everyone in the world physically and spiritually, and the task is too weighty, so he appoints assistants in each place: the physicians to kill physically and the false leaders to kill spiritually" (*Avanehah Barzel* p.43 #64).

Master of Prayer since he is the one who channels it to them. Thus they are in his debt, as it were. Now it is a talmudic principle that "a person does not act impudently towards his creditor" (Bava Metzia 3a). As a debtor, the false leader is ashamed in front of his creditor, the Master of Prayer, who is thus able to recognize him for what he is. Since the ability to recognize the false leader comes through prayer, the main issue is therefore how to attain true prayer. It is in the course of his discussion of this issue that Rebbe Nachman will explain the power of prayer to channel healing (sections #9-11). The foundation of true prayer lies in the Godly awe and awareness in our hearts. It is therefore necessary to cleanse our hearts of our material cravings for wealth, food and sex, which destroy this awe and awareness.

The knowing heart: *Yerushalayim*

#4. The way to recognize which of the famous leaders owe their position to brazen impudence is through "rebuilding Jerusalem," i.e. the heart.[13] For Jerusalem, ירושלים (*Yerushalayim*), is יראה שלם (*yir'ah shalem*), perfect awe of God.[14] This depends upon the heart, as the Rabbis said, "Wherever a mitzvah is entrusted to the heart of the individual [because no one else can know what his true motives are] the Torah adds the words 'and you shall fear God'" (*Kiddushin* 32b), proving that the place of fear and awe is in the heart.

Three destructive cravings

But there are three traits which destroy Jerusalem, i.e. the heart, weakening one's awe of God. These three traits are: the cravings for wealth, food and sexual pleasure.[15] The power of these three desires to weaken one's awe of God

---

13. **"rebuilding Jerusalem," i.e. the heart** Jerusalem is the heart of the world. As the place of the Holy Temple, gathering place of all the Jewish souls, it corresponds to the Throne of Glory. The three "feet" of the throne are the three "foot" festivals, when all the Jews are commanded to make the pilgrimage to Jerusalem. Thus Jerusalem is rebuilt through observing the three festivals.

14. **perfect awe of God** *Yir'at shamayim*, reverential awe of Heaven, is the foundation of the entire pathway set forth in this discourse. Intellectual knowledge that God exists is of little value without heartfelt awareness of God's awesome greatness and His power to requite us for our actions in this world, good or evil. Rebbe Nachman once said, "I am the treasure house of awe of heaven" (*Tzaddik* #294).

stems from the fact that they are all centered in the heart. The proof that the craving for wealth is centered in the heart is found in the verse, "The blessing of God is what makes a person wealthy,[16] and toil (עצב, *ETZeV*) adds nothing to it" (Proverbs 10:22). This "toil" is felt in the heart, as it is written, "And it grieved Him (ויתעצב, *vayitATZeV*) in His heart" (Genesis 6:6). Of eating, it is written, "And bread sustains the *heart* of man" (Psalms 104:15). Sexual desire is also in the heart, because sexual desire is governed by the passion coming from the blood in the hollow of the heart. It is because all these three cravings are rooted in the heart that they weaken the awe in a person's heart, "*Yerushalayim.*"

In the light of this we can understand the saying of the Rabbis: "The night is made up of three watches, and the Holy One, blessed be He, sits over each one and roars like a lion, as it is said, 'God will roar from on high and let out His cry from His holy habitation, He will roar mightily because of His fold' (Jeremiah 25:30). The sign of the first watch is the braying of the ass; the sign of the second, the barking dogs; the sign of the third, the baby sucking from his mother's breast and a woman talking intimately with her husband" (*Berakhot* 3a).

---

15. **These three traits are: the cravings for wealth, food and sexual pleasure** The essence of material desire is the search for one's own self-gratification. This is the opposite of the self-effacing humility that is necessary in order to see the glory of God and "take hold of the throne." The pathway Rebbe Nachman explains in this discourse is not only one of healing but also of preventive healthcare. The cravings for wealth, food and sexual pleasure are among the main destroyers of people's health. The stress and tension involved in the battle to increase earning power play a prominent role in heart disease, the main killer in "advanced" countries. Another major factor in heart disease is excessive intake of fat, which, together with other unhealthful dietary habits, is also responsible for many other diseases. Giving way to excessive sexual craving can lead not only to venereal diseases, AIDS, etc. but also causes distortions in interpersonal relationships that engender deep unhappiness and eventually find expression in all manner of actual physical illnesses. Conversely, moderation and self-discipline are among the best guarantors of sound, good health.

16. **"The blessing of God is what makes a person wealthy..."** The real blessing is to recognize all the good God has given us and to be grateful for it. This is true wealth, for "Who is rich? The one who is satisfied with his portion" (*Avot* 4:1). The "toil" (*etzev*) which those who lack this blessing suffer is *atzvut*, tension and depression, which take an especially heavy toll on the heart, as alluded to in the verse Rebbe Nachman quotes presently, "it grieved Him in His *heart*" (Genesis 6:6).

The darkness of night signifies obstacles, i.e. the three cravings: for wealth, food and sex. These are the "three watches." The sign of the first, the braying ass, alludes to the craving for wealth.[17] Thus Jacob's blessing to Issakhar as "a large-boned *ass*" (Genesis 49:14) is translated by Onkelos as indicating that he will be "rich in possessions." The barking dogs who mark the second watch signify the craving for food, as it is written, "The dogs are *greedy*, they don't know when they've had enough" (Isaiah 56:11). The double sign of the third watch, the baby sucking from his mother's breast and a woman talking intimately with her husband, both have sexual connotations. Thus the sight of a woman conversing intimately with a stranger is considered grounds for suspicion of a liaison between them (*Ketuvot* 13a). As regards the baby sucking from his mother's breast, sexual desire is related to breast-feeding.

A baby who feeds from the breast of an immodest woman will suffer from excessive sexual desire in later life, because the milk in the breasts is formed from congealed blood (*Bekhorot* 6a) and the impurities in the blood of an immodest woman will harm the suckling child, engendering the passion in the heart that causes excessive desire. On the other hand, when a child sucks the milk of a modest woman, his heart is quiet within him[18] (cf. Psalms 109:22) and has only the little passion necessary to fulfil God's commandment to be fruitful and multiply. Thus the Rabbis said, "David did not deserve to succumb to his desire for Batsheva, since he had reached a level where he could say of himself (Psalms *ibid.*) 'My heart is quiet within me'" (*Avodah Zarah* 4b). The initial letters of

---

17. **The sign of the first watch, the braying ass, alludes to the craving for wealth** "The craving for wealth is called 'the first watch' because money-making is the main preoccupation of most people in this world. Next comes eating, which is the 'second watch.' People tend to be more secretive about their sexual cravings, and thus it is the 'third watch'" (*Parpara'ot LeChokhmah* #3).

18. **his heart is quiet within him** The parents of R. Judah the Prince had him circumcised despite the fact that the Roman rulers in Israel had prohibited circumcision. The Roman governor sent the baby R. Judah with his mother to Rome to appear before the Emperor. But before they went in to him, a gentile friend of R. Judah's mother who had also recently given birth to a baby boy told her to take *her* baby, who was uncircumcised, and show him to the Emperor. On seeing the uncircumcised baby, the Emperor sent R. Judah's mother home, threw out the governor for slander, and revoked the decree against circumcision. When R. Judah's saintly mother took the gentile baby into the Emperor she fed him with her own milk. Drinking this milk influenced this boy for life, and when he grew up, he learned Torah and had himself circumcised. He became the Emperor Antoninus, R. Judah's lifelong friend (*Tosafot* on *Avodah Zarah* 10b, s.v. amar ley).

the Hebrew words in the phrase, "my heart is quiet within me" — ל'בי ח'לל ב'קרבי, *Libi Chalal Bekirbi* — spell out the word חלב (*ChaLaV*), "milk": i.e. it was because of the milk of a modest woman that his heart was quiet within him and he did not suffer from an excess of this desire. It was because David was in this category that he did not deserve what happened with Batsheva. On the other hand, the milk of an immodest woman engenders excessive passion. For this reason the initial Hebrew letters of the phrase "my heart waxed hot within me," חם ל'בי ב'קרבי (*Cham Libi Bekirbi*) (Psalms 39:4) also spell out the word חלב, *ChaLaV*.

The Rabbis said that "over each watch the Holy One, blessed be He, sits and roars like a lion…" — i.e. over the destruction of awe. For "The lion roars: who will not *fear*?" (Amos 3:8). For these three cravings, which are the "three watches," prevent the rebuilding of Jerusalem, i.e. the perfect fear of heaven which depends upon the heart.

Bringing *da'at* into the heart

Rebbe Nachman will now explain how to cleanse the heart of its cravings for wealth, food and sex — by filling the heart with deeper knowledge and awareness of God, da'at. It is not enough to know God intellectually: one must bring this knowledge into one's heart, the seat of one's passions, in order to turn the whole of one's life into a unitary quest for God. In Torah psychology, perfect da'at, "knowledge," is a synthesis of the higher spiritual-intellectual faculties of Chokhmah, "visionary wisdom," and Binah, "rational understanding." Although accessible at all times through Torah study, prayer and performance of the mitzvot, Chokhmah, Binah and Da'at are revealed especially at the three high points of the year, the three festivals of Pesach, Shavuot and Sukkot. In Temple times the entire Jewish People would then go up to Yerushalayim (Jerusalem), ascending to yir'ah shalem, perfect awe of God, and attaining enhanced knowledge and awareness of God. Celebrating the festivals with due honor is thus a way to fill the heart with da'at and thereby rectify its material cravings.

#5. The way to rectify these three cravings is by bringing deeper knowledge and awareness of God, *da'at*, into one's heart[19]: "Know this day and put it into your *heart* that HaShem is God…" (Deuteronomy 4:39). One must draw this

---

19. **bringing…** *da'at* **into one's heart** Da'at is the knowledge and awareness that everything in the world is under God's direct control and providence, including the

knowledge and awareness into the heart, and this is how these three cravings are rectified, because *da'at* actually contains all three parts of the mind, [*Chokhmah, Binah* and *Da'at* — wisdom, understanding and knowledge — corresponding to] the three cavities of the skull. These correspond to the three pilgrim festivals, Pesach, Shavuot and Sukkot. On each festival new levels of Godly awareness shine forth to rectify these three cravings. Each of the three festivals rectifies one of them, and for this reason one must take great care to give due honor to the festivals and celebrate them fittingly,[20] because it is

---

so-called laws of nature, which God has the power to suspend at will. As we have seen, the concept of *da'at* plays an important role in Rebbe Nachman's spiritual pathway of healing (see pp. 219ff.). But it is not enough to have this knowledge and awareness on a purely intellectual level. We have to bring it into our hearts so that we actually *feel* God's power and presence (*cf. Likutey Moharan* I, 34).

Reb Noson writes: "The darkness of night symbolizes these three cravings, which are the three watches of the night. Each day we have to fill ourselves with the Godly awareness engendered by the three festivals in order to bring these three cravings under control. Godly awareness, *da'at*, is the 'light of day,' and it comes from the three festivals, which are called *Yom Tov*, a good day. For the light of day is good, as it is written, 'God saw the light that it was *good*' (Genesis 1:4). *Da'at*, the 'light of day,' puts the darkness of night — the three cravings — to flight. The way to fill ourselves with *da'at* is by studying Torah at night, i.e. getting up for *Chatzot* (the midnight service) in order to break the darkness of night. For *Chatzot* is the middle point of the night, when the darkness is at its most intense. By forcing ourselves to get up, we break the power of the 'three watches,' i.e. the three cravings. We then study Torah in order to draw *da'at* into our hearts to rectify the three cravings. *Chatzot* is a lament over the destruction of the Holy Temple, because the Temple is the source of *da'at*" (*Torat Nathan* #5).

20. **one must take great care to give due honor to the festivals and celebrate them fittingly** Honoring the festivals is one of the most important pieces of practical advice in this discourse. It emerges that celebration of the festivals is one of the keys to healthcare and healing! It is characteristic of Rebbe Nachman to teach us to fight the negative — here the three cravings — by emphasizing the positive (see *Tzaddik* #354). The concept of the festivals also includes Shabbat, which is called "the first of the holy convocations" (see *Parpara'ot LeChokhmah* #9). Unlike the festivals, the fixing of Shabbat has nothing to do with the phases of the moon (which is one of the major underlying themes of this discourse), but even so, in Leviticus ch. 23, where all the festivals are listed, Shabbat comes first.

In Temple times the festivals were occasions for the Jewish People to make a physical pilgrimage to a holy *place*, the Sanctuary. But Shabbat and the festivals can themselves be seen as "sanctuaries in *time*" — sacred time when we pause from the mundane activities that keep our minds focussed on the material in order to direct ourselves to the spiritual

through fulfilling the commandment of the three festivals[21] that we are able to rectify these three cravings.

---

and build our *da'at*. The purpose is that this enhanced *da'at* should then shine into our everyday lives so as to elevate them to a higher plane. We must learn to turn *every* day into a "Yom Tov" — by finding and enjoying the good in it (*cf. Likutey Moharan I, 33:3*). The key to finding the good is to put all our powers of concentration into the three daily prayer services, which correspond to the three patriarchs and the three festivals. This is how we fill ourselves with Godly awareness so as to "know this day and put it into your *heart* that HaShem is God...."

Rebbe Nachman's discussion in this discourse about observance of the festivals as the way to bring *da'at* into the heart seems to be related to his discussion of the festivals in his discourse on "The Ravens" (*Likutey Moharan II, 4:6*), which was given later in the same year. Rebbe Nachman says there that the key to awe of heaven is to know that everything in the world is governed by God's will, and this is revealed on the three festivals, all of which commemorate the striking revelation of God's providential control over the world in taking the Jewish People out of Egypt, giving us the Torah and surrounding us with clouds of glory in the wilderness. As we have seen, healing is also an important theme in "The Ravens" (see pp. 93ff.). When we count Shabbat as the first of the festivals, we can also discern a link between the current discourse and that entitled "The days of Chanukah are days of thanksgiving" (*Likutey Moharan II, 2*) where Rebbe Nachman discusses Shabbat in relation to the concept of perfected speech, i.e. prayer, which is the central theme of the present discourse.

21. **through fulfilling the commandment of the three festivals** We find repeating patterns of triads in this discourse. Having dealt with the three cravings that destroy Jerusalem, Rebbe Nachman now discusses how the three festivals are the remedy for these cravings. Later in the discourse (#10) Rebbe Nachman will discuss three other traits that destroy prayer. This pattern of triads seems to be bound up with the main motif of the discourse, the Throne of Glory, which according to tradition has three main legs (corresponding to the patriarchs Abraham, Isaac and Jacob, and to the sefirot of Chesed, Gevurah and Tiferet) and a fourth leg corresponding to King David and to the sefirah of Malkhut. Chesed, Gevurah and Tiferet correspond to the elements of Water, Fire and Air, while Malkhut corresponds to the element of Earth.

We have seen that Rebbe Nachman viewed illness as being bound up with disharmony among the four elements of which the body is composed (see Chapters 12 and 19). It seems that the triadic spiritual remedies discussed in this discourse — breaking the three cravings, honoring the three festivals and nullifying the three destroyers of prayer — are designed to restore balance and harmony among the three higher elements of Water, Fire and Air, while the release of prayer from its exile is bound up with the rectification of the Earth element, which for Rebbe Nachman is the main key to healing, as discussed in his discourse, "Sound the Shofar — Faith" (see next chapter). The triads discussed in this

On Pesach the craving for wealth is rectified. Thus when the Jewish People left Egypt, "God gave the people favor in the sight of the Egyptians and they made them take [jewels etc.]" (Exodus 12:36) — "against the will of the Jews themselves" (Berakhot 9b), because they had no desire for them at all, since the craving for wealth was rectified then.[22] On Shavuot sexual craving is rectified,[23] for "the blood was congealed and turned into milk"[24] (see *Shaar HaKavanot, Sefirat*

---

discourse may also be related to the "three hands" in each of the three higher worlds, *Atzilut, Beriyah* and *Yetzirah*, that sweeten severe judgments in *pidyon nefesh* (Likutey Moharan I, 180, see p.193).

We see from the present discourse that the redemption of prayer, which is the foundation of healing, depends upon drawing *da'at* from the head into the heart. This seems to be connected with the idea of bringing healing to the body by vitalizing the pulses governing bodily functioning (the heart) through restoring the flow of spiritual influence from the ten sefirot of Abba (the head), as discussed earlier (see Chapter 12).

22. **since the craving for wealth was rectified then** The Jews abandoned the advanced material culture of Egypt in favor of the life of the spirit: they went out into the wilderness to receive the Torah. Today we spend money liberally to keep Pesach — it is the most expensive of the festivals — but the climax of Pesach is when we eat *lechem oni*, the "bread of poverty"! In preparation for the festival we give money for the poor to buy matzot, and we invite all who are hungry to come and eat. Charity rectifies the craving for wealth (*Likutey Moharan* I, 22:9).

23. **On Shavuot sexual craving is rectified** On Shavuot we celebrate the Receiving of the Torah. "This is the Torah — man" (Numbers 19:14). Not only does the Torah teach man how to lift himself above the physicality of this world. It also contains all the secrets of the form of the Supernal Man, in Whose image man was created. Devotion to Torah study is thus the perfect remedy for cravings for the physical human form.

24. **"the blood was congealed and turned into milk"** Milk is formed in the breast from nutrients that ultimately derive from the mother's blood. The concept of blood alludes to God's aspect of severity and concealment (*gevurot*), while milk alludes to His *chesed*, love and kindness. Prior to the revelation of the Torah, God was almost totally concealed from the world, and his aspect of severity was predominant. But at the time of the Giving of the Torah, God revealed Himself to the Jewish People from every direction, and they saw that even His aspect of limitation and severity is ultimately an expression of His love and kindness. Thus severity turned into kindness and the "blood" turned into "milk." The true milk of God's kindness is the Torah, which is called milk (Song of Songs 4:11). In the light of this, the earlier passage discussing the relationship between the milk a baby drinks and the intensity of his physical desires in later life (#4) can be interpreted not only literally but also on a spiritual plane to refer to the way that the quality of the Torah teachings ("milk")

HaOmer 9). On Sukkot the craving for food is rectified,[25] because Sukkot is called the "festival of ingathering" (Exodus 23:16) when we harvest all kinds of foods. This rectifies the craving for food, because "there's no comparison between a person with bread in his basket and someone without" (Yoma 74b) — someone who has what he needs does not feel the same insecurity and craving as someone who lacks it.

In the following paragraph, Rebbe Nachman brings supporting texts demonstrating that the three cravings for wealth, food and sex are all bound up with the concept of "names," or words. We can see an allusion here to the way that people who are sunk in these cravings often tend to use language in a distorted manner in order to enhance the objects of their desires and give them legitimacy. Thus the reverent terms in which people often speak of wealth in its various forms tends to add to its mystique, while the whole purpose of our advertising culture is to praise material products and give them a name. The world of gourmandise has an elaborate language of its own designed to whet the appetites of devotees of food. In the same way, sexually-charged language is used to arouse people's desires. From a spiritual point of view, all such uses of language debase and degrade the divinely-given faculty of speech, whose true purpose is to reveal the power of God in creation so that we should come to "fear this glorious and awesome Name of the Lord your God" (Deuteronomy 28:58).

In the phrase describing Korach's supporters, "the chosen men of the assembly, men of renown" (Numbers 16:2), the "men of renown," *anshey shem* (lit.

---

a Jew imbibes from his teacher affects his spiritual outlook and orientation. If the "mother" — the teacher (see *Likutey Moharan* I, 4:8) — is one of those whose influence is founded on brash self-assertiveness, his teachings will simply fan the flames of his followers' material cravings. The remedy is to turn the *gevurot* into *chasadim* by receiving the Torah from the true Tzaddik.

25. On Sukkot the craving for food is rectified The mitzvah of succah involves eating all our meals in the succah. The concept of the succah is one of constantly striving to attain higher and higher levels of spiritual perception and connection. By bringing the satisfaction of our physical needs within the shade of holiness, we are emphasizing that the true purpose of eating is not merely to gratify our bodily appetites but to give us the strength to pursue our spiritual purpose in this world. The other main mitzvah of Sukkot is that of the four species. We take the etrog (citron), which is a food, but instead of eating it, we put it aside in order to use it for the mitzvah.

"men with a name") denote these three cravings.[26] In each case we find the concept of "names" in relation to the objects of these cravings. With regard to wealth, it is written, "In every place where I cause My *Name* to be mentioned, I will come to you and *bless* you" (Exodus 20:21), and "The *blessing* of God is what makes a person wealthy" (Proverbs 10:22). With regard to eating, it is written,

---

26. **"men with a name" denote these three cravings** The concept of names and words recurs in several places in this discourse. Most important of all is the Name of God. God in Himself is intrinsically unknowable, and only through His Name can we come to know and revere Him. Bound up with the Name of God are the names of the great tzaddikim (*Likutey Moharan* II, 67). This is because the whole mission of the tzaddikim is to spread the knowledge of God and His Name throughout the world, and indeed the actual names of many of the tzaddikim mentioned in the Bible, Talmud, etc. are associated with the various names of God through *gematriot*, letter combinations, etc. The main advice in this discourse is that we should attach ourselves to the known leaders of the Jewish People — those who have a "name" — and the central issue is how to distinguish the true leaders from those who owe their name and reputation to brazen self-assertiveness.

When false leaders "have a name" and enjoy notoriety, the effect is to throw the name of the true tzaddikim into shadow, and with it the Name of God. Instead of people honoring God and those who truly fear Him, they give all the honor to false celebrities. The phrase "men with a name" actually refers to Korach and his associates, who although they were initially distinguished leaders, eventually stumbled and tried to besmirch the name of Moses. Korach and his associates were thus the archetypal false leaders of the Jewish People. The false leader fails to inspire his adherents to make genuine efforts to curtail their material cravings: on the contrary, the effect of his teachings is more likely to be to intensify them. Thus the "men with a name" also alludes to our material cravings, which tend to overshadow the spiritual side of our being.

The recurrent theme of names in this discourse is intimately bound up with the theme of healing. Rebbe Nachman discussed the significance of names in various places in his writings (see *Rabbi Nachman's Wisdom* #44 & #95 and *Rabbi Nachman's Tikkun* pp. 100-4). In these sources we see that a person's vitality is channeled to him through his name, which is rooted in the Name of God, the source of all vitality. Illness is caused by a lack of vitality. This results from a flaw in the flow of vitality from the ten sefirot of Abba, which shine through the letters of the associated Divine Name and vitalize the pulse (see pp.138-43). The flaw in the flow of energy from Abba may be caused by sin, which causes "men with a name" — materialistic desires — to come to the fore, causing the spiritual to become concealed. The art of healing is to restore the flow of holy vitality to the sick person. This is accomplished by giving honor to God's Name through prayer — to "fear this glorious and awesome Name of the Lord your God" (Deuteronomy 28:58).

"And call a *name* in Beit Lechem²⁷ (lit. the house of *bread*)" (Ruth 4:11). With regard to sexual desire, it says, "except if the king delighted in her and she were called by *name*" (Esther 2:14). The awe in the heart is also bound up with the concept of names, i.e. the Name of God, as it is written: "to fear this glorious and awesome Name of the Lord your God" (Deuteronomy 28:58). The Hebrew words for "the chosen men of the assembly," קראי מועד (*keri'ey mo'ed*), allude to calling (קרא, *kara*) and announcing the festivals²⁸ (a מועד, *mo'ed*, is an appointed season, a

---

27. **"And call a *name* in Beit Lechem"** "It is also written, 'And you will eat in plenty and be satisfied and you will praise the *name* of HaShem your God' (Joel 2:26). The purpose of eating is to give us the strength to come to know God through Torah study and to praise and give thanks to His Name in our prayers and blessings" (*Parpara'ot LeChokhmah #7*).

28. **calling and announcing the festivals** The timing of the festivals — days of light — is bound up with the phases of the moon, the luminary God created to light up the darkness of night. The Torah lays down on which date in the month each of the festivals falls, but when the month actually begins depends on the phases of the moon. As long as there was a Sanhedrin (supreme rabbinic court) in Eretz Israel, witnesses who had sighted the new moon would come and testify before the court, after which the head of the court would declare, "Sanctified," and all those present would also call out, "Sanctified." The fixing of the dates of the festivals thus depends upon "calling and announcing" the new moon.

The moon is a recurrent motif in this discourse (see #9 and #14). Unlike the sun, which constantly radiates with light of its own, the moon has no light of its own and sends us only reflected light. While the surface of the moon facing earth is sometimes fully visible, there are other times when it is only partially visible or even disappears completely. The relationship between the sun and the moon parallels the relationship between the upper sefirot — which send a constant flow of Godly light into the worlds — and the sefirah of Malkhut, which has no light of its own and is the focus of a struggle between the forces of holiness on the one hand and those of impurity on the other. At times the earth itself stands in the way of the light radiating from the sun, throwing the moon into shadow. To the extent that the "earth" — physicality and materialism — stand in the way of the flow of light from the higher sefirot, Godliness is concealed in this world and the forces of darkness and unholiness gain the upper hand. On the mystical level, the concept of the phases of the moon is integrally bound up with the struggle between good and evil in this world, which is what gives man his free will.

The power of the three cravings for wealth, food and sexual pleasure is rooted in the concealment of Godliness in this world, and therefore the remedy is to bring the light of *da'at* into the world. This comes about through honoring the festivals, and we can now understand why they all begin when the moon is either full or waxing, and why the timing of the festivals depends upon the sighting of the *new* moon, which signifies that the light of the moon is now beginning to increase.

festival). According to the above explanation, we see that implicit in the phrase "the chosen men of the assembly, men of renown," is the concept of announcing and celebrating the festivals in order to rectify the three cravings, which are called "men of renown."

Prophecy

In Temple times, when the Jewish People went up to Jerusalem for the pilgrim festivals, many reached high levels of prophetic inspiration. For the Temple, like the Sanctuary in early biblical times, was the source of prophetic spirit. This emanated from between the two cherubs over the Ark of the Covenant. Similarly, through the spiritual "rebuilding of Jerusalem," i.e. filling the heart with awe of God, the individual becomes receptive to prophetic spirit, which, as we will see presently (section #8), brings about the release of prayer from its "exile" (see Chapter 2).

#6. And through the rebuilding of Jerusalem, i.e. developing complete awe and reverence in the heart,[29] an angel is created[30] who sends down prophetic inspiration[31] to the vessels of prophecy. For prophecy comes from the

---

29. **the rebuilding of Jerusalem, i.e. developing complete awe and reverence in the heart** "The ultimate goal of the spiritual pathway explained in this discourse is to come to true humility. Only with humility can one gain any perception of God's glory. Humility is the key to awe and reverence for God, for 'the heel of humility is awe of God' (Proverbs 22:4), and when one attains humility, God accepts one's prayers" (*Torat Nathan #7*).

30. **an angel is created** We thus see that by rectifying the three cravings one already has power over the angels! After the conclusion of the text of this discourse as printed in the Hebrew edition of *Likutey Moharan*, we find the following: "Regarding prophecy, there is a question, because the angel that sends down prophetic inspiration, i.e. 'the angel who saved...' is *below* the place from which prophecy emanates, for this angel is the Shekhinah [= Malkhut] (see *Zohar* I, 166, 170, 228b etc.) and the Shekhinah is below the sefirot of Netzach and Hod, which are the sources of prophecy. Profound issues are involved here, because the Shekhinah rises up above them, and it is then that she sends down prophecy, but this is not our current concern."

31. **prophetic inspiration** We saw in Chapter 13 that Rebbe Nachman taught that the spirit of prophecy rests upon the prophet through the "hand" of the "musician" (= *simchah*, joy), which sifts the "good air," the good spirit, from the bad spirit of depression and animality (*Likutey Moharan* I, 54:6). The ability to find and see the good is integral to the celebration of the festivals, which are called Yom *Tov* (good), and which are times of special joy (Deuteronomy 16:14), and this is how we rectify the bad spirit of depression — our animalistic cravings — thereby attaining prophetic inspiration.

"cherubs," as it is written, "He heard the voice... from between the two *cherubs*" (Numbers 7:89). The cherubs had the faces of little children (*Zohar* I, 18b) and they receive the flow of blessing from the angel, as it is written, "And the *angel* who saved me from all evil will bless the children" (Genesis 48:16) — i.e. the cherubs, which have children's faces. The root of this angel lies in heavenly awe, which is why the letters of the Hebrew word for angel, מלאך (*MaL'AKh*), are the initial letters of the words כ'י א'ין מ'חסור ל'יראיו (*Ki Ein Machsor Li'yreyav*), "for nothing is lacking[32] to those who *fear* Him" (Psalms 34:10). Prophetic inspiration then comes into the world, and even children can prophesy — "And your sons and your daughters will prophesy" (Joel 3:1).

#7. But one must be very cautious about being appointed to a position of authority. A person who attains heavenly awe has a strong yearning to be appointed to a position of authority.[33] This is because "When a person has fear of heaven, his words are listened to" (*Berakhot* 6b), and because his words are listened to, he longs for a position of authority. But one must strongly guard oneself against this, because such a position holds back the flow of prophecy which comes from the angel created through awe. This explains why, when Joshua heard that "Eldad and Meidad are prophesying in the camp" (Numbers 11:27), he said "My lord Moses, close them up (כלאם, *KeLA'eM*)" (ibid. 28).[34] The Rabbis explained Joshua's words as meaning, "Make them take responsibility for the affairs of the community and they will automatically stop" (*Rashi ad loc.* and *Sanhedrin* 17a). The reason is that having responsibility for community affairs, i.e. a position of authority, stops the flow of prophecy, and the letters of the word מלאך (*MaL'AKh*), angel, are rearranged to form the word כלאם (*KeLA'eM*), "close them up."

---

32. **nothing is lacking** When a person experiences cravings, something is lacking. But when a person brings his cravings under control, nothing is lacking: all is harmony and balance.

33. **a strong yearning to be appointed to a position of authority** Someone who yearns to influence others because he is God-fearing and therefore his words are listened to would seem to be the opposite of a false leader. However, it often happens that people begin a career of leadership with the best of intentions but later become corrupted, as happened in the case of Korach, who turned against Moses, and Jeraboam ben Nevat (Kings I, 11-14).

34. **"My lord Moses, close them up"** Moses replied to Joshua, "If only all the People of God would be prophets, when God will put His spirit upon them" (Numbers 11:29). The true Tzaddik wants all Jews to come to their ultimate destiny and rise to the level of true prophecy and holy spirit (*Parpara'ot LeChokhmah #9*).

The redemption of prayer

Rebbe Nachman now turns directly to the subject of prayer. The flow of prophetic inspiration that comes through the "rebuilding of Jerusalem" brings about the release of prayer from its "exile," and when people rediscover the pathways of true prayer there is no more need for medicine, because healing power can be drawn down through prayer alone.

#8. And through the flow of prophetic inspiration,[35] even though there may be no one to actually prophesy, the very fact that prophetic inspiration is present in the world brings about the release and redemption of prayer.[36] For prayer is most exalted,[37] but human beings take it lightly, and when they stand

---

35. **the flow of prophetic inspiration** Having prophetic inspiration does not necessarily mean that one knows the future, but that one has attained an exalted level of holy spirit and attachment to God. "When a person concentrates intently on his prayers, directing his heart to Heaven and pouring out his soul to God as if speaking to Him face to face... this is the spirit of prophecy" (*Parpara'ot LeChokhmah* #11, and see *Likutey Moharan* I, 138).

36. **the release and redemption of prayer** "The redemption of prayer and the release of the souls from the three kinds of servitude discussed below (#10) are one and the same thing" (*Biur HaLikutim* #26).

37. **prayer is most exalted** Prayer is the very center of Rebbe Nachman's healing pathway. He will point out later (#11) that it was because King Hezekiah redeemed prayer that he was able to put away the Book of Remedies. The true dominion of the Jewish People is exercised through prayer. Today prayer is in exile and its power is largely unknown. But when prayer is redeemed, all Jews will be able to bring about exalted wonders through their prayers, just as the Baal Shem Tov did (*Keter Shem Tov* #1).

It is noteworthy that in this discourse about the redemption of prayer, Rebbe Nachman alludes to all thirteen intermediate blessings of the main prayer in the Jewish liturgy, the *Shemoneh Esrey* (*Amidah*, or standing prayer). The subject of the first blessing is *da'at*, which Rebbe Nachman speaks about in #5 of this discourse. In the second blessing we ask God to bring us near to His service. Rebbe Nachman discusses the concept of "service" in #9 and #10. Forgiveness for sin, the theme of the third blessing, is discussed in #14, while redemption, the subject of the fourth blessing, is discussed in the current section (#8). Healing, for which we pray in the fifth blessing, is the theme of #9-11, and from Rebbe Nachman's discussion of the relationship between the redemption of prayer and healing, we can understand why the blessing for healing immediately follows the blessing for redemption. Rain, for which we pray in the sixth blessing, is discussed in #12, while the ingathering of the exiles, subject of the seventh blessing, is heralded by the blast of the shofar of redemption (#14 end), and is also bound up with guarding the Covenant, the abuse of which causes divine sparks to be exiled and scattered throughout the creation.

up to pray they want to get it over with. Thus the Rabbis, in their comment on the verse, "When that which is exalted is held cheap among the sons of men" (Psalms 12:9), said, "This refers to words that stand on the exalted summit of the world [i.e. prayer], but the sons of men despise them" (*Berakhot* 6a). But through the flow of prophetic inspiration, prayer is released from its exile. Thus it is written of Abraham, "For he is a *prophet* and he will pray for you"[38] (Genesis 20:7). Prophecy brings about the perfection of prayer, for prayer itself is a form of prophecy (נבואה, *NeVu'ah*), as it is writtten, "He creates the fruit (ניב, *NiV*) of the lips" (Isaiah 57:19).

Healing power from the "Word of God"

#9. And when prayer is freed and redeemed, the whole of medicine falls, because there is no need for medicines.[39] All medicines are derived from plants,

---

Guarding the Covenant is discussed in #10. The discussion about judgment in #14 relates to the eighth blessing for the restoration of our judges, while the references to faith in #10 relate to the ninth blessing against atheists and heretics. The entire discourse is concerned with the tzaddikim, who are the true leaders of the Jewish People, for whom we pray in the tenth blessing. The eleventh blessing is a prayer for the rebuilding of Jerusalem, which is discussed in #4, while the twelfth blessing is a prayer for Mashiach, discussed in #12. The thirteenth intermediate blessing of the *Shemoneh Esrey* is a general appeal to God to hear our prayers, and prayer is the central theme of this entire discourse.

38. **and he will pray for you** This verse was spoken to Avimelech when he was sick (see pp. 22-4). Abraham's prayer was for healing.

39. **there is no need for medicines** It seems that some people feel threatened by Rebbe Nachman's warnings against going to doctors because they cannot imagine how illness might be cured without medicine, and they fear that without it they would be left with no weapon with which to combat ill health. But here Rebbe Nachman is saying that when prayer is truly redeemed, medicine simply becomes unnecessary and superfluous because healing can come about through the power of words and prayer alone. If the world is seen as nothing but a mechanistic system determined by inexorable laws of nature, it is certainly hard to imagine how healing can come about through mere words. Yet we all know the power of words to destroy people's happiness and indeed their very lives, and "if you believe you can destroy, believe that you can repair" (*Likutey Moharan* II, 112).

Rebbe Nachman's teachings in this discourse about the power of words to bring about healing relate to ideas he developed in his discourse, "*The days of Chanukah are days of thanksgiving*" (*Likutey Moharan* II, 2) given a few months later, when he discussed how speech is perfected by letting the light of truth radiate to the mouth. "And with perfect speech

and every single plant receives its powers from its own particular planet or star, because "there isn't a single plant that doesn't have a planet or star that strikes it and says, 'Grow!'" (*Bereshit Rabbah* 10). Every planet and star receives its power from the stars above it, and the highest stars from the higher powers, until they receive power from the supreme angels, as we are taught (*Tikkuney Zohar* #44, #79b), "All the stars borrow one from another: the moon borrows from the sun, etc. 'for one higher than the high guards, and over them are those who are even higher' (*Ecclesiastes* 5:7)." All of the stars borrow one from the next, until they receive and borrow from the supreme angels, and the angels receive from the powers beyond them, one higher than the other, until they all receive from the root of all things, which is the Word of God,[40] as it is written, "Through the word of God the heavens were made and all their hosts by the breath of His mouth" (*Psalms* 33:6).

This explains why, when we attain prayer, there is no need for plant-based medicines. The reason is that prayer is "the Word of God," which is the root of all things. Thus the four letters of the Hebrew word for prophet, נביא (*NaVIE*), are related to the initial letters of the four words נ'עשו ש'מים י' ב'דבר (*Bid'var YHVH Shamayim Na'asu*), "Through the word of God the heavens were made."[41] Three of the four words in this phrase start with three of the letters in the word נביא (*NaVIE*) — i.e. 'י ב' נ' — while the ש (*shin*) of the fourth word, שמים (*Shamayim*, "heaven"), corresponds to the א (*aleph*) in נביא (*NaVIE*), because "*aleph* is the firmament (heaven) separating between the waters and the waters" (*Tikkuney Zohar* #5 & #40). For through prophecy we attain prayer, which is "the Word of God." Thus, "He sent His word and healed them, and delivered them from their abominations" (*Psalms* 107:20). "He sent His *word* and healed them" — i.e. all cures are received only through the Word of God, namely prayer. And then, "He saved them from their abominations (שחיתותם,

---

one can accomplish whatever one wants through words, and one can change nature at will" (*ibid.* #6).

40. **the Word of God** The kabbalists point out that this phrase alludes to the Shekhinah (*Iggeret HaKodesh* #25).

41. **Through the word of God the heavens were made** The "heavens" symbolize the soul (*Sanhedrin* 91b). The soul is "made" — cultivated and developed — through the Word of God, i.e. prayer, for by expressing our yearning and desire to serve God in words of prayer, we actualize our spiritual potential (*Likutey Moharan* I, 31). And it is the soul that brings healing to the body.

shechitotam)" — i.e. from their herbs,[42] as in the phrase "harvesting for fodder (שחת, *shachat*)" (*Menachot* 71a) because there is no longer any need for medicines produced from herbs.

The bread and water cure

In the preceding section, Rebbe Nachman set forth the central concept of his healing pathway, which is that true prayer, the "Word of God," channels healing power directly from the very source of all creation without the need for herbs and medicines. In the course of the following sections of the discourse Rebbe Nachman uses this concept to explain a number of key biblical and rabbinic texts on the subject of healing. The first is the verse, "And you will serve the Lord your God, and He will bless your bread and your water; and remove sickness from among you" (Exodus 23:25).

"And you will serve the Lord your God, and He will bless your bread and your water; and I will remove sickness from among you" (Exodus 23:25). "And you will *serve* the Lord your God" — "*service* means prayer" (*Bava Kama* 92b). And then, "He will bless your bread and your water, and remove sickness, etc." In other words, you will be healed through bread and water,[43] because they will

---

42. **abominations, i.e. herbs** Medicinal herbs are amazing and miraculous, but when man depends on them exclusively and allows himself to become their servant, they become as abominable as the objects of idolatrous worship. It is also obvious that when medicines are administered wrongly they can be extremely destructive.

43. **you will be healed through bread and water** The body is a physical entity, and from Rebbe Nachman's words here it appears that when the body is sick, healing may have to be channeled to it through some physical means. The late Lubavitcher Rebbe, R. Menachem Mendel Shneerson, related: "I heard once from the previous Rebbe that a very sick person came to the Alter Rebbe (R. Shneuer Zalman, the founder of ChaBaD), and he healed him with a piece of *shemurah matzah* (used to fulfil the mitzvah of eating matzah on the first night of Pesach) and half a glass of water. You see, at any rate there has to be at least some involvement with nature" ((*Refuah Shelemah* p. 33).

Even those who want to depend primarily on faith and prayer for healing still often wonder how much effort they need to make in the physical realm in order to create the necessary "vessel" through which healing energy can be channeled into the body. From the current discourse it seems clear that in Rebbe Nachman's view, the main effort must be in the spiritual realm, and then even one's regular food and drink ("bread and water") can serve as the channel to bring healing energy into the body. On another level, "bread and water" can be seen as an allusion to Torah study and prayer. Thus Rebbe Nachman

receive blessing from the root of all things, namely the Word of God — prayer — and bread and water will have the same power to heal as herbs. For the division and allocation of the various powers, which give one plant the power to cure one kind of illness and another a different illness, is found only in the lower world. But above, at the root of all, that is the Word of God, everything is unity,[44] and there is no difference between bread and water and plants and herbs. When one grasps the root, the Word of God, meaning prayer, one is able to channel curative powers into bread and water,[45] and one can be healed through bread and water, "and He will bless your bread and water, and remove sickness...."

---

said, "Happy is the person who eats many chapters of Mishnah (Torah) and drinks many Psalms (prayer)" (*Rabbi Nachman's Wisdom #23*).

44. **at the root of all... everything is unity** The root of all is the Word of God, i.e. prayer. Thus Rebbe Nachman teaches that hisbodedus *"includes everything, because no matter what one needs in one's service of God... one can put it into words and ask Him for it"* (*Likutey Moharan* II, 25).

45. **one is able to channel curative powers into bread and water** As we have seen, bread and water were the food of the Simpleton in Rebbe Nachman's story of the *Sophisticate and the Simpleton* (*Rabbi Nachman's Stories* pp. 168-73, and see above pp. 115-6). Rebbe Nachman told this story towards the end of the winter of 1808-9, just a few months after giving the current discourse. The Simpleton's ability to taste all the tastes in the world in his bread and water is clearly related to the concept of grasping the root of all things, i.e. the Word of God, where "everything is unity and there is no difference between bread and water and plants and herbs... and one is able to channel curative powers into bread and water."

The way we actually channel blessing into our literal bread and water and other foods is through the blessings we make over what we eat and drink. Thus Reb Noson writes: "The various blessings we make are the 'Word of God.' Through the blessing, the item of food or drink is elevated to its source — the Word of God — and this is the essential purpose of the blessing. This is why, when we make a blessing over our food and drink, we have no need to take anything else in order to be cured of illness. For the blessing itself is a prayer — the concept of prayer includes all our various blessings and expressions of thanksgiving to God. As a prayer, the blessing is the 'Word of God,' which is the Supreme Source of all things. When the Supreme Source, the Word of God, is aroused, the individual item over which we make the blessing returns to its source, and here all the powers that are separate in the lower worlds are merged in perfect unity. This is why we need nothing else in order to be healed, because we can draw curative powers into our usual food and drink by means of the Word of God. This is why the verse says, 'He will *bless* your bread and water and remove sickness from within you' — for all the necessary curative powers are drawn into one's regular food and drink" (*Torat Nathan #14*).

Three destroyers

As we have seen, prayer is "service." But just as the three cravings for wealth, food and sexual pleasure destroy the awe and awareness of God in the heart, so there are three other forms of "service" that destroy prayer. These are: looking down on other people, idolatry (flawed faith) and sexual immorality. Rebbe Nachman will bring supporting texts to show that these three are all forms of "servitude." Thus we see that those who despise other people become locked into an attitude that divides the world into superior and inferior people, and inevitably they themselves feel subordinate to those they consider superior. As regards idolatry, we have already seen that Rebbe Nachman viewed dependence on the means of healing, making a living, etc. rather than upon God, as a form of idolatry (Likutey Moharan I, 62:6). Thus people tend to become enslaved to their businesses, medicines and all the other things they look to as their means of salvation and security in various areas of life. When it comes to immorality, it is easy to see how people become enslaved to the dictates of their passions. In the course of his discussion of these three forms of servitude, Rebbe Nachman gives a novel explanation of a second key Torah text on healing, the rabbinic statement that "One can be cured by any means except idolatry, immorality and bloodshed" (Pesachim 25a). Literally this means that any Torah prohibition besides these three may be violated to treat a critically sick person.

#10. But there are three forms of "service" which destroy prayer.[46] These are three negative traits: (1) Looking down on other people, failing to live by

---

46. three forms of "service" which destroy prayer The true service is prayer, but the three forms of servitude Rebbe Nachman discusses here are really slavery. Thus (1) when a person lacks faith that God is in control of everything and provides him with what he needs, he puts his faith in the *means* by which he makes a living, seeks to be cured of illness, etc. and feels as if he has no option but to do whatever seems necessary to secure what he needs through these means, as if God would not be able to provide his needs through other means. Because of his lack of faith, he becomes a slave to the means. (2) At the outset a person can control his sexual thoughts and desires and turn his mind elsewhere, but if he indulges them, they soon become compulsive and he becomes their slave. By turning the physical body into an object of worship he degrades both the objects of his passions and himself. (3) When a person looks down on others, his false perceptions prevent him from viewing the world as it really is and seeing God's glory in all people. Instead, he becomes a slave to his own misconceptions. In addition, "Anyone who tarnishes others is himself tarnished" (*Kiddushin* 70a), and by looking down on others, he is really looking down

the injunction, "Don't despise anyone" (*Avot* 4:3);[47] (2) Idolatry — and anything less than perfect faith in God is also tantamount to idolatry; (3) Immorality, failure to guard the Covenant properly. Each of these traits is an unholy form of "service" and destroys the true service, which is that of prayer. Thus we find

---

on himself and putting himself into the category of an inferior, a slave. These three traits are an insult to the dignity of man, *Adam,* and those who are sunken in them are therefore unable to "take hold of the throne," which is the "seat" of the Supernal Man, in Whose image man is made. "These three forms of servitude are themselves responsible for the exile of prayer, causing prayer itself to seem weighty and burdensome. As Rebbe Nachman said earlier in the discourse (#8): 'When they stand up to pray, they want to get it over with.' Prayer itself comes to be experienced as a form of servitude!" (*Biur HaLikutim* #25).

Reb Noson writes: "It is striking that the Rebbe enumerates sexual desire twice in this discourse: the first time as one of the three cravings that destroy Jerusalem, and the second time as one of the three forms of 'service' that spoil prayer. But there is an important difference between the three kinds of slavery discussed here and the three cravings discussed earlier. For the three forms of slavery are traits that must be totally broken and removed. On the other hand, the three cravings for wealth, food and sexual satisfaction contain both good and evil, and our task is to sift out the good while rejecting the evil. Thus greed for wealth is certainly evil, but we need money in order to provide for our true needs and to keep the mitzvot. Similarly, excessive indulgence even in permitted sexual activity with one's spouse is destructive, yet the sexual relationship is one of the foundations of married life and is obviously indispensable in order to fulfil the command to 'be fruitful and multiply,' and we must do so in holiness and purity. So too, overindulgence in food is evil, yet it is impossible to survive without food, and we must eat with dignity and holiness, especially on Shabbat and the festivals. But when it comes to the three forms of slavery, idolatry, immorality and despising others, we must totally remove them from ourselves. Even a seemingly minor flaw in faith is tantamount to idolatry and must be removed. In the same way we must totally cleanse our minds of all sexual thoughts and desires that involve forms of sexual activity that are not permitted by Torah law. And so too, we must certainly never despise anyone in the world..." (*Torat Nathan* #11).

47. **"Don't despise anyone"** Reb Noson writes: "This applies to the way we look at ourselves as well. Just as we must not despise others, in the same way we must not look down upon ourselves. For we don't even know our own place, let alone the place of anyone else. For we certainly do not know the root cause of everything we have gone through in all our incarnations, or the true source of all our evil thoughts and desires. For this reason, we must never give up hope or criticize ourselves excessively and lose our self-respect. On the contrary, we must judge ourselves positively" (*Torat Nathan* #13). As we have seen, searching for one's good points in order to attain simchah is an integral part of Rebbe Nachman's healing pathway (see pp.163ff.).

that despising other people leads to slavery. Joseph's brothers despised him and did not believe he would be king. As a result they fell into slavery and eventually said to him, "Here we are, your slaves" (Genesis 50:18). Idolatry is the religion of slaves. Thus it is written, "I am the Lord your God Who brought you out of the land of Egypt, out of the house of slaves" (Exodus 20:2). For Egypt was full of idols and cults, and for that reason is called the "house of slaves." Thirdly, a person who violates the Covenant and succumbs to immorality also falls into slavery, which is associated with Ham, the father of Canaan,[48] of whom it is said, "Cursed be Canaan, let him be a slave of slaves to his brothers" (Genesis 9:25).

Only when one emerges from these three forms of slavery, i.e. from these three traits, can one attain prayer. One can then be cured with anything in the world, even bread and water.[49] We can now see a new dimension of meaning in the Torah principle that, where there is a threat to life, one may violate any prohibition except three: "One can be cured by any means except idolatry, immorality and bloodshed" (*Pesachim* 25a). "One can be cured by any means" — i.e. one can be cured by anything in the world. But there is a condition: "excepting idolatry, immorality and bloodshed." These are the three evil traits discussed above, which are three forms of slavery. When one becomes free of them, "one can be cured by any means," even with bread and water, because

---

48. **Ham, the father of Canaan** When Noah became drunk and was uncovered in his tent, his son Ham, the father of Canaan, "saw the nakedness of his father," and, according to the Rabbis, castrated him or lay with him (Genesis 9:22 and *Rashi ad loc.*), which is why Noah cursed him. Thus Ham, whose name means "hot" or "passionate," is associated with sexual misdemeanor.

49. **Only when one emerges... One can then be cured with anything in the world...**
Rebbe Nachman summed up the essence of the healing pathway elaborated in this discourse in the first item in the chapter on Healing in his *Aleph-Bet Book*: "Know that each herb has a unique power to heal a particular illness. But all this is only for the person who has failed to guard his faith and morality and has not been careful to avoid transgressing the prohibition against despising others (*Avot* 4:3). But when someone has perfect faith, guards himself morally, and lives by the principle of not looking down on anyone at all, his healing does not depend on the specific herbs that have the power to cure his illness. Such a person can be healed through any food and any drink, as it is written, 'And He will bless your bread and your water, and remove sickness from you' (Exodus 23:25). Such a person does not have to wait until the specific remedy for his illness is available" (*Aleph-Bet Book*, Healing #1).

when one emerges from these three forms of slavery one attains the service of prayer, and can then be healed through anything in the world.

Prevention and cure

In the following section, Rebbe Nachman explains a third key Torah text on healing: "If you will listen carefully to the voice of HaShem your God and do what is right in His eyes, and give ear to His commandments and keep all His statutes, I will put none of the diseases upon you that I have put on the Egyptians, for I am HaShem your Healer" (Exodus 15:26). Through careful textual analysis Rebbe Nachman will show that the three aspects of devotion mentioned in this verse — doing what is right in God's eyes, giving ear to His commandments, and keeping His statutes — are the remedy for the three forms of "slavery" that destroy prayer, as discussed earlier. Rebbe Nachman addresses the apparent contradiction in the key verse: if God "will put none of the diseases upon you that I have put on the Egyptians," why is He "your Healer"? There should be no illnesses to heal! In answering this, Rebbe Nachman points out that an illness may be present in the body in an embryonic state of development even when it is not detectable in the form of overt physical symptoms. The path of prayer can bring healing to incipient or latent illnesses as well as to those that are fully developed. The path of prayer is thus preventive, conferring immunity, as well as being a healing pathway when an illness has already developed. This section of the discourse is of particular interest in view of the contemporary recognition of the importance of a strong immune system in healthcare.

#11. And know that there are different kinds of illness. There is a kind of illness which develops the way a plant does. When a seed is sown in the ground the husk decomposes and a fatty substance emerges which turns into strands which steadily multiply and become the root. From this emerge branches, and from them more branches, until eventually the fruit blossoms. In the same way there is a form of illness that develops in a person over the course of years. On the other hand, there are certain illnesses that people are born with, inheriting them from their parents, though the illness may not manifest itself until old age. During the developmental stages of the illness, it is hidden and concealed from the eye of all living, and nobody knows of it, although the person with the illness may begin to feel certain sensations that are symptomatic of the illness.

There are also differences between medicines.[50] There are illnesses that can be cured by a single herb, but more serious illnesses may require compounds of a variety of herbs in order to cure them. Sometimes the illness calls for drugs that grow in far-off places. And there are illnesses which no medicine has the power to cure, because the illness is too strong to be cured by herbs. In the initial stages of its development, before it spread and manifested itself outwardly, it could have been cured quite easily, but then it was hidden and concealed from the eyes of all, and nobody knew of it except for God.

Yet when one attaches oneself to the Word of God, prayer, one can be cured by anything in the world, even bread and water, because "One can be cured by any means," as discussed above. One can be cured even when the disease is still in its early stages of development,[51] while it is still hidden from the eyes of men, since one has no need for medicines at all as one's "medicine" is bread and water. Therefore even then, when the illness is not revealed, one can also be cured through the bread and water one eats at the time.

It is written, "If you will listen carefully to the voice of HaShem your God and do what is right in His eyes, and give ear to His commandments and keep all His statutes, I will put none of the diseases upon you that I have put on the Egyptians, for I am HaShem your Healer" (Exodus 15:26). All the commentators raise the obvious question: If He will not put the diseases upon us, what need is there for healing? (See *Rashi, Ramban* and *Kli Yakar ad loc.* and *Sanhedrin* 101a.) But in the light of the above discussion, the question is resolved quite satisfactorily. "I will put none of the diseases upon you..." i.e. He will not bring you to an actual illness, because He will heal you beforehand, while the illness is still developing. "For *I am HaShem* your Healer" — i.e. during the developmental

---

50. **differences between medicines** Rebbe Nachman's statements in this section of the discourse bear out our earlier contention (p. 218) that he did accept, at least in principle, that medicines have the power to cure.

51. **One can be cured even when the disease is still in its early stages of development...** It is nothing but miraculous that our bodies are constantly prey to all kinds of incipient illnesses, yet in most cases they are cured before anything serious develops. This is what we thank God for in the *Nishmat* prayer: "You spared us from severe, numerous and enduring diseases" (Shabbat and festival liturgy). Nevertheless, we are usually unaware of the extent of such miracles, because "the person for whom a miracle is performed does not recognize the miracle" (*Niddah* 31a).

stages of the illness, when no one knows of it except for God,[52] then *"I will heal you"* through the Word of God, prayer. It will never reach the stage of an actual illness,[53] because it will be cured before this, while still developing.

All this depends upon prayer with true devotion, which entails emerging from the three kinds of slavery[54] discussed above. Rectifying these three traits is alluded to in the same verse: "If you will listen carefully to the voice of HaShem your God and do what is right in His eyes, and give ear to His commandments and keep all His statutes...." Doing "what is right (ישׁר, *yashar*) in His eyes" is the opposite of despising other people. For someone who abuses another person will eventually have to repent and "ישׁר (*yashor*), come before men and say, 'I have sinned and perverted what was right (ישׁר, *yashar*)...'" (Job 33:27 and see *Yoma* 87a). The idea of "giving ear to His *commandments*" is that of guarding the Covenant, which is the foundation of all the commandments,

---

52. **when no one knows of it except for God** Rebbe Nachman's discussion here helps us to understand the wording of the blessing after relieving oneself (*Asher yatzar...*): "It is *revealed and known before Your Throne of Glory* that if just one [of the many openings and cavities in the body] were to be ruptured or blocked, it would be impossible to survive and stand before You even for a brief moment." This is revealed and known before God's Throne of Glory, but it is not revealed to anyone else, because God alone knows of it! The reference in the blessing to the Throne of Glory also becomes understandable from this discourse.

53. **It will never reach the stage of an actual illness** Clearly Rebbe Nachman's pathway in this discourse is one of prevention just as much as cure. It is true that Rebbe Nachman endorsed the use of medical means of prevention in the case of the smallpox vaccination (see above pp. 203f.). Yet it is evident from this discourse that he viewed the spiritual pathway elaborated here as being the true foundation of good health and prevention. This point of view is virtually identical with that of the Ramban, who wrote: "When the Jewish People are in a state of spiritual perfection, their physical bodies... are not governed by nature at all. This applies to the nation as a whole and to each individual Jew. For God 'will bless their bread and their water, and remove illness from their midst.' They will have no need for doctors, *nor will they have to follow medical procedures even as precautionary measures*, 'For I, God, am your healer'" (Ramban, Commentary on the Torah, Leviticus 26:11; see above p. 195).

54. **emerging from the three kinds of slavery** Rebbe Nachman does not seem to give an explicit explanation of how to overcome these three forms of servitude, but the answer is implicit: through striving to follow the spiritual pathway taught by the true Tzaddik, who is totally clean of all three traits, and is the perfect exemplar of faith and purity, and judges everyone favorably.

and thus "Abraham circumcised Isaac his son when he was eight days old just as God *commanded* him" (Genesis 21:4). "And keep all His *statutes*" implies developing one's faith to perfection, the opposite of idolatry and imperfect faith, of which it is said, "the *statutes* of the nations are vanity" (Jeremiah 10:3).

When we fulfil all this, then "I will put none of the diseases upon you that I have put on the Egyptians, for I am HaShem your Healer." For then one attains perfect prayer and can be healed by the Word of God through anything in the world, even before the illness becomes outwardly manifest — "One can be cured by any means." (And even when the illness has already developed, as in a case where a person has not merited healing beforehand, even so, he can still be cured through the Word of God, even from a fully developed illness, as it is written, "And He will bless your bread and your water; and I will remove *sickness* from among you," i.e. even a fully developed illness, because through the Word of God one can always be cured through anything in the world.)[55]

King Hezekiah and the Book of Remedies

Rebbe Nachman's essential point about healing in this discourse is that by redeeming prayer from its "exile" it is possible to heal without recourse to medicine. Rebbe Nachman now shows that this is precisely the pathway

---

55. **And even when the illness has already developed... one can always be cured through anything in the world** The few lines printed here in parentheses are printed in the Hebrew version of *Likutey Moharan* as a gloss at the side of the main text. The point expressed here is of the utmost importance, because it proves that the pathway explained in this discourse is not only one of health and prevention but also one of actual healing from fully developed illnesses. It is difficult to understand why such an important point was inserted as a gloss rather than being incorporated in the main text. It is out of the question that Reb Noson, who authored the glosses on *Likutey Moharan*, would have inserted such a comment on his own initiative unless he was perfectly certain that Rebbe Nachman had made this statement. Possibly Rebbe Nachman did not make it when he originally taught the discourse on Rosh Hashanah 1808, but instructed Reb Noson to add it when he subsequently brought his transcription to the Rebbe for checking, as he usually did. (There are numerous other places in *Likutey Moharan* where we find that Rebbe Nachman made emendations and additions to his discourses after they had been transcribed.) Of course, if the whole world followed this pathway as a way of life, no illness would ever develop, and then indeed the fact that this pathway also has the power to cure actual illnesses would indeed become merely academic.

instituted by King Hezekiah, who "put away the Book of Remedies" (see above pp. 18f.).

When King Hezekiah fell sick and prayed to God, he said, "I have done what is good in Your eyes" (Isaiah 38:3). Our Rabbis said he was referring to the fact that he "joined redemption and prayer" (i.e. he introduced the rule that the Amidah prayer should be recited directly after the blessing of Redemption that follows the *Shema*) and he put away the Book of Remedies (Berakhot 10b). It is all one idea, because through joining redemption and prayer, i.e. through redeeming prayer from its exile, he was able to put away the Book of Remedies. For when prayer is redeemed, all the medicines fall away, because one can be healed through the Word of God. And then all the doctors are ashamed of their remedies,[56] because no medicine has any power, as all the healing plants put their power back into prayer, which is the Word of God, their supreme Source.

For all the plants and herbs of the field are obliged to do this. When a man rises to pray — and this is the Word of God, their supreme Source — they give back their power and put it into the prayer, which is their supreme source. When a person prays for a cure to an illness, the herbs which have the power to cure that illness are obliged to give back their power and put it into the prayer, which is their source, the Word of God. Thus "Isaac went out to pray (לשוח, *laSuaCh*) in the field" (Genesis 24:63): his prayer was *with* the herbs (שיח, *SiaCh*) of the field, because all the herbs of the field returned their power and put it into his prayer,[57] which was their root.

---

56. **ashamed of their remedies** A person feels shame when he becomes aware of his own shortcomings, especially in an area in which he previously experienced feelings of pride. The implication is that spiritual healing is superior to any medical cure. The idea that medicine has no *power* when prayer is redeemed seems to be linked with Rebbe Nachman's teaching that in time to come, when the world will be seen to be governed only through divine providence and prayer, the natural order will no longer operate as such, for (Isaiah 51:6) "the heavens will vanish away like smoke and the earth will be worn out like a garment" (*cf. Likutey Moharan* I, 250; see *Supplementary Readings* pp. 436-7). The shame of the doctors over the powerlessness of their remedies is parallel to the shame experienced by the false leaders in the face of the true Master of Prayer as discussed in #13 of the discourse.

57. **all the herbs of the field put their power into his prayer** This idea is connected with Rebbe Nachman's teaching that "when the summer begins to approach, it is very good to meditate in the fields... When every bush of the field begins to return to life and grow, they all yearn to be included in prayer and meditation" (*Rabbi Nachman's Wisdom* #98 and cf. *ibid.* #144 & #227, and *Likutey Moharan* II, 11). Reb Noson writes: "The idea that the various forces in the

Mashiach

With the above reference to Isaac's prayer "with the herbs of the field," Rebbe Nachman concludes his direct treatment of the theme of healing in this discourse, though some of the later sections have an important bearing on the subject. The redemption of prayer from its exile is nothing less than the redemption of the Jewish People by Mashiach from their servitude to the nations and to the laws of nature. The implication is that Mashiach is the true Master of Prayer, and all the prayers of individual Jews feed into Mashiach's prayers. For each individual Jew is a "plant" or "tree" in the "Garden of the Souls," and his prayers are the "fragrant scent" emanating from the plant. Mashiach, who is the "Master of the Field" (see Garden of the Souls), *goes out to pray "in the field," as it were, and the "herbs of the field" — the souls — return their power and put it into his prayer, which is their root, as discussed above.*

---

lower worlds, such as the herbs and plants and the angels above them, are obliged to give back their power to its source, the Word of God, is connected with the kabbalistic concept that the lower worlds rise up step by step through our prayers until they become merged with their source, for the multiple powers down below must all rise upwards and return to their unitary source, which is the Word of God, i.e. prayer" (*Torat Nathan* #8).

Reb Noson also writes: "The main thing is that whenever a person derives any kind of energy or vitality from things in this world, such as when he eats or drinks, wears clothes, uses money, etc., he must know and believe that everything derives from the 'Word of God,' i.e. the prayers of the true tzaddikim. For everything in the world ultimately comes from the earth: everything that grows comes from the earth, as do silver and gold and everything else. The earth in turn receives everything it gives us from higher powers, all of which receive and borrow from one another, until eventually all of them borrow from the Great Lender. Therefore anyone who takes anything from the world is receiving it in the form of a loan — a loan that he must pay back to the Great Lender. The way to repay him is by pouring all the strength and vitality gained from what he has taken from the world into his prayers. He must bind his prayers to the Great Lender, so that his prayers, together with all the power and energy they contain, will become part of the prayer of the Great Lender. The prayer of the Tzaddik then has the power to rise higher and higher, and sends greater and greater power back into the lower worlds. The more people pay their debts to the Tzaddik, who is the Great Lender, the more he is able to channel blessing and goodness back into the world. The recipients must then return all this power to the Tzaddik, who can then in turn channel ever greater blessings and goodness back into the world. If everyone were to play their part in this, the Jewish People would again enjoy all goodness and blessing!" (*ibid.* #10)

#12. When the plants and herbs return their powers and put them into prayer, Mashiach[58] shines forth. For all things are differentiated from one another by their appearance, taste and scent — which is why the Hebrew word for "rain," which is what causes all vegetation to grow, is מטר (*matar*): the letters of מ'ט'ר are the initial letters of the Hebrew words for appearance, taste and scent, מ'ראה (*Mar'eh*), ט'עם (*Ta'am*) and ר'יח (*Rei'ach*). Of these, the most important is scent, because it is only from a thing's scent that the *soul* has enjoyment, as our Rabbis taught: "What is it that the soul enjoys but not the body? Fragrant odors" (*Berakhot 43b*). Now prayer emanates from the soul, as it is written, "Let every *soul* praise God" (Psalms 150:6). Mashiach receives all the prayers [to elevate them to God], because Mashiach is the "nose," as it is written, "The breath of our *nostrils*, God's annointed (*Mashiach*)" (Lamentations 4:20). It is the nose which receives all the scents, i.e. the prayers, because prayer, which comes from the soul, feeds from the scent, as we noted above. Thus prayer is associated with the nose, as it is written, "And My praise is that I will restrain My anger (אחטם, *eChToM*) for your sake" (Isaiah 48:9). [The literal meaning is that God is to be praised for patiently bearing the sins of the Jewish People, but the verse is also teaching that prayer, "My praise," requires a long breath of patience before one sees results.[59] Thus prayer is an aspect of "the nose" (חוטם, *ChoTeM*), through which we breathe.] This is why he is called משיח, *Mashiach*, because he receives his "nourishment" from the herbs (שיח, *Si'aCh*) of the field, i.e. from all the scents[60] which come into the prayer, which

---

58. **Mashiach** "The pathway explained in this discourse, which is intended to lead to the repair of the whole world, was begun by King David, who gave birth to Solomon, שלמה, *ShLoMoH* (the Hebrew letters of whose name spell out המשל, *HaMoSheL*, the Ruler). Shlomo sat upon the throne and ruled over the angels above as well as all the hosts in the lower worlds. Nevertheless the ultimate rectification, which is nothing less than the establishment of God's kingdom upon earth and the dominion of Israel, can be completed only by Mashiach" (*Biur HaLikutim #22*).

59. **prayer requires a long breath of patience before one sees results** cf. *Likutey Moharan* I, 2 for the concept of the long breath of patience.

60. **all the scents** The Hebrew for scent is ריח (*ReYaCh*). This word is made up of the same letters as the ירח (*YaReiaCh*), the moon. As we have seen, the moon is one of the most important recurrent motifs in this discourse (see note #28). Of Mashiach it is written, "*VehaReYCho* — his delight will be in the fear of God" (Isaiah 11:3). Mashiach's task is to bring the world to know God — i.e. to bring *da'at* from the "head" down into the "heart." This is accomplished through prayer, the rectification of which depends upon honoring the three festivals, which are fixed according to the phases of the moon.

is the "nose" (*ChoTeM*), as in the verse, "My praise (prayer) is a long breath (*eChToM*)." Mashiach receives them, for he is "the breath of our nostrils, God's annointed."

Recognizing false leaders

On the basis of all the concepts discussed in the discourse from section #4 until this point, Rebbe Nachman now gives his answer to the question of how to recognize the false leaders who owe their position to self-assertiveness. As already mentioned, the essence of the answer is that when a person attains true prayer, the "Word of God," which is the source from which all the forces within creation receive their power, all these forces owe their power to him and are in his debt, as it were. In accordance with the talmudic principle that "a person does not act impudently towards his creditor" (Bava Metzia 3a) the false leader is ashamed in front of the Master of Prayer, who is thus able to recognize him for what he is.

#13. A person who attains true prayer finds favor in the eyes of all, as we find with Esther: "And Esther found favor in the sight of all who looked upon her" (Esther 2:15). The Rabbis explained this to mean that "everyone who saw her imagined she was from his own nation" (Megillah 13a). In the same way this Master of Prayer, who attains the Word of God, which is the supreme Source from which all the different powers and all the hosts of heaven receive, finds favor in the eyes of all of them. Every single one of them imagines that he is "from his own nation,"[61] and is only concerned about him, because all of them are receiving from him.

He can then recognize which of the famous leaders owe their position to brash self-assertiveness, because their brazen shamelessness falls away in his presence.[62] For when a person attains true prayer, the Word of God — which

---

61. **Every single one of them imagines that he is "from his own nation"** People often wonder how Mashiach will be universally accepted by all the different groups within the Jewish People, such as the Ashkenazim and Sefardim, Chassidim (Belzer, Gerer, Satmar, Vishnitzer...), Mitnagdim, Conservative, Reform, nonaffiliated, etc. Here Rebbe Nachman indicates that Mashiach will have a unique grace that will endear him in the eyes of all.

62. **their brazen shamelessness falls away in his presence** "Only the Master of Prayer himself understands how their brazen shamelessness falls away in his presence, for this happens on a highly subtle spiritual level, and only temporarily. For immediately afterwards [the false leaders] stand up against him once more and try to stir up opposition

is the supreme Source from which the highest angels and all the hosts of heaven receive their power — all the angels and the hosts of heaven become his debtors. For "all the stars borrow one from another, etc." and thus all of them are debtors, right up to the supreme Source, which is the Word of God, which the Master of Prayer has attained. He is thus the Great Lender, to whom all the hosts of heaven and all the powers in the world are in debt.

"And the hosts of heaven bow to You" (Nechemiah 9:6): all the hosts of heaven bow down to and humble themselves before their root, which is the Word of God, which the Master of Prayer has attained. For this reason the initial letters of the four Hebrew words in this verse, וצבא ה'שמים ל'ך מ'שתחוים (*Utzeva Hashamayim Lecha Mishtachavim*), spell out the word מלוה (*MaLVeH*), which means a creditor. For all these forces borrow from one another until they receive from the Great Lender, the Master of Prayer, who has attained the root of all things, the Word of God. The reason why he is able to recognize which of the famous leaders owe their position to brazenness is that "a person does not act impudently towards his creditor" (*Bava Metzia* 3a). Because of this, their brazen impudence falls away before the Master of Prayer, who is the Great Lender — because they are all in his debt.

Moses was the archetypal leader of the Jewish People, and a veritable Master of Prayer. God said to Moses, "You have found favor in My eyes and I know you by name" (Exodus 33:17). The concept of "names" was discussed earlier in the discourse, at the end of section #5. Rebbe Nachman now returns to this idea again, using the above-quoted verse to draw together some of the main strands of the discourse as a whole.

God said to Moses, "For you have found favor in My eyes and I know you by *name*" (Exodus 33:17). When "all the hosts of heaven bow to you [i.e. the Master of Prayer]" because they all receive and borrow from him, through this he finds favor in their eyes, since "each one imagines he is from his own nation." And through finding favor in the eyes of all, then: "I know you *by name*" — i.e. you will be able to know and recognize all the famous leaders who have made a "name" for themselves. For a famous leader who owes his name and fame to brazenness falls down before the Master of Prayer, as explained above.

---

against him" (*Parpara'ot LeChokhmah* #14). Thus we find that Moshe Rabbenu suffered repeated episodes of opposition during the forty years of wandering in the wilderness, for example the revolt caused by the report of the spies and the rebellion of Korach.

On the positive side, "I know you by name" also relates to the concept of attaching oneself to the roots of the souls, through which one is saved from the accusation of the angels. For the "name" is the soul,[63] as it is written, "the soul of every living creature is its name" (Genesis 2:19). For through attachment to the true leaders one is bound to all the souls and can "grasp the face of the throne" — i.e. one is bound to the roots of the souls, who are the Throne of Glory.

Judgment and mercy

This discourse was given on Rosh Hashanah 1808, and Rebbe Nachman now turns to the implications of Rosh Hashanah as the Day of Judgment. Yet, as the Rebbe says, any time that a person sits down to talk about another person is a "day of judgment." The theme of judgment relates to the earlier sections of this discourse in several ways. The idea that we should not judge others negatively — and this applies to ourselves as well — is a further development of the idea discussed above (section #10) not to despise anyone (Avot 4:3). The Rabbis warned not to judge another person "until you have reached his place" (Avot 2:5). But only God, Who is beyond space, knows the true place and situation of each and every person, and can thus judge favorably and charitably. Rebbe Nachman adds that those who grasp the Throne of Glory also rise to a level that is "beyond space" and can also judge favorably. This discussion has an important bearing on healing, since essentially healing comes through joy, which is attained through judging oneself positively and finding one's good points (see Chapter 13). As we have seen, illness is essentially a "decree" or "judgment" (see above pp. 188ff.). The key to healing lies in sweetening the harshness of the decree through pidyon nefesh, "redemption of the soul," which can only be accomplished by a Master of Prayer who can intercede and plead with God to judge the sick person with mercy and kindness. Rebbe Nachman here provides us with a powerful argument to use in our prayers and appeals to God to forgive us for our backsliding and to send healing.

#14. And then one can celebrate Rosh Hashanah,[64] the New Year. For when a person sits down to talk about another person, this is "Rosh Hashanah,"

---

63. **For the "name" is the soul** See *Rabbi Nachman's Wisdom* #44.

64. **And then one can celebrate Rosh Hashanah** "The root of all the remedies discussed in this discourse is Rosh Hashanah, which is the first of the Ten Days of Repentance, i.e.

which is the Day of Judgment — for he is sitting in judgment over his fellow man. One must be very cautious about this and examine oneself carefully to see if one is fit to judge one's fellow man. For "the judgment is God's" (Deuteronomy 1:17), for God alone is fit to judge people, as our Rabbis said: "Don't judge your fellow man until you have reached his place" (*Avot* 2:5). Who can understand and project himself into the place of his fellow man[65] except God? For "God is the Place of the world, but the world is not His place" (*Bereshit Rabbah* 68 and *Rashi* on Exodus 33:21). Each individual has a place with God, and therefore He alone can judge a person, because God is supreme in compassion and certainly fulfils the maxim to "judge everyone favorably" (*Avot* 1:6).

Underlying the next paragraph is the rabbinic teaching that the sun and the moon were originally created equal, but when the moon complained that the heaven and earth could not have two luminaries of equal size, God made the moon smaller, which is why, after full moon, the moon begins to wane until it finally becomes invisible at the end of the month (Bereshit Rabbah 6:3). *This midrash relates to the idea that God created the lower world (the realm of the "moon," malkhut) with the intention that ultimately Godliness should be revealed there as fully as in the upper worlds (the realm of the "sun," the higher sefirot), but that this purpose could be accomplished only by first screening and hiding the divine light in the lower world in order to challenge man to discover it for himself by overcoming his materialistic impulses. If man is often*

---

the start of repentance. For the truth is that the first step toward repentance is very hard and burdensome. It is so hard to know where to start. The way to conquer our cravings for wealth, food and sexual pleasure is by celebrating the festivals in holiness and purity, but how can we do so when we are still sunk in our material cravings? This is why the root of this whole pathway is Rosh Hashanah, when we start serving God" (*Torat Nathan* #16).

65. **Who can understand the place of his fellow man** Rebbe Nachman's teaching of "*Azamra — I will sing!*" (*Likutey Moharan* I, 282) is based on the verse (Psalms 37:10): "And in a little bit the sinner is not; you shall reflect upon his place and he will not be there." "In a little bit" — in virtue of a tiny redeeming good point — "the sinner is not" — he is no longer a sinner! The key to finding the redeeming points is to "reflect on his place," and consider the circumstances that caused him to become what he is. But even while taking his situation into account as it appears to us, we must be aware that "a person's true place is not determined merely by his place and situation in this world, but by the deepest roots of his soul, which lie in the Throne of Glory. These are known only to God and to those who have followed the pathway explained in this discourse to the ultimate level" (*Biur HaLikutim* #34).

defeated by the obstacles confronting him, it can be argued in his favor that God Himself is responsible for the "flaw" in creation that causes man to sin.

We see God's compassion in the fact that he ordained that Rosh Hashanah, the Day of Judgment, should fall on the day of the New Moon. This is an act of great mercy, because how could we raise our heads to ask Him to grant us atonement? He therefore had mercy on us and set the Day of Judgment, Rosh Hashanah, on the day of the New Moon, when He Himself, as it were, asks for atonement [for making the moon smaller.[66] The Rabbis learned this from the fact that, uniquely among all the other festival sin offerings, the sin offering brought on the appearance of the New Moon is called "a sin offering for God" (Numbers 28:15)], as if God were saying, "Bring atonement for Me" (*Chullin* 60b). For this reason we are not ashamed to ask for atonement on the Day of Judgment, since God Himself then asks for atonement. In addition, the very fact that God Himself came to the point where He had to say, "Bring atonement for Me" — i.e., He did something that gave Him cause to regret, as it were, and say, "Bring atonement for Me" — makes it possible for us to come before Him without shame and beg atonement for *our* sins and express *our* regret, because

---

66. **atonement for making the moon smaller** "The moon was made smaller because she was *jealous* of the sun. This links with the jealousy of the angels, which causes the souls of Israel to become 'smaller' because of the material cravings they inject into them. The fact that all our sins are ultimately rooted in this primordial sin of jealousy provides us with an argument in our defense, and we can now ask for atonement" (*Biur HaLikutim* #28).

Reb Noson writes: "All the concepts in this discourse are tightly bound together. The underlying concept is that of the waning and waxing of the moon. For the three traits that destroy the reverence in the heart are rooted in the dark side of the moon, which is the source of the power of the *sitra achra*, the unholy side of creation, and the root of all evil cravings, especially these three. It is because they are rooted in the dark side of the moon that the Talmud refers to them as the three watches of the *night*. They destroy the reverence in the heart, which is 'Jerusalem,' '*Malkhut*,' the 'small light.' The diminution of the moon is rectified by the festivals, which are a concept of full light as opposed to shadow. Through honoring the festivals we can come to prophetic spirit and prayer. All this is accomplished through the rectification of the moon and of *Malkhut*, which is the source of the angel that sends prophecy....

"In the Rebbe's discussion about how the lower planets borrow from the higher stars, it could be asked why he takes as his example the way that the moon borrows from the sun. The answer to this question is that the heavenly order as a whole is patterned after this borrowing by the moon from the sun. The underlying concept is the diminution of

He too did something that He came to regret. We thus see His great compassion. And therefore He alone is fit to judge the world, because He knows the place of each and every person, because all their different places are with Him since He is the Place of the world, whereas the world is not His place.

The reference to the moon in the last paragraph connects thematically with the earlier discussion about how the lower planets receive their light from the higher stars, etc. (#9), and also with the discussion about rectifying our cravings for wealth, food and sexual pleasure through celebrating the three festivals (#5): the dates of the festivals are fixed by counting the days from the start of the month, which according to the Jewish lunar calendar depends upon the appearance of the new moon. Pesach and Sukkot both begin on the 15th of the month — full moon — while Shavuot falls when the moon is waxing. Thus the festivals rectify our material cravings, which have a hold over us only because of the "diminution of the moon," the muting of the light of Godliness in this world.

In the next three paragraphs Rebbe Nachman further explores the idea that God is the "place of the world," which is why He can judge everyone favorably, as He knows the place of every single person. The discussion here about the Temple also connects thematically with earlier references to the rebuilding of Jerusalem and to the sanctuary as the source of the prophetic inspiration that redeems prayer. The Temple, the House of Prayer, is the

---

Malkhut: the darkness of the moon represents the concealment of God's kingship, the Word of God, and then all have to borrow, one from the other. But when God's kingship, the Word of God, is revealed, all the loans are annulled, because it is then revealed that there is really no law of nature at all but that all receive only from the Great Lender, the Word of God, and 'His kingship rules over all.' Just as the highest spheres receive from the Word of God, so does the lowliest blade of grass. For the Master of Prayer reveals God's kingship down below in this lowly world. This is the ultimate perfection of the moon. And then all the herbs return their power to their root, the Word of God. And then Mashiach can shine forth.

"The waxing of the moon symbolizes the dominion of Mashiach. For when Mashiach comes, the Jewish People will be renewed like the moon, and then 'the light of the moon will be like the light of the sun.' And then one can celebrate Rosh Hashanah, because Rosh Hashanah falls on Rosh Chodesh, the New Moon, when God Himself asks for atonement, as it were, giving *us* an opening to ask for atonement. Thus Rosh Hashanah itself depends on the rectification of the moon..." (*Torat Nathan #4*).

interface between our finite, time- and space-bound world, and the upper worlds that are beyond time and space as we know them. Through prayer it is possible to rise beyond finite time and space, and this is the concept of "grasping the Throne of Glory," with which the discourse began.

For although we find places where the Divine Presence dwelled, as in the Holy Temple, the idea is not that His Godliness was contracted there, God forbid, for as King Solomon said, "Behold, the heaven and the heavens of heaven cannot contain You, how much less this house" (Kings I, 8:27). It means, rather, that the Temple contained things of great beauty, for "the Holy Temple had the same form as the work of creation and the form of the Garden of Eden" (Introduction to *Tikkuney Zohar*), and God therefore drew down His holiness to there. But as for God in Himself, the world is not His place, although He is the Place of the world. This is why He can celebrate Rosh Hashanah, the Day of Judgment, for He fulfils the prescription, "Don't judge your fellow man until you have reached his place," since He is the place of the world.

This idea is expressed in the verse, "Holiness is becoming to Your house, O God, for the length of days" (Psalms 93:5). "Holiness is becoming to Your house," i.e., God drew only His holiness down to the Temple because it contained beautiful objects, but as for God Himself, the world is not His place, but rather He is the Place of the world. And therefore, "O God, for the *length of days*,"[67] i.e. God can celebrate Rosh Hashanah, the two days of which are considered one long day (*Beitzah* 4-6 and *Shulchan Arukh, Orach Chaim* 393).

And someone who grasps the Throne of Glory, the root of the souls, is also the "Place of the World," as it is written, "He raises the poor out of the dust... to make them sit with princes, and inherit the *Throne of Glory*, for the pillars of the earth are God's and He has set the world upon them" (Samuel I, 2:8). In other words, through grasping the Throne of Glory, the roots of the souls, one rises to the level of the Place of the World, for "He has set the world *upon them*" and therefore one can celebrate Rosh Hashanah.

Rebbe Nachman concludes the discourse by showing how all of its main themes are alluded to in the key verse: "Sound the shofar on the new moon, at the time appointed for our festive day" (Psalms 81:4).

---

67. **"O God, for the *length of days*"** Length of days, without illness!

"Sound the shofar on the new moon, at the time appointed for our festive day".

Sound (תקעו, *TiK'u*): this is the concept of dominion, "I will fasten him (ותקעתיו, *uTeKativ*) as a peg in a sure place." **On the *new* moon:** this is the renewal of Godly awareness that shines on the three pilgrim festivals, the times of which are fixed according to the New Moon, because "He made the moon to mark the seasons" (Psalms 104:19). **The shofar (שופר, *horn*):** this symbolizes the heart, which is nourished by the choicest beauty (שופרא דשופרא, *shufra deshufra*) (Zohar IV, 216 & 221, and see *Tikkuney Zohar* #21 & #49). **The shofar** also alludes to awe of heaven, as it is written, "Shall the *shofar* be blown in the city and the people not *tremble*?" (Amos 3:6). **The shofar** also symbolizes prophecy, as in "Raise your voice like a *shofar*" (Isaiah 58:1). **The shofar** also signifies prayer: "Out of the narrow straits I called on God, He answered me with great expansiveness" (Psalms 118:5). Thus one blows into the *narrow* end of the shofar and the sound comes out of the *wide* end. **The shofar** also alludes to the way the herbs of the field put their power back into the prayer, as when "Isaac went out to pray in the field." The shofar is called a יובל (*yovel*), as in "when they make a long blast with the ram's horn" (Joshua 6:5). The letters of the word יובל, YOVeL, are the initial letters of the words ו'יצא י'צחק ל'שוח ב'שדה (*Vayetze Yitzchak Lasuach Basadeh*), "Isaac went out to pray in the field." And through all these categories, we come to **the time appointed for our festive day,** i.e. Rosh Hashanah, for through attaining these levels one can celebrate Rosh Hashanah.

In brief

1. *"Sound the Shofar — Dominion"* teaches not only a pathway of healing but a way of *life* that can bring every Jew to the *takhlit*, the ultimate purpose — complete fulfilment in this world and the next.

2. First and foremost, "bind yourself to the true Tzaddik" by regularly taking time to study his teachings and doing your best to follow them in practice. This is how to conquer all the obstacles and barriers that stand in the way of spiritual fulfilment.

3. Let your goal be to "build Yerushalayim" — to fill yourself with awareness of God in all your activities, especially when satisfying your material needs for livelihood, food and sexual satisfaction. There are many mitzvot connected with making a living, eating and marital life. Give special attention to halakhic study of the details of these mitzvot, and make every effort to carry them out in practice.

4. When making a living, let your aim be to have the means to give charity and lead a Torah life. Eat wisely in order to enhance your spiritual faculties and have the strength to pray, study and fulfil the mitzvot. Cherish your spouse and seek to procreate in order to bring into the world holy Jewish souls who will grow up to know God and serve Him.

5. The key to sanctifying all your mundane activities is through celebrating Shabbat and the festivals joyously with due honor through the year, and, on a daily basis, by giving pride of place to the three prayer services and to hisbodedus. This way you build a sanctuary of Godly service in your very heart — a worthy place for prophetic spirit to rest. You will learn to draw all your needs in life from God through "prayer to the God of my *life*" (Psalms 42:9).

6. In order to perfect your prayer, work on refining your faith in God, fight against all immoral desires, and train yourself to respect and cherish all people, searching for their good points. Be sure to search for your own good points as well, and take the greatest joy in them. It's a great mitzvah to be happy always!

*

Chapter 19

Faith

During the two years from the time of giving the discourse "*Sound the Shofar — Dominion*" until his death in the fall of 1810, Rebbe Nachman further developed and expanded on many of its themes in his major teachings (see pp. 91-102). In "*Sound the Shofar — Dominion*," Rebbe Nachman taught that we can only come to true prayer by bringing deeper knowledge and awareness of God — *da'at* — into our hearts. But even more basic is the foundation on which this knowledge and awareness necessarily rest: simple faith in God.

Not only is faith the cornerstone of the whole of Judaism. It is also the root of Rebbe Nachman's path of healing, because without faith, prayer is meaningless. Moreover, for Rebbe Nachman, the key to health and healing is *simchah*, joy, and as we have seen, the only way to develop a truly joyous outlook in a world where good and evil are mixed up is by cultivating strong faith that everything is under God's providence and that therefore, no matter what happens, ultimately everything must be for the very best (see above pp. 117ff.).

The subject of faith pervades "*Sound the Shofar — Dominion*": flawed faith — "idolatry" — is one of the negative traits that destroys prayer, and must be countered by cultivating perfect faith in God (#10). During the last two years of his life, Rebbe Nachman put ever stronger emphasis on faith, and he made it the central theme of his longest teaching, "*Sound the Shofar — Faith*," (*Likutey Moharan* II, 5), given on Rosh Hashanah (September 11) 1809. The bulk of this discourse is devoted to a detailed exploration of all the *tikkunim* (rectifications) that have to be accomplished in order to bring about the complete restoration of faith within the Jewish People and indeed in the entire world (see above pp. 97ff.). But the first section of the discourse, a translation of which is provided below, explicitly discusses the relationship between faith (or the lack of it) on the one hand and illness and healing on the other.

Before turning to "*Sound the Shofar — Faith*," let us first consider what Rebbe Nachman actually means when he talks about "faith." One of the clearest expositions of the fundamentals of faith as taught by Rebbe Nachman is contained in a short work entitled "Seven Pillars of Faith" by R. Yitzchak

Breiter (1886-1943?). R. Yitzchak brought Breslover Chassidut to pre-war Poland and was the leader of the Breslover movement there until his death in Treblinka at the hands of the Nazi persecutors. The following is adapted from *Seven Pillars of Faith*.

Fundamentals of Faith

1. God controls everything

The first principle of faith is to know and understand that everything in the entire universe is under God's control. This includes everything that happens to you personally, both spiritually and materially, including what you yourself do, whether deliberately or unwittingly, wilfully or under compulsion: everything is from God.

Appearances may sometimes seem to suggest otherwise, yet faith is "blind" in the sense that the believer does not pay attention to the external appearance of this world but to the underlying reality. There may be many philosophical questions about faith, but most of them are unanswerable. If you are prepared to accept the Torah unconditionally, you will eventually see with your very own eyes the truth of what you believe in.

Sincerely following the Torah pathway enables us to experience a dimension of existence which is otherwise simply inaccessible. You may be surrounded by radio waves, but you need a receiver to convert them into something you can experience with your senses. Faith is the "receiver" through which you experience the Divine. The essence of faith is believing that the One God controls everything.

2. Freedom

What we ourselves do is ultimately controlled by God, but this is concealed from us by our own egos, which give us the sensation of being independent and separate from God. It is inherent in our make-up to think that our thoughts and actions are our own, and that it is *"my* power and the strength of *my* hand" (Deuteronomy 8:17) that makes things happen in our lives.

God created us like this in order to give us free will. Our task is to turn to God of our own free will, in order to discover the truth for ourselves and see that, in actual fact, God controls everything, including our thoughts, feelings and actions. In this world, we are given the freedom to make our own choices.

Then, depending on the choices we make, God either reveals Himself to us or conceals Himself even more, according to a system of strict justice.

3. Action

Even though all things in both the spiritual and material realms are in God's hands, this does not mean that our role is passive, waiting for God to do everything. God arranged the universe in such a way as to give us freedom of action, whether in regard to carrying out the mitzvot, earning a living, finding a marriage partner, etc. We have to act — but always with the understanding that our need to act in this world is a test, to see whether we will exercise our free will in accordance with the Torah or not.

Whether in carrying out the mitzvot or in acting in the material world to make a living and attend to our other needs, we have to understand that, although it is up to us to take the initiative and act *as if* everything is up to us, ultimately everything depends on God. No matter what we feel we ought to do, whether in our spiritual or material lives, our first step should always be to ask God to guide us in what we do and to bless our efforts with success.

4. Reverses

When things appear to turn out badly for us, we have to accept that this is God's will and that whatever happens is for the best. Even when things go wrong because of something we ourselves may have thought, said or done, we have to accept that this was also brought about by God. While we should feel contrite about our sins and make every effort to do better in the future, it is pointless to live with regrets about the past, because ultimately whatever happened came about through the will of God. Even when you observe the mitzvot and pray but feel that God is not responding, you must have faith that God is paying attention to everything you do, and that "if you get no answer, this is also an answer."

Other people are also free agents, yet, paradoxical as it may seem, everything they do is ultimately controlled by God. Therefore you should understand that if someone insults you or harms you in some way, this has been sent to you from God. If you respond by getting upset and venting your anger, it is a sign that you do not have complete faith in God's control over every detail of the Creation. When people insult you, it is God's way of cleansing you of your sins. If you respond with anger, it is as if you are refusing to accept His reprimand.

If things go against you, be patient. Take a deep breath and accept this as God's will. If somebody hurts you in some way and you keep silent, accepting it as atonement for your sins, this causes the outer veil of concealment to be removed, and God's control over the entire Creation becomes manifest.

5. Personal growth:

Your spiritual development is also under God's control. You may feel a desire to grow in a specific area and accomplish something holy, but as long as you are not ready to achieve what you want, things will be arranged in such a way as to hold you back — either by external obstacles or through some idea that becomes implanted in your own mind to prevent you from reaching your goal. This does not mean that God is rejecting you, but He knows that, in the long run, this will be the best way to bring you to the ultimate good. The purpose of holding you back is to prompt you to cry out to God to help you rise from your current level and to bring you nearer your true goal.

Even when you experience a breakthrough in your spiritual growth, do not imagine that from now on you will always be able to maintain your new level. Anything you may have achieved until now came about only through the love and help of God, and the only way you will be able to stand up to future challenges is also through His help.

While you must always try to do your part to develop and deepen your observance of the mitzvot, the central focus of your efforts should be your prayers to God for *His* help. Prayer reveals that everything is in God's power and that "it is in His hand to cause all things to grow and become strong" (I Chronicles I, 29:2). Ask God that no matter what may happen to you, you should always remember that the main thing is to pray.

6. Revelation and guidance:

Since God is everywhere and in all things, everything we experience is actually a communication from God. This includes our inner thoughts and feelings. Even negative thoughts and feelings — heaviness, lack of enthusiasm, depression and the like — are from God. Whatever you hear, see, or experience in life, whether from people you know or from complete strangers — everything is a call to you from God. Through these communications everything you need in order to grow and attain spiritual perfection is sent to you.

We often find ourselves faced with unclear or even contradictory messages. These are also sent to us with a purpose: to give us free will and thereby to test us. The way to sort out which messages to follow and which to ignore is through evaluating everything in the light of Torah teaching. The more you familiarize yourself with the Torah outlook on life, and especially the Halakhah, which gives clear guidance about what is right and what is wrong, the more you will be able to interpret the various messages.

7. The Wise Man-Tzaddik:

Faith in God includes faith in the tzaddikim whom God sends into the world to teach us how to transcend our lowly state and fulfil our spiritual destiny. It is not enough to accept that God gave the Torah to Moses on Sinai. The Torah tells us that in every generation we can resolve our doubts and questions about what is the right path to choose only by turning "to the judge who lives in those days" (Deuteronomy 17:9).

God sends Wise Men in every age to lift Jewish souls out of our exile. "You must do according to what they tell you... take care to act in accordance with everything they teach you... Do not turn aside from what they tell you either right or left" (*ibid.* 10-11).

The main thing is faith

"*Sound the Shofar — Faith*" is far too long and complex to be translated here in its entirety. The subject of healing is addressed directly mainly in the first two sections of the discourse, which make up about one seventh of the teaching as a whole. These two sections are presented here in full.

In the opening section Rebbe Nachman tells us that the collapse of faith causes terrible afflictions to come into the world, and he gives a careful analysis of why, in the absence of faith, neither medicine, prayer, ancestral merit or even the cries and groans of the invalid are of any avail. This analysis is important for the light it throws upon Rebbe Nachman's understanding of the causes of illness: the idea of disharmony among the four bodily elements of air, fire, water and earth is discussed here more fully than anywhere else in his writings.

One of the striking features of the concept of faith as Rebbe Nachman presents it is that not only does faith or the lack of it affect the life and outlook of the individual. More than this, it has a profound influence on the workings of the physical world. Thus in discussing the healing powers of medicinal plants and herbs, Rebbe Nachman tells us that not only do the rains necessary for plant growth fall in the merit of faith, but that even the strength of the healing powers of plants as governed by the seasons and the locations in which they grow also depends upon faith. Moreover, faith is the key to maintaining harmony among the four bodily elements, and in the absence of faith, no medicine has the power to restore harmony among them so as to bring true healing.

Since faith is the vital element in all healing, the only remedy is to "dig down for the waters that nurture faith": these are the "waters of counsel" — the spiritual pathways that enable us to deepen our faith. "Like deep waters, so is counsel in the heart of man, but a man of understanding will draw it up" (Proverbs 20:5). Many of the later sections of "*Sound the Shofar — Faith*" are concerned with this "man of understanding" who offers wise counsel: this is the Tzaddik, whose Torah teachings guide us in building and deepening our faith. But when the crisis of faith is very deep, the first step towards reclaiming and restoring our shattered faith must be to cry and scream from the heart alone without words. Rebbe Nachman's evocative teaching about the wordless "cry from the heart" strikes home very powerfully in our own confused times, when words seem so inadequate to express the pain in the hearts of so many. (For excerpts from Reb Noson's prayer in *Likutey Tefilot* based on this discourse, see p. 423ff.)

Sound the Shofar — Faith

Likutey Moharan II, 5

#1. The main thing is faith. Every person must search within himself and strengthen himself in faith. For there are people suffering from the most terrible afflictions, and the only reason they are ill is because of the collapse of faith. It is written: "God will send you wondrous plagues, great and *faithful* plagues and great and *faithful* sicknesses" (Deuteronomy 28:59). The plagues and sicknesses are called "faithful," because they come on account of a lack of faith. The collapse of faith causes "wondrous" plagues, for which neither medicine nor prayer nor the merit of the fathers are of any avail.

For Rebbe Nachman, medicine, prayer and ancestral merit all have the power to bring healing. But in his careful analysis in the following paragraphs, he shows that each of them depends upon faith, which is why, with the collapse of faith, there can be no cure for the "wondrous" plagues he speaks of.

Medicines

In the next two paragraphs Rebbe Nachman gives two reasons why medicines have no power in the absence of faith. For one thing, our faith and our prayers to God are preconditions for the orderly rainfall needed for the growth of medicinal plants. Secondly, their medicinal powers depend upon the seasons in which they mature (time) and the locations in which they grow (space), and for Rebbe Nachman, the temporal and spatial order of the plant kingdom depends on faith. Further on ("And it is because of this very fact itself...") Rebbe Nachman adds a third reason for the ineffectiveness of medicines when faith is lacking: this is that the harmonious balance of the four bodily elements depends upon faith (see also *Likutey Moharan* I, 57:1, below pp. 430-2).

For all medicines are based on herbs and plants, and these grow only through faith, as our Rabbis said (Taanit 8a): "The rains come down only in the merit of faith, as it is written (Psalms 85:12), 'Truth sprouts forth from the earth and righteousness looks down from heaven'" [i.e. when there is truth and faith in the world below, God responds with righteousness and sends the rains]. When there is faith, the rains come down and the plants grow and then there are medicines. But through the collapse of faith there are no rains, and then there are no medicines.

In addition, the healing powers of the various herbs and plants depend on factors relating to the natural order of the plant kingdom, in particular the places and seasons in which the different herbs and plants grow. There are plants whose healing powers are present only when the plants are harvested before they reach a third of their full growth: after this their potency leaves them and they have no power to heal. Other herbs possess healing powers only when they mature and fall by themselves. Each plant develops according to its own unique timetable as laid down by the natural order. Similarly, plant life is governed by location. One place is suitable for one kind of plant while another place favors different plants. The curative powers of herbs and plants depend entirely on the order of the plant kingdom as governed by factors of time and space. And the order of the plant kingdom depends upon faith. This we see from the saying of the Rabbis: "'Faith' (Isaiah 33:6) — this is the Order of Seeds" (Shabbat 31a, where each of the six concepts mentioned in Isaiah 33:6 is associated with one of the six Orders of the Mishnah). Faith maintains the temporal and spatial order of the plant kingdom, thereby giving plants their powers to heal. Therefore, because of the collapse of faith, medicines are of no avail.

Prayer and the merit of the fathers

Prayer is also a matter of faith, as it is written, "And his hands were *faith*" (Exodus 17:12), which the Aramaic Targum translates to mean "he spread them forth in *prayer*."

Even when a person has little or no merit in his own right, the merits of his ancestors may stand in his favor to mitigate the divine judgment against him and bring him healing.

The merit of the fathers is also revealed only through faith, as it is written, "The flowers appear in the earth" (Song of Songs 2:12). "The flowers" are the patriarchs (Zohar, Introduction 1b) and they appear and are revealed "in the earth," which symbolizes faith, as it is written, "Dwell in the *land* and feed off *faith*" (Psalms 37:3). For faith corresponds to the earth element, and "earth is the vessel for all [of the other three elements, viz. water, fire and air, which correspond to the patriarchs Abraham, Isaac and Jacob]" (Tikkuney Zohar #70, 120b). *[Rebbe Nachman now summarizes the main point, which is that none of the three factors discussed so far can effect a cure when faith is lacking.]* We therefore see that through the collapse of faith neither medicine nor prayer nor ancestral merit can avail the sick person, because all of them depend on faith.

Cries and groans

Rebbe Nachman now adds a new point: without faith, the sick person cannot be helped by cries and groans. This is because, as we will see below (#2, penultimate paragraph), the voice is made up of the three higher elements of fire, water and air [the voice is air, and when it comes out of the mouth it is warm (= fire) and moist(= water)]. But these can only be revealed in all their power through the earth element, which is faith. Without faith, cries and groans have no power to heal.

Neither can the sick person be helped by cries and groans. Sometimes such cries can help a sick person by arousing pity for him [in Heaven]. But because of the collapse of faith this too is of no avail, since these groans and cries are a voice without words. The voice is in the category of the patriarchs, because the voice is made up of fire, water and air (Tikkun 69) which are the three fathers. But they are revealed only through faith, the earth element, which is the vessel of all of them. Because of the collapse of faith these cries also cannot help.

The four elements

In the following section Rebbe Nachman adds a further point: faith, the earth element, is necessary to maintain harmony among the three higher elements of air, fire and water. Illness is the result of disharmony among the elements, but although medicines have the power to strengthen or weaken one or other of them and thereby influence the balance between them, lasting harmony depends upon faith, and without it, medicines are of no avail.

And it is because of this very fact itself [that the earth element is the vessel of the three higher elements] that medicines cannot help. For basically a person is healed through bringing harmony among the elements. There are four elements: fire, water, air and earth. It needs a great expert who understands through his medical expertise how to balance the elements contained in each of the different herbs in order to produce the remedy needed by this particular invalid given the particular element which is weak and damaged in his case. (The harmony of the elements is also involved in projecting the voice properly.) When faith is lacking, the balance of the four elements is undermined, since all of them are revealed through the earth element, which is "the vessel of all of them," and therefore there is no cure for him.

The waters of counsel

Having diagnosed the essential problem, which is the collapse of faith, Rebbe Nachman now begins his explanation of the remedy, which is to rebuild and restore it. The key is to discover the "waters of counsel" that nurture faith. The world needs the guidance of an outstanding Sage in order to return to faith. The whole of the remainder of this discourse is devoted to an elaborate, detailed examination of all the steps that are necessary in order to restore faith among the Jewish People and in the world as a whole. But to initiate the whole process and find the "waters of counsel," it is necessary to cry out silently to God from the very depths of our hearts.

#2. The remedy is to dig down until we find the waters which nurture faith. These are the waters of counsel — the spiritual pathways which enable us to deepen our faith, as it is written, "I will acknowledge Your Name, for You have done wonders, [sending] *counsels* from afar, nurturing *faith*" (Isaiah 25:1). True spiritual counsel nurtures faith, enabling it to grow.

True counsel springs from the depths of the heart. When the crisis of faith is so great that even cries without words cannot help, one has to cry from the heart alone: "Their *heart* cried out to God" (Lamentations 2:18). The heart alone cries without our letting out a sound. "From the depths I call out to God" (Psalms 130:1) — from the depths of the heart. And from the depths of the heart comes guidance, for "like deep waters, so is counsel in the heart of man" (Proverbs 20:5). When shouts and screams no longer help because faith has collapsed, one must cry from the depths of the heart without letting out a sound. This is how true counsel is revealed, for "like deep waters, so is counsel in the heart of man."

And through the true guidance and counsel that are revealed in the world (i.e. each person knows in his own heart what he has to do) faith is able to grow, as it is written, "*Counsels* from afar, nurturing *faith*." Then everything discussed above can be put right. For true counsel is a "wonder" — "I will acknowledge Your Name, for You have done *wonders, counsels* from afar...." This makes it possible to heal the "wondrous plagues" sent by God. Prayer also brings about "wonders," as it is written, "Awesome in praises [i.e. prayer], doing *wonders*" (Exodus 15:11). The same is true of ancestral merit: "In front of their *fathers* He performed *wonders*" (Psalms 78:12).

All these ideas are expressed in the verse, "And I taught Ephraim to walk, taking them by their arms; but they did not know that I healed them" (Hosea 11:3). "And I taught Ephraim to walk (תרגלתי, *tiR'GaLti*)": this is the concept of counsel, as in "the people that follow in your *footsteps* (ברגליך, *beRaG'Lecha*)" (Exodus 11:8) — i.e. those who follow your counsel (see *Rashi ad loc.*). "Taking them by the *arms*" is an allusion to the merits of the fathers, for the patriarchs are called the "arms of the universe" (Deuteronomy 33:27). "But they did not know that I *healed* them" — for in truth, all this brings healing.

Dark night and the light of day

The following passage depicts dawning faith as the light of day that dispels the darkness of night. Many people who have suffered illness know only too well the agonizing trials and torments suffered during long nights. Yet it is precisely during the darkness of "night" — the night of exile, personal and national — that we must strive to deepen our faith in God. The light of the dawning day is the light of divine redemption and the revelation that God is in complete control of the entire creation on every level.

The search for guidance is like the creation of the world, at first dark and then light. The absence of guidance is "darkness," as it is written, "Who is this who *darkens* counsel with words?" (Job 38:2). But afterwards, when guidance and counsel, "deep waters," are revealed, God "reveals deep things out of the darkness" (*ibid.* 12:22). The greater the light of guidance and counsel, and the more that darkness, doubt and confusion are put to flight, the stronger faith becomes. It is written, "and Your faith *in the nights*" (Psalms 92:3). It is "in the nights" that faith grows. That is to say, the more the night advances and the closer we come to the light of day, the stronger faith becomes. As the night continues to advance and we come closer and closer to the light of day, so faith keeps growing little by little, until with the light of day, faith is complete, as it is written, "New in the *mornings*, great is Your *faith*" (Lamentations 3:23).

And with the light of day comes healing, as it is written, "Then your light will break forth as the morning, and your healing will spring forth speedily" (Isaiah 58:8). In short, as true guidance and counsel are revealed and the "light" shines forth out of the "darkness," faith grows and matures, bringing healing: "Then will your light break forth as the morning, and your healing will spring forth speedily."

This explains the meaning of the saying of the Rabbis: "What is the reason why the goats walk at the head of the flock and only afterwards come the sheep? It is like the creation of the world: at first darkness, and then light" (*Shabbat* 77b). The idea of the "goats" (עזים, *IZim*) is an allusion to faith, as it is written, "God is clothed, He has *girded* Himself with strength (עז, *OZ*)" (Psalms 93:1), and "righteousness will be the girdle of his loins, and *faith* the *girdle* of his reins" (Isaiah 11:5). "And afterwards the sheep": the word for "sheep" (אמרי, *IMRi*) is an allusion to healing: "אמר, *AMaR* — God said, and I will *heal* him" (Isaiah 57:19). The three letters of the word א'מ'ר, *AMaR*, are the initial letters of א'ש (*Esh*), מ'ים (*Mayim*) and ר'וח (*Ruach*), "fire, water and air," from which healing comes.

In other words, on a deeper level, the question about the goats and the sheep is one about why healing essentially depends upon faith: why it is first necessary to develop one's faith, and only then does healing come? The answer the Rabbis give is, "Like the creation of the world: at first there was darkness, and then light." That is, the concept with which the question is answered is that of the creation of the world, where first there was darkness and then the light was revealed. Similarly, true counsel and guidance are revealed out of the darkness: "uncovering deep things out of the darkness." It is through counsel and guidance that faith grows strong. Only with the "light of day" is faith perfect. This is why healing can come only through faith, because healing comes only with the light of day: "Then will your light break forth as the morning, and your healing will spring forth speedily."

*

SECTION 7

The Wings of the Sun

Chapter 20

The Wings of the Sun

After Jacob was struck on the thigh by the angel, the sun shone on him to heal him (Genesis 32:32, see *Rashi ad loc.*). Said R. Huna in the name of R. Acha: "The sun healed Jacob our father but burned up Esau and his generals. The Holy One, blessed be He, said to Jacob: You are a sign for your children. Just as the sun healed you while burning up Esau and his generals, so the sun will heal your children and burn the idolators. For your children — 'There will shine upon you who fear My Name a *sun of charity with healing in its wings*' (Malachi 3:20). But as for the idolators (*ibid.* v.19), 'Behold the day is coming blazing like a furnace....'"

(*Bereshit Rabbah* 78:5)

Rebbe Nachman said:

"It is best for the sick to trust only in God. They should trust that saying the Psalms will help them. Faith is a support and a staff. You can lean on God and depend on Him just as you would lean on a staff or cane. King David said, 'God has been my *staff*' (Psalms 18:19). He could lean on God like a physical support! It is written, 'If he rises and walks about outside on his *staff*, then he shall be cleared' (Exodus 21:19). Healing comes through the staff of faith.

"It is also written, 'And a *staff* shall come forth from the stock of Jesse' (Isaiah 11:1). This refers to the Mashiach, who will be David's descendant. The Mashiach will hold the healing staff of faith. It is also written, 'The *breath* of our nostrils, God's Mashiach' (Lamentations 4:20). The staff of healing will arise through the holy spirit that King David placed in the Psalms.

"In the time of Mashiach — 'There shall yet sit old men and women in the broad places of Jerusalem for many days, every man with his *staff* in his hand' (Zechariah 8:4). From this verse the Talmud learns that in the time of Mashiach, the Tzaddikim will resurrect the dead (*Pesachim* 68a). The staff they will hold will be the one that Elisha used to resurrect the son of the Shunamite (Kings II, 4). And thus it is written, 'And you shall place the *staff* on the boy's face' (*ibid.* v.31). This is the healing staff of faith" (*Rabbi Nachman's Wisdom* #98).

293

For Rebbe Nachman, faith, prayer and joy are such sure remedies that we can actually lean on them the way people support themselves on a walking stick. For many suffering with medical problems, nothing is more reassuring than to be able to take a pill or some other treatment in the hope of finding relief. People's very confidence in the power of medicine can itself effect a cure, as is seen in the well-documented "placebo effect," where surprisingly high percentages of patients given dummy pills recover just as well as those taking real medications. If faith in a pill has such a power, how much greater is the power of firm faith in the Healer of all flesh. For Rebbe Nachman, prayer, introspection, taking responsibility for one's life, searching for the good points and reaching out to God are more dependable than any medicine. One can lean on them as surely as on a staff.

Yet Rebbe Nachman indicates that the truth of these spiritual remedies will be revealed in all its glory only in the future. This will be when the Mashiach brings back into the world the holy spirit that King David put into the Psalms, with their ten kinds of healing melody.

A world of amazing wonders

Rebbe Nachman evoked the new world order that is to be revealed in time to come in the very last discourse he ever gave, "*Sound the Shofar — Reproof*" (*Likutey Moharan* II, 8), delivered on Rosh Hashanah 1810, eighteen days before his death. It was in this final discourse that he spoke about the "sun of charity with healing in its wings" that will shine in the future, as prophesied by Malachi (3:20).

This will occur when the whole world is finally rectified, and God's glory will radiate in full splendor like the light of the sun. "And with the renewal of the world in the future, the world will be governed by 'wonders,' that is, by God's providence alone and not by the law of nature" (*Likutey Moharan ibid.* #10). The very visibility and immediacy of God's providence in our lives will bring us to the wholehearted embrace of our spirituality, thereby freeing us from subjection to the natural order and lifting us above sickness and disease, which are within nature.

Rebbe Nachman's discussion of these themes in "*Sound the Shofar — Reproof*" can be seen as a further development of his previous teachings. The glory of God was the central theme of "*Sound the Shofar — Dominion,*" given exactly two years earlier. There the key idea is to "grasp hold of the Throne of Glory." But during the period of exile God's glory is concealed. Nevertheless, through faith it can be revealed even then, and thus Rebbe Nachman focussed on how faith can be restored to the world in *"Sound the Shofar — Faith."* Finally, in *"Reproof,"* the Rebbe looks forward to the future, when God's glory will be revealed to perfection.

Parts of *"Reproof"* deal with the destruction of evil and the rectification of sin and lust. It is perhaps to balance this that the discourse opens with a caution on giving criticism:

> "While it is true that giving moral guidance and criticism is most important, and every Jew is obliged to guide his fellow Jew if he sees him acting improperly, nevertheless not everyone is fit to offer criticism. When guidance and criticism are given by someone who is unfit to give them, not only are they ineffective; worse still, they spoil the fragrance of the souls towards whom they are directed, turning them putrid. These souls become weakened, and this holds back the blessing from all the worlds that depend on them. Only those who can *add* to the fragrance of the souls they guide are fit to criticize the Jewish People and rebuke them for their sins. The voice of rebuke must be the 'voice that waters the Garden of Eden,' for this is where all the fragrances grow and where holy awe takes root. This is the sound of the melody destined to be sung in the future" (*Likutey Moharan* II, 8:1).

Reb Noson points out that Rebbe Nachman is speaking here not only about criticism offered to others but also about how we criticize ourselves. "We see time and time again that when people castigate themselves for their own wrongdoing they often fall down even more badly as a result.... Even when examining and criticizing oneself, it has to be in the spirit of the song of kindness that will be revealed in time to come. That is, one has to tilt the scales towards kindness and judge positively, as the Rebbe taught in his discourse on '*Azamra* — *I will sing'*" (*Likutey Halakhot*, Tzitzit 5:3).

We see that Rebbe Nachman's teachings even in his very last discourse are rooted in his teaching of *"Azamra"* (*Likutey Moharan* I, 282). Whether judging ourselves or others, we must do so in the spirit of the "voice that waters the Garden of Eden," garden of the souls. This voice is the "song of kindness" that will be sung in time to come: the "simple, double, triple, quadruple song" that will be played on an instrument of seventy-two strings (*Tikkuney Zohar* #21). One plus two plus three plus four make ten — the ten kinds of melody. The "instrument of seventy-two strings" alludes to חסד (*chesed*, kindness), the Hebrew letters of which have the numerical value of 72. This is also the value of the "expansion" of the letters of the Tetragrammaton with *yud*'s, signifying the perfect revelation of God's unity on every level (see above pp.142f.).

The way to hear this future song is through prayer, which redeems all the holy sparks devoured by the forces of evil. God's glory then shines forth like the light of the sun. A spirit of prophecy will spread throughout the world, bringing perfect healing. With this spirit of prophecy we will clarify and purify our faith, thereby revealing a new world order in which everything will be governed by miracles and wonders, and the hand of God's providence will be manifest in all things (*Likutey Moharan* II, 8:2-10).

The House of Prayer

Likutey Moharan II, 8:6

"The revelation of God's glory is the 'rising sun,' — 'And the glory of God has *risen* upon you' (Isaiah 60:1). And with the shining of the rising sun will come healing, as our Rabbis said, 'When the sun is high, the sick are relieved' (*Bava Batra* 16b), as it is written, 'But to you who fear My name *the sun of charity will rise, with healing in its wings*' (Malachi 3:20). For the spirit of prophecy that spreads as God's glory is revealed is itself the healing brought by the rising sun, for 'A man's *spirit* sustains him in his illness' (Proverbs 18:14).

"The revelation of God's glory comes about through prayer, which causes the 'clouds' — the forces of unholiness and impurity — to disperse and disappear. The nations of the world turn to God, and His glory is revealed. Through abundant prayer, sin is forgiven, and then the sun rises and shines, bringing healing. For sin is a 'cloud' darkening the light of the sun. Sins are dark in their very nature — 'And their works are in the *dark*' (Isaiah 29:15). Sin and illness are bound up with each other, because illness is basically caused by sin, as our Rabbis said: 'There's no suffering without sin, as it is written (Psalms 89:33), "I will requite their transgressions with the rod and their iniquity with plagues"' (*Shabbat* 55a). Sins are the 'clouds' that darken the healing light of the sun.

"But prayer brings atonement for sin, because prayer takes the place of sacrifices, as it is written: 'And I will bring them to My holy mountain and make them joyful in My House of Prayer; their burnt offerings and their sacrifices will be acceptable on My altar; for My house will be called a House of Prayer for all peoples' (Isaiah 56:7). Through the atonement of sin, the 'clouds' disperse and disappear, for 'I have blotted out your transgressions like a thick cloud, and your sins as a cloud' (Isaiah 44:22). The sun then rises, bringing healing. For illness is bound up with sin, which is a dark cloud hiding the healing light of the sun. When the sins are forgiven, the cloud disappears and the sun rises and shines, bringing healing. And all this is accomplished through prayer, which brings atonement for sin.

"The prayer that brings forgiveness and saves from illness comes about when a new 'neighbor' joins the community of Israel. With every new neighbor who comes, the prayer is enormously enhanced and magnified. The greater the multitude of Jewish souls gathered together, the greater and more magnificent the House of Prayer. For 'three stones build six houses, four stones build twenty-four houses, five build a hundred and twenty... until the mouth cannot utter it or the heart conceive it' (*Sefer Yetzirah* 4:16). With every single stone that is added, the number of houses is multiplied exponentially out of all proportion. Now the 'stones' are the souls — 'the holy stones have been poured out' (Lamentations 4:1), while the houses are 'My house, the House of Prayer.' Thus with every single soul that joins the ingathering of the Community of Israel, the House of Prayer is vastly expanded and magnified. The addition of yet another soul creates an incalculable number of totally new and different combinations.

"Every time a new neighbor joins an existing community of Jews, the prayer is expanded and magnified amazingly, for one more soul has been added. And it is the abundance of prayer that brings forgiveness and healing, so that 'The neighbor will not say, "I am sick"' (Isaiah 33:24). For the addition of a new neighbor is what saves everyone from illness, for (*ibid.*) 'the people that dwell there will be forgiven their iniquity'" (*Likutey Moharan* II, 8:6).

*

The Wings of the Sun

Ultimately the roots of sickness lie in mankind's "fallen" state as a result of the eating of the fruit of the tree of knowledge of good and evil, which caused illness and death to the soul and the body (see above p. 131). For this reason, perfect healing can come only with Mashiach, who will complete the rectification of sin, inaugurating the era when God "will remove death forever and wipe off the tears from all faces" (Isaiah 25:8).

As we saw in "*Sound the Shofar — Dominion*" (#14), sin is at root the result of the "diminution of the moon," the muting of the light of Godliness in this world. In its diminished state, the moon is the battleground of good against evil, as symbolized in its ever-repeated waxing and waning phases. In "*Dominion*" and many of his other teachings, Rebbe Nachman taught the way to "rectify the moon" — to elevate the materialism that casts a shadow over Godly revelation, in order that the "moon," *Malkhut*, this world, can come face to face with the radiant sun of God's glory and receive the light in full, bringing perfect healing and everlasting life.

The "sun" is a sun of *charity*, because God's beneficent Will to reveal Himself to His creatures — to share His goodness with them and grant them healing and life — is itself the greatest charity. In order to elicit this divine charity, man must first effect an "arousal from below" by giving charity himself. Through the act of charity, man breaks his innate selfishness and cruelty, redeeming himself from his lower cravings, bringing first atonement for sin, and then healing and life. Giving charity takes an act of will on our part, and this brings about the revelation of the supreme Will of God underlying all creation. Man's charity thus brings about the revelation of God's charity, which is His true glory — the healing "sun of charity."

What are the *wings* of the sun? We normally think of wings as the limbs with which birds, angels and the like propel themselves through the air. However, the Hebrew word כנף (*KaNaF*), although usually translated as "wing," also has the connotation of a "cover" (see Isaiah 6:2). While a cover may hide that which lies behind it, it can also serve to reveal something important about it at the same time (cf. *Likutey Moharan* I, 63). Thus our clothes serve to cover over our nakedness, but they also reveal important information about our personalities, social status, aspirations and so on.

The "wings" of the sun clothe God's glory in order that it can be revealed to His creatures. The wings (כנפים, *kenafayim*) are the "garments" through which Godliness is revealed, as it is written (Ecclesiastes 10:20), "That which has *wings* will tell the matter, *DaVaR*" — the *DeVaR HaShem*, the Word of God through which the Heavens were formed (cf. *Likutey Moharan* I, 60 end). The wings of the sun are the perfected "vessels" of Godly revelation, finally rectified after the "shattering of the vessels" that caused the "diminution of the moon." The wings of the sun that bring healing are the teachings of the true Torah Sage, who fashions perfect vessels with which to reveal to us God's glory and His presence in our lives.

The prayer that brings forgiveness for sin and dispels the clouds hiding the sun is the prayer offered by the assembly of the souls, "neighbors" united in the common purpose of serving God without selfishness. The ingathering of all the souls to serve God with one accord is the ultimate rectification of mankind. Speech is redeemed from its exile, and all the blessings are channeled into the world through the Word of God, prayer, bringing healing. The key is "good neighborliness," binding ourselves to our fellows in mutual respect and love — by finding the good points in everyone.

Arousing the dawn

> "Be strong as a lion to get up in the morning to serve your Creator. *You* be the one to arouse the dawn!"
>
> *(Shulchan Arukh, Orach Chaim* 1:1)

To some, Rebbe Nachman's healing teachings will be deeply meaningful and of practical relevance. Others, however, may still find them strange and mysterious, and may have difficulty conceiving how the ultimate liberation from sickness, ageing and death will come not from the medical laboratories and superclinics of the future but through simple faith, prayer, hisbodedus and joy.

Yet in some ways the world may be more ready for this pathway now than it has been at almost any time in modern history. With all the sophistication of contemporary medicine, the medical services are in deep crisis. The very expense of conventional treatment and insurance is forcing more and more people to look for alternative approaches. The reappearance of old diseases together with the emergence of new, sometimes strange and often lethal conditions has led many to question old assumptions. New scientific research is confirming the crucial role of mental, emotional and spiritual factors in all kinds of physical conditions, leading to widespread interest in therapies involving meditation, self-expression, music and so on.

Barring major cataclysms, it seems unlikely that patients will suddenly abandon the hospitals and clinics *en masse* in favor of synagogues and prayer halls. In any case, it would be absurd to throw away the great benefits offered by modern medicine, both conventional and alternative. However, there is no need to view the medical and spiritual approaches to illness as mutually exclusive. Even while receiving medical treatment, it can be only beneficial for patients to meditate, pray and search for the redeeming points that will give them the courage to take themselves in hand and *live*. And those who are blessed with good health should cherish and foster it by putting all their energy into a life of Torah, mitzvot, prayer and joy as the best guarantors of long-term immunity.

The pathway of simchah is there, ready and waiting. The cost in terms of money is almost negligible: faith, prayer and hisbodedus are free, and we are in any case obliged to give charity. If kindness, charity, faith and joy are the path mankind will take on the dawning future day, it is surely up to us to awaken from our sleep already and to *rouse the dawn* by carrying out these teachings in practice *now!*

Much remains to be discovered about Rebbe Nachman's healing pathway, which is really a very old path, the path which our ancestors walked (see Chapter 6). The concepts of the four elements, the ten pulses and the ten kinds of melody warrant careful research. Our study of excerpts from the Rebbe's discourses on healing is only a start. Every one of his teachings, and especially the discourses dating from the last three years of his life, could be explored at length for deeper insights into the meaning of joy, faith, speech, prayer, charity, Shabbat and festivals, etc., in relation to healing.

Another subject on which we have hardly touched at all is holy dance, which Rebbe Nachman saw as a powerful means of *pidyon nefesh* (see *Likutey Moharan* I, 41) and the ultimate *tikkun* for illness. Dance is mentioned in Rebbe Nachman's teaching on the great mitzvah of simchah (*Likutey Moharan* II, 24, see above pp. 123-4). Dance would presumably have been a central theme in the final section of the Story of the Seven Beggars, the tale of the Beggar with no feet. However, the Rebbe did not complete the story, and said it would not be told until the coming of Mashiach (*Yemey Moharnat* p.32b).

Reb Noson said that when Mashiach comes, educational centers will be established for the study of Rebbe Nachman's teachings (*Avanehah Barzel* p.90). Without doubt, the Rebbe's healing pathway will then be formally taught and widely practiced. But as yet there seems to be no Jewish spiritual equivalent to a medical school or hospital. It is far from clear who the professors and doctors would be, how a simchah clinic might function, how hisbodedus will become a universal Jewish practice, and so on. Still, this should not prevent rabbis, counsellors, psychologists, therapists, etc. from using Rebbe Nachman's teachings in their work with the sick, and indeed with the healthy. Jewish doctors and other healing professionals can encourage their patients to follow the pathways of faith, joy, prayer, hisbodedus and so on, even while continuing to treat them medically at the same time.

The challenge to all of us is to study and contemplate Rebbe Nachman's teachings, and to make every effort to put them into practice when healthy and in times of illness. The Rebbe's Torah is "deep, deep, who can find it?" (Ecclesiastes 7:24) But "the main thing is not the theory but the *practice*" (*Avot* 1:16).

And in the merit of our efforts to reveal and follow this new-old pathway, may the Holy One fill us with awe of His Name and shine upon us with the "sun of charity." May He open our hearts, minds and souls to His radiant light, and bring us to genuine faith, true simchah and perfect healing of the soul and the body, quickly in our times. Amen.

*

In time to come the Holy One, blessed be He, will make amazing changes in the world. God Himself will light up the world, and 'the sun will no longer light up the day' (Isaiah 60:19). God will make the sun shine forty-nine times as strongly as today, as it is written, 'The light of the moon will be like the light of the sun, and the light of the sun will be seven times seven...' (*ibid.* 30:26). If anyone is sick, God will command the sun to heal him, as it is written, 'But to you who fear My Name the sun of charity will rise, with healing in its wings' (Malachi 3:20). God will send living waters from Jerusalem and they will heal all the sick, as it is written, 'Wherever the rivers will come, every living soul there will live and be healed' (Ezekiel 47:9). God will make the trees bear fruit every single month, and those who eat the fruits will be healed, as it is written (*ibid.* v.12), 'And by the river shall grow every tree for food, and its leaves shall not wither, neither will its fruit fail.... It will bring forth new fruit every month... and its fruit will be for food and its leaves for healing' (*Shemot Rabbah* 15:21).

*

Part II

IN PRACTICE

Chapter 21

Keeping Healthy

"When you go out in the street, you should think of yourself as having been handed over to a policeman to be taken for trial. If you have a headache, you should think of yourself as having had your neck put in chains. If you fall ill and have to go to bed, you should look on yourself as if you've been brought up to the execution block. Anyone on the execution block can be saved if he has sufficiently powerful advocates. If not, there's no escape. And who are a person's advocates? Repentance and good deeds. Even if a person has nine hundred and ninety-nine accusers and only one defender, he will be saved, as it is written (Job 33:23-4): 'If he has *one defending angel out of a thousand* to vouch for his righteousness, then God will show him favor and say, Save him from the pit, I have found a ransom!'"

(Shabbat 32a)

Rebbe Nachman's healing pathway is very exalted, especially as expressed in "*Sound the Shofar — Dominion*" (Chapter 18, pp. 237-78). Some people may feel that "grasping hold of the Throne of Glory" and "attaining the Word of God" would be far beyond their capabilities. Yet Rebbe Nachman always put the main emphasis on carrying out his practical advice with the utmost simplicity. No one seeking a medical remedy would expect to be cured merely by studying a medical textbook: without some background, the average layman would find such a work quite baffling. As every doctor would tell his patients, after all the explanations, what really counts is actually swallowing the pill. So too with Rebbe Nachman's teachings. In the words of Reb Noson:

"While it is certainly true that the Rebbe's discourses contain awesomely profound ideas, plumbing the deepest mysteries of the Torah, even so, he put the main emphasis on their simple meaning. The Rebbe's lessons are not in heaven. 'The main thing is not the theory but the *practice*' (*Avot* 1:17). Anyone can carry out what he says and accomplish great things. All that's needed is truth and sincerity. Open your heart to the simple meaning of his words and you will find a pathway to God. You may study some of his discourses and think that they apply only to those who have reached exalted spiritual levels. At first you may not be able to find anything that seems to apply to you personally. But look more carefully .

Open your eyes and heart, and you will certainly find guidance and a way that you too can follow" (*Rabbi Nachman's Wisdom* #131).

Ultimately, all Rebbe Nachman's pathways are simple: sincere personal prayer from the heart in one's own words; turning one's thoughts to the good side of things; inspiring oneself with a joyous melody; making regular gifts to charity according to one's means; mouthing out the words, "I believe in You...."

Can simple methods really help? Rebbe Nachman once said to his followers:

"Didn't the prophet Elishah say to the leprosy-stricken Naaman (Kings II, 5:13), 'Wash [in the River Jordan] and be purified'? Yet Naaman didn't want to believe that he could be cured through something so simple, and he said, 'Aren't Amana and Pharpar, the rivers of Damascus, better? May I not wash in them and be purified?' But his servants said to him, 'My father, if he had told you to do something great, wouldn't you have done it? How much more so when he tells you to wash and be purified.' Only then did Naaman listen. He washed in the Jordan seven times, 'and his flesh came back and was clean.' You are the same. You believe that in order for you to be healed I have to prescribe onerous devotions. You don't have faith that through something simple that I tell you to do, you can be completely healed — healed in your very souls!" (*Tzaddik* #492).

Spiritual healthcare

It's not worth waiting till you fall sick before starting to take care of yourself. By then it can be far more difficult to restore and maintain bodily health, and sometimes it may be just *too* late. Rebbe Nachman held that even when illness has already struck, it is certainly possible to be healed through the pathway of joy, faith and prayer. Yet it is far preferable to follow this pathway as one of *prevention*, so that any latent problems are cured long before they develop into actual illnesses.

The key is to develop healthy habits, spiritually and physically, and to make simchah, Torah, prayer, hisbodedus, charity, kindness and all the other mitzvot an integral part of one's life every day. As a way of health and prevention, the spiritual pathway Rebbe Nachman teaches is none other than the path of faith, Torah and prayer discussed in all his writings (see *Advice, Rabbi Nachman's Wisdom*, etc.). The Rebbe once said, "When you're healthy, devote all your strength to 'do and do' in serving God" (*Avanehah Barzel* p.44 #64). This is because serving God *is* life, "for they are your *life and length of days*" (Deuteronomy 30:20).

Torah study, prayer, self-development, love of others, kindness, charity and all the other mitzvot connect us with the Life of life. They are our best investment not only for long-term life and sustained good health, but for rich vitality every day.

"One mitzvah leads to another" (*Avot* 4:2). When we strive to carry out the mitzvot not as soulless acts of duty but as heartfelt gestures of outreach and connection with God on every level of our being, in thought, word and deed, then every successive step we take opens up new dimensions of the mitzvah at hand and other related mitzvot. This leads to higher and higher levels of devotion in prayer and hisbodedus, fresh horizons in our understanding of Torah, and ever-enhanced self-refinement. Making the mitzvot into an all-encompassing pursuit in the home, at work, with family and friends, in the community and in the wider world *is* the life of simchah that brings glowing health and healing.

The Breslover Chassidim point out that the four Hebrew letters of the word שמחה (*SiMChaH*) are the initial letters of the Hebrew words for four key practices that are at the heart of Rebbe Nachman's pathway: ש'לחן ערוך, *Shulchan Arukh* — the study of Jewish law; מ'קוה, *Mikveh* — ritual immersion; ח'צות, *Chatzot* — *Tikkun Chatzot*, the midnight lament over the destruction of the Holy Temple, and ה'תבודדות, *Hisbodedus* — private prayer and meditation.

Hisbodedus

The single most important spiritual habit to cultivate is daily hisbodedus. In essence, hisbodedus is private time that a person takes from his or her daily activities in order to confront the basic issues of life: "What is my purpose in this world? What am I doing with my life? What are my true goals? To what extent am I achieving them, and if I am not, why not? What are the internal and external problems and obstacles that are holding me back? And how, with God's help, can I overcome them in order to attain complete self-fulfilment?" Facing these questions helps us to accept the fact of our own mortality and value the gift of life so that we live it to the fullest.

Unless we take regular breaks from the immediate business of living in order to work out *how* to attain what is most important to us, we are liable to become helplessly swept up by one current after another, and we may never come to true fulfilment. Hisbodedus is a daily workshop in which we take ourselves and our lives in hand in a creative partnership with God. It is the time to make contact with our inner thoughts and feelings, to work out our priorities, and to ask God for everything we need, spiritually and physically. As we have seen, man achieves his true dignity when he draws all his needs in life through prayer (see p. 219). Hisbodedus is the time to search for the good points within ourselves and in all the different situations we confront, and this is the very key to joy, health and healing (see Chapter 13, pp 163-73).

The ideal would be to practice hisbodedus for about an hour every day. For those who find this impossible, even sessions of ten to fifteen minutes can be highly valuable, and are certainly far better than nothing. Like life, the agenda of hisbodedus is constantly changing. By definition there is no uniform method, because each person's situation is completely unique. Just about the only rules are (1) to be completely truthful at all times, and (2) to persist. How each person turns to God is a very individual matter, and each of us must find our own way, whether through quiet meditation, contemplation, personal prayer, cries, tears, song or any other appropriate form of self-expression (see *Outpouring of the Soul, Under the Table* pp. 101-144 and *Crossing the Narrow Bridge* Chapter 9).

Shulchan Arukh: **Jewish Law**

> "The Academy of Eliahu taught: Everyone who studies *halakhot* every day is assured of a place in the World to Come."
>
> (*Megilah* 28b)

Study of the halakhah, Jewish law, is crucial for sound spiritual development, because without objective guidelines for our choices in life, we become ready prey for our own whims and misconceptions. The halakhah is the guide to what the Torah is actually asking us to *do* in life, giving clear directives for dealing with any and every situation with which we may be confronted at any time. While the halakhah relating to unusual and intricate cases is the special province of trained Rabbis, every Jew is duty bound to become familiar with the basic laws relating to everyday life, prayers and blessings, Shabbat and festivals, kashrut, family purity, interpersonal relationships, purity of speech, charity, business practice, etc. Moreover, regular study of the halakhah is a most powerful spiritual remedy. In the words of Rebbe Nachman:

> "When a person sins, good and evil become mixed together. But a legal opinion is a clear separation between the permitted and the forbidden, the clean and the unclean. When you study religious law, good is once again separated from evil and the sin is rectified" (*Rabbi Nachman's Wisdom* #29; cf. *Likutey Moharan* I, 8:6).

Rebbe Nachman teaches that the Torah contains the roots of the entire creation, including all forms of conflict in the world. Even unholy conflict, such as the war of the evil urge against the soul, is also ultimately rooted in the Torah — in this case in the holy disputes between the mishnaic and talmudic Sages. The remedy for these holy disputes is the halakhah, which "makes peace" between the Sages, steering a steady path amidst their opposing viewpoints in order to reach a clear legal decision. "And through study of the halakhah, a person becomes attached to the peace that reigns in the realm of holiness. The holy disputes are resolved, and then the unholy turmoil in his heart caused by the evil urge is automatically removed, and he is able to serve God with all his heart" (*Likutey Moharan* I, 62:2).

We have seen that, according to Rebbe Nachman, all illness is caused by conflict among the bodily elements (see p. 125 and p. 287). Since the study of halakhah connects one with the holy peace that is the remedy for all forms of conflict in creation, halakhah is clearly a powerful means of promoting peace and harmony within the self and in our very bodies, and thus a way of promoting good health.

Rebbe Nachman urged everyone to study halakhah every day without fail (*Rabbi Nachman's Wisdom op.cit.*). Those who are able to study the *Shulchan Arukh* with its commentaries should aim to go through the entire work in order and then review it again and again. For those who are unable to study the original, a wide variety of clear and easily understandable halakhic texts is available in English covering all the mitzvot of everyday life (see *Under the Table* pp.293f.). Make a list of the main areas you should be familiar with, and work through the relevant texts one after the other. When you are fully familiar with them, move on to more comprehensive works.

Mikveh

In the absence of the Holy Temple, immersing in the mikveh (ritual bath) is not mandatory today except for married women after *niddah* (ritual impurity) and for men on the eve of Yom Kippur (the Day of Atonement). However, chassidic literature in general and Breslov literature in particular emphasize the tremendous spiritual benefits that come from regular immersing in the mikveh prior to the morning prayers and in preparation for Shabbat and festivals. It is a practice that leads to the utmost personal sanctity, removing the impurity caused by sin, and bringing freedom from troubles, physical and spiritual. For "God is the *hope* (מקוה, *mikveh*) of Israel. He saves them in times of trouble" (Jeremiah 14:8).

Besides the spiritual benefits of the mikveh, Rebbe Nachman also pointed out the physical benefits:

"Immersing in the mikveh is not harmful at all, and any doctor who says the mikveh is harmful is no doctor at all. On the contrary, immersing in the mikveh is very beneficial for physical health. There are innumerable tiny ducts in the skin through which the sweat is secreted. It is important to open them, because if the sweat ducts are closed up, a person can become very weak. Immersing in water opens the sweat ducts, and this is very beneficial for physical health — as long as the water is not excessively cold, because then the water stops up these ducts. But when the water is not too cold, immersing is very healthy" (*Likutey Moharan* II, 123).

Tikkun Chatzot

Tikkun Chatzot is a special prayer service recited in the small hours of the night throughout the year to express our grief and concern over the destruction of the Temple and the Jewish exile. Interrupting our sleep in the middle of the night for prayer and devotion helps break the darkness of night — the night of exile — thereby initiating the redemption of the individual and the nation and the restoration of Jerusalem (see *The Sweetest Hour* for full details). Like immersing in the mikveh, *Tikkun Chatzot* is not a mandatory practice, but it is without question a central element of a life of true devotion and service of God.

The theme of *chatzot*, "midnight," comes into "*Sound the Shofar — Dominion*" (#4, and see note 19). We see there that Jerusalem — *Yerushalayim* — is not only a physical place but also a spiritual ideal that we must seek to realize in our own hearts: *yir'ah shalem*, complete awe and awareness of God (see pp. 243ff.). Thus the *Chatzot* prayers over the destruction of Jerusalem "do not refer only to the historical past. More important, they refer to what each individual is going through in the present. When you realize this, you can find all your own inner conflicts and your struggles with the evil urge expressed in the prayers of *Chatzot*" (*Likutey Moharan* II, 101).

Tikkun Chatzot is the time to look deep into one's heart and, while grieving over one's many flaws and imperfections, to search for the redeeming sparks of good. "'I will remember my song in the night; I will converse with my heart and my soul will search' (Psalms 77:7). This teaches that the main time to search for the 'good spirit' is at night. Through the melody and joy that come from searching for the good, one can keep one's mind focussed on one's ultimate purpose in this world. This stirs one to pour out one's heart and speak to oneself about one's eternal destiny in the World to Come, and to seek and find one's good points, in order thereby to return to God" (*Likutey Moharan* I, 54 end, and see pp.163ff.). This is the work of building *yir'ah shalem*, which, as we see from "*Sound the Shofar — Dominion,*" is the foundation of true prayer. Prayer is the channel for genuine healing and freedom from illness. Thus *Tikkun Chatzot,* which is all about rebuilding *Yerushalayim*, *yir'ah shalem*, is one of the key components of Rebbe Nachman's healing pathway.

Rebbe Nachman said that the time for *Tikkun Chatzot* always begins exactly six hours after nightfall, both in the summer and in the winter, and continues for two hours (*Likutey Moharan* I, 149). Even today, many Breslover Chassidim are in the habit of retiring fairly early after the evening prayers in order to get up at the proper time for *Tikkun Chatzot,* following it with hisbodedus or Torah study. Some go back to sleep afterwards, while others remain awake until the morning, praying with the first light of day and then taking a nap for an hour or more to ready themselves for their daily activities.

Rebbe Nachman had one follower who found it quite impossible to get up at the right time for *Tikkun Chatzot.* Rebbe Nachman said to him: "Get as much sleep as you need.... Your *Chatzot* is at 3.00 a.m." (*Kokhvey Or* p.25). Instead of telling this chassid to abandon the idea of getting up for *Chatzot* altogether, the Rebbe gave him a way of carrying out the mitzvah that *was* possible for him. Those who find themselves unable to manage with less than seven or eight hours of uninterrupted sleep at night can still try to get to bed earlier in the evening in order to wake up an hour or two before the light of day for early morning sessions of hisbodedus and Torah study.

Rising regularly for *Tikkun Chatzot* can be fairly demanding, and some people may feel it to be altogether beyond their capabilities. But even those who feel unable to practice *Tikkun Chatzot* are urged to explore the possibility of arranging their schedule in such a way that they can rise early in the morning on a regular basis. The very first halakhah in the *Shulchan Arukh* tells us to "be strong as a lion to get up in the morning to serve your Creator. *You* be the one to arouse the dawn!" (*Orach Chaim* 1:1). This attests to the value and importance of early rising in the life of the spiritual seeker. Those who do so regularly know the unique blessing of the quiet hours of the early part of the day, and find that they can accomplish far more of the things that really count in life than they can by staying up very late at night and starting late in the morning (see *Azamra!* pp.19-46).

Physical healthcare

Does Rebbe Nachman's emphasis on spiritual remedies imply that as long as we devote ourselves to prayer, Torah and mitzvot with all our hearts, our bodies will somehow take care of themselves, so that diet, exercise, hygiene and other aspects of physical healthcare can simply be ignored?

Rebbe Nachman's profound respect for the physical body is expressed in the closing words of his beautiful poem, *Shir Na'im* ("Pleasant Song"), printed at the beginning of *Likutey Moharan*:

> "Let us apply our hearts to wisdom and seek to understand the design of our body, the proportions of its bones and joints and the arrangement of its organs.
> This understanding, which is so necessary, helps one to know the Creator and Former of all these creations,
> Who heals all illnesses and each person's pains: the blind, the lame, the leper and the smitten, those who are anxious and those who are in pain.
> Let us eat only for the sake of our souls, minimizing our physical lusts."

The body is a living teacher about God. "From my flesh I see God" (Job 19:26): the limbs and organs of the physical body, its structure and proportions all allude to aspects of divinity. Moreover, it is only with the physical body that we can carry out the mitzvot and accomplish our mission in this world. Without doubt, the soul is the essential self, while the body is secondary. But the body has to be properly cared for in order for the soul to be able to carry out its mission.

As a physical organism, the body has needs of its own. As Rebbe Nachman said, "It is completely impossible to be attached to the Torah all the time, day and night, without a moment's interruption. Every Torah scholar and even the greatest spiritual master must necessarily interrupt his devotions for a certain time to attend to the needs of the body, etc." (*Likutey Moharan* II, 78). Guarding our health is itself one of the mitzvot: "Take care of yourself, and guard your soul diligently" (Deuteronomy 4:9). This is a positive duty. In the Hebrew, the word translated as "diligently" is מאד (*me'od*), which literally means "very much." We are duty bound to take the utmost care of our physical health. Good health is a precious gift of God, and it is incumbent upon the recipient to guard and protect it in every way possible.

Moreover, as we have seen, Rebbe Nachman taught in "*Why do people get sick?*" that "when a person curbs his desires and submits to a medical regime... his soul sees that he has the power to control his impulses in order to achieve a certain goal, and she therefore comes back to him in the hope that he will curb his desires for the sake of the true purpose" (*Likutey Moharan* I, 268, see pp. 179ff.). This implies that a sound regime of diet and exercise, etc. can itself enhance our spiritual powers and become the foundation for a disciplined lifestyle that can lead to complete self-fulfilment. This is attested to by the many people who have found that a sensible program of diet and exercise greatly increases their mental tranquillity, clarity, energy levels and zest for life.

Abuse

Rebbe Nachman warned his followers never to smoke, and he told them not to drink except on Shabbat, festivals and other religious celebrations, and then only in great moderation. It goes without saying that he would have been opposed to all other kinds of substance abuse. In the ever more complex world in which we live, there are innumerable other things that are hazardous, from asbestos to zirconium. In the words of the *Shulchan Arukh*:

> "It is a positive duty to take all due precautions and avoid anything that may be a danger to life, as it is written, 'Take care of yourself, and guard your soul diligently.' The Sages prohibited many things that involve a risk to life. Anyone who violates such prohibitions, saying 'I'm only putting myself at risk — what business is that of anybody else?' or 'I'm not particular about such things,' deserves a lashing" (*Choshen Mishpat* 427:8-10).

It is a rabbinic principle that "a danger to life must be treated with greater stringency than a ritual prohibition" (*Chullin* 10a). Besides obvious physical dangers, the Rabbis also warned against various other practices deemed hazardous to physical and/or spiritual health, such as things that cause forgetfulness and certain other harmful practices in connection with eating and drinking, dress, bathing and grooming, sleep, travel, marriage, illness, death and burial, etc. (see *Kitzur Shulchan Arukh* #33 and Y. Y. Lerner, *Shemirat HaGuf veHaNefesh*, *passim*).

Diet

As we have seen, one of the greatest ever Breslover Chassidim, Reb Avraham Chazan, said: "Since the Rebbe warned us against doctors and medicine, we have an obligation to make every effort to eat only healthful foods" (*Siach Sarfey Kodesh* #3-539). What we eat and, equally, if not more important, *how* we eat, has a profound effect on our mental states, our thoughts, feelings, moods, general morale, energy levels and, of course, our physical health. Eating the wrong foods, or even the right foods in the wrong ways, can cause mood swings, tension, fatigue, negativity and depression, as well as long-term debilitation and degeneration of bodily organs and tissues.

The talmudic dictum that "more people are killed by the cooking pot than suffer from starvation" (*Shabbat* 33a) shows that the Rabbis were fully aware of the dangers of bad eating habits. Rebbe Nachman saw proper eating as a mark of basic human dignity: "A person who eats more than he needs is eating like an animal. One of the marks of human dignity is to eat only what one needs. To eat more than that is to act like an animal, who eats and chews the whole day, and this can bring on a fever" (*Likutey Moharan* I, 263).

Besides pointing to the physical dangers of excessive indulgence, Rebbe Nachman also emphasized its negative spiritual effects: "Eating properly subdues the tendency towards folly, enhancing one's intellectual and spiritual faculties. But when one overindulges and eats like a glutton, folly will get the upper

> The table, as the place where we eat, should be a central focus in our quest for health and healing. Thus the Hebrew letters of the word שלחן (*ShuLChaN*), "table", have the same numerical value as the Yiddish phrase צו רפואה (*Tzu ReFU'AH*), "for healing" (*Tzaddik* #476).

hand and overcome one's intellectual and spiritual faculties" (*ibid.* I, 17:3). "Our states of mind directly correspond to the food we eat. When the body is pure, the mind is clear and one is able to think properly and to know what to do in life. But impurities in the body cause putrid gases to rise to the brain, throwing the mind into such confusion that it becomes impossible to think straight" (*ibid.* I, 61:1).

Rebbe Nachman said little about what foods to eat and what to avoid, though he did warn against eating unripe fruits and raw onions (*Likutey Moharan* II, 88; *Rabbi Nachman's Wisdom* #265). Rabbinic guidance on basic principles of diet can be found in *Kitzur Shulchan Arukh* (32:2-19), in the Rambam's *Mishneh Torah* (*Hilkhot De'ot* 4:6-13) and at greater length in his *Hanhagat HaBri'ut* (#1). A more extensive Hebrew compendium of rabbinic lore on various aspects of diet, including the nutritional qualities of many different kinds of foods, is included in *Tav Yehoshua* (see *Sources and Further Reading*). However, in view of the innovations in food production in the modern era and the consequent changes in eating habits, we cannot necessarily expect direct guidance from classic Torah sources about how best to nourish ourselves today.

People's physical constitutions vary enormously. Different people have their own individual food needs, and may react to specific foods in very different ways. In the words of the *Kitzur Shulchan Arukh*: "Every individual should consult with medical experts to choose the foods best suited to his or her particular constitution, place and time" *(Kitzur Shulchan Arukh 32:7)*. For those who wonder what Rebbe Nachman would have thought about turning to medical experts for nutritional advice, it is worth noting that the Ramban, who was equally opposed to going to doctors, considered the giving of such advice to be the one valid function of the medical profession! (Ramban, Commentary on the Torah, Leviticus 26:11, see Chapter 15, p. 195) Those unable to turn to a competent nutritionist would be advised to consult contemporary works offering sensible nutritional guidance.

An obvious problem when seeking such guidance is that there are so many controversies among nutritionists of various schools over vitamin and mineral supplements, refined flour and sugar, meat-eating vs. vegetarianism, food combining, pesticides and any number of other issues. There is no option but to pray for clear guidance as to what and how to eat in order to keep ourselves fit and well to serve God. And when we find out which foods are best for us, we must then pray for help to keep to our diets.

Since Rebbe Nachman taught that a person can be healed through bread and water alone, it seems likely that in general he would have advocated simpler foods with a minimum of additives and supplements. When it came to religious stringencies, Rebbe Nachman's advice was not to be unnecessarily strict but simply to follow Jewish law *(Rabbi Nachman's Wisdom #235)*. Presumably he would also have been opposed to turning diet into a fetish. He taught that the food of Shabbat is in a completely different category from that of the six working days, and he encouraged his followers to eat plentifully and enjoy their food on Shabbat *(Likutey Moharan I, 276 & 277; ibid. II, 17)*.

Besides urging moderation, the Rebbe put great emphasis on *how* we eat. "Be careful not to gulp your food down hurriedly. Eat at a moderate pace, calmly and with the same table manners you would show if an important guest were present. You should always eat in this manner, even when you eat alone" *(Tzaddik #515; for a fuller discussion of diet, see Under the Table pp.74-82)*.

Exercise

The importance of exercise as an integral part of health maintenance needs particular emphasis, because it is still insufficiently appreciated in many circles. In the words of the Rambam: "Exercise is the most important fundamental in maintaining good health and keeping up our resistance to the majority of illnesses. Through exercise it is even possible to neutralize the damage caused by many bad habits" (*Hanhagat HaBri'ut* 1:3). "Even if you eat good foods and take proper care of your health in other respects, if you sit back comfortably and do no exercise you will suffer from constant aches and pains and your strength will decrease" (*Mishneh Torah, Hilkhot De'ot* 4:15).

Rebbe Nachman did not discuss exercise directly. Perhaps he didn't need to: his followers certainly didn't go everywhere by car like many people today, and most of them didn't have their own carriages either. They must have walked about in the fresh air far more than most people in our urbanized, technological world, and they were probably considerably more physically active! Rebbe Nachman recommended going out into the meadows for hisbodedus. This was primarily for the spiritual benefits, but it is also a fact that walking in the countryside is one of the best forms of exercise there is. We find that when he became sick, the Rebbe himself would take walks in the fields for his health (*Rabbi Nachman's Wisdom* #144).

Rebbe Nachman explicitly mentions that a good sweat helps remove illness-generating toxins from the body and brings a person to joy (*Likutey Moharan* II, 6, see Inset on facing page). The Rebbe was specifically referring to sweating over a holy task (such as dancing at a wedding, baking matzot, etc.). Exercise enthusiasts might argue that exercising in fulfilment of the mitzvah of "Take care of yourself..." would also come into the same category, and they could cite this teaching as further endorsement of the value of a regular workout!

What kind of exercise? The Rambam writes: "Not every bodily movement is 'exercise.' Exercise is defined as any form of movement — whether vigorous, gentle, or a combination of both — that involves some effort and causes an increase in one's breathing rate" (*Hanhagat HaBri'ut* 1:3). This would seem to correspond to what we today would call aerobic exercise: a steady, non-stop activity that leads to an increased pulse rate yet without putting strain on the cardiovascular system. Aerobic exercise helps develop cardiovascular endurance, the sustained ability of the heart, blood vessels and blood to carry oxygen to the cells and remove waste products. A balanced exercise program

A Good Sweat

"A good sweat (as when one sweats over a holy task) leads to joy — festive joy, as it is written, 'And you will rejoice on your festival' (Deuteronomy 16:14). (This need not necessarily be on an actual festival: any day which contains good is a *yom tov*, literally a 'good day,' i.e. a 'festival.') The reason is that joy depends on the state of the blood. Depression is caused by the spleen [whose functions include filtering the blood]. Malfunctioning of the spleen gives rise to impurities in the blood. An excess of impurities in the blood causes illness. When the impure blood in the spleen is within normal limits it is beneficial, because the spleen removes the impurities in the blood-stream, leaving the blood pure. But when too much impurity builds up in the spleen, it causes illness.

"The remedy is to sweat, because the illness-generating toxins in the blood are exuded in the sweat, and the blood is left pure. One can then come to joy. The reason is because depression is caused by the build-up of impurities in the blood and the spleen. Now that the impurities have been flushed out through the sweat, one comes to joy. And thus the letters of the Hebrew word for sweat, זיעה (ZeY'AH), are the first letters of the words in the phrase ז'ה ה'יום ע'שה י' (Zeh Hayom Asah YHVH), 'This is the day God made' (Psalms 118:24). This is the festive joy brought about by a good sweat. This explains what we often see, that as soon as a sick person sweats, he feels happy — because the sweat brings about joy" (*Likutey Moharan* II, 6; for Reb Noson's prayer based on this teaching, see p. 420).

should also include exercises that promote muscular strength and endurance and flexibility of the joints.

It is essential to tailor a physical fitness program to one's state of health, fitness and other individual factors. No one should begin any program of exercise without first consulting a competent authority. The body is a most wonderful, subtle, delicate instrument that has to be treated with the utmost care and respect. Those who have not exercised for a long time and are out of condition must be very gentle and patient while slowly encouraging stiff joints and weak muscles to start working again.

One of the most perfect forms of exercise is chassidic dance, in which all parts of the body are moved with grace and joy in praise of the Creator. In Rebbe Nachman's teaching on the healing power of joy, he points out that the Hebrew word for a sick person, חולה (*choleh*), is also the word for a "dance circle," and thus the dance circle of the Tzaddikim in time to come will mark the ultimate triumph over illness (*Likutey Moharan* II, 24, see Chapter 12, pp. 123f). The implication is that chassidic dance is a most powerful weapon in our healthcare armory. Reb Noson told one of his students, "I'll give you a pathway to repentance: dance every day!" (*Avanehah Barzel* p.62 #29). What better way of combining physical and spiritual exercise than to make it a regular practice, six days a week, to play tapes of your favorite *nigunim* and to dance free-style for seven to twelve minutes or more? (For a fuller discussion of exercise, see *Under the Table* pp.95-99.)

Relaxation and breathing

The relationship between chronic tension and poor health is now well established. In the stressful world in which we live, it is important to learn how to release anxiety and tension and relax. The best foundations for genuine relaxation are faith and trust that everything in our lives is sent from God and that no matter what might happen, God will always take the best care of us. With these basic attitudes, physical relaxation techniques can be an excellent way of unwinding, getting in touch with one's thoughts and feelings, and re-energizing. Even brief periods of relaxation can be an excellent preparation for prayer, hisbodedus, Torah study and many other activities. (For relaxation techniques, see *Under the Table* pp.64-72.)

Excessive tension is often a factor in faulty and inhibited breathing, which can give rise to low energy levels, lack of clarity, nervousness and a lowering of resistance to disease. It is most valuable to learn to breathe freely and fully, and to make it a habit to pause periodically in the course of one's daily activities in order to re-energize with a few long breaths. (For a full discussion of breathing, see *Under the Table* pp.83-95.)

General healthcare

The Rabbis put great stress on general cleanliness and hygiene, not only because of their importance for our physical health but also because "everyone who is careful about these matters brings extra holiness and purity into his soul and refines his soul for the sake of God's Name, fulfilling the command

(Leviticus 11:44) to 'sanctify yourselves and be holy, for I am holy'" (*Mishneh Torah, Hilkhot Maakhalot Asurot* 17:32). It is most desirable to gain a basic knowledge of the workings of the human body and to make a study of the fundamentals of self-care, including diet, fitness, dental care, how to prevent injury at home, outdoors and at work, stress management, precautions when traveling, and so on.

On the other hand, Rebbe Nachman was against going to extremes in such matters. For example, there were people who used to spend much time in the lavatory attempting to cleanse their bodies totally prior to their morning prayers. Rebbe Nachman ridiculed this practice because "the Torah was not given to ministering angels" (*Berakhot* 14a; *Rabbi Nachman's Wisdom* #30; *Tzaddik* #498). From his comments on this subject we can infer that while it is clearly desirable to take proper care of ourselves, it would be wrong to allow this to become obsessive.

Preventive medicine

We have seen that Rebbe Nachman insisted that his followers have their children vaccinated against smallpox (see Chapter 15, pp. 203ff.). This was a procedure that had proved itself, and it would seem reasonable to infer that Rebbe Nachman would have readily endorsed other tried and tested preventive procedures that have been developed since his time, such as immunization against diphtheria, tetanus, polio and so on. Nevertheless, in view of the controversies among doctors over the necessity and safety of certain vaccinations, one should seek expert advice in all questions concerning immunization.

Regular physical check-ups and screening are obviously recommended since the chances of recovery from cancer and other serious illnesses are far greater when they are detected at an early stage. Diagnostic testing of many different kinds has become increasingly common in contemporary medical practice. Besides well-established blood tests, urine analysis and screening for breast, cervical and colon cancer, many other advanced diagnostic methods are now available using ultrasound, magnetic resonance imaging (MRI), biochemical markers, etc. It is possible to identify many subtle conditions that could not have been found a few decades ago. However, it should be remembered that by no means are all tests offered by medical centers necessary. Studies indicate that certain diagnostic tests often detect trivial anomalies that may well remain dormant for life or even disappear, while the treatment offered may be ineffective or even dangerous.

We should always be aware that our lives are ultimately in God's hands and that our health is a precious gift that we are duty bound to cherish and protect by doing our part. Even when resorting to medical procedures, we should offer a prayer and take the opportunity to inwardly reaffirm our commitment to the spiritual pathway of faith and joy, and to sensible diet, proper exercise and other forms of self-care. Each day, when reciting the blessing said after relieving oneself, we should remind ourselves of God's awesome kindness in giving us our health and contemplate the amazing wisdom with which He fashioned the human body and the wondrous way in which He heals all flesh. (For text of the blessing *Asher yatzar*, see p. 13.)

Chapter 22

Dealing with Common Problems

1. Minor Upsets

Rebbe Nachman taught that all of life is necessarily a constant succession of ups and downs. This is certainly true of our spiritual lives, which are marked by an unending ebb and flow of highs and lows. And it is also true of our physical functioning. Our ever-fluctuating states of mind and spirit are intimately bound up with all kinds of other irregularities in our lives — an unusually late night, a skipped meal, the rich food of Shabbat or Yom Tov, an unaccustomed bout of physical exertion, stressful situations in the home or at work, economic and political developments, changes in the weather and any number of other factors. They can influence our bodily functioning in all kinds of ways.

Health could be loosely defined as the body's ability to maintain a stable internal environment — "harmony among the elements" — in face of the various external changes to which we are constantly exposed. The adaptive process is not necessarily always comfortable, yet the bouts of fatigue, stiffness, minor aches, stomach upsets, constipation, diarrhea, etc. we are all prey to as part of this process are not the same as illness.

In the words of the Rambam: "Even with the utmost care and caution it is impossible to avoid constant minor fluctuations in our physical functioning. Sometimes the stools become a little soft, sometimes a little dry. One day a person may find a change in his digestion or feel a mild headache or a slight pain in some other part of his body, and so on. Don't be in a hurry to take medications for these kinds of minor problems. Nature will take care of them without any need for medicines. Follow your normal health regime. If you try treating these minor ailments, either you will do the wrong thing and cause harm or, if you do the right thing, while you may succeed in restoring the normal balance, you have also taught your body to become lazy, and it will no longer function properly without outside assistance" (*Hanhagat HaBri'ut* 4:3).

Despite this sage advice, multimillion dollar industries are founded on the sale of innumerable over-the-counter remedies for hosts of minor, everyday problems: heartburn, flatulence, constipation, headaches, congestion, sore throats, coughs and many more. Certainly any unusual or persistent symptom calls for a thorough assessment by a competent doctor. But we should not let drug advertising deceive us into thinking that every minor fluctuation in our physical functioning calls for a remedy — and this would apply to herbal and other non-conventional medical remedies as well.

All kinds of minor physical symptoms may be related to poor diet, improper self-care, stress and other problems in our lives. Quick-fix remedies may bring immediate relief, but over the long term it would be far better to investigate the deeper roots of such problems, since if left unattended they may lead to more serious conditions. For example, vast quantities of antacids, digestive aids and laxatives are consumed in our societies. But when used to excess they can be counterproductive, and many of the problems they are supposed to aid would be far better tackled by a thorough review of one's dietary habits.

> Once Rebbe Nachman's daughter Sarah had a bad toothache. The Rebbe advised her to be happy. "How can I be happy?" she thought, feeling that her pain was too much to overcome with positive thinking. But the Rebbe said, "Even if it's hard to be happy, you must force yourself. If you pretend to be happy despite the pain, you'll eventually come to such a state of true joy that you'll dance, and this will cure you." Sarah took her father's advice to heart. Closing the shutters of her house, she began dancing, and before long the pain disappeared (Oral tradition).

Headaches of various kinds may be caused by all kinds of factors, from stress, tension, repressed emotion, strenuous activity, poor posture, bad lighting and certain food substances to heavy smoking and drinking. "The heart knows its own bitterness" (Proverbs 14:10): each person must decide for himself when a headache is bearable and when to take a pill. But almost all headache drugs have undesirable side effects, and where headaches are a persistent problem it would be preferable to try non-drug techniques as far as possible, such as relaxation, massage, hot or cold pads, etc. Insomnia is a distressing problem for many people, but sleeping pills disrupt the body's natural sleep cycle and can have undesirable side effects. Sleep problems may often be bound up with dietary factors, inadequate exercise, stress, or a lack of fulfilment in life.

Minor cuts, scrapes and grazes can be attended to at home, but where a wound is very deep and may have hidden dirt or debris in it, or if bleeding comes in spurts (indicating that an artery may have been cut), it is vital to seek prompt medical attention. The same applies to serious burns, possible fractures or dislocations, dog and snake bites and any insect sting that gives rise to nausea, vomiting, flushing, irregular heartbeat and difficulty in breathing.

Every household should have a reliable home medical and first aid guide providing clear information about which symptoms require medical attention and what to do in an emergency. Every home should

> Reb Noson was once at an inn eating his evening meal when a bone became stuck in his throat and he started choking. He opened his mouth wide the way people do when choking. At last the bone was dislodged and Reb Noson was safe. He said to the person who was with him, "Did you notice that when the bone was stuck I looked up to Heaven? No matter what happens, the only recourse is to turn to Heaven for help. Even when one cannot speak, one should at least look upward to Heaven" (*Kokhvey Or p. 71 #8*).

also have a basic first-aid kit, including a clinical thermometer, scissors, tweezers, antiseptic cream, antibiotic ointment, cotton, adhesive bandages, sterile gauze pads, bandages and safety pins. Emergency information should be readily accessible, including telephone numbers of local doctors, clinics, hospitals, drugstores, poison control center, details of one's medical insurance company, and details of persons to contact in an emergency.

2. Healing Crises

At some time or another almost all of us face health problems that are not necessarily dangerous but which make it impossible to continue with our normal activities: a particularly severe cold, a prolonged bout of 'flu, a bad infection, an incapacitating sprain, a torn muscle, a fracture or some other kind of problem or injury requiring medical attention, possibly a small operation, and bedrest. Work, engagements, plans and timetables all have to be suspended, and often there seems to be little one can do except lie low and put up with the pain, discomfort and disruption to one's life.

The natural tendency is to focus on the physical condition as the essential problem and view it as an unfortunate interruption — a medical problem that simply has to be treated in the appropriate manner until it "goes away" and we can return to normal life, hopefully as quickly as possible. But to look at such occurrences as purely physical phenomena is to ignore their spiritual dimension. The physical problem is often an alarm signal indicative of a more extensive malady with ramifications on the emotional, mental and spiritual planes of our being. It is the very pain and disruptiveness of the physical problem that make the message so emphatic.

"Nobody bruises so much as a finger here on earth unless it was decreed against him in Heaven" (*Chullin* 7b). Some may find it disquieting to think that an unseen tribunal is monitoring all our activities and imposing decrees and penalties. But this rabbinic teaching should not be taken to mean that all physical problems are simply vindictive "punishments." God may send suffering as a way of arousing us to search for Him or to cleanse us of sin. But even then, "Everything that the Loving One does is for good" (*Berakhot* 60b): everything God sends is planned and executed with the greatest compassion.

Godly awareness in exile

In the hustle and bustle of everyday life we are too often pushed into doing all kinds of things that go against our own better judgment. Even when we know that what we are doing is unwise, we often drive our subliminal doubts and reservations out of our conscious minds, giving ourselves all kinds of specious reasons to justify our actions. Yet at times it's as if there is a higher power — one that is beyond us but at the same time working *within* and *through* us — that will not let us get away with our efforts at self-deception. Something brings us to a halt. It may be a nexus of external circumstances and events that conspire against us, or something we do in spite of ourselves — an impulsive act of self-sabotage — that stops us in our tracks. And at times it's an illness or injury that in some way we ourselves, or our "souls," or a "heavenly finger," bring upon us, forcing us to pause and take stock.

A sin is a prime example of an action a person takes against his better judgment, allowing considerations of short-term gain (the immediate pleasure of the sin) to outweigh those of longer-term pain (its evil consequences). This is what the Sages meant when they said that "a person transgresses only because a spirit of madness enters into him" (*Sotah* 3a). The "spirit of madness" is the rash injudiciousness that leads the person to make such a choice. Indeed, the superficial rationale that justifies a sin has an uncanny power to charm the person who does it until, after repeating it once or twice, it seems perfectly permissible (*Yoma* 86b). Every sin drives out the Godly soul from a person to some degree or other. At first he may experience the separation from holiness and feel contrition. But each time he sins he descends to a lower level of spiritual consciousness, until he is no longer even aware that he is separated from God (see *Likutey Moharan* I, 56:3).

Da'at is a person's awareness of God and his sense of connection with Him. This is what is driven into "exile" by a person's sins. His *da'at* is still there *in potential*, and can be restored if he repents. But until he does so, his conscious mind is numbed to the Godly dimension of existence, and a this-worldly consciousness takes over instead. Yet God wants the person to repent and return to his heritage of Godly consciousness. He may therefore send him a "slap," in the form of a physical injury or illness — a stark fact that the person cannot deny. If he recognizes it as a message, he can then make the necessary efforts to recover his *da'at*.

"Through the blow itself God sends healing"

The classic case of illness in the Torah is *tzara'at*, "leprosy" (see pp. 24ff.). The *metzora* succumbed to *lashon hara*, speaking disparagingly about others in order to show himself in a positive light. The pleasure of not having to confront his own flaws may have been an immediate gain of his *lashon hara*, but the flaws remain, while the slander destroys the slanderer, the one slandered and the person who hears the slander (*Erkhin* 15b). Someone who regularly speaks disparagingly about others develops a distorted view both of his own righteousness and of the flaw-ridden characters of others: his holy *da'at* leaves him, and a false consciousness comes to the fore.

But the highly visible leprous mark on the *metzora*'s body is a flaw he cannot deny. How will he take it? Precisely because his *da'at*, his higher spiritual sensibility, is in exile, leaving him in a state of *mochin d'katnut*, constricted consciousness, it is very possible that he will take it on its own terms as a purely physical ailment that he will try to have treated medically in the hope that it will just "go away." This is why the Torah requires him to show his mark to the priest — a *moral* figure — and spend a period in isolation from the rest of society in order to reflect. The physical symptom is an invitation to the *metzora* to search beneath the surface of his conscious mind in order to rise to *mochin d'gadlut*, expanded consciousness, recover his *da'at*, and understand that casting aspersions on God's creatures is as ugly a flaw on the soul as the leprous mark on his body.

Nevertheless, the physical symptom is no more than a hint: the person is always given the freedom to evaluate it as he will. This is because God wants us to be masters of our own good, and He gives us freedom of choice in every aspect of life. For this reason, physical symptoms can always be viewed in two ways: as purely natural phenomena, or as having psychological and spiritual ramifications. By taking the latter view we can understand the saying of the Rabbis that "the Holy One sends healing through the very blow itself" (*Mekhilta Beshalach* 15:25).

The blow — the injury or illness — is an invitation to the sufferer to rouse himself to do the spiritual work that will bring healing to the *whole person*, including the spiritual maladies to which the physical problems point. The outbreak of such a problem could be called a "healing crisis" (to borrow an expression used somewhat differently by naturopathic doctors).* A crisis is a moment of climax when various interconnected problems and tensions that may have been developing over long periods of time finally come to a head. The ailment that puts a person out of action is indeed a "crisis." But it is a *healing* crisis — an invitation to employ the sudden rupture in one's normal routine to bring one's life to a higher level, thereby healing the deeper, spiritual malady.

When to call a doctor

This is not to say that introspection and prayer are all that's needed when a person is suffering from illness or injury. Where a condition requires medical attention, it would be dangerous and irresponsible to neglect it. Conditions that should be reported to a competent doctor include: a temperature above 103° F. (39.5° C.) or one that remains over 100° F. (37.5° C.) for three days; severe pain in the chest, stomach, head or ears; enlarged neck glands; any fever, sore throat, cough or severe runny nose that persist for more than a week; severe or persistent muscle pain, swelling or spasm; pain centered in a bone or joint; decreased mobility of a joint or inability to move it at all; stabbing or radiating

---

*Some alternative healers use the term "healing crisis" to refer to outbreaks of symptoms such as tiredness, weakness, mild fever, etc. experienced in the months after embarking on a health regime. In their view these are to be taken not as an indicators of bodily malfunctioning and pathology, but rather as signs that, after so much neglect, the body is rebounding in response to the new regime and cleansing itself of accumulated waste and toxins.

pain; numbness or tingling, and any other unusual or persistent symptom. (See pp.354f. on choosing a doctor.)

Where medical treatment is deemed necessary, bear in mind the advice of the Rambam: "If the patient can be treated through diet alone he should not be treated with medicines. If it is impossible to control the illness without medications, the first choice should be medicines that are nourishing and foods that have medicinal properties. When using medicines, one should begin with mild ones. If these are sufficient, well and good. Only if they are insufficient should one use stronger medicines" (Rambam *Hanhagat HaBri'ut* 2:21-22).

Even where medical remedies are called for, we must still look to God to guide the physician as to how to restore physical balance. Ultimately physical healing depends on the amazing self-regulating mechanisms God has planted in the human body, even where these are aided and strengthened by medicines. After taking medicine or receiving treatment, we must still depend on God and wait for the healing process to follow its course. It takes time for the body to rebound, for damaged tissues to mend and normal functioning to return. This is time that can be used for the spiritual work of healing.

> On taking medicine or receiving medical treatment, one should offer a short prayer:
>
> יהי רצון מלפניך ה' אלקי שיהא עסק זה לי לרפואה
> כי רופא חנם אתה.
>
> "May it be Your will, HaShem my God, that this medicine/treatment should bring me healing, for You send healing as a free gift."
>
> After treatment, one should say: ברוך רופא חולים, "Blessed is the Healer of the sick" (*Shulchan Arukh, Orach Chaim* 230:4).

Spiritual strategies

The key to the spiritual dimension of healing is the attempt to transcend *mochin d'katnut*, the "constricted consciousness" that fills a person when his holy *da'at* goes into exile, and to rise to a state of *mochin d'gadlut*, "expanded consciousness" and manifest *da'at*. This is because the physical problem is itself symptomatic of the exile of the person's *da'at*. One of the main ways to channel spiritual healing is through seeking deeper insight into the spiritual, emotional, social, economic and other issues in one's life calling for attention and making fresh efforts to resolve them through prayer and practical action.

Someone suffering from a severe infection, fever, aching muscles or acute pain and discomfort in the wake of an injury may feel like doing very little except trying to sleep! But even simply crying out to God because of the pain and frustration is a major step towards *da'at*, expressing one's awareness that the trial is from God and that God alone has the power to send true salvation and healing. Fever, pain, exhaustion and the like may make sustained introspection and prayer difficult, especially when a person is taking medications and painkillers. Yet "the Divine Presence is above the head of the sick person" (*Nedarim* 40a), and such trials can engender a unique sense of closeness to God, drawing forth cries and prayers from the very depths of one's heart. Physical suffering can also be strangely conducive to flashes of profound insight and self-understanding, especially during the long periods of half-waking, half-sleeping restiveness so often experienced during recovery.

Simchah

Genuine spiritual insight is hardly likely to come from brooding anger, self-reproach and the like. On the contrary, these make the Godly soul cringe and wilt. The subtle, delicate Jewish soul rises to her level not through negativity and harshness, but out of joy. Simchah frees the mind and soul from exile, bringing *yishuv hada'at*, settled consciousness and spiritual awareness.

We have seen how the Rambam emphasized the key importance of cheerfulness in the healing process:

"The physician should make every effort to see that everyone, sick and healthy alike, should always be cheerful, and he should seek to relieve them of the spiritual and pychological forces that cause anxiety. *This is the first principle in curing any patient*, especially if his illness is bound up with his mental and emotional state, as in the case of those who are gloomy and depressed. In all such cases *the physician should do nothing before improving the patient's state of mind....* The physician should not think that he can alter these emotions through his medical knowledge and expertise. This can be achieved only through moral guidance and the religious teachings we have received from the prophets" (*Hanhagat HaBri'ut* 3:13-14; see p. 41).

The Rambam gives practical suggestions as to how to foster a good mood:

"One should never forget to strengthen the patient's physical vitality with nourishing food, and to strengthen his spiritual powers with fragrant odors, with music, by telling him happy stories that expand the heart, and by distracting his mind with things that make him and his friends laugh. The people chosen to take care of him should be those who know how to cheer him up" (*ibid.* 2:20).

As one of the ultimate goals of the spiritual seeker, true simchah is an exalted state of *devekut*, devotion and attachment to God that bring an expansive sense of joy at His overwhelming goodness and kindness. But as Rebbe Nachman stresses many times, simchah starts with little things. Pleasant surroundings, wholesome, tasty food, beautiful flowers, fragrant odors, joyous and inspiring music, interesting conversation and amusing jokes all have the power to lighten our moods. When it comes to fun and jokes, Rebbe Nachman said: "If you want to joke, there are three conditions: (1) you must be careful not to insult anyone; (2) you must not use vulgar language; (3) your intention should not be to show yourself in a good light at the expense of others. Now you can joke!" (*Siach Sarfey Kodesh* I:13)

The foundation of true simchah lies in the "ten kinds of melody" (see Chapter 13, pp. 166-9). On one level this means quite literally music that delights and inspires. Music has tremendous power to open the heart and help one get in touch with one's inner feelings. Those recovering from an illness or injury should try to keep tapes or discs of their favorite joyous and inspirational music readily accessible to lift their spirits and keep themselves in a positive frame of mind.

On another level, the concept of the "ten types of melody" means prayer and devotion of all kinds. Rebbe Nachman taught that the entire Book of Psalms is built upon the ten kinds of melody, and these are the very key to healing. It is good to keep a copy of the Psalms at hand. If possible, try to recite at least a few Psalms each day. The Ten Psalms making up Rebbe Nachman's *Tikkun HaKlali*, the "General Remedy," contain all ten kinds of melody and are therefore a powerful spiritual remedy. (The Ten Psalms are listed on p. 153.)

Periods of bed-rest may provide an excellent opportunity for reading that one may not usually have time for, and this can also often be a catalyst for spiritual insight and growth. The Rabbis said: "Someone with a headache should busy himself with Torah; someone with a sore throat should busy himself with Torah; someone with stomach pains should busy himself with

Torah; someone with aching bones should busy himself with Torah.... And if his whole body is aching, he should busy himself with Torah" (*Eruvin* 54a).

A person recovering from illness or injury may find it difficult to concentrate on serious reading for any length of time, but the short items in books such as *Restore My Soul, Rabbi Nachman's Wisdom* and *Tzaddik* provide plenty of food for thought. *Rabbi Nachman's Stories* can be highly refreshing and also contain the profoundest healing wisdom. Where patience is short, the single-sentence items in the *Aleph-Bet Book* and *Advice* do not require sustained concentration, yet are highly interesting and thought-provoking. Someone who finds it difficult to read may enjoy listening to tapes of Torah talks and classes.

Vidui: Acknowledgement

A positive mental state is the best foundation for the introspection and hisbodedus needed to confront the deeper issues that are so often bound up with physical illness or injury. Even a common cold may be associated with personal, family, social, economic and other pressures, and the same is true of many other problems. All kinds of accidents and injuries occur at times of particular stress and difficulty. Under the pressures of everyday life, we are often so anxious to get on with immediate business that we feel forced to ignore the various tensions within ourselves or in our relationships with those around us. We tend to mask them even from ourselves, sending our *da'at* into exile. The physical crisis is often a signal that we need to take a break from routine in order to look within ourselves and seek more effective ways of tackling our problems.

When things come to a head in a "healing crisis," the point is to penetrate *behind* the mask and flush out one's accumulated frustration and negativity in order to restore *yishuv hada'at*, clarity and spiritual awareness. Just as a boil needs to be drained of infected waste matter, so it is necessary to release the various blocked emotions and inner frustrations that may be bound up with problems in one's spiritual life, with family or friends, at work, in the community, and so on.

The process of penetrating beneath the surface of everyday consciousness in order to get down to the roots of our problems is what today is called "therapy," a word that literally simply means "treatment" or "cure." For most people therapy means going to talk about one's problems with a trained psychotherapist, but in fact "therapy" was known and practiced long before the twentieth century. Anyone who feels troubled and goes to pour out his heart to a trusted friend or a more experienced elder and ask for counsel is practicing a form of therapy, as is the Jew who goes to a Rav, Rebbe, etc. to discuss his problems and ask for wise advice. And so too is the person who practices hisbodedus, pouring out his anguish and suffering to God and crying out for help.

In Torah terms, the process of pouring out the heart is called ודוי (*vidui*), which is related to the Hebrew root ידה meaning "admit" or "acknowledge." The conventional rendering of this word as "confession" has confusing connotations for many Jews, who associate this with non-Jewish religious practices and are unaware that *vidui* is a Torah mitzvah (Leviticus 26:40, and see Rambam, *Hilkhot Teshuvah* 2:2) and an authentic Jewish spiritual pathway followed by Jews for thousands of years. The idea of *vidui* is not to wallow in guilt and self-recrimination. It is to give frank and honest expression to one's often conflicting thoughts and feelings, and to own up to and take responsibility for one's personal shortcomings and for any mistakes one has made. This is what lays the foundation for more positive attitudes and behavior in the future. Until one gives verbal expression to one's negative thoughts and feelings, they remain "inscribed on one's bones" and may continue to give rise to actual physical symptoms (*Likutey Moharan* I, 4:5 and see p.183).

Vidui need not be a formal ritual of special prayers and breast-beating. A few spontaneous words of honest self-expression are also considered *vidui*. The key is to be sincere and truthful. The very pain, discomfort and suffering caused by illness and injury can be the starting point. It's *hard!!!* "Hard" in Hebrew is קשה (*kasheh*). "I'm in pain! I'm hurting all over! Why is this happening to me? What does it mean?" The very hardship (קושי, *KoShI*) itself elicits these questions to God. A question is a קשיא (*KuShYA*). *KuShYA* is made up of the initial letters of the words שמע י'י ק'ולי א'קרא (*Shema YHVH Koli Ekra*), "God, hear my voice — I call" (Psalms 27:7; see *Likutey Moharan* II, 46 and *Rabbi Nachman's Wisdom* #146). The very purpose of the trouble is to force one to cry out to God. And the cry itself can elevate and strengthen one's faith, until eventually all the difficulties are resolved.

The literature on hisbodedus discusses the various ways of expressing oneself to God, talking through one's problems and difficulties and praying for help and guidance (see *Outpourings of the Soul, Under the Table* pp. 101-144 and *Crossing the Narrow Bridge* pp. 147-160). Also most valuable is *sichat chaverim*, heart-to-heart conversation with a good friend. In times of illness it can be tremendously beneficial to unburden oneself to a trusted friend. If you have been having difficulties in your relationship with your spouse, a parent, a child or other family member, or a friend or colleague, etc., part of the therapeutic process may be to discuss the problems with that person honestly, constructively and in a spirit of reconciliation.

Expanding one's *da'at* through introspection, hisbodedus and *sichat chaverim* is an ongoing process of exploration and gradually deepening awareness and understanding. The discomfort and fatigue experienced during recovery may make it difficult to think in a concentrated way, especially since part of oneself may be resisting the whole process. At the same time, such periods can provide many rich insights into oneself and one's life. It can be helpful to keep a notebook at hand to record passing thoughts or capture fleeting insights. Often they may come while one is half asleep or dreaming. Over time, it should be possible to connect the various ideas and understand the broader picture.

3. The Meaning of Symptoms

Psychologists and doctors are becoming increasingly aware of the influence of psychological factors on physical health in general. There is also growing recognition that specific personality traits and emotions are frequently associated with particular kinds of physical problems. Thus many studies indicate a close relationship between grief, suppressed anger, sense of failure, etc. and vulnerability to cancer, while the link between tension and heart disease is now well established. Many psychotherapists and some of the more psychologically-aware doctors now encourage patients to explore the possible role of such factors in their illnesses in the hope that bringing buried emotions to the surface and resolving inner conflict will help promote actual physical healing.

In the Torah view, physical ailments may be bound up not only with worldly psychological factors but also with spiritual flaws. In biblical times saintly individuals took physical ailments as signs of spiritual shortcomings, and would seek out a prophet for insight and practical guidance (Ramban on Leviticus 26:11, see pp. 194-5). The Rabbis taught that certain physical conditions, such as *tzara'at*, were visitations caused by particular sins (see p. 25). The story of how the Ari diagnosed the spiritual roots of one man's shoulder pain (p. 181) is an example of the way an outstanding latter-day tzaddik viewed a physical problem.

The Rabbis said that "when someone sees that suffering has come upon him, he should carefully examine his behavior" *(Berakhot 5a)*. Clearly this is a prescription for making a general spiritual accounting in times of trouble and illness. But should the actual physical symptoms themselves be looked upon as pointers to the specific nature of the underlying spiritual problem?

Rebbe Nachman taught: "Every thought, word and deed that God sends you every day is a hint intended to help you draw closer to Him. God Himself is infinite and without end, but He 'contracts' Himself, as it were, to our level, using all the experiences that He sends us every day as a way of signaling to us and guiding us. It is up to us to search for and recognize the messages contained in our various thoughts and conversations and all the other events in our lives. They are all sent to help us reach deeper levels of insight and draw closer to God" *(Likutey Moharan I, 54:2)*.

It should be noted that Rebbe Nachman himself warned against giving excessive attention to such hints to the exclusion of other sources of spiritual guidance, especially Torah study *(ibid.)*. Nevertheless, this teaching indicates that it is perfectly valid to view physical ailments as allusions to deeper spiritual issues, and to devote some attention to pondering their significance. Thus the late Lubavitcher Rebbe, Rabbi Menachem Mendel Shneerson, wrote to one sick person: "You have surely heard the saying of the Baal Shem Tov that everything that happens to a person and everything he sees or hears contains buried guidance about ways of serving God, and this is especially true in the case of a major event like your eye problem" *(Refuah Shelemah p.110)*.

The mitzvot and the parts of the body

How does one discover the possible spiritual implications of specific physical problems? We know that the 613 limbs and arteries, etc. of the human body correspond to the 613 mitzvot. If a person has a problem in a particular part of his body, does this suggest a possible flaw in his fulfulment of the mitzvah corresponding to that body part? Do we even know which mitzvot correspond to each of the different parts of the body?

Nowhere in rabbinic literature is there an exhaustive one-to-one listing of *all* the limbs and organs of the body and their corresponding mitzvot. However, the classic 16th century *Sefer Charedim* contains a lengthy discussion of the various positive and negative Torah and rabbinic mitzvot dependent on the heart, eyes, ears, nose, mouth, respiratory system, digestive system, arms, legs, head and sex organ *(Sefer Charedim, chapters 9-32 & 35-51; see Inset on next two pages)*.

(continued on p. 336)

Selected mitzvot associated with major limbs of the body

Based on *Sefer Charedim*, chapters 9-32 & 35-51

The Heart:

Have faith in God; love and fear God; attach yourself to God; trust in God; sanctify God's Name; concentrate on the *Shema* and the prayers; revere and honor parents; love your neighbor; judge others fairly; repent and have contrition over sins; don't forget God; don't become angry, hate, bear a grudge or take vengeance; don't listen to slander; don't entertain sinful thoughts.

The Eyes:

Look at the tzitzit; weep over the death of a tzaddik; read the Torah; don't look at statues of idols; don't gaze lustfully.

The Ears:

Study the Torah aloud; listen to your prayers as you say them; hear the shofar on Rosh Hashanah; listen to reproof; listen to prophets and judges; don't listen to false prophets or tempters; don't listen to slander.

The Nose:

Don't savor the scent of someone with whom sexual relations are forbidden.

The Mouth and Respiratory System:

Recite the grace after meals, blessings and prayers, kiddush and havdalah; study Torah aloud; recount the story of the Exodus on Pesach; count the Omer; mention the Exodus daily; remember the command to blot out Amalek; confess verbally; tell the truth; comfort the sick and oppressed; swear in God's Name; don't take God's Name in vain; don't mention names of idols; don't practice divination; fulfil vows; cry to God in times of trouble; don't take part in communal strife; don't oppress others verbally or shame them; don't lie, flatter or use vulgar language.

The Mouth and Digestive System:

Don't eat before feeding your animals; eat on Shabbat and festivals; eat matzah on Pesach; eat in the sukkah; fast on Yom Kippur; don't consume forbidden fat, blood, unclean or improperly slaughtered animals, birds, fish, worms, insects, fruit from an immature tree (*orlah*), idolatrous wine or *chametz* on Pesach.

The Hands and Arms:

Give charity; practice kindness; give loans; wear tzitzit; put on tefilin; fix a mezuzah where required; put a protective railing around a roof; pay wages on time; bury the dead; save your fellow from danger; send away the mother bird from the nest when taking eggs or chicks (*shiluach haken*); return stolen goods; return lost property; redeem the firstborn; write a Torah scroll; kasher and immerse utensils purchased from a non-Jew; destroy idolatrous shrines; don't make idols; don't murder, steal or rob; don't take interest on loans to a Jew; don't take a pledge by force; don't encroach on others' property; don't blot out God's Name; don't waste food; don't take bribes; don't cut your *peyot* or razor-shave your beard; don't hit others; don't imitate gentile dress or customs; don't have yourself tattooed; don't delay payment of charitable pledges; don't perform forbidden labors on Shabbat or festivals.

The Feet and Legs:

Stand up before elders and Sages; stand up before a Torah scroll; give testimony standing; escort guests out of the house; attend to the needs of the sick and needy; escort the dead; sit in the sukkah; *chalitzah*; don't walk beyond the Shabbat boundaries; don't bow to idols; pray to God standing.

The Sex Organ:

Circumcision; marital relations; personal sanctity; don't engage in forbidden sexual relations.

*

The discussion in the *Sefer Charedim* provides much food for thought about the possible implications of certain localized problems.

Another rich source of information about the spiritual connotations of the various body parts is to be found in Kabbalah and Chassidut, which are founded on the principle that man was created in the image of God. "From my flesh I see God" (Job 19:26): the various parts of the human body correspond to various aspects of the higher, spiritual worlds, and the Kabbalah is replete with references to the spiritual significance of various parts of the body (see *Anatomy of the Soul* by R. Chaim Kramer).

However, an extensive knowledge of Kabbalah and Chassidut is not essential in order to consider the possible spiritual implications of particular ailments. In hinting to people to draw closer to Him, God "contracts" Himself to the level of each and every person, sending messages that each one is capable of understanding in the light of his or her existing knowledge. One should ask oneself: "What does this problem mean to *me*? What could it be telling me? What mitzvot or Torah teachings do I associate with this body part or perform with it? How have I been carrying them out?"

Can one know if one's intuitions about possible connections are correct? It would be unrealistic to expect absolute certainty of the kind that masters of *ruach hakodesh* like the Ari, the Baal Shem Tov and Rebbe Nachman possessed. But precisely because many ailments are sent as hints to the individual *on his or her level*, it is sometimes enough to devote just a little thought to one's life and activities in order to become strongly aware that a particular ailment is bound up with a specific shortcoming or area of neglect. It is true that "a person does not see his own blemishes" (*Sifri Behaalotkha* 12:12). Even when faced with the clearest hints, people sometimes resist confronting certain painful issues. In order to overcome such resistances, those sincerely wishing to explore the spiritual dimensions of a physical problem would be advised to do so with the help of a trusted friend, a sympathetic counsellor or therapist, or an understanding rabbi.

If you become aware of having neglected a particular mitzvah or of having acted wrongfully against God or a fellow human, you should verbally acknowledge the wrongdoing and make a firm commitment not to repeat it. You should also make every effort to take all necessary steps to make amends for the wrong. It can be helpful to focus on Torah teachings relating to the part of the body that is afflicted. Thus the Baal Shem Tov taught: "Sometimes one can draw beneficial influences through words alone. For example, if a person has an ailment in a particular limb, he should speak about the corresponding aspects of the upper sefirot. When a person has a pain, he should attach himself to God, i.e. God's attributes [= the sefirot] and he will not feel the pain" (*Keter Shem Tov* II, #299).

The all-encompassing mitzvot

We should not necessarily expect to find simple answers and direct correspondences between particular maladies and specific spiritual flaws. Many illnesses affect several body parts and systems at once. Any illness should alert us to the need for introspection and spiritual reckoning, but especially where a problem is more generalized, the search should be not for a single magic solution but for deeper insight into the main areas needing improvement in one's life as a whole. One should give thought to one's connection with God and mitzvah-observance in general, with special emphasis on those mitzvot that encompass all the others: faith, prayer, Torah study, charity and kindness. As the Lubavitcher Rebbe wrote to one sick person: "We need God's blessing in everything, and at times when we are in need of extra blessing it is necessary to add in matters of Torah and mitzvot. The more one adds, the greater the blessing that will come from God" (*Refuah Shelemah* p.117).

First and foremost is charity. In the words of Rebbe Nachman: "It is through charity that all blessings flow into the world" (*Likutey Moharan* I, 31). "Charity is the remedy for all wounds" (*ibid.* II, 4:12). The quest for spiritual healing involves prayer, hisbodedus, Torah study and fulfilment of the mitzvot — and charity is the key to all of them. "Charity has the power to widen the entrance to holiness. When a person wants to embark upon a certain path of devotion, he first needs to make an opening to enter on this new path. This is why all beginnings are hard. But giving charity makes the entrance wider" (*ibid.*).

At times of illness and injury, one should, if possible, aim to give extra charity according to one's means. (Regarding *pidyon nefesh*, see below p. 361.) As we have seen, the Chafetz Chaim would distribute food to the needy when there was an illness in his family (see p. 197). Rebbe Nachman taught that "when a person gives charity to the Tzaddik, it is as if he gives charity to many, many Jewish souls" (*Likutey Moharan* 17:5). This is because the Tzaddik has a general soul which includes the individual souls of all those under his influence. One of the highest forms of charity is to support the spreading of the Tzaddik's teachings through books and publications, which provide spiritual food for innumerable Jewish souls. It is a good idea for a sick person to keep a charity box within easy reach and to try to give small amounts before prayer and hisbodedus.

The sick person is in special need of God's kindness and compassion, and it is his acts of love and kindness to others that make it possible for God's love to be channeled to him. As the Rabbis taught: "Everyone who shows love for God's creatures is himself shown love" (*Shabbat* 151b) (see Inset). It may be difficult for someone who is ill or injured to carry out practical acts of kindness, but even thoughtfulness, consideration, kind words and smiles are also forms of *chesed*.

One who shows love to others is himself shown love

"When a person is in special need of God's love, God sends him an opportunity to show love to someone else. This is what makes it possible for God's love to be channeled to the person himself, because 'Everyone who shows love for God's creatures is himself shown love' (*Shabbat* 151b). Thus it is written, 'And He will give you love [i.e. He will give you the opportunity to show love to someone else] and [then] He will show you compassion' (Deuteronomy 13:18).

"A person's ability to show love depends on his level of *da'at*, Godly awareness. Someone who has Godly awareness will have compassion. For anger, the opposite of compassion, is rooted in foolishness: 'Anger rests in the bosom of fools' (Ecclesiastes 7:9). Accordingly the Rabbis said, 'It is forbidden to show compassion to anyone who lacks *da'at*' (Berakhot 33a). This is because a person who lacks *da'at* is himself lacking in compassion (since 'anger rests in the bosom of fools'). This is why it is forbidden to have compassion on him, because 'Everyone who shows love for God's creatures is himself shown love,' but if a person lacks compassion, it is impossible to have compassion on him. Thus a sick person who is in need of God's compassion needs to have compassion on others, and this depends on *da'at*.

"A special flow of *da'at* comes into the world on Shabbat... On Shabbat everyone is given extra *da'at*. This is why it is customary for those visiting the sick on Shabbat to say, 'Shabbat has the power to show compassion' (*Shabbat* 12a). Shabbat is a time when *da'at* shines to all, and thus the Shabbat itself has the power to make the sick person have compassion on others because of the extra *da'at* that shines into the invalid on Shabbat. And once the sick person has compassion on others, he will certainly receive compassion from Heaven, because 'Everyone who shows love for God's creatures is himself shown love'" (*Likutey Moharan* I, 119).

4. Getting out of a rut

Almost all of us go through periods when we find ourselves feeling generally low physically and spiritually. We may not be able to put our finger on any specific problem. We just feel inexplicably tired, weak, uninspired and apathetic. Prayer, study, mitzvot, work and other responsibilities all become burdensome, and things that never used to be so problematic suddenly seem to weigh excessively. We find ourselves moody, impatient, cynical, angry, rebellious, tense and anxious, or just gray and clouded.

Such periods are often marked by physical problems of various kinds — headaches, stiffness, pains, rashes, nausea, digestive problems and so on — and these may often be exacerbated if we start eating badly and neglecting basic self-care. Yet we may not feel that there is any specific medical problem as such, although apparently minor symptoms and general malaise can sometimes be the first signs of serious illness. Indeed, chronic frustration and depression can themselves lead to physical illness, which is itself a good reason to make strong efforts to overcome them. But in most cases the weariness and general sense of discouragement that characterize these kinds of ruts in our lives are transient phenomena, perhaps a reaction to a particularly exhausting period we've gone through, a demanding project, a major move or change of direction, a new arrival in the family, and so on. At other times such ruts may *precede* an important advance in our lives, spiritually or otherwise. But until we actually take the next step forward, we may experience only the negativity.

What can we do to get out of such ruts? Often we are quite well aware of what we *ought* to do: put more strength into our prayers and meditation, give more time to our Torah study, eat properly, exercise, take ourselves and our lives in hand and be *joyous*. But we just can't get ourselves to move. We may feel we've tried again and again, only to see all our efforts thwarted. How can we possibly be joyous when we feel so low and the problems we face seem so intractable?

In some shape or form depression is ubiquitous in our societies. Many try to smother it with food, sex, shopping, entertainment, alcohol, drugs, gambling and other distractions. But since depression is at root a spiritual problem, the quest for solutions in the external, material world is doomed to failure. Millions of dollars worth of tranquillizers and antidepressants are consumed every year, but they simply mask the underlying problems while often producing new ones, including psychological dependence, anxiety and further depression. Medications can undoubtedly help alleviate certain mental conditions, but all too often they are prescribed indiscriminately for problems that are rooted in far deeper levels of people's being than simply their body chemistry.

Atzvut

Anxiety, tension, frustration and depression are precisely the ailments of the Princess in Rebbe Nachman's story of the Beggar who had no hands (*Rabbi Nachman's Stories* pp. 410-34; see pp. 149-52). The Princess is the divine soul in every Jew. In flight from the cruel king — the evil force sent to challenge us in this world by seeking to turn us away from our holy mission — the Princess tries to enter the amazing, beautiful Water Castle: this is the Torah, to which we turn as a salve for the ills and pains of life. Seeing her flee, the king orders his troops to shoot her with their ten types of poisonous arrows, and she falls unconscious. The ten types of arrows symbolize the entire gamut of negative feelings and emotions that poison people's lives, including the futility, sadness, unease and foreboding so many experience, as well as far deeper complexes of frustration, anger, shattered hopes and dreams, grief and despair, of which we may often be barely conscious.

Rebbe Nachman said: "Only a great Tzaddik has the power to enter every place where the soul has fallen and remove all ten arrows from her" (*Rabbi Nachman's Wisdom* #273). If only it were possible to pour out our hearts to such a Tzaddik and receive true, sage advice! For many people today one of the greatest sources of frustration is the feeling that they have no one they can really talk to. The few known tzaddikim are often practically inaccessible, while many of the people to whom we do have access give us the feeling that they simply won't understand. If only there was one kind, sympathetic Sage who could answer the deepest questions of our lives, or just *encourage* us! Rebbe Nachman told of one saintly man who said, "If only someone, *anyone*, no matter who, had just said to me when I was starting on my way and going through all the trials of rejection and confusion, 'Be strong, brother! Hold yourself!' I'd have gone *running* forward with all my might" (*Likutey Moharan II*, 48).

All this should at least teach us to make every effort to play a supportive role for others when we see them going through *their* moments of discouragement and depression. When struggling with our own problems and difficulties, it is certainly most important to seek the help and support of any trusted friends and counsellors we can turn to: one of the main pillars of Rebbe Nachman's healing pathway is to bind oneself to other souls, especially to the tzaddikim. Even if it seems impossible to find the right person to speak to, we can and should search in the literature of mussar and chassidut for guidance from the outstanding luminaries of the past. But when it comes to putting their advice into practice, there may be no option but to play the role of helper/counsellor to ourselves. In any case, when it comes to taking the necessary steps to get out of the rut, we have to do the actual work ourselves!

Tracing the causes

It is tempting to look for a quick fix — a crash diet, an intense burst of exercise, some magical *segulah* or a single *tikkun* that will quickly lift us out of our low. It is true that certain cases of malaise can indeed be traced to some fairly simple underlying cause, spiritual or physical. Fatigue, for example, may sometimes be directly related to a particular dietary deficiency, an allergy, toxicity, an infection, a postural fault or some other physical cause. Once this is identified and properly treated, the fatigue may just disappear. Poor diet in general is often a factor in mood and fatigue problems. Many people believe their diet to be fairly wholesome without being aware that their two or three seemingly innocent daily cups of coffee, their late-night snacks or some other aspect of their eating habits may be playing havoc with their physical, mental and emotional life. Another frequent cause of fatigue problems is chronic lack of exercise, which can lead to muscle weakness, joint stiffness, poor circulation, sluggish metabolism and a build-up of toxic wastes in the body.

Certain cases of depression, malaise or other problems may be traceable to a single spiritual factor, such as an invalid mezuzah or tefilin, some faulty practice in relation to Shabbat observance, giving charity, kashrut, family purity, etc., or some other spiritual flaw. There have been cases where severe depression has been dissipated simply by inducing the suffering individual to take care to perform the first mitzvah in the daily life of the Jew — washing the hands three times on rising in the morning (*negelwasser*) in order to dispel the impure spirit that clings to the fingers after sleep.

However, in many other cases of depression and malaise the underlying causes are far less simple and straightforward, and may involve complex syndromes of interconnected problems on numerous different planes. Domestic, work, financial, family and other difficulties may conspire with inner emotional and other factors to disrupt the daily hisbodedus, prayer and

Torah study that are vital to inner balance. All this may adversely affect our celebration of Shabbat and performance of other mitzvot. The general stress and tension this causes may then lead us to eat badly and neglect or abuse ourselves in other ways. This is likely to leave us feeling unfit, out of condition, strained and fatigued, which makes us all the more liable to make mistakes and less able to cope with our problems. We become increasingly frustrated, tense and angry... and so the cycle continues — until we may find ourselves in a state of deep gloom and despair.

Making a start

Many of the problems involved in such syndromes are likely to have been long in the making and will not necessarily be able to be solved quickly. The first step in climbing out of this kind of rut is to find some way to sidestep the discouragement and despair that throw everything else into shadow. However, for more lasting solutions it is also necessary to confront the more long-term problems involved and to institute the necessary changes in your life.

As in any enterprise in life, the first step is to give charity, even just a coin or two, and to pray. The mitzvah of charity brings a flow of kindness into creation, forging a channel for the divine love that will sweeten the situation you confront and release you from the constricted consciousness that is preventing you from seeing your way out. Keep a charity box within easy reach at all times, and get into the habit of making frequent contributions throughout the day. Even when no charity box is at hand, you can always assign one of your pockets or wallet compartments to serve as such temporarily. By frequently making small donations you draw a constant flow of divine love to yourself.

Turn to God for help. Cry out and ask Him for everything you need, materially and spiritually. If you find it hard to talk to God out loud, you can still whisper in your heart: "*Ayeh???* Where are You? Where is the place of Your glory?" (see *Ayeh?*). Rebbe Nachman stressed that not a single word of prayer ever goes to waste. Even the prayers you offer with little inner conviction still leave their mark. You can always say a few simple words asking God to help you make a new start even if you can't yet see how you'll take the first step. You may not feel like embarking on a session of hisbodedus, opening a Torah text, beginning that diet, doing some exercises or taking whatever other steps are necessary in order to heal yourself and bring your life to a higher level. But you can still tell God what you would *like* to do. You can still express your *yearning* to do it.

Turning self-healing into an ongoing project

The moment someone takes his or her problems to a doctor, be it a physical doctor — a physician — or a spiritual doctor — a tzaddik, counsellor, or therapist, etc. — getting cured becomes a definite, ongoing *project*. In the same way, when you have to play the role of doctor to yourself in order to lift yourself out of a rut, it is helpful to turn your quest into a definite project: self-healing. In order to give continuity to the healing process, why not start a special file in which you collect all the material relating to this project: your private notes, relevant cuttings and articles, inspiring quotations, etc. One of the main keys to self-healing is deeper insight and self-understanding. But insights come and go in the mind. They may come at any time of the day or night. Writing them down as they occur and keeping them together in a place where you can refer to them easily should make it much easier to follow them through and integrate them into your life.

Such a file does not have to be a literary journal. It is often sufficient to note down just a few key words in order to keep track of your thoughts and feelings, define the issues and problems in your life as you currently perceive them, and list ideas to which you want to give further attention. Some people think better in pictures than in words. If this is true for you, why not try drawing simple pictures of yourself, those around you, your house, place of work, synagogue, yeshivah, etc. in order to get in touch with your thoughts and feelings about them and gain deeper understanding of the issues you face?

Making time: regular hisbodedus

If you want to go to a doctor for a consultation or treatment, you normally have to make an appointment. In the same way, you should set appointed times for yourself in order to work on your self-healing project. Fix regular hisbodedus sessions to enable you to unwind from everyday pressures and to work seriously on bringing your life to a higher level. If you feel beset by many problems and find your morale to be low, try to schedule a break from your daily activities — whether for an hour or two, an afternoon, or even a few days if possible — to take yourself to a quiet spot for a brief retreat in order to pray, meditate and start to clarify your goals. If your self-healing strategy includes a physical dimension, such as a cleansing diet, a new exercise routine, etc., such a retreat might be the ideal time to give these special attention.

Trying to diagnose and overcome your own problems when caught up in the middle of them can be one of the hardest and most frustrating aspects of spiritual self-healing. The problems themselves, together with the many associated negative thoughts and emotions, may be keeping you locked in *mochin d'katnut*, the very state of constricted consciousness that you need to transcend in order to find your way out of them. Quiet meditation and introspection can help you get in touch with levels of your higher self that may have been crowded out by the daily pressures in your life. But you also need to cry *out* to God, to call out *beyond* the situation that traps you, appealing for a helping hand to lift you to *mochin d'gadlut*, expanded consciousness.

A good way to focus the search for insight and understanding is to use questions that you address to God and to yourself: "Where am I in the world? What am I thinking? What am I feeling? What is my health problem? What are my other problems? What do I want in life? What is my purpose in this world? What are my aims and goals? What is holding me back from them, and how can I overcome the obstacles and attain my purpose?" etc. Putting key questions into words and asking them out loud makes it easier to think about the issues involved, to redefine them where necessary, and to start seeing solutions. Use this method over several sessions of hisbodedus in order to focus on the central issues you face in your life. (See Guiding Questions for Self-Awareness and Change, pp. 347-9.)

Sometimes insight and answers may come quickly; at other times the process of gaining deeper understanding of your problems and seeing how to overcome them may be long-drawn out and uneven. Flashes of expanded consciousness and moments of release and joy may be followed by long periods when the problems seem as bad as ever, if not worse. Many of Rebbe Nachman's writings deal precisely with this aspect of the spiritual journey and are the ideal support when facing the constant ups and downs it involves (see *Outpouring of the Soul, Restore My Soul*, etc.). Each time you fall down, you must start over again, giving a little charity, offering a few simple prayers, returning to Torah and hisbodedus, and persisting until God sends complete salvation.

Many problems are best solved by learning to change the way you view them. There are all kinds of things in life that cannot be changed — your body, your family, past mistakes, certain social and economic factors, and many others. But where these are problematic for you, the solution often lies in learning to alter your perceptions and finding ways of turning seeming limitations into advantages. The principle shift in perception needed in practically all the problems we face in life is to recognize that they have been sent to us by God out of love.

A healing worksheet

It can be very helpful to develop a personal healing worksheet listing the principle issues and difficulties you are grappling with and the practical steps you intend to take in each area. Summarize the main goals of your life as a whole. Next, list your particular goals in the current period together with specific projects you are working on. These could include spiritual projects (e.g. conquering anger and other negative traits, embarking on daily study of the *Shulchan Arukh*), current projects connected with the home, family, work, friends, the community, etc., creative projects, and also any specific health projects you are working on (e.g. losing weight, overcoming fatigue, getting back into condition).

Now list the main components of your self-healing plan, including both physical strategies (e.g. diet, exercise, treatment for specific problems) and spiritual strategies (e.g. giving charity, regular hisbodedus, daily Torah study). Beside each item, briefly note the specific practical steps you plan to take to implement your strategy (e.g. diet — check out sound literature on nutrition; exercise — seek expert advice about appropriate plan). In another section of your worksheet, list the main issues you want to work on in your hisbodedus and all the things you would like to pray for regularly.

Your self-healing worksheet could prove to be one of the most important documents in your healing file. Mapping it out will help you to define the issues and problems you want to work on and to clarify the strategies you need to follow. Seeing all your goals and strategies concisely listed before you will help you keep them at the forefront of your mind and assist you in organizing your monthly, weekly and daily schedule in order to accomplish what you want. You will probably wish to take your worksheet through a number of successive drafts as you deepen your self-understanding and make progress with your various projects.

Have your worksheet before you during hisbodedus, and ask God to help you attain your goals and to assist you at every step of the way in all your various projects and activities. Ask Him to give you whatever you need, and to inspire you with the willpower and determination to carry out your plans in practice.

Every word of your prayers, each expression of holy longing and yearning, every good thought, and even your very cries and sighs will become "notes" in the holy melody of joy that will steadily subdue the negative, depressed spirit, bringing true healing of the spirit and the body (see Chapter 13, pp. 163ff.).

*

Guiding questions for self-awareness and change

Where am I in the world?

Where am I? What is troubling me? What is frustrating me? Which thoughts and feelings constantly recur? What do I find myself dwelling on? How do I see the problems and issues in my life? How do others see them — my spouse, parents, children, brothers and sisters, friends, colleagues, teachers, employer, doctor, therapist, wider family, people in the community...?

Physical problems

Can I define specific problems and symptoms? What are my general health problems (e.g. fatigue, overweight, out of condition, discomfort...)? How do I feel about my body? My appearance? Do I think of my body as basically healthy or unhealthy? Do I have particular thoughts and feelings about the condition of particular organs: my heart, lungs, stomach, liver, pancreas, intestines, kidneys, bowels, brain, nervous system, sex organs...? What about my skin, blood, bones, joints, muscles, arms, hands, legs, feet? Which parts of my body do I feel to be unhealthy? Which parts are sound? What are the effects on my body of my way of life and behavior — diet, exercise or lack of it, work, family activities, social life, vices, addictions... ? What long-term changes do I need to institute? What three things could I do immediately to improve my health?

General problems and issues

Relationships: with spouse, parents, children, brothers and sisters, relatives, friends, teachers, colleagues, boss, employees, others. Are my relationships easy/difficult, simple/complicated, fulfilling/frustrating?

Livelihood: work, career, obligations, commitments, debts... *ma'aser* (tithes) and charity.

Spiritual and emotional issues: self-image; personality traits, positive and negative; security vs. insecurity; calm vs. anxiety and tension; joy and enthusiasm vs. negativity, depression and despair. Creativity. Intellect. Level of knowledge in Torah, other areas. Devotion in prayer. Fulfilment of mitzvot. What are my fears? What beliefs do I have about life, death, God, the world, myself...? Which of my beliefs (e.g. about myself, what I am capable of, what people think about me, etc., etc.) limit my ability to achieve? What bad or self-destructive habits do I have? What mistakes do I make over and over? What have I done wrong in my life? My failures? Major sins? How are past mistakes affecting my current situation? How can I make amends?

Life-fulfilment: goals, projects: Torah study, mitzvot, career, family, community, organizations, the nation, the world.... What do I want in life? What do I yearn for? What is my purpose in this world? What are my unique capabilities (e.g. spiritual, intellectual, creative, artistic, domestic, scientific, mechanical, business, social, interpersonal)? What can I contribute to my family, friends, organization, community, the nation...? Am I coming closer to achieving my goals or drifting further away? Where *am I* in the world? How do the issues in my life relate to the Jewish People? Eretz Israel? The world as a whole?

Thinking positively

What do I have to be thankful about? What do I have to rejoice about? What is good about me? What are my good points? What are my growth points? How can I change my view of the things I see negatively and look at them in a more positive light — myself, my past, family matters, my economic and social situation, work, the community, situation of the Jewish People, that of the world? To what extent are my definitions of certain problems or ways of looking at them actually *creating* those problems? What is positive about the problems? How can I see them as part of God's plan for my ultimate good? What can I learn from my problems? How can I use them positively? How can I turn shortcomings, faults and flaws into advantages, assets and merits?

Changing things

What can I do practically to change what I want to change? What is up to me? What is up to others? What do I need to do in cooperation with others? What can I change in myself? What can I change in my home, at work, in my family, organization, community, country, the world in general?

What information do I require? What questions do I need to ask? What sources of information do I have (e.g. libraries, bookstores)? Who can I turn to for guidance and advice (e.g. rabbis, teachers, counsellors, specialist advisers, health experts)? What are the things that most inspire me (which books, music, etc.)? What can I do to inspire myself? What decisions do I have to make? How can I harness my motivational system to stop doing the things that are destroying my self and my life and to do the things that will bring me to the ultimate good?

Practical steps

What practical steps do I have to take to change myself and my life? **What changes do I need to make in my lifestyle and daily routine:** hisbodedus, prayer, Torah study, work, family life, general healthcare, diet, exercise...? **Developing a game plan:** goals, strategy and tactics. In order to accomplish my long-term goals, what will I need to do first? Long-term projects, short-term tasks. What things will

I have to wait for to come about in due course, and what practical steps can I myself take *now*? What is important? What is urgent? What should take priority? What is of secondary importance? What do I want to accomplish this year? This month? This week? Today? Now? Writing a tasklist, workplan, timetable. **Hisbodedus:** What do I have to pray to God for? What do I have to emphasize and "nag" about persistently every day and in every prayer?

Some suggestions

Schedule **hisbodedus today.** Plan a **stroll** in a quiet park or the woods for an hour or so, or possibly longer. Arrange a **weekend spiritual retreat**. Schedule **regular Torah study**, including chassidut. Enroll in a class. Seek a study partner. Take a few minutes of **quiet relaxation** every day. **Dietary changes**: reduce or eliminate intake of coffee, refined sugar, excessive fat, etc.... Give more emphasis to grains and vegetables. Stop smoking and substance abuse. Do I need support to overcome an addiction? Start a **regular exercise routine**. Check out exercise plans.

Do I need to take a **new step** in my career, change my job, investigate a new synagogue or community, etc. etc.? Do I need help to develop a game plan to get out of debt? Do I have **"unfinished business"** with a parent, spouse, sibling, child, friend, colleague, acquaintance...? What practical steps can I take to **heal relationships** in the family, with friends, at work, in the community?

Choose **one mitzvah** to emphasize: e.g. Shabbat, tzitzit, tefilin, mezuzah, one of the festivals, visiting the sick, charity, acts of love and kindness.... Choose **one trait** to work on: e.g. selfishness, anger, insensitivity to others.... Try to put a little **more time and effort** into prayers and blessings. Rejoice over them! Sing an inspiring **melody**. Have **faith and trust in God!**

*

Chapter 23

Facing Serious Illness

Perhaps it was just a minor ache or pain at first, or a lump you preferred to ignore... until eventually you *had* to see a doctor. And then, when the results of the tests came back, suddenly everything changed. You have a life-threatening illness — a gaunt fact that overshadows all else. Will you ever again be able to enjoy anything without having to think about this knife held at your neck?

How many different thoughts and feelings pass through the mind of a person who has just found out that he or she has a dangerous illness! Gut fear. Images of death and the grave. Grief. Anger: "Why *me*?" Disbelief: "It can't be true! There must be some mistake!" A sense of betrayal by the body. Nightmare images of attacking snakes and spiders. Worries about what's going to happen: "Will I suffer pain? Will I be disfigured? Incapacitated? How are my dear ones going to manage... without me?" Strange feelings of recklessness: "I don't care! I'd rather die than go through the pain, the torment of all the treatments, the shame of disfigurement and disability!" Terror and helplessness. "Get somebody to *do* something! Cure me! Just take this illness away!"

Since God is beyond nature and runs the world providentially, Rebbe Nachman rejected the materialistic notion that a life-threatening illness must inevitably take its course. It is a fact that by no means do all cases of dangerous illness lead to death. There are many long-term survivors from serious heart disease. At least fifty percent of those diagnosed with cancer recover from it, and modern medical diagnosis and treatments are extending survival time in many cases of other serious illnesses.

But no one can give you any guarantees. With a knowledge of your history, your general state of health and the type and stage of your illness, doctors may offer an assessment of the possible course of the disease based on statistical probability. But no doctor alive can honestly predict exactly what is going to happen to *you*. Nor is the Torah healing pathway of faith, prayer and joy a magical solution offering greater certainty of physical recovery. Indeed, the Torah reminds us that our lives are totally in God's hands: "I kill and I make alive, I wound and I heal, and there is no one that can deliver from My hand" (Deuteronomy 32:39).

King Hezekiah said: "Even if a sharp sword is pressing on your neck, don't despair of pleading for God's mercy" (*Berakhot* 10a, see p. 17). Rebbe Nachman taught us always to be positive and optimistic. But this does not mean engaging in wishful thinking and pretending there's no threat. The foundation of Rebbe Nachman's pathway is truth and honesty. In the case of serious illness this entails facing your fears and accepting the reality. Being positive means searching for the good in the situation as it actually is. This is the only sound basis for true joy, for only when we accept the reality of death can we really live.

Illness is a call to *live!*

In our societies, serious illness and death are subjects most people don't like to talk or even think about, preferring to lead their lives in the pretense that death will never come. From the news with which we are being constantly bombarded about fatal accidents, war, terrorist attacks, epidemics, famine and other disasters, we are all aware of death in theory. If a close relative, friend or acquaintance dies, it brings the meaning of death home in a far more powerful way. But serious illness brings us face to face with the stark reality of our own mortality. "*My* life is going to end!" Yet the fact is that, seriously ill or not, in this world we are *all* condemned to death, and none of us knows when his or her time is going to come — "who will die at his destined time and who before his time, who by water and who by fire, who by the sword, who by a wild beast, who by famine, who by thirst, who by a storm, who by plague, who by strangulation and who by stoning..." (from the High Holiday liturgy).

The Rabbis said, "Repent a day before your death" (*Avot* 2:10) — which means *every* day, since we never know which day will be our last. The ancient Rabbis wanted us to keep our mortality at the forefront of our minds. So did Rebbe Nachman, who reminds us about it in conversation after conversation (see *Rabbi Nachman's Wisdom* #51, #77, #83, #84, etc.). This is because only when we know clearly where this life leads to — the grave and the Next World — can we really make the most of our lives in *this* world. Only when we understand that our time here is limited do we truly value it.

We must be willing to face our deepest fears and come to terms with the prospect of death in order to use the time we have left in the best possible way. For the fact that we cannot control death does not mean we cannot choose how to live in the face of it. The idea is not that you should spend all your time morbidly preparing for death. On the contrary, you should shift from being a passive victim of fear and anxiety to actively taking charge of your life. Take stock of yourself. Where have you been and where are you going? Work out your priorities. Drop whatever is meaningless and wasteful. Say what you want to say to your friends and dear ones. Fix what is in your power to fix in this world — and *live*.

The purpose of life is to come ever closer to God, and indeed, death is simply the next stage in life. It is death only in relation to the material world. But for the essential *you* — your soul — death is the gateway to a higher, more intense and infinitely more joyous level of life. This is because of the greater intimacy of the soul's connection with God when divested of the physical body. If the prospect of death is so fearsome, essentially this is because God Himself is fearsome. The proximity of the encounter with the Living God is awesome. Serious illness thrusts upon us the awareness that the next step up in life is ahead of us.

Illness is a call to *live*, and it should be taken as such: as a call to live fully in this world and the next. This is the true healing. There can be no guarantee of physical healing: it may come about and it may not. But even if you recover, fully or partially, the only purpose of being well is to *live* — to strive to come ever closer to God day after day. By making the decision to *live* in every way possible, even under the limitations of serious illness, you are indeed preparing yourself to live in better health. The decision to *live* is thus the key to healing: to live every moment as best you can, coming closer to God in every way, in thought, word and deed.

Job and Elijah

In Uman it was customary to whisper the following to a sick person: "Job went on a journey and met Elijah the Prophet. Elijah said to him, 'Why are you sick?' He replied, 'Because of my head and because of my whole body.' Elijah said to him, 'Go to the River Dinur and immerse in it, and you will be healed.' Job went to the River Dinur and immersed, and he was healed. And just as Job was healed, so will all sick Jews be healed." This custom is said to have been instituted by Rabbi Pinchas of Koretz (1726-91) (*Siach Sarfey Kodesh* 5-457).

[The River Dinur (Daniel 7:10) is formed from the sweat of the *chayot* (*Chagigah* 13b). The *chayot* bear the Throne of Glory, which is the subject of "*Sound the Shofar — Dominion*" (see Chapter 18).]

1. Medical treatment

The last thing Rebbe Nachman would have wanted would be for anyone who genuinely needs medical treatment to feel guilty and anxious about taking it because of the Rebbe's comments against doctors. The medical profession is still open to many criticisms, but without question medical knowledge, techniques and standards of care have vastly improved since Rebbe Nachman's time. Contemporary medicine saves many lives and can also often greatly improve the *quality* of life of the seriously ill and chronically sick. Even as you go for medical treatment, the most important thing to remember is that everything is only in God's hands.

Many patients try to ignore that first ache, lump or sign of bleeding, putting off visiting the doctor as if pushing the problem out of mind will somehow make it disappear. This is very foolish and dangerous, because the more a disease spreads in the body and the later it is diagnosed, the more of a threat it becomes and the harder it is to treat. Don't ignore unusual developments in your bodily functioning because you are afraid of finding out what they might mean. This would be a flight from reality. It is better to face up to the truth, however unpleasant, than to be confronted with a far more catastrophic situation later on. Knowing exactly what is happening enables you to take positive action to deal with any problem instead of just worrying about what it might be.

Choosing a doctor

As we have seen, Rebbe Nachman's main advice to those needing medical treatment is to make sure to get the very best (*Siach Sarfey Kodesh* I:8; see p. 4). Many patients take far more care in deciding where to go out to eat or which clothes to buy than they do in choosing a practitioner who may have a major influence on the length and quality of their lives. More often than not, they select a hospital or clinic merely because it happens to be the nearest, and the institution itself chooses a physician for them from its roster of specialists. For financial reasons and because of the limitations imposed by insurance companies, etc., it is often difficult for people to insist on the medical treatment of their choice. But remember: it is your life that is at stake. You owe it to yourself and your dependants to do everything in your power to get the best possible treatment.

Today's medical market offers a bewildering variety of approaches to illness and treatment: orthodox, naturopathic, herbal, homeopathic, chiropractic, osteopathy, acupuncture, reflexology, kinesiology and shiatsu to name but a few. There is growing acceptance even in the orthodox medical establishment that so-called alternative therapies may often successfully complement conventional surgery and drug therapy. However, in many cases the different approaches to treatment are based on radically different theories of illness. Even in orthodox medicine most courses of treatment involve difficult decisions about risks versus benefits.

Rebbe Nachman did not offer any guidance about the merits or lack of merits of different approaches to medical treatment. As in all the agonizing decisions we face in life, we must first and foremost pray to God for true guidance (see Inset). As we have seen, the Talmud tells us that Heaven decrees which medicine and doctor will be the agents of healing in each individual case of illness (*Avodah Zarah* 55a, see pp. 185ff.). Turn this into a prayer that God should help you find the doctor and treatment *you* need quickly and easily, and that he should do his work with the utmost proficiency. Make enquiries wherever you can and discuss your problem with reliable people who have experience with similar problems. Many rabbis encounter a wide variety of medical problems in the course of their duties, and it

> Rebbe Nachman was once talking with one of his followers when they heard someone reciting the evening prayers. The man was saying the words ותקננו בעצה טובה מלפניך, "and remedy us with good counsel from before You." The Rebbe said to his follower, "Listen to the way this man is just running through the words. Doesn't he realize that one must say the words 'remedy us with good counsel' with the utmost intensity and feeling from the very depths of the heart? We must always beg God to have mercy and grant us good advice and guidance so that we will know what is right!" (*Rabbi Nachman's Wisdom* #238).

may be helpful to consult with them. In the Torah-observant community there are a number of well-known figures who have made it a specialty to keep abreast of current medical developments and who can often give advice about the best specialists and clinics in various areas.

What makes a good doctor?

What makes a "good" doctor? We can gain some insight into this from a comment by the Maharsha on the mishnaic dictum that "The best of doctors are destined to go to hell" (*Kiddushin* 82a). The Maharsha explains (*ad loc. s.v. tov*):

"The 'best of doctors' means a doctor who considers himself to be the best. He relies only on his own expertise. There are times when his haughtiness and conceit cause him to diagnose an illness mistakenly, resulting in the death of the patient. The doctor should make it a habit always to consult another physician, because a *life* has been placed in his hands."

Presumably a "good doctor" is one with the greatest medical expertise, but from the Maharsha's comment it is clear that expertise itself depends not only on profound study and rich experience, vital as these are, but also on *humility*. A true healer is always conscious of the awesome responsibility he bears and his own human limitations. He recognizes the amazing intricacy of the human body. Knowing the difficulty of diagnosing accurately and determining the most suitable treatment, he weighs every decision he makes with the utmost care.

Another factor is the doctor's optimism. On the saying of the Rabbis that "the Torah gave the doctor license to heal" (*Berakhot* 60a), the Tzemach Tzedek (the third Lubavitcher Rebbe, 1789-1866) noted the Torah gives him authority only to heal, not to make the patient despondent" (*Refuah Shelemah* p.25).

To a large extent, judgments about different doctors' levels of expertise, humility and optimism are bound to be subjective. In any case, a doctor who is good for one person may be useless for somebody else. Which characteristics are important to *you*? Would you feel comfortable with a male or female? A young person or someone with more maturity? Which count more to you: impressive medical credentials and aggressive style, or affability, compassion and good bedside manner? Is it important to you that your doctor should have a feel for religion?

Many people develop all kinds of complexes about their doctors, becoming strangely inhibited in their presence and wary of raising their doubts and questions for fear of antagonizing them. Perhaps this is because, consciously or unconsciously, they look to the doctor as their savior, investing him with a power he does not possess. If you always keep in the forefront of your mind that God is the only healer, this should enable you to relate to doctors and other medical personnel as human beings and to interact with them in the same way as you would with professionals in any other field. Especially where you face serious decisions about treatment options, it is your absolute right to consult more than one doctor. If you are uncomfortable with your doctor, whether for professional or personal reasons, find someone with whom you feel more comfortable.

Don't be shy. Don't be afraid of imposing on the doctor's time: it's *your* life that is at stake, and the doctor is being paid to serve you. List your questions in advance of your appointment in order not to forget anything. Ask about anything you need to know. Don't hide any symptoms. Speak frankly about any anxieties you have, such as whether you face disability or disfigurement, will you suffer pain, etc. Everybody has worries of one kind or another; this is nothing to be ashamed of. The doctor may be able to dispel some of your fears or offer practical suggestions for dealing with any problems that are likely to arise. Don't forget to express your appreciation to your doctors and other members of the healthcare team.

Your role in the healing process

Having chosen your doctor and course of treatment, take good care to carry out the doctor's advice. Don't use Rebbe Nachman's negative comments about doctors and medicine as an excuse to be lax in taking medications and following other instructions. If you don't trust your doctor's judgment or have doubts about the value of the treatment you are receiving, go to another doctor and get a second opinion. But be sure to persist with medical treatment if that is what you need. Following the prescribed course of treatment conscientiously is part of the mitzvah to "take care of yourself, and guard your soul diligently" (Deuteronomy 4:9).

That is not to say that, having found a doctor, you can simply leave your health entirely in his hands and wait for the treatment to take effect. More and more orthodox doctors and clinics now accept that in many different illnesses, lifestyle changes by the patient in such areas as diet, exercise, relaxation, etc. play a major role in restoring health. Even when it comes to medical treatment *per se*, the doctor may be the agent and the medications the means, but for true and complete healing, you must look only to God. This is another aspect of the mitzvah to "guard your *soul* diligently."

Try to turn your thoughts to God at every stage of treatment. Take a copy of the Psalms with you to the clinic and read from it while waiting. Pray for an accurate diagnosis. Ask God to guide the doctor in prescribing the best course of treatment. When taking medicines or receiving treatment, believe not in the means but in God, and recite the prayer for healing (see above p. 327). Where possible, choose a hospital that can provide you with kosher food and take account of your need to observe Shabbat and other religious requirements. Wherever possible, use medicines that are kosher, and try to avoid treatments that may lead to sterility or otherwise affect future mitzvah observance.

Doctor's appointments, visits to clinics and hospitalization provide many opportunities to serve God. Your primary purpose may be to receive treatment, and you may be uncomfortable or in pain. But you can still use those of your faculties that are still intact — your speech, your smile, and so on — to sanctify the name of God. Talk about Torah and serving God. Share your faith with nurses, doctors and other patients. Offer comfort and encouragement to those who are also suffering. You can make use of your own experience to help others and to deepen your human relationships, elevating yourself in the process.

Spiritual healing strategies

Every doctor will first seek to diagnose the problem or illness — to give it a name. However, it is vital to recognize that the doctor's diagnosis is nothing but a way of classifying your physical condition: into which category of known medical problems does it fall? Your physical condition is unquestionably of the utmost importance, having a decisive effect on everything else in your life. Yet the physical is only one plane of your being as a whole. Just as the state of your body is affecting the way you feel, think and act, so your thoughts, feelings and activities in the past have played their part in influencing your current physical condition. And so too, how you direct them now will affect your state of health and the course of your healing both now and in the future.

Don't let the medical label become the definitive statement of who you are — a "case" of this or that — because this will limit the way that you (and others) look at yourself. As a soul, a *whole person* living in multiple dimensions, your situation goes far beyond the strict medical diagnosis of your physical condition. As you work on yourself, be sure to take into account the broader ramifications of the physical problem. Bodily illness generally indicates disharmony in other planes of life besides the physical, such as the stress bound up with career and livelihood, long-standing tensions in the family or other close relationships, deep inner frustrations and other emotional and spiritual wounds. The healing you need is not only healing of the body but healing of the soul.

2. Faith

As we have seen, Rebbe Nachman emphasized that all the spiritual pathways of healing are ultimately founded on faith (see Chapter 19, pp. 284-9). But no one should say, "Well, I just don't have sufficient faith, so how can I follow these pathways?" For the very process of healing itself is precisely about *developing* and *deepening* our faith. In times of health we often take our bodily functioning for granted. Only when our bodies fail in some way and we become sick do we suddenly see how frail and helpless we are, and we begin to recognize how totally dependent we are on God's mercy. Illness is thus a prompt to reach out to God, and we must direct our cries of pain and suffering to Him.

Use your mouth to affirm your faith. You can do this even if you feel your faith to be shaky, or even non-existent. "Even if you have doubts about your faith in God, say out loud: 'I believe with perfect faith that God is One, first, last and always'" (*Rabbi Nachman's Wisdom* #142). The Jewish mystical tradition associates the mouth with *malkhut*, kingship. Use your mouth to lead and rule over yourself; your thoughts and feelings will eventually follow. When talking about your illness and treatment and hopes of recovery, be sure to use phrases like *"im yirtzeh HaShem*, God willing," "everything is in God's hands," and "God is the Healer."

Have firm trust that every detail of your illness and recovery is in God's hands. God controls the entire universe, and nothing can stand in His way. The Lubavitcher Rebbe wrote to one sick person: "Regarding your quotation from the Rambam that the Holy One, blessed be He, does not perform miracles going beyond the bounds of nature for a single individual, the fact is that we have seen with our own eyes miracles beyond nature performed for individuals, especially in the last few years, and especially in the case of medical problems in the interior of the body. Again and again the doctors have been wrong in their diagnoses even after all the tests" (*Refuah Shelemah* pp.35-6).

Does this imply that having faith means believing you will definitely be completely cured and everything will turn out as you wish? This kind of thinking is dangerous because it can lead to crushing disappointment if the situation deteriorates. Some people might feel guilty for not having believed strongly enough, while others might conclude that their "faith" didn't work, which might lead them to abandon it altogether. To insist that everything will turn out exactly as we might choose is not faith but wishful thinking. True faith means knowing that whatever happens is from God, and that everything God does is for the very best. Our task is to *search* for God's goodness. Have faith that every last detail of what is happening to you is sent by God — every ache and pain, every twist and turn, and every step in the healing process. Know that God is good, and therefore everything will turn out for the best, even if you cannot see how right now.

Don't feel bad about feeling bad

Believing that everything is for the best does not mean that you are not allowed to feel bad. The pressure put on ill people to keep their spirits up and think only good thoughts can make them feel very isolated from those trying to "cheer them up." They may even come to feel ashamed if they see that things are getting worse rather than better. The last thing you need is to feel bad about feeling bad. Don't feel guilty if you feel miserable and sorry for yourself. But turn your cry of pain and misery to God: "*Ayeh mekom kevodo?* Where is the place of Your glory? Where are You? Come down to me and help me!" We should believe that everything God sends is for good, but that does not mean we may not ask for what we believe to be better!

> "The essence of God's compassion is when 'the Eternal God will grant *you* compassion' (Genesis 43:14) — i.e. when God puts the compassion in our hands. Even when God sends a serious illness or other kinds of suffering, it may in fact be out of compassion, because certainly everything God sends a person, even extreme suffering, is only out of love. However, we often cannot comprehend God's compassion and are unable to bear it when He expresses His compassion for us in the form of suffering. We therefore ask God to put the compassion in *our* hands and to show us compassion in the way that we understand it in the literal sense of the term — to be healed of illness, etc. This is alluded to in the very name of the Jewish People, ישראל (*YiSRaEL*), which is made up of the initial letters of the Hebrew words of the above verse, א'ל ש'די י'תן ל'כם ר'חמים (*El Shadai Yiten Lakhem Rachamim*), 'the Eternal God will grant *you* compassion'" (*Likutey Moharan* II, 62).

The essence of a positive attitude is not to pretend that you're fine if you're far from it, but rather to keep yourself from sinking into a quagmire of morbid negativity by having faith in God's goodness even at the hardest moments. The worst suffering is easier to bear when you know that it comes for some purpose, such as to cleanse you of your sins. In the words of Rebbe Nachman: "When things are very bad, make yourself into nothing. Close your mouth and eyes — and you are like nothing. Sometimes you may feel overwhelmed by evil thoughts, finding it impossible to overcome them. You must then make yourself like nothing. You no longer exist, your eyes and mouth are closed. Every thought is banished. Your mind ceases to exist. You have nullified yourself completely before God" (*Rabbi Nachman's Wisdom #279*).

It is striking that in the last of Rebbe Nachman's tales, "The Seven Beggars," not only are all seven heroes the lowest of the low on most people's scale of success, since they're all beggars. In addition, each of them appears to have a terrible disability. One is blind, another deaf, another dumb, one has a crooked neck, one is a hunchback, one has no hands and one has no legs. Yet each one has turned his apparent disability into a most amazing advantage in the world of truth. And they all owe their success to their very social disadvantage, because, being beggars, they all know that they have nothing in this world and must depend on God for everything. This comes to teach us that we must ask God to show us how to take advantage of even the worst situations, including severe disability and chronic illness.

Can you still talk? Use this divine faculty to pour out your heart to God and reach out to Him as never before. Sing. Cheer yourself up. Speak to the people around you and cheer *them* up. Talk on the phone: call people you know who are lonely and unhappy. Use your own experience to help you understand what other people are going through. Encourage them to talk. Be a good listener. Talk about faith and simchah.... And if it's hard for you to talk, you can still *think* about God and pray to Him in your heart. And when you do this you are *alive*, because faith and prayer connect us with the Life of life.

3. *Pidyon Nefesh*: Redemption of the Soul

All illness has a spiritual as well as a physical dimension, and in order to heal you therefore need not only your physician but also a doctor of the *soul* — a tzaddik — both to intervene on the spiritual plane through his prayers, and to give guidance about *tikkunim*, changes in your life or shifts of emphasis that may help bring long-term health to the whole person.

The first priority is *pidyon nefesh*, redemption of the soul, because the sick person is under a cloud of *dinim*, heavenly judgments, as manifest in the pain, discomfort and mental constriction that accompany so many illnesses. The Talmud says, "Someone who has a sick person in his house should go to a Sage and ask him to request mercy for him" (*Bava Batra* 116a). The true Sage is the Tzaddik, who works to "sweeten" the harsh judgments. As we have seen, Rebbe Nachman taught that "when a person is sick, a redemption is the prerequisite of any cure. Only after the redemption has been made does the Torah give the doctor permission to cure" (*Likutey Moharan* II, 3; see Chapter 14, pp. 186ff.).

It is not necessary to wait until illness strikes before giving money for a *pidyon*. This can be done at any time. In the words of Rebbe Nachman: "It is a good practice to give money regularly for a *pidyon*. This sweetens any harsh judgments and gives constant protection against them. Even when no one in the house is sick and you have no particular problems, it is still good to give money for a *pidyon* in order to prevent any problems or illness, God forbid" (*Tzaddik* #539). A suitable time to give money for a *pidyon* is on the eve of Rosh Hashanah (*Rabbi Nachman's Wisdom* #214). Some may wish to do so when they feel themselves to be in a rut or face particularly difficult problems, after a frightening dream or some other bad experience, such as a near accident, a mugging or terrorist attack, etc.

> "There are prayers which are not accepted above until one gives a sum of money that is numerically equivalent to the letters of the relevant prayer. For example, when a person prays 'Give me children,' he must give a sum of money equivalent to the numerical value of the letters of the words תן לי בנים (*ten li banim*, 'Give me children,' numerically 592)" (*Aleph-Bet Book* Prayer II:9). [The numerical value of the letters of the words שלח רפואה שלמה (*shelach refuah shelemah*, "send complete healing") is 1005.]

How much money should one give? In some cases a tzaddik may suggest an appropriate sum, but it is impossible to lay down general rules. How much is your life worth? In many cases illness brings heavy expenses leading to acute financial pressures, especially when the patient is the main bread-winner. At such a time a sizeable contribution for a *pidyon* may seem out of the question. But considering the massive sums that are often spent on medical treatment, it is strange how tight-fisted some people with means become when it comes to charity. Yet "charity saves from death" (Proverbs 10:2 & 11:4, and see *Tzaddik* #10).

To whom should one give the *pidyon* money? Rebbe Nachman spoke about the great wisdom and effort required to accomplish a redemption (see p. 192). Some people wonder whether any known tzaddik today has the power to do everything necessary to bring about a *pidyon*. However, "The Bible compares

Gideon, Samson and Jephthah to Moses, Aaron and Samuel. This is to teach you that Gideon was to his generation as Moses was to his; Samson was to his generation as Aaron was to his; Jephthah was to his generation as Samuel was to his. This comes to teach you that no matter how lowly a person may be, once he is appointed leader of the community he is like the noblest of the noble" (*Rosh Hashanah* 25b). Thank God, there are many saintly tzaddikim in the various Jewish communities. The Breslover Chassidim often send money for a *pidyon* to leading elders of the movement.

The Prayer for Redemption

When money is brought to a Tzaddik for a *pidyon*, the Tzaddik places his two hands upon the redemption money and says:

יהי רצון מלפניך שימתקו הדינים והגבורות הקשות מעל פלוני בן פלוני על ידי פלא עליון שהוא חסדים גדולים ורחמים גמורים ופשוטים שאין בו תערובת דין כלל. אמן.

May it be Your will to sweeten the harsh and severe judgments against (...) the son/daughter of (...) through *Pelé Elyon*, the Supreme Wonder, where there is nothing but utter mercy and complete, simple love, with no mixture of severity at all. Amen. (*Likutey Tefilot* I, 123; see above p. 193.)

By his own testimony, Rebbe Nachman himself possessed the power to bring about redemption of the soul (*Rabbi Nachman's Wisdom* #175), and "the tzaddikim are greater after their death than during their lifetime" (*Chullin* 7b). For this reason, in cases of serious illness, many Breslover Chassidim endeavor to send someone to pray at Rebbe Nachman's grave in Uman.

Other means of *pidyon nefesh*

Rebbe Nachman writes that "filling the mouths of Torah scholars with wine has the same power as a redemption and can sweeten harsh judgments" (*Likutey Moharan* I, 41). On the literal level this would mean presenting a gift of wine for genuine Torah scholars to drink. In addition, since "'wine' refers to Torah" (*Tanchuma, Vayechi* 10), this can be taken to mean that a *pidyon nefesh* can be effected by helping to spread the "wine" of the Tzaddik's teachings as widely as possible so that they are on the lips of multitudes of Jewish souls.

Rebbe Nachman also teaches that "rising for *Tikkun Chatzot*, the midnight prayer, has the same power as a redemption" (*Likutey Moharan* I, 149). *Tikkun Chatzot* clearly has an important place in Rebbe Nachman's healing pathway (see pp.310f.). This is because the purpose of the midnight prayer is to initiate the restoration of Jerusalem by mourning over the destruction of the Temple. As we have seen in "*Sound the Shofar — Dominion*," the "rebuilding of Jerusalem" is the foundation for the redemption of prayer that brings true healing (see pp. 243ff.). Mourning for the Temple, which is the source of *da'at*, is bound up with mourning over the concealment of the true Tzaddik, who is the very embodiment of *da'at* (*Likutey Moharan* II, 67). Since it is the Tzaddik who brings about *pidyon nefesh*, there is a close connection between *tikkun chatzot* and *pidyon nefesh*.

The quiet that reigns in the small hours of the morning can be most conducive to clear insight and heartfelt prayer. Many people with serious illnesses find that their sleep patterns are disturbed, and they often lie awake for long periods during the night. It can only be beneficial to take the opportunity to recite a few portions of *tikkun chatzot* and offer your own personal prayers to God.

Stories about the Tzaddikim

"Telling stories about the Tzaddikim showing their greatness and extraordinary powers sweetens harsh judgments and brings lovingkindness into the world" (*Tzaddik* #479).

Once when Rebbe Nachman's daughter Adil (1787-1864) was sick, the Rebbe cured her by telling her the following story about the Maharsha (see p.35): "In Ostrog, where the Maharsha died, there was a monastery by the side of the road leading to the Jewish cemetery. Whenever there was a funeral, the monks used to ring the bells and pelt the mourners with stones, and it often happened that the Jews were forced to abandon the corpse and flee. Prior to his death, the Maharsha gave instructions that a copy of his talmudic commentary should be placed on his bier. When the funeral procession reached the monastery, the monks came out as usual, but just as they were about to start throwing stones, the Maharsha sat up and began turning the pages of his work. The terrified monks fled, and the monastery sank into the ground, and from that time on was left abandoned." Adil subsequently told this story to several sick people and they were cured, and later Breslover chassidim would also tell the story to the sick (*Avanehah Barzel* p.37 #53).

According to Rebbe Nachman, *pidyon nefesh* is the very key to healing. But the object is not to throw all the responsibility for healing onto the Tzaddik and simply wait for salvation to come. People make the same mistake about medicine — "Doctor, cure me!" — hoping that the treatment will make the patient well again without his having to take the trouble to make any changes in his lifestyle, drop bad habits, quit smoking and drinking, modify his diet, exercise properly, etc. Turning to the Tzaddik for spiritual healing involves more than just asking him to pray. One must also make a deep study of his teachings as a guide to the changes one must make in one's life in order to bring about true healing on all levels.

4. Fear

The first shock of discovery of a life-threatening illness usually passes within a few days, but is often followed by a phase of anxiety and depression as the news begins to sink in. This period may be marked by a loss of interest in eating and other activities, sleep disturbances, difficulties in concentration and general apathy. But in most cases these reactions tend to become less intense within a couple of weeks or so as you adapt to the new reality, resume some of your normal activities and actively confront the various problems you face, such as those involving treatments and their effects on day to day life.

Still, it is very likely that you will continue to experience many different kinds of fears: apprehensiveness about visits to the doctor or medical tests and their results, nervousness about treatments and their side effects, dread of pain, disfigurement and disability, trepidation about the future, and, most of all, fears of death. Every new ache or pain may give rise to further worry about what is happening. Fears for oneself are often complicated by other factors, such as anxiety about the impact of the illness on other members of the family or financial worries at a time when income may be seriously reduced.

There is nothing unusual or improper about such fears. Everyone with a serious illness wonders whether he will die of it. Fear of pain and other anxieties are only natural. Indeed, confronting your fears and coming to terms with them are important parts of the healing process. Some of your concerns will be able to be dispelled through frank discussion with your doctor, family members, friends, rabbis and counsellors who may be able to give you support, offer practical advice or provide you with valuable information about options you may not be aware of. When it comes to the possibility of physical deterioration and death, these are an inescapable part of our existential situation. Those who are willing to confront and accept them with equanimity are immeasurably enhanced as human beings.

Standing outside the feeling

In order to release yourself from the grip of fear and escape the paralytic sense of helplessness it engenders, the first step is to learn to stand outside the feeling. If you find yourself in the throes of an attack of fear, accept that you are afraid and recognize the intensity of the feeling. But at the same time, remind yourself that your degree of fear is not necessarily a reflection of the severity of the real problem. In order to think about your problems more rationally and to develop a practical strategy for coping, it can be most helpful to discuss your concerns openly and honestly with others.

> ## Overcoming fear
>
> "It is not the person who fears, but something else within him. You may clearly realize that the thing you fear cannot harm you. Still, you cannot help being terrified of it. This is because of that something within you that is responsible for your fear.... If you learn to understand yourself, you can rid yourself of all fears. You must only realize that something else within you is responsible for them. Understand this and you can overcome everything. You have free will. You can easily train your mind to avoid the thing inside you that is responsible for your fears" (*Rabbi Nachman's Wisdom* #83).

You should discuss any anxieties about possible pain and disability with your doctors, because they may well be able to set your mind at rest. Contemporary medicine offers highly sophisticated techniques for controlling pain and overcoming disability that did not exist in the past. If you are worried about what is likely to happen in the event that your illness worsens, ask your doctor for clear information about what you might have to face. You may find it helpful to work out contingency plans for dealing with situations that concern you, such as what medical treatment you would want to receive if your physical and mental stamina declines to the point where you are unable to make decisions. Many people facing serious illness find one of the best forums for dealing with their fears and concerns to be support groups made up of those in similar situations. Your clinic or hospital should have information about suitable groups.

If you are worried about family matters, financial problems and so on, try to discuss them openly with those concerned, or talk them over with a good friend or a rabbi, etc. Owing to the strong taboos in our society against speaking about illness and death, even very close friends and family may feel inhibited about discussing sensitive issues. You may sense that some of those around you are simply unable to deal with the situation. But with those to whom you feel you can talk, you may be able to set the tone for serious discussion by bringing up words like "illness" and "death" yourself in order to let them know that such topics are not taboo. Be prepared to cry together and express strong feelings with dignity.

"Why should you be afraid about dying? The world there is far more beautiful than here" (*Tzaddik* #445).

As far as possible, try to resolve outstanding family matters and attend to unfinished business. Settle old grievances and say what you need to say to loved ones and friends. One of the most positive things that can come out of a serious illness is the open expression of feeling and support it can engender, leading to greater intensity and cohesiveness in family and other relationships. On the other hand there are some relationships that cannot be deepened, and you should learn to say "no" to social obligations that are devoid of any real value in order to invest your energies in relationships and activities that are more meaningful.

Try to attend to what needs doing sooner rather than later. Even those in the best of health are advised to consider the purchase of a burial plot, which in Jewish lore is regarded as a *segulah* for long life. Write a will stating exactly how you wish your possessions to be distributed. It is desirable to attend to such matters not because you are necessarily going to die soon, but on the contrary, because when all your affairs are in order you can *live* to the fullest without having a clutter of unresolved issues weighing on your mind.

Turning fear into awe

No matter how much support you have from those around you and how many issues you resolve, it is very likely that many of your fears will rear their heads again and again, including some you thought you had overcome. Many of our deepest fears are necessarily private. Pain, disability and, most of all, death are all things that we ultimately face alone. Indeed they *are* fearsome, especially death, which is not just a matter of ceasing to live in this world, but of going before the heavenly court and facing the Creator of the universe.

Fear is one of the main ways in which God's attribute of stern justice — to which the sick person is particularly subject — manifests itself in his or her consciousness. Indeed, fear is sent to us precisely to bring us to a deeper awareness of and connection with God. Chassidism calls the experience of gut fear *"fallen* fear" — fallen, because it is on a lower level than the faculty of reverential awe of God that is the mark of the mature soul. The point is to elevate gut fear and turn it into awe of God and awareness of His presence. Fear is a signal to repent and to fix what has to be fixed in order to attain a deeper connection with God. This does not mean getting into a morbid state of waiting to die, but rather preparing yourself to *live,* by reaching out to God through intense prayer and devotion, Torah and mitzvot.

Fear and love

The Baal Shem Tov taught: "The various fears a person has are really rooted in the hand of Godly love and kindness that is stretched out to him. Such fears are only sent to rouse him to fear God. And when a person understands that his fears are signs of God's kindness and are sent only to awaken him, fear turns into love — the love with which he receives God's kindness — and his fears leave him. Fear is to be found among all God's creatures and in all the worlds. The ultimate root of all the different types of fear found throughout the creation is Godly awe. The lower fears that come upon a person are sent only to stir him to this heavenly awe, and they are sent out of love. They are a *request* to the person to rouse himself to fear God, as it is written (Deuteronomy 10:12), 'What does God *ask* of you except to fear God'"
Keter Shem Tov I, #38).

Rebbe Nachman taught that the way to elevate fear and turn it into awe is through self-judgment: examining yourself, surveying your life and evaluating your behavior, activities and involvements.

"When a person fails to examine and judge himself, he is examined and brought to judgment from on high. God has many ways of executing His judgments: He has the power to clothe them in anything in the world, because all things are His messengers, and He can use any means He chooses to execute His judgments. We can actually see this in practice. When something bad happens to a person, the particular cause which precipitates the problem is often apparently quite insignificant. One would never have expected a small thing like this to bring on such a train of consequences — illness, suffering and the like. The explanation is that the divine decree against the person has been clothed in these mundane circumstances in order to give him his deserts.

"But when you yourself take the initiative to examine and judge yourself, this removes the heavenly decree. There is no need for you to be afraid of anything. Worldly objects and events will no longer be used as a cloak and veil for executing God's decree, because by bringing yourself to a reckoning you remove the judgment above. You are already sufficiently spiritually awake without needing things of this world to shake you. This is what is meant by elevating fear to its root. You are afraid of nothing except God" (*Likutey Moharan* I, 15:2).

You may well feel bad about certain aspects of yourself or guilty that you didn't do this or that differently. But does this mean you should feel guilty about being ill, as if it's your fault? People certainly do often perceive illness as a punishment because of the associated suffering and the unpleasantness of many of the treatments. In some cases one can identify specific activities or habits that brought on the illness. But the point is not to castigate yourself for having caused your illness: God's ways are ultimately inscrutable, and it would be presumptuous for anyone to state definitively what purpose He has in sending a particular illness. Far more important is to view the illness as a prompt to fix what lies within your power to fix *now*, and to bring your relationship with God to a new level of intensity.

Make your peace with God. Look back over your past and confess what you know to be your sins, mistakes and personal shortcomings. You should feel contrition, certainly, but this does not mean that you should engage in an orgy of self-castigation. After taking responsibility for past mistakes, ask God to help you understand what He wants of you *now* and how you can come closer to Him through your illness. This process of introspection and self-judgment may be a lengthy one. Even after you have worked hard to use your fears to bring you to *teshuvah*, don't be surprised if they return again and again. Each time you experience fear and anxiety, know that they are nothing but a prompt to cry out to God again *now*, for "Now, Israel, what does God ask of you except to fear God, to walk in all His ways and to love Him and to serve God with all your heart and all your soul" (Deuteronomy 10:12).

5. Patience

Illness can bring many trials besides the physical pain and suffering which are often a part of it and which can be so exhausting and enervating. To those for whom even the simplest everyday activities such as going to the toilet, washing, dressing, etc. are suddenly impossible, the sense of helplessness and dependence on others can be a source of terrible humiliation. Because of the emphasis we put on our physical appearance, even minor disfigurement can cause extreme embarrassment, as can the need to use a wheelchair, catheter or other external apparatus.

Then there are the more subtle trials. Other people often don't know how to react appropriately to those who are sick and in pain. Even close friends may have little understanding of what you are going through, leaving you feeling estranged and isolated. Cancer and certain other illnesses are so feared that even the best-intentioned people often tend to shy away from those afflicted as if they were contagious. Ironically, the feeling of having been reduced to the status of a second-class citizen is often most pronounced when having to deal with the medical system itself. No doubt unwittingly, doctors, nurses, medical secretaries and insurance company staff often treat patients with the grossest insensitivity and lack of understanding.

You can certainly be forgiven for being upset and distressed by this added suffering. "A person cannot be called to account for the way he reacts at his time of suffering" (*Bava Batra* 47b). But if you can bring yourself to accept these trials with patience, you will draw rich blessings upon yourself, as the Rabbis taught: "Of those who suffer their humiliation without humiliating others, who hear themselves insulted yet do not answer back, who act out of love and rejoice in their suffering — of them the verse says (Judges 5:31): 'And those who love Him are as the sun when it comes out in its might'" (*Shabbat* 88b etc.).

In order to experience God's glory, which as Rebbe Nachman teaches is the ultimate destiny of the Jew (see pp. 237ff.), it is necessary to set aside our own dignity. We are often so full of our own of self-importance and so determined to be in control of our lives and environment that we lose our awareness of God's presence and His power and control over us. But the humiliation and suffering that are so often part and parcel of illness whittle away this pride, opening our hearts to God.

"You must make yourself into nothing, like a wasteland that people trample over. Pay no attention whatever to any opposition or to the contempt with which people may treat you. Be aware of the wrong you have done and accept that even the suffering and murderous opposition you may have to encounter in your quest for truth are perfectly just. Train yourself to be silent and to be able to hear yourself insulted without answering back. Someone like this is called 'wise' and will come to complete *teshuvah*, *Keter*, the Crown, which is the highest of the sefirot. This is the way to true and enduring glory, the glory of God" (*Likutey Moharan* I, 6:2).

Why are remedies so bitter?

"Healing requires rebirth of the soul. When a person is sick or injured, the soul goes out of his body, or at least out of the part that is wounded. The wound can therefore be healed only through the birth of the soul in order for new vitality to enter the part of the body from which the soul has gone out. This is why one of the Hebrew words for healing is from the root חיות (*chiyut*), 'vitality,' as in the phrase ותחלימני ותחייני (*vetachlimeyni utechayeyni*), 'heal me and cure me.'

"Since healing requires the birth of the soul, all remedies come only from God's 'mighty hand,' through which the souls are born (see *Likutey Moharan* I,67), as it is written, 'I wounded and I will heal' (Deuteronomy 32:39). Thus the Rabbis said that the Holy One, blessed be He, heals with the very hand with which He strikes — 'striking and healing' (Isaiah 19:22). This means that healing comes about through the hand with which God wounds, the 'mighty hand' which is the source of all severe judgments and punishments.

"This is the reason why all remedies involve bitter herbs and suffering — because healing comes through the 'mighty hand,' which is the source of all suffering and injuries. Accordingly, the healing that comes from there also necessarily involves suffering and bitter drugs. For the same reason women experience great pain during childbirth. This is because the soul of the new child is born through the 'mighty hand'" (*Likutey Halakhot, Chovel beChavero* 3:4).

6. Pain

Lingering pain can be totally debilitating, making it virtually impossible to enjoy most of the activities that give pleasure and meaning to life, leaving one irritable, helpless and depressed. Thank God, the medical resources for managing pain are far better and more sophisticated than they were even a couple of decades ago, especially in cases of acute pain, where the underlying cause can usually be rapidly identified and treated. Yet, effective as modern analgesic medications and surgical or other techniques may be, they are certainly not a panacea. Analgesics do not always work, and they sometimes have troublesome side effects, such as drowsiness and confusion. In many cases of chronic pain, even the most sophisticated diagnostic tests may give little indication about the causes, and people often come to the end of long and frustrating courses of treatment involving surgery and drugs of all kinds, only to be told by their doctors that they will have to "learn to live" with their pain.

> One of Rebbe Nachman's followers was once very sick. He suffered greatly from tremendous pains in his teeth, and was almost on his deathbed. The torture continued to grow worse until his agony was beyond description. His face was terribly swollen and the doctors had to resort to all sorts of agonizing methods to remove his teeth. His internal organs were also affected, torturing him beyond all measure. The Rebbe said to this man: "You have suffered the most severe and bitter pains all these years. But it is still better than one burn in Gehennom. One such singe is worse than all this" (*Rabbi Nachman's Wisdom* #236).

Pain control: psychological techniques

Physical and occupational therapy, acupuncture, massage and the like can often help alleviate certain types of chronic pain. But experience in growing numbers of stress and pain reduction programs continues to confirm the value of psychological techniques such as relaxation, meditation, visualization and self-hypnosis in increasing control over pain and reducing the physical tension that often accompanies mental anxiety.

By utilizing the power of the mind over the body many patients find that they can cut their dosages of analgesics, reduce the undesirable side effects of chemotherapy and other treatments, rehabilitate faster after surgery and control a wide range of other problems, from back pain and asthma to warts, psoriasis and irritable bowel syndrome. On average, psychological techniques can reduce pain by some 10 to 40 percent, and while this may not seem very much, those suffering from chronic pain find comfort in the knowledge that they can modulate it to a point where it is manageable.

Before embarking on the use of psychological techniques to reduce pain, it is vital to understand that pain is one of the body's most important messengers. At times, pain may be the body's way of telling us that there is a serious problem that requires immediate medical attention. Pain control should be used not as an alternative to medical treatment where this is called for, but as a complement to it.

In learning to control pain, it is valuable to grasp the distinction between pain and suffering. Pain is a physical signal, while suffering is one of many possible responses to such a signal. Even a mild pain can produce great suffering if we are afraid it may indicate a tumor or some other dangerous condition. But the very same pain may be seen as nothing more than a minor inconvenience if all the tests turn out to be negative. This shows that it is not necessarily the pain itself so much as the way we react to it that determines the degree of suffering we experience. This does not mean that the pain does not exist and is all "in your head." What it does imply is that while your pain may be a very real physical sensation, you can influence the way you experience it by mobilizing your mental and spiritual resources.

If your pain is causing you anxiety, this can produce muscle tension that may itself increase the pain. You can see this from the fact that you can produce painful sensations in an uninjured part of your body simply by tensing your muscles. Since muscle tension can increase the physical component of pain, you have it in your power to reduce your pain by consciously relaxing your muscles. Progressive relaxation techniques are now taught in many pain and stress control programs (and see *Under the Table* pp. 65-69). Deep relaxation can be greatly enhanced by the use of visualization, such as imagining your body floating somewhere safe and comfortable. One of the most important principles in pain management is to deal with an attack early. It is far more effective to employ relaxation and other techniques to deflect an attack of pain before it becomes established than to reduce severe pain that has been troubling you for some time.

We are constantly exposed to unending streams of stimuli of all kinds, external and internal. However, we are not consciously aware of most of them because our minds are focussed elsewhere. Pain is the most compelling of all sensations. Yet it is still possible to reduce the amount of pain you actually feel by learning to shift your attention away from the physical signals. Rather than insisting that the pain should go away, try to imagine yourself taking a warm bath or using ice or cold water or some other remedy that usually works for you. Alternatively, try concentrating on the sensations in other, non-painful parts of your body, such as the delicate sensations in your fingertips as you rub them together. Another technique is to picture yourself in some place you particularly enjoy or engaged in some pleasurable activity. The principle is the same as when you are so caught up in a good book that you lose all awareness of your surroundings. The more engrossed you are in one object of attention, the more likely you are to ignore others.

Two generations ago, in the days before sophisticated anesthetics, R. Chaim Ozer Grodzenski of Kovno (d.1941) went through a lengthy surgical operation without drugs of any kind by mentally working through

"During the three years of Rebbe Nachman's final illness his torments grew worse than ever. He said, 'When the pains strike I grit my teeth so hard, I could bite through a wooden board!' Yet he also said, 'My suffering is always in my power.' Whenever he wanted, he could accept the agony and feel it in full measure. But when he wished to, he could negate it and be totally oblivious to all pain" (*The Praise of Rabbi Nachman* p.27).

an intricate talmudic *sugya* with the utmost concentration. Such a feat may be beyond the capabilities of most of us, but the average person can learn to focus his or her attention on a familiar passage, such as Psalms 23 and 121, *Adon Olam*, etc., concentrating intently on each of the words in turn in order to shift conscious awareness away from pain. The deeper trust and faith engendered by intense prayer at such a time will also aid muscular relaxation. One present-day chassid successfully endured a series of treatments that most people find excruciating by singing a succession of lively *nigunim* at the top of his voice from the beginning of each session to the end!

*

Transcending Pain

Likutey Moharan I, 65:3-4; see Garden of the Souls pp. 43ff.

"Even when bad things happen and you are beset with troubles and suffering, God forbid, if you look at the ultimate purpose, you will see that these things are not bad at all. On the contrary, they are really a great favor, because all suffering is sent from God for your own ultimate good, whether to remind you to return to Him or to cleanse and scour you of your sins. If so, the suffering is really very beneficial, because God's intention is certainly only for good. Whatever evil and suffering you go through, God forbid, if you will just look at the ultimate goal — God's purpose — you will not experience it as suffering at all. On the contrary, you will be filled with joy at so much good when you look at the purpose of this suffering. For the ultimate purpose is entirely good, all unity. And the deep truth is: there is no evil at all in the world, everything is good.

"Why then do we feel pain when we suffer? People experience pain only because their *da'at* — divine awareness and understanding — is taken from them, making it impossible for them to focus on the ultimate purpose, which is entirely good. It is then that they feel pain. But when one has *da'at* and keeps one's attention fixed on the ultimate goal, one does not feel pain or suffering at all.

"This helps us to understand a deep mystery. Why is it a natural reflex-response for people to screw their eyes up and shut them tight when suffering intense pain, God forbid, as when having a limb amputated for example? We know from experience that when we want to look at a far-away object, we screw up our eyes in order to focus our vision on the object we wish to see. Vision is the agent of the mind sent to bring information about the object in question into the brain. But when something is very far away, our power of vision may be inadequate to reach there to bring it back into the brain. We tend to be distracted by the various things we see from the side, and in addition our vision is diffused over such a great distance. This is why we have to narrow our eyes to see a distant object: we have to limit our vision so that other things should not interfere, and we have to focus it on the desired object in order to

(Transcending pain, cont.)

strengthen our vision and avoid its being diffused. Then it is possible to see the far-off object.

"So too, when we want to look at the ultimate goal of creation, which is all good, all unity, we have to close our physical eyes and focus our inner vision — the vision of the soul — on the goal. For the light of this ultimate goal is very far away. The only way to see it is by closing our eyes and keeping them firmly shut. Then we can gaze on this ultimate goal. In other words, we must turn our eyes away from *this* world and close them to it completely. We must pay no attention to the vanity of this world and its mundane temptations. Then we can see and apprehend the light of the ultimate goal, which is all good. And then the suffering will disappear. For the main reason why a person suffers is that he is far from this goal.

"That is why it is a natural instinct to screw up one's eyes when undergoing pain — in order to escape the suffering and nullify the pain by gazing at the ultimate goal, which is entirely good. For the only way to see this goal is by closing one's eyes. And even though the individual may be totally unaware of what he is doing, the soul knows everything. That is why it is stamped within our nature to close our eyes when suffering pain. And it really is true that at the moment of *bittul* — the state of self-transcendence when one becomes nullified within the ultimate goal, which is all good, all unity — at that moment the pain and suffering are nullified and actually disappear. However it is not possible to remain in this state of *bittul* all the time, because that would be beyond the limitations of our human existence. In this lifetime *bittul* can be experienced only for limited periods, the way the angels in Ezekiel's prophecy of the Chariot are described as 'running and returning' (Ezekiel 1:14). They 'run forth,' transcending their limitations for a moment, rising towards God, but then they 'return' again to their separate selves.

"When a person returns from the state of *bittul* to normal consciousness, the conscious mind comes back to the brain, which is the seat of the mind. But the limited human brain is unable to hold the transcendent state of *bittul*, because the latter is *Ein Sof*, limitless Infinity, which is the ultimate goal: all unity, all good. As a result, the brain now feels the pain of the suffering, because it is in the brain that all sensations

(Transcending pain, cont.)

of pain and suffering are felt. Nerve passages extend from the brain to all the limbs in the body, and through them the brain is aware of pain in whatever limb is afflicted.

"Indeed, after returning from the state of *bittul* to normal consciousness, the pain and suffering may attack even more strongly than before. This may be compared to two fighters who are wrestling with one another. If one of them sees that the other is getting the upper hand, he fights back even harder. Similarly when the forces of judgment gripping a person see that he wants to overcome his suffering and nullify it through *bittul*, absorption in the ultimate goal, they attack even more strongly. This is why afterwards, when one returns from the state of *bittul*, the suffering is felt even more intensely than before, because the forces of judgment fight back against one, since one wanted to escape them.

"Afterwards, however, the suffering is lightened and we can derive a measure of consolation from the new spiritual insights we achieve as a result of the suffering. The reason why suffering leads to spiritual insight is that suffering brings one to *bittul*, and while in this state of nullification to the ultimate goal, one realizes that one's pain and suffering are actually of great benefit. As a result one becomes filled with joy, and joy is the 'vessel' for receiving new Torah insight. Then afterwards, even though one returns from *bittul* to normal consciousness, a trace of the *bittul* still remains, and from this trace comes Torah insight. It is the deepening of Torah insight resulting from the remaining joyous trace of the *bittul* that later cools the intensity of one's suffering. For Torah quenches the thirst of the soul, namely the experience of pain and suffering.

"'Happy is the man whom God chastises and from Your Torah you teach him' (Psalms 94:12). The very chastisement — the suffering — is what brings one to greater Torah insight. And indeed, if out of suffering you come to enhanced understanding, this is a sign that you have accomplished something and that you have dealt with the suffering in the proper way. Your deepened spiritual awareness is a sign that you were able to use the suffering to attain the state of *bittul*, nullification to the ultimate goal, because the trace that remains after the *bittul* is what gives rise to the enhanced Torah understanding."

7. Mind over Body

We have seen how techniques like visualization and the wilful focussing of attention can utilize the power of the mind to counter physical pain. Can the power of the mind and soul also be harnessed to promote actual physical healing in the body? It would seem that if mental and spiritual factors have the power to bring on illness then they should have an influence in healing it as well. This of course is the principle behind Rebbe Nachman's statements that the main reason why people become sick is because they are depressed, and the great healer is joy (*Likutey Moharan* II, 24, and see Chapters 12 and 13).

In recent years there has been a burgeoning of interest, not only among psychologists and alternative practitioners but also among growing numbers of conventional physicians, in the use of specific mental techniques that appear to promote healing. Foremost among them is "meditation." This is a word that different people understand in different ways. Basically, meditation simply means "thinking in a controlled manner... deciding exactly how one wishes to direct the mind for a period of time, and then doing it" (R. Aryeh Kaplan, *Jewish Meditation* p.3). According to this definition, there are as many different types of meditation as there are ways of directing the mind. The kinds of meditation that have received most attention in connection with healing essentially involve *non-doing* — relaxing the body and, rather than trying to direct one's thoughts, detaching oneself from them in order to attain a state of inner calm.

Benefits of meditation

It is obvious that relaxation and meditation of this kind directly affect the somatic nervous system, which is under our conscious control, reducing tension in the skeletal muscles, leading to a greater sense of tranquillity. But the implication of recent studies is that meditation can also influence the autonomic nervous, endocrine and immune systems, which are generally thought of as being less subject to our conscious control, yet which play a vital role in many aspects of bodily functioning, directly affecting the working of organs like the heart, lungs, blood vessels, stomach, intestine and bladder.

A number of studies have indicated that regular meditation can reduce hypertension (high blood pressure), which is implicated in the vast majority of heart attacks and strokes, and that it can also lower abnormally high levels of cholesterol in the blood (another primary risk factor for heart attacks, since excess cholesterol in the blood is directly linked to the fatty plaque deposits that clog the arteries leading to the heart). Other studies indicate that regular meditation may substantially increase blood levels of certain important immune-system hormones, while reducing levels of the stress hormones that have been linked to many diseases. In addition, meditation is said to be of benefit for migraine, various kinds of back pain, digestive disorders, arthritis, diabetes and thyroid problems.

That the salutory mental states induced by relaxation and passive meditation have a positive effect on physical functioning and health only confirms the truth of Rebbe Nachman's teachings about the vital role of *simchah* in physical well-being. But besides passive meditation, can more active kinds of meditation and the like be used as ways of "communicating" directly with the autonomic nervous and immune systems, etc., in order to stimulate the healing process?

Visualization

One of the most often discussed techniques is visualization, in which the patient enters a state of deep relaxation and concentrates on vivid mental images representing the physical effect he or she wishes to achieve. For example, some patients imagine their immune system cells "swallowing up" invaders in the body. Visualization practitioners claim that the imagination can be used to influence physiological processes as varied as salivation, skin resistance, muscle tension, respiration, heart rate, blood pressure, gastrointestinal activity, blood glucose levels and blister formation.

Rebbe Nachman discussed the power of intense concentration and visualization, though not specifically in connection with healing. He said: "Thought can bring about many things.... When thought is intensely concentrated it can exert great influence. Every faculty of the mind, both conscious and unconscious, down to the innermost point, must be focussed without distraction. To accomplish this, the concentrated thought must spell out every step of the desired result in detail" (*Rabbi Nachman's Wisdom* #62).

Although Rebbe Nachman does not appear to have directly addressed the subject of visualization as a method of healing, the Bible itself provides an instructive example of what might be called a visual cure. In the course of the Children of Israel's forty years of wandering in the wilderness, the people complained against God and Moses, causing a plague of poisonous serpents. In response to Moses' prayer for help, God told him to make a serpent and place it on a pole. "And everyone who has been bitten will see it and live. And

Moses made a bronze serpent and put it on a pole, and if the serpent had bitten a man and he gazed at the bronze serpent, he lived" (Numbers 21:8-9). After the Jewish People came into Eretz Israel, the bronze serpent was preserved. However, in later times it turned into an object of cult worship, and we find that King Hezekiah, besides putting away the Book of Remedies, also "broke in pieces the bronze serpent that Moses had made, for until that time the Children of Israel used to make offerings to it" (Kings II, 18:4).

Hezekiah's objection to the bronze serpent can perhaps be understood in the light of the famous rabbinic comment on the episode in the wilderness: "Does a serpent kill and does a serpent give life? No! When the Jewish People looked upwards and submitted their hearts to their Father in Heaven they were healed, and if not, their bodies rotted" (Rosh Hashanah 29a). It was not the bronze serpent that healed. Its only value lay in helping the sick to direct and focus their attention on God as the true source of healing. As soon as people attributed healing power to the image itself, they turned it into an idol, the negation of our faith, and as such it had to be destroyed.

Magic and manipulation

The story of the bronze serpent teaches that true spiritual healing is not a matter of attempting to employ spiritual techniques in place of drugs, surgery, etc. as a way of making adjustments in the natural world: this would turn spirituality into little more than a form of magic. Rather, spiritual healing means opening ourselves to the beneficial spiritual influences God is constantly sending into the world to bring harmony, health and healing. They will indeed do this if we will just allow them to work without interference. God created the human body to be healthy, and He revealed a code of conduct — the Torah — that, when faithfully and joyously observed, fosters balance on every level, spiritual and physical. Diverging from this code leads to imbalance, which may cause physical illness. In order to be healed, it is necessary to turn our eyes back to God and His Torah in order to open ourselves to the spiritual influences that can restore harmony.

Rather than trying to manipulate nature, the spiritual approach is to put our main effort into seeking to influence that which most lies within our power to affect — our own hearts. Our task is to re-establish and deepen our attachment to God and to the Torah code that brings balance and health. Perhaps it is significant that the meditation practices that have proved the most effective in promoting healing (and are also the least disputed even among orthodox practitioners) are those that are more passive, involving *non-doing* — opening oneself to salutory mental states and leaving the divinely created body to adjust itself without interference, rather than actively trying to manipulate the physical realm through some kind of spiritual technique.

Visualization has proved itself in fields as wide apart as athletics, salesmanship and childbirth. Rebbe Nachman advocated the use of visualization as an aid in accomplishing spiritual goals. "For example, you can concentrate on the fact that you want to complete the four sections of the *Shulchan Arukh* (Code of Jewish Law). If you study five pages each day, you will finish all four sections in one year. Picture in your mind exactly how you'll go about this course of study. Concentrate so strongly that you are literally obsessed with the thought. If your desire is strong and your concentration intense enough, your plans will be fulfilled. This same concept can also be applied to other areas" (*Rabbi Nachman's Wisdom ibid.*).

Here visualization is being used to gear oneself for dynamic action, which can be of tremendous value as a part of healing when it comes to rehabilitation or making necessary lifestyle changes. In these cases one is trying to change oneself and enhance one's own performance as opposed to seeking to affect autonomic bodily processes. It may be that visualizations for the latter purpose can sometimes be effective. If you feel that they are of value for you in your personal healing pathway you should certainly use them. But it would be a mistake to believe that you can force your body to heal through the intensity of your visualizations — "*my* strength and the power of *my* hands" (Deuteronomy 8:17). Rather you should use mental images as a means of focussing your sight on God's healing power and allowing it to work within you.

The power of words

The same distinction between working to open oneself to God's healing power as opposed to trying to manipulate physical processes would also apply in the case of the most potent of all spiritual weapons: words. As we have seen from "*Sound the Shofar — Dominion*" (Chapter 18), the power of speech is at the very core of Rebbe Nachman's healing pathway. Does this mean that words can be used to channel healing directly into the physical body?

Rebbe Nachman told R. Shmuel Isaac, one of his most prominent followers, that "during hisbodedus he should speak in turn to each of the limbs and organs of his body, explaining to them that all material desires are futile, because in the end man is destined to die. Eventually R. Shmuel Isaac reached a level where any limb or organ he spoke to individually was so responsive to his words that the very life would ebb out of it, leaving it completely devoid of strength or sensation. This was actually visible in the case of his external limbs, such as his fingers and toes. Regarding the vital internal organs, such as his heart, etc. he actually had to hold back when speaking to them for fear that the life would quite literally leave them, God forbid" (*Tzaddik* #442).

This passage implies that through words alone a person has the power to influence the vitality or lack of it, not only in his external limbs but even in his internal organs. This might suggest that someone who is sick could try talking to (or singing to or otherwise communicating with) the affected body parts in order to encourage them to heal and function properly. There is indeed evidence that for certain types of physical conditions, sounds or vibrations of various kinds can be used to promote healing. Sounds, chants, prayers and music play a role in many healing traditions. Soundwaves may well have a direct effect on certain aspects of bodily functioning. But when it comes to the use of words to "communicate" with the body, far more important than seeking to affect physiological processes would be to try to influence the spiritual soul that animates the body — the *nefesh* — and to fire yourself with a will to *live* and to use your physical faculties to fulfil the Torah and mitzvot (cf. p. 47).

Jewish law strictly forbids addressing prayers, psalms or other biblical verses, etc. to the body or particular body parts, as this is akin to using spells and witchcraft. "Those who whisper biblical verses over a wound or to stop a child panicking, or who place a Torah scroll or tefilin on a child to make him sleep, are not only sorcerers but heretics as well, because they want to use words of Torah as a form of treatment for the physical body, whereas they are essentially a remedy for the soul, as it is written 'And they will be life for your *soul.*' However it is permissible to recite verses and psalms in order that the merit of one's recitation should protect one from harm and suffering" (Rambam, *Mishneh Torah, Hilkhot Avodat Kokhavim* 11:12).

8. Prayer

The closing words of the biblical account of Creation speak of "His work which God created *to do*" (Genesis 2:3). God created the entire universe, but He left His work unfinished as it were, leaving it to man "to do" — to take an active role in completing the task so as to have a share in the work of creation.

to our level of understanding. Sometimes people pray for someone to be healed and he or she dies. This does not mean that all their prayers were wasted, because God takes these prayers and may use them for the healing of that person's soul in the upper worlds, or for some other purpose.

The quest for connection

As the principle spiritual pathway of healing, prayer involves far more than simply asking repeatedly for physical healing. True healing is the healing of the *whole person*. Our essential illness is our distance from God, and this is what prayer — the quest for *connection* with God — comes to heal. The pathway of prayer that brings healing is precisely the pathway Rebbe Nachman taught for all Jews at all times: putting all our strength into the set blessings and daily prayer services, reciting many psalms and other additional prayers, and talking to God in our own words in hisbodedus.

> Rebbe Nachman once told a man who had a sickness in his family to rise before daylight and recite the entire Song of Songs. The Rebbe said, "Every remedy in the world is contained in the Song of Songs." The man did this, and his relative immediately took a turn for the better and regained his health (*Rabbi Nachman's Wisdom* #243).

The set blessings and prayer services have an effect on at least two levels. For one thing, by concentrating on the many different expressions of praise of God and His power as manifest in the Creation, we heighten our own consciousness of God's presence in our lives and in the world around us. This can only strengthen our attachment to God and our desire to follow His code of law, which is the key to balance and healing. But in addition to this, the very letters and words of the set prayers are a most powerful means of channeling divine influences to ourselves and to creation in general. The prophets and sages who arranged the prayers were masters of *Lashon HaKodesh*, the Holy Language, and provided us with sequences of holy names that bring divine blessing into all the worlds. The prayers "work" even without our understanding the mystical *kavanot* (intentions) that lie behind them (see *Under the Table* pp. 166-88). In the same way, the Psalms are not only profoundly inspiring in themselves but also bring all kinds of beneficial influences into the world in general.

Try to put as much strength and concentration as you can into your daily prayers and blessings. If it is not possible for you to recite the services in full,

(continued on p.388)

Channeling healing energy through prayer

1. "The hosts of heaven bow to You"

"During the morning prayers, when reciting the words וצבא השמים לך משתחוים, 'The hosts of heaven bow to You' (Nechemiah 9:6), it is appropriate to intend them as a prayer for anything one needs. For all the different herbs and plants receive their healing powers from the stars and planets, which are the 'heavenly hosts.' Each star or planet gives power to the particular herbs that come under its influence, and thus they are the source of the healing powers of the various curative herbs and plants. When a person needs a cure of some kind, various forces channeled by a number of different stars and planets combine together. One star puts power into one kind of herb, another into a second, and so on. They all join together to create the compound of herbs and plants that make up the medicine. For this reason, when saying the words, 'The hosts of heaven bow to You' — at which moment they all come to prostrate and give praise and thanks to God — it is good to have in mind that God should command them to channel the powers one needs for one's healing into one's slice of bread or some other food item, and this way one will be healed. Amen. So may it be His will" (*Likutey Moharan* I, 231).

2. Blessings before and after eating

"The blessing we recite before eating any item of food elevates that item to its supreme Source, which is the 'Word of God.' All the blessings we make over the various kinds of food we eat are essentially declarations that God created this particular item and that it derives from the supreme Source, the 'Word of God.' And through the blessing, the item returns to its supreme Source. Thus when one makes the blessing properly before eating, one is eating from the table of the Almighty, the supreme Source of all the different powers manifest in creation.

"After finishing eating we then recite another blessing. This channels the energy we need into our bodies. For example, when a person is in need of healing, after he finishes eating, as the nutrients begin to be distributed through his body to vitalize and strengthen his various limbs and body parts, recital of the blessing after food channels the necessary energies and

(Channeling healing energy through prayer, cont.)

remedies from the supreme Source, the 'Word of God.' For this reason all of the various blessings we recite after different kinds of food and drink refer to the way food brings vitality into the body. Thus the blessing בורא נפשות (*borey nefashot*, recited after cheese, meat, vegetables, most fruits and beverages, etc.) speaks of how God 'creates many souls and their deficiencies,' and goes on to thank Him 'for everything You have created to maintain the life of every living being...' While reciting the blessing, the inner intention should be to draw energy, vitality and healing power into the body through the food one ate.

"Most of the foods people eat are not medicines, but even so, the blessing, which is the 'Word of God,' has the power to channel healing energy into the body through ordinary food, as it is written, 'And He will bless your bread and your water, and I will remove sickness from among you' (Exodus 23:25). This explains the wording of the above-quoted blessing: 'for everything You have created to maintain the life of every living being...', i.e. God gives life to the souls through *everything* He created. Even though a particular item of food may not be specially suited to a particular person's needs according to strict medical or nutritional principles, even so God gives vitality to the soul through all that He created. With every single item God created, no matter what, He gives life to all kinds of souls. This is brought about through making the blessing, which is the 'Word of God,' through which the particular item of food returns to its supreme Source. Any kind of food can thus channel healing energies to a person in accordance with his individual needs.

"In the same way, the intention of *Birkat HaMazon*, the Grace after Meals, is to bless the food as it passes through the digestive system in order to channel nutrients and energy to the limbs of the body and bring satisfaction. This is why the Grace includes the verse, 'You open Your hands and satisfy the desire of every living being' (Psalms 145:16). That is, we gratefully request that God should satisfy the desire of every living being by channeling to each one the energy and strength it needs by means of the 'Word of God.' For through the 'Word of God,' all the various kinds of energies each individual needs can be channeled through any kind of food and drink" (*Likutey Halakhot, Birkat HaRei'ach* 2:3).

ask a competent rabbi for guidance as to which sections you should endeavor to say, and where possible, add any other passages from the Siddur, the Psalms, *The Fiftieth Gate — Likutey Tefilot*, etc. that are particularly meaningful to you. Depending on your condition, there may be times when it is hard for you to focus for very long. Pause whenever necessary, and allow your own thoughts to weave in and out of the text of the prayers. This will serve to keep your mind directed towards God.

Psalms for Healing

Among the Psalms that are particularly appropriate in times of sickness are: 3, 6, 13, 20, 23, 30, 38, 39, 41 and 121. The Ten Psalms of Rebbe Nachman's General Remedy are 16, 32, 41, 42, 59, 77, 90, 105, 137 and 150.

The divine conversation

In addition to the set blessings and prayers, your own private prayers in your own words are most important: not only your prayers for physical recovery, but also your prayers to *live* as a Jew, to refine your personality, develop your love and awe of God and other traits — kindness, generosity, truthfulness, honesty, moral purity, diligence, joy and so on — and to fully observe the mitzvot in all their details: charity, Torah study, Shabbat, Yom Tov, kashrut, tzitzit, tefilin, etc. Give voice to your longing and yearning to serve God. Even if at present you feel uncomfortable, sore, tired, weak, sick and disheartened, you can still quietly talk or whisper to God about all the holy tasks you would like to accomplish in your lifetime, and ask and plead with Him to help you complete them.

These conversations with God are the true "service of the heart" (*Taanit* 2a) in which you work to submit your innermost will and desire to God and His Torah. As we have seen, Rebbe Nachman taught that "the yearning and longing for something holy are themselves very precious. The soul of the Jew is actually formed through the yearning and desire which he feels for God and his good intentions to serve Him. Regardless of his level, each individual has a desire to reach a higher level. It is through this yearning that his holy soul is formed" (*Likutey Moharan* I, 31, and see Chapter 18, p. 234). Affirm your will to *live* and serve God joyously and with vigor. The expression of holy desire and longing in hisbodedus builds and strengthens the soul, and it is the return of the soul to the body that brings new vitality and healing.

Instead of focussing on the illness, this avenue of prayer concentrates on the *life* you look forward to when you will be well — life that you can already start living *now* by offering many prayers and carrying out as many mitzvot as you are capable of with as much strength and intensity as you can command. Don't eat, drink and breathe your illness. It may be an unwelcome part of your life, but don't let it take you over.

In the words of the Lubavitcher Rebbe: "As far as possible divert your attention from thinking too deeply about the subject of your health" (*Refuah Shelemah* p.31). "I stand by my opinion that one of the best medicines is to divert one's attention to other things. And since a person's thoughts are constantly racing around, the way to divert your attention is by focussing on Torah and service of God, and fulfilling the prescription to 'serve God with joy' (Psalms 100:2). Service of God has to be constant, as it is written, 'I have set God before me *constantly*' (*ibid.* 16:8). This is what the entire Code of Jewish Law starts with (*Orach Chaim* 1:1). Therefore you must contemplate something that will bring you to a state of joy, such as the thought with which we begin each day, '*Modeh ani lefanekha* — I gratefully thank You, living and eternal King....' Focus on the fact that we are constantly before the King" (*Refuah Shelemah* p.57).

9. Recovery

Today blocked arteries can often be successfully opened. Certain cancers can be completely removed. Some types of infections can be totally eliminated and some chronic conditions successfully reversed. But there are still many cases of illness where the answer is far less clear: it may be possible to slow the advance of the illness or reduce the damage it causes, but the disease itself or the threat of its return cannot be altogether removed. This means that you cannot expect that your life will simply go back to what it was before you became ill.

Every cardiac patient worries what effect a little excess exertion or stress might have on the heart. Every cancer patient fears that some new ache or lump may mean the illness has come back or is spreading. Those with diabetes, arthritis, osteoporosis, multiple sclerosis and many other chronic conditions wonder what the future bodes. It can help to have a plan ready for what you would do in the event of a new crisis. If a pain or some other problem is on your mind, instead of just worrying about it, ask your doctor what it might mean and what, if anything, can be done. Often there may not be any simple solution. But even if there is nothing else to do, at least you can always use your aches and pains and your very fears as a reminder to keep your eyes turned towards God. See them as a spur to you to persist in your prayers, Torah and mitzvot.

Keeping happy does not mean that you have to deny any frustration you may have over the constraints imposed by your illness, or grief over your inability to do all the things you once did. Express your feelings openly and honestly to God, while at the same time being thankful for the gift of health you enjoyed in the past. You should also recognize that although you may be more limited in some ways, your intrinsic value as a person and a *soul* is unchanged. There are other ways you can build your life and serve God.

Look ahead to what you can do *now*. Concentrate on your good points: search for the good that remains (see pp. 79f.). Remember Rebbe Nachman's Seven Beggars, who found ways to turn what others may have seen as disabilities into great advantages. For example, the fact that you have been through this experience puts you in a very strong position to help and support others in similar situations. When *you* encourage other patients and tell them, "You can get through this," you speak with an authority that even the most experienced doctor does not have. Use the tests and trials you have been through to deepen your human relationships.

After the crisis

Most people expect to be relieved when the immediate crisis passes, after surgery or when they complete a course of chemotherapy or other treatment. But ironically, when treatment ends and the reality of the situation begins to sink in, the experience is often one of renewed anxiety and loneliness. For some, leaving the womb-like security of a hospital can be a traumatic experience. Having made friends with the staff and having had everything done for you, you are suddenly on your own in the outside world facing a host of problems, new and old. Just when those around you are expecting you to be feeling better and to act accordingly, inside you may be feeling more vulnerable than ever.

This may be a good time to join a support group for those with a similar condition. Yet even with the best support from friends, family, doctors and therapists, there are still likely to be many challenges that you will have to face on your own, with only your faith and prayers to rely on. Every day may bring an endless succession of ups and downs in both your physical state and your morale. Each step in recuperation and recovery — going home, starting to do more for yourself, beginning to get out, going back to work, etc. — is likely to bring new stresses. After completing treatment, what many patients find most stressful of all is that they live in constant fear that their illness will recur, yet they feel they aren't *doing* anything to fight it.

Of course there are many things you *can* do to build your health, and you surely owe it to yourself to put extra effort into the mitzvah of "Guard your soul" (Deuteronomy 4:9, and see Chapter 10, pp. 105-114). Make sure you take proper care of yourself. Eat properly and get your sleep. After serious illness, surgery, chemotherapy, radiation and the like, exercise must be approached with the utmost caution. But in due course, efforts at sensible regular exercise in consultation with your doctor may boost your health considerably. Take advantage of rehabilitation programs, which often provide excellent guidance and practical assistance in regard to suitable exercise, correct diet and the like.

Alternative therapies — diet therapy, massage, acupuncture, osteopathy, etc. — may also help in a variety of chronic conditions, whether as a complement to conventional medical treatment or instead of it. Among the conditions where such therapies may be relevant are: allergies, arthritis, asthma, chronic backache and postural faults, deafness, diabetes, heart problems, high or low blood pressure, irritable bowel syndrome, migraine, muscular dystrophy and atrophy, multiple sclerosis, osteoporosis, peptic ulcers, polio, psoriasis, rheumatic aches in muscles and joints, thyroid problems and vision problems.

As Rebbe Nachman taught, a serious health regime can be an important key to healing. This is because when a person "curbs his desires and submits to a medical regime, his soul sees that he has the power to control his impulses in order to achieve a certain goal. She therefore comes back to him and revitalizes his body in the hope that he will discipline himself in order to attain his true purpose — which is to carry out the will of the Creator" (*Likutey Moharan* I, 268, see p. 179).

Healing means *living*

A sensible program of diet and careful exercise can greatly enhance your sense of well-being and give you new strength and zest for life. But at the same time as you take steps to advance your physical healing, be sure to move forward with your spiritual healing, which will automatically benefit your body. Essentially this means *living now*. Living is what healing is ultimately all about — for why do you want your health if not to *live* and fulfil yourself? If this is what you want, you have to take the initiative and start living *right now*. It's like physical rehabilitation: when you're ready to start getting back the use of stiff, painful joints and muscles after injury, illness, surgery, etc., the way to do it is not by waiting for them to spring miraculously back to life. No; you must gently *initiate* the process with small but increasingly adventurous movements in the right direction, even when it is uncomfortable. In the same way, when you want to *live*, you must start *now* by taking small, sure steps despite the fact that you may still be feeling weak, tired and disheartened.

Real life is the life of Torah and mitzvot — "for they are your life and the length of your days" (Deuteronomy 30:20), because the mitzvot connect us with the Life of life, giving us long, full days in this world and the next. The ultimate healing is the day-to-day life of the Jew: the life of tzitzit and tefilin, prayer (see Inset), Torah study, charity, family and community life, Shabbat and festivals, etc. These are what bring us to our true fulfilment and destiny.

It may be hard for you to concentrate on your prayers, open a Torah text or get up to do that mitzvah. But know that every single prayer or Psalm, each word of Torah you study and every other mitzvah you perform is a *pill of life*. Unlike mundane activities relating to the finite material world, every word of Torah and each mitzvah is a connection with the Infinite, kindling a lamp that shines forever. In the words of Rebbe Nachman: "Every single item of knowledge you acquire in Torah law — whether in the mitzvot between man and his fellow or those between man and God — brings success to the soul" (*Aleph-Bet Book*, Torah Study #10). "Every single mitzvah a person does becomes a lamp with which the soul can later search in the treasure house of the King, which is the ultimate delight of the World to Come" (*Likutey Moharan* I, 275).

Making a start

Rebbe Nachman well understood how difficult it is to make a start. It's a new challenge every single day, every hour and every moment. "When you begin each day, at first the day is very short — in the sense that the spiritual

(continued on p. 394)

The joy of prayer

"We should try to pray all the main services in a *minyan* of ten, because ten people praying together arouse all of the ten types of melody, which together bring perfect joy. This is why one should make every effort to pray with the community, because then one can easily be saved from sadness and depression. The great joy of all these people coming together has the power to turn even sorrow and depression into joy. Even the sadness and depression in which a person is enmeshed can be transformed into joy through the power of the group. This is why prayer is a remedy for everything, because all healing comes about through joy.

"This explains why we make no break between the closing words of the *Shema* and the blessing of Redemption that follows it (*Orach Chaim* 66:5). For the *Shema* is our affirmation of faith, and faith is the foundation of joy, as it is written, 'I will *rejoice* in God' (Psalms 104:34). The *Shema* contains 248 words corresponding to the 248 limbs of the body and the 248 positive mitzvot. For to have true joy a person must experience every level of joy. Therefore, after our affirmation of faith, we recite 248 words in order to draw the joy into all the 248 limbs of our bodies and so complete the entire edifice of joy corresponding to the 248 positive commandments.

"After this we immediately recite the blessing of Redemption. For redemption comes about essentially through joy, as it is written, 'For you will go out in *joy*' (Isaiah 55:12). And then, directly after this arousal of joy, we rise for the *Amidah* prayer. For true prayer requires a state of joy. The rabbis said, 'Everyone who makes no interruption between the blessing of Redemption and the *Amidah* prayer will come to no harm all day' (*Berakhot* 9b). The reason is that when we start the prayer immediately after the blessing of Redemption with no interruption, we are able to pray with joy (see Rashi *ad loc.*). And joy protects us from all harm and injury, because these occur only when there is a flaw in our joy. But when we pray joyously, this brings complete healing and salvation" (*Likutey Halakhot, Kriat Shema* 2).

tasks you must accomplish today seem to weigh so very heavily. It takes tremendous determination not to be discouraged as you feel the weight of the devotions you have to undertake today. But be courageous and don't lose heart! Make a start — even if at first things seem heavy, strained and difficult. If you are determined, they will become easier and you'll find that you *can* accomplish what you must in God's service. With every hour that passes, see to it that you enrich that hour and 'lengthen' it by filling it with extra holiness. Do the same with every new

You have only today

"Think only about today. Think only about the present day and the present moment. When someone wants to start serving God, it seems too much of a burden to bear. But if you remember that you have only today, it won't be such a burden. Don't push off serving God from one day to the next, saying, 'I'll start tomorrow — tomorrow I'll pray with proper concentration, etc.' All a person has is the present day and the present moment. Tomorrow is a whole different world. '*Today*, if you will listen to His voice!' (Psalms 95:7)" (*Likutey Moharan* I, 272)

day of your life. Let each day be filled with more holiness than the day before. Then you will be blessed with length of days — long life!" (*ibid.* 60:2)

Obviously you cannot expect to be able to take on a full routine of Torah observance right away. Recognize that your resources are limited, and allocate your energy where you need it most. Set realistic goals for yourself, and have a plan of action — at the same time being ready to grasp at unexpected opportunities. If your plans are not working, try something else. There are bound to be reverses. Just don't let them deter you. Set your goals for *today*, and pray to God to help you at every step. In the words of Rebbe Nachman: "As

When the Baal Shem Tov visited the town of Uman, he instituted among other things that a person who recovered from illness should make a thanksgiving feast for a *minyan* of at least ten needy people and give them charity as well (*Siach Sarfey Kodesh* I-329).

each day begins, I place my every movement in God's hands, asking only that I should do His will. I then have no worries. Whether or not things go right, I am totally dependent on God. If He desires otherwise, I have already asked that I should only do His will" (*Rabbi Nachman's Wisdom* #2).

The blessing of thanksgiving

On recovery from a serious illness one should recite *Birkat HaGomel*, the blessing of thanksgiving, corresponding to the thanksgiving offering that was offered in Temple times by those who had been spared from a life-threatening situation. The blessing of thanksgiving should be recited in the presence of a *minyan* of ten men, preferably including two Torah scholars, and if possible within three days of the event. It is customary to recite the blessing in synagogue during the Torah reading. Where the blessing is to be said by a man, he is called to the Torah reading (though this is not obligatory) and recites the blessing of thanksgiving immediately after his concluding blessing over the Torah.

ברוך אתה ה' אלקינו מלך העולם הגומל לחיבים טובות שגמלני כל טוב.

Blessed are You, HaShem our God, King of the universe, Who bestows good things upon the undeserving, Who has bestowed every goodness upon me.

The congregation responds:

אמן. מי שגמלך כל טוב הוא יגמלך כל טוב סלה.

Amen. May He Who has bestowed every goodness upon you continue to bestow every goodness upon you forever.

*

Chapter 24

Care of the Sick

Visiting the sick (*bikur cholim*) is one of the greatest of all the mitzvot. It is one of the mitzvot the fruits of which a person enjoys in this world while the principal remains intact for him in the World to Come (*Shabbat* 127a).

*

Visiting the sick is included in the mitzvah to "go after HaShem your God" (Deuteronomy 13:5). It is impossible for man to literally "go after" the Divine Presence as "HaShem your God is consuming fire" (ibid. 4:24). Going after God means following in God's ways. We find that the Holy One visits the sick, as in the case of Abraham, to whom God appeared as he recovered from his circumcision (Genesis 18:1). In the same way, we too should visit the sick (*Bava Metzia* 30a).

*

"Once one of Rabbi Akiva's students became ill. None of the other students visited him, but Rabbi Akiva personally went to see him and swept and cleaned his room. This literally revived the student, who said, 'Rabbi, you've brought me back to life!' As soon as Rabbi Akiva left, he taught: 'If a person does not visit the sick, it is as if he shed blood!'" (*Nedarim* 40a)

*

"Someone who visits the sick gives him life because he prays that he should live. But a person who does not visit him does not know what he needs and therefore does not pray for him" (*ibid.*).

*

"Everyone who visits the sick is saved from the judgment of hell, as it is written (Psalms 41:2-3): 'God will save him on the evil day.' And what is his reward in this world? 'God will protect him' — from the evil inclination — 'and preserve him in life' — from suffering — 'and he will be praised in the land' — all will feel privileged to be associated with him" (*Nedarim ibid.*).

*

1. Laws of Visiting the Sick

(based on Yoreh Deah #335)

When someone becomes ill, relatives and close friends should visit immediately. But except in the event of a sudden, serious illness, other people should not visit until after the first three days so as not to give the sick person the "name" of an invalid, which may have an adverse effect on his *mazal*. Each visitor takes away one sixtieth of the illness (*Bava Metzia* 30b). Even an important person should visit someone of lesser importance. A man may visit a woman and vice versa, as long as the two are not completely alone together. One should not visit an enemy so that he should not think one is glad about his suffering. One may visit the same person even several times in one day, and the more one visits, the more commendable it is — as long as it is not a burden on the patient. Where it is impossible to visit in person, one may fulfil the mitzvah by speaking on the telephone (Rabbi Moshe Feinstein).

The three main components of the mitzvah of visiting the sick are:

1. To check if there is anything the patient needs and to attend to it.

2. To lift the patient's spirits. Choose conversational topics that will bring him joy and vitality. Avoid anything that might give rise to depression and negativity. It is quite proper to suggest that he should put his affairs in order, and there is no reason for him to fear that this would be like preparing to die, because keeping one's affairs in order is an obligation even in times of good health. However, one should not tell the patient to confess his sins unless his condition is very serious. Be careful not to burden the patient. Be as sensitive as possible to his feelings. Sometimes it may be hard for him to talk but he feels obliged to do so out of respect for the visitor. Or he may have to attend to his needs but feel too ashamed to say so. Some conditions are highly embarrassing to the patient. In such cases, rather than going into the patient's room to see him in person, it is better for the visitor to stay outside and ask other members of the household if there is anything he can do for him.

3. To pray for the patient. Someone who visits a sick person but does not pray for him or her has not fulfilled the mitzvah. For this reason the Sages advised against visiting the sick in the first three hours of the day because most patients experience a certain improvement in their condition at that time and one may not realize the importance of praying for them. Similarly the Sages advised not to visit in the last three hours of the day because there is often a deterioration at this time and one may despair of praying. When praying for the sick, one should include him or her

among all sick Jews, because their collective merit makes the prayer more acceptable. The traditional prayer for the sick is:

יהי רצון מלפניך ד' אלקי ואלקי אבותי שתתשלח מהרה רפואה שלמה מן השמים רפואת
הנפש ורפואת הגוף ל-(patient's name) בן/בת (mother's name) בתוך שאר חולי ישראל.

"May it be Your will, HaShem my God and God of my forefathers, that You should quickly send complete healing from heaven — healing of the soul and healing of the body — to (patient's name), son/daughter of (mother's name), among the other sick members of the Jewish People."

The face of kindness

"Underlying the mitzvah of visiting the sick is the idea of showing them a face of radiant kindness. Rather than staying buried in our own homes and hiding our faces from the patient, we must visit him, attend to his needs and speak to his heart. By showing him a smiling face and radiating kindness, we draw down to him the light of God's countenance — 'the light of the countenance of the Living King' (Proverbs 16:15), the light of the Shekhinah — and this is what gives him the new vitality he needs to be healed.

"'The Shekhinah is above the head of the sick, as it is written (Psalms 41:4) "God will sustain him on the bed of sickness"' (Shabbat 12b), i.e. specifically *because* he is sick, the light of the Shekhinah shines upon him. This is the light of the true Tzaddik, who takes care of all the sick, and especially those who are the sickest; he watches over them more than over anyone else in order to heal them physically and spiritually, and to bring them to higher and higher levels of knowledge of God. The true greatness of the Tzaddik lies in the fact that he makes such a great effort to heal those who are sickest of all. Because they are so sick, the Shekhinah — i.e. the light of the Tzaddik — is above their heads.

"Thus it was that when Abraham was sick, 'God appeared to him in the plains of Mamre' (Genesis 18:1). Precisely because he was sick, it was necessary to visit him. The revelation Abraham attained was in the same category as the perceptions of Godliness attained by the sick through the light of the Tzaddik, which is the light of the Shekhinah" (*Likutey Halakhot, Hashkamat HaBoker* 4:14).

On Shabbat one says, "Today it is Shabbat, which is not the time to cry out. Healing will soon come! God is overflowing in kindness! Shabbat Shalom!"

When someone in the house is sick, one should go to a Sage in the town and ask him to pray for the patient and bless him. It is customary to bless the sick in the synagogue during the Torah reading, which is a time of divine favor. In a case of serious illness it is customary to give the patient a new name (i.e. add a name), since a change of name may annul a bad decree (*Rosh Hashanah* 16b, and see *Rabbi Nachman's Wisdom* #95).

*

2. The Human Connection

When writing disparagingly about doctors and medicine, Reb Noson frequently uses the phrase רופאי אליל (*rophey elil*), "worthless doctors" (*Likutey Tefilot* II, 1; 3; *Alim Literufah* #4, #391 etc.). The phrase is taken from the book of Job (13:4), and it is illuminating to examine it in its context, because it contains a vital lesson for all those involved in caring for the sick, whether privately or in some professional capacity.

As Job sat grieving over the terrible tragedies and illnesses that had befallen him, the three friends who had come to comfort him urged him to accept that he must have done something to deserve his plight since God is just in all His ways (see pp. 26ff). Yet far from giving Job any solace, his friends' lengthy speeches only exacerbated his pain. It was not that Job doubted God's perfect righteousness, but he knew he had done nothing to deserve all this suffering. Not one of his friends was willing to grapple with the deep mystery that was troubling Job: Why should a just God send suffering to those who do *not* deserve it? Perhaps his friends had listened to Job's words, but none of them had really *heard* what he was saying. They had not heard *him*.

This was why he cried out, "You are all plasterers of lies, *worthless doctors* all of you! If only you would keep completely quiet — that would be your wisdom! Please! *Hear* my argument and *listen* to what my lips are struggling to express" (Job 13:4-6). It was not his friends' words and interventions that Job needed. He was not necessarily looking for answers. What he craved more than anything was for his friends to *be quiet* — to listen and receive. He was pleading to be *understood*. This was what could have brought him some relief from his inner torment. It was because his friends were not willing even to try to comprehend him that they were "worthless doctors."

Trying to understand

No matter what the problem is in life, it is not enough to have an impressive armory of powerful remedies and solutions. The most ingenious remedy is worthless if it is not properly tailored to the problem that needs to be solved. And therefore, as every true doctor knows, *before* offering treatments and solutions, the first thing is to understand exactly what the problem *is*. One who would heal must first observe, examine and probe, scrutinizing every detail for signs, hints and clues about the true nature of the problem in all its breadth and depth.

Especially where spiritual, mental and emotional factors are involved, it is vital to hear the suffering person out and to attend not only to what he says but also to what he leaves unsaid. What unspoken messages are contained in his choice of images and symbols, his tone of voice, his hesitations and silences, facial expressions, posture, gestures, movements...? Without sensitivity and receptivity to all this and more, the would-be healer will miss the essence of the problem, and all his remedies will be worthless.

At some point in our lives each one of us may be involved in caring for the sick and troubled. Certainly nobody should ever put himself forward as a healer without having a deep understanding of the art of healing. Yet there is a sense in which the Torah asks *all of us* to be healers — because we all have the obligation to carry out the mitzvah of *bikur cholim* when necessary. The Sages taught that visiting the sick gives them *life* (Nedarim 40a), and since life is what healing is all about, this means that *bikur cholim* is a vital part of the healing process. The principles of *bikur cholim* apply not only when paying a visit to a sick relative or friend. They are relevant to everyone involved in care of the sick, including both those tending cases of short- or long-term illness at home and those involved in some aspect of sickcare as a vocation, from doctors (conventional or alternative), therapists, nurses, paramedics, receptionists, secretarial and medical insurance staff to rabbis, psychologists, social workers, volunteer helpers, educational and other personnel.

The impressive achievements of modern medicine have been taken as license for the medical establishment to virtually appropriate for itself the concepts of curing and healing, as if genuine healing can occur only when the physician opens his box of tricks and intervenes with drug therapy, surgery or some other form of treatment. The main focus of aggressive, high technology modern medicine is on attacking the disease. But the *person* who has the disease is largely ignored! Even those vested with the task of seeing to patients' human needs tend to look on their role in the healing process as being merely secondary to that of the prestigious warrior doctors on the battlefront.

Reaching out to the person

Job's lesson is that reaching out to the *person* who has the illness is in fact the very essence of healing, and the "healer" whose remedies and treatments fail to touch that inner person is a *rophé elil*, a worthless doctor. All the science and technology and hands-on skills are lacking when something far more elemental is absent: basic human understanding. The qualities that count here are not slickness and sophistication but sensitivity, empathy and the ability to reach out and make a human connection.

It is significant that several large-scale epidemiological studies have shown a definite link between physical health and the social support in people's lives — family ties, marriage, friendships, group affiliation and the like. The number of regular social relationships people have correlates with a lower risk of dying at a given age. For example, those who have an extensive and caring social network have been found to be three times more likely to recover from a heart attack than those who are socially isolated!

In Torah terms, the sick person is in a kind of exile: a spiritual flaw on some level prevents his soul from radiating to the fullest, resulting in both his physical symptoms and a corresponding constriction in his mental and emotional state. What is necessary is to penetrate behind the manifest symptoms to the underlying spiritual flaw. In order for the sick person himself to be able to understand what the flaw is and to work to correct it, he must rise beyond his mental constriction to a higher state of *da'at*, spiritual awareness and insight. But "a prisoner cannot release himself from prison" (*Berakhot* 5b), and therefore the sick person needs the help and support of those around him in order to escape his spiritual exile.

For this reason the mitzvah of *bikur cholim* involves more than simply seeing that the patient's basic physical needs are taken care of. Certainly it is essential to ensure that he or she receives the best medical treatment possible and is properly cared for in other ways. But equally important are the other two components of the mitzvah: lifting the sick person's spirits and praying for his or her recovery. Praying for the patient is an integral part of *bikur cholim* because although healing is ultimately in God's hands, it is up to *us* to forge a channel for His blessings and draw them to the patient through our prayers on his or her behalf. And while we must rely on God for what is up to God, we are still obliged to do what lies within *our* hands, which is to show the patient the face of human kindness and support in order to help him come to the simchah that is the key to all healing.

The human connection is an essential part of Rebbe Nachman's healing pathway as explained in *"Sound the Shofar — Dominion"* (see pp.237-78). It is when a person is alone and isolated that he is vulnerable to the "accusation of the angels" as expressed in the vicissitudes of material existence, including physical illness. The power to withstand these attacks comes through bonding and connection with other souls, especially with that of the Tzaddik, who has a collective soul. The Tzaddik is the exemplar of *tzedakah*, outreach and kindness to all who are in need, and is thus the central figure in the Jewish healing pathway. Having struggled successfully to cleanse his own heart of the worldly attachments that throw the light of spirituality into shadow, the Tzaddik has the power to radiate insight and understanding to others and help them rectify their spiritual flaws in order to be healed.

> ### How to pray for the sick
>
> On Rebbe Nachman's last Rosh Hashanah in Uman, his four-year-old grandson Yisrael was with him. The Rebbe was in a very serious condition, and said to his grandson, "Yisrael, pray to God that I should get better." The little boy said, "Give me your watch and I'll pray for you." The Rebbe said, "You see, he's already a Rebbe because he tells me to give him something in order for him to pray!" The Rebbe gave him the watch, and the little boy turned aside and said, "God! God! Let my *zeida* be well!" The other people in the room smiled, but the Rebbe said, "This is exactly how we have to ask things of God. What other way is there to pray to God?" The essence of prayer is total simplicity: to speak to God like a child talking to his father or the way a person talks with a friend (*Tzaddik* #439).

Breaking through the walls of the heart

To give the necessary direction to each soul, the Tzaddik must undoubtedly have profound knowledge of each one's roots and its place in the *merkavah*, the "chariot" through which God governs creation (see *Biur Halikutim* II, 1:2; above p. 242, Note 11). But to form his personal connection with each individual soul, the Tzaddik needs more than this esoteric wisdom. He must also have simple, down-to-earth human sensitivity. This is what Rebbe Nachman was talking about when he said, "People bring money to a man as a *pidyon*, a redemption, asking him to intercede for them on high. They tell him their illness and suffering and other problems. It's a wonder to me that the man accepting the redemption doesn't suffer as much as the sick person himself!" (*Rabbi Nachman's Wisdom* #188). Reb Noson tells us that the Rebbe "actually felt the pain and suffering of the sick for whom he prayed. He literally felt their every ache and pain" (*ibid.*).

Rebbe Nachman made it very clear that this sensitivity is not simply a natural gift that some are born with and others not. It is something one has to work on. The Rebbe said, "When I first began, I asked God to let me feel the pain and suffering of others. Sometimes a person would come to me and tell me his troubles but I would feel absolutely nothing. But I prayed to God that I should feel this Jewish suffering. Now I feel the other person's suffering even more than he does!" (*ibid.*).

Moreover, this acute sensitivity is not something only tzaddikim are required to have. Rebbe Nachman insisted that all of us should cultivate it. "You should be able to feel another person's troubles in your own heart. This is especially true when many are suffering. It is possible to have a clear intellectual understanding of another person's anguish and still not feel it in your heart. If you don't feel it, you should strike your head against the wall! *You should strike your head against the walls of your heart.* This is the meaning of the verse '*Know* this day and put it into your *heart* that HaShem is God...' (Deuteronomy 4:39). You must bring the realization from your mind to your heart. Undertand this well. This is what is meant by 'Hezekiah turned his face to the wall' (Isaiah 38:2). The face he turned was his awareness, bringing it inside the walls of his heart. For a person's true face is his mind, which illuminates the face from within" (*Rabbi Nachman's Wisdom* #39).

It is significant that Rebbe Nachman connects the idea of bringing understanding from the head into the heart with King Hezekiah's turning his face to the wall, an act that encapsulates the Torah healing pathway in its entirety (see p. 17). Literally, Hezekiah's turning to the wall means that he turned aside to pray. He was sick, and he was praying for his own recovery — and certainly anyone who is sick should try to break through the walls and barriers in his own heart in order to emerge from his spiritual exile and heal. Bringing deeper knowledge and awareness of God into the heart is thus one of the central themes in "*Sound the Shofar — Dominion,*" where it is presented as the key to the redemption of prayer, which makes it possible to channel healing without the need for medicines (*Likutey Moharan* II, 1:5-8, see above pp. 246ff.).

But breaking down the blockages in the heart is a task not only for the sick but also for those who are healthy, who are charged with the responsibility of caring for the sick, visiting them and praying for their recovery (see Inset). As we have seen, this applies to all of us at one time or another since we are all commanded to carry out the mitzvah of *bikur cholim*. Empathy with the sick person is an essential part of this mitzvah. Bringing *da'at* into the heart so as to "know this day and put it into your heart that HaShem is God" means more than simply cultivating an awareness of God "out there," as it were. Equally important, it involves recognizing the Godly sparks within each and every one

---

I am the obstacle!

Rebbe Nachman told one of his leading followers, R. Yudel, that praying for a friend with troubles keeps a person from arrogance. R. Yudel said, "But it would seem that, on the contrary, I would just become more arrogant. If I'm praying for my friend, the implication is that I am more important than my friend!" The Rebbe answered with a story:

"There was a king who was angry with his son and sent him away. Afterwards, the prince placated his father, who agreed to have him back. The same thing happened several times, until at last the king was so angry that not only did he send his son away, but he also told one of his ministers that if the prince were to come along wanting to placate him, the minister should not allow him to enter. The minister obeyed, but he saw how much the prince was suffering because of not being able to get into his father to placate him. The minister realized that the king was also suffering, and he said to himself, 'Surely *I* am the cause of all this since I am the barrier between them. I myself will go to the king and beg him to forgive the prince and allow him back.' The minister did so, and the king immediately agreed.

"The meaning of the story is obvious. Whenever a friend of ours is suffering, physically or spiritually, we should say, 'Without doubt *my* sins are the cause of all this. The Holy One, blessed be He, constantly desires to bestow blessings of goodness upon His children. But my sins are a barrier holding all this back. The solution is for *me* to plead with the King on behalf of my friend.' When a person thinks like this, he will certainly not come to arrogance because he knows that the only cause of his friend's deficiency, spiritual or material, is the screen he himself has erected between his friend and the Holy One, blessed be He" (*Tzaddik* #447).

of His creatures, seeing and *feeling for* each one as a unique individual with his or her supreme value. This is why Rebbe Nachman gives such emphasis in "*Sound the Shofar — Dominion*" to the rabbinic teachings never to look down on other people and not to judge them until you truly understand their situation (*ibid. #10 & #14, pp. 260ff. & 272ff.*).

The good points

Who *is* this person? What has made him the way he is? Where is the good in him? How can I connect with it? The teachings on human connection in "*Sound the Shofar — Dominion*" are essentially an elaboration of the pathway Rebbe Nachman taught in "*Azamra — I will sing!*" (*Likutey Moharan* I, 282; see pp. 79f.). Searching for the good points in all people and judging them positively is more than a mere cognitive stance, a mode of viewing other people that need not necessarily affect the way we actually behave towards them. On the contrary, the sensitivity we cultivate to the divine sparks in people must suffuse every facet of our relationships with them, governing, for example, the things we talk about, the activities we share, etc. The way we relate to people has a decisive effect on the way they relate to themselves. Rebbe Nachman said: "By finding even a modicum of good in another person, you *really do elevate him* and you can actually bring him back to God!" (*Likutey Moharan* I, 282).

While the need to search for people's good points applies in all of our relationships in life, it is of special importance in our caring relationships with the sick. In the medical

> ### From a letter of the Lubavitcher Rebbe to a doctor
>
> "...You surely follow the practice of many other God-fearing doctors who, when patients turn to them for medical advice, take the opportunity to give them encouragement to heal the soul. Everyone needs this, particularly in this orphaned generation... especially since we see with our own eyes that an improvement in a person's spiritual health quite literally leads to an improvement in physical health..." (*Refuah Shelemah* pp.24-5).

paradigm the sick person is treated primarily as a *patient*, a passive victim of an illness who must now passively submit to treatment in order to be cured. But this can encourage the patient to evade his own responsibilities and simply wait to be cured by medicine. However, where self-neglect, bad habits, negative traits and the like have played a part in the development of illness, true healing requires a willingness to change on the part of the sick person himself. In addition to receiving any necessary medical treatment, he must also be ready to take his own life in hand and make the adjustments in outlook, attitudes, lifestyle and behavior that are needed for long-term balance and health.

One of the primary aims of those involved in care of the sick at any level should thus be to strengthen the sick person spiritually in order to help him overcome the backlog of discouragement, demoralization and depression that may be standing in the way of his trying to make changes and take new initiatives. In addition to providing for the patient's medical and other physical needs, a central focus of care of the sick must therefore be to help him attain deeper self-understanding and spiritual insight and assist him in developing his motivation and marshaling the inner resources he needs for new growth. This is precisely what searching for and working with the "good points" —

the spiritual growth-points — is all about. The very phrase *bikur cholim*, "visiting the sick," contains an allusion to the search for the good points, because the root meaning of the word ביקור (*bikur*) is "searching."

A full exploration of the applications of Rebbe Nachman's teaching on searching for the good points in human relationships in general and in care of the sick, therapy, rehabilitation and counselling, etc. in particular would require a complete study on its own. When it comes to practice, the essential challenge is to maintain our sensitivity to the feelings of others even when we are

With happiness you can give life

"With happiness you can give a person life. A person might be in terrible agony and not be able to express what is in his heart. There is no one to whom he can unburden his heart, so he remains deeply pained and worried. If you come to such a person with a happy face, you can cheer him and *literally give him life*. This is a great thing and by no means an empty gesture" (*Rabbi Nachman's Wisdom* #43).

under sustained pressure. Care of the sick and *bikur cholim* are such great mitzvot because of the enormous difficulty of fulfilling them adequately. Caring for a sick child, a spouse, a parent, a dear friend or a neighbor can be extremely draining, especially when the illness is protracted or where the burden of extra duties is made even weightier by emotional or financial problems. For the professional doctor or healthcare worker, simply being faced with a never ending succession of suffering, anxious, lonely and demanding patients can itself be overwhelming, causing many to seek refuge behind a thick exterior of brisk matter-of-factness and superficial banter, rather than to risk opening the gates of human feelings.

In asking us to "know *today*" and turn our heads to the walls of our hearts, Rebbe Nachman is asking us to make the effort to remember at all times that those in our care are not just "patients" but real live people. Each one is a *living soul*, an entire universe with a past, a future, and an infinitely subtle, complex mesh of thoughts and tender feelings. Being empathic does not necessarily have to consume tremendous amounts of time. All that's needed is to take that second or two to try to put ourselves in the other person's place. Instead of merely throwing out a jaunty "How are you today?" without really wanting to hear the full answer, let us have the courage to make a human commitment by taking that extra moment to smile, to look kindly into this person's eyes, to make a connection, and to say, even without words: "I am here for you. I will support you. I won't try just to impose my own categories on you. I am willing to open myself to who *you* are and what *you* need."

All this can be accomplished even while delivering a tray of food, tidying around the bed or taking the patient's temperature or blood pressure.... Healing is more than just a matter of conducting tests and prescribing medicines. With all the science and technology, healing will always remain an art — the art of rebuilding the sick person by uncovering his growth points so that he can take his destiny into his own hands and live. And the only way to build anyone is through a sensitive, caring *human* relationship.

3. Children's Illness

How do Rebbe Nachman's teachings on healing apply to children? It is quite clear that Rebbe Nachman saw illness in adults as a call for spiritual arousal on the part of the person who is ill, which is obviously not relevant when a baby or a very small child is sick, God forbid. But the rabbis taught that little children sometimes suffer illness because of the sins of the generation (*Shabbat* 33b, see Inset on next page), and this indicates that children's illnesses should certainly be taken as a call for serious thought and introspection on the part of their parents and other adults around them and the community in general.

Nothing can be more agonizing than the anguish of parents when a dear child is ill. Which father or mother wouldn't rather take the illness and suffering upon themselves if only they could? It would be distasteful in the extreme to make glib moralistic judgments about the meaning of tragedies like stillbirths, crib deaths, deformities, serious children's illnesses and deaths. Why such things happen involves some of the most deeply hidden secrets of God's providence, and none of us is qualified to "utter that which we do not understand, things too wonderful for us, which we do not know" (see Job 42:3).

"Why are little schoolchildren stricken with illness? When there are Tzaddikim in the world, they suffer for the sins of the generation. But when there are no Tzaddikim, the little children suffer for the sins of the generation. This is hinted at in the verse, 'If you do not know where to graze, O fairest of women, go in the footsteps of the sheep and pasture your tender kids by the shepherds' tents (משכנות, *MiShKeNot*)' (Song of Songs 1:8): the little kids are taken as a pledge (ממושכנין, *meMuShKaNin*) instead of the shepherds" (*Shabbat* 33b).

Rebbe Nachman alluded to such mysteries of providence in speaking about the illnesses that struck his own small children and grandchildren (see pp.70ff.). When his baby Shlomo Ephraim was sick with tuberculosis, Rebbe Nachman indicated that it was the very preciousness of the boy's soul that aroused the jealousy of the *sitra achra*, the forces of unholiness, which attacked the boy to prevent a great spiritual light from being revealed in the world. This was perhaps one of the main reasons why the Rebbe put so much effort into praying for the boy and begged his followers to do the same. The only way to fight such an attack by the forces of evil is by concerted efforts to strengthen the power of holiness in the world through prayer and good deeds.

Even if certain cases of children's illnesses can be viewed in a moralistic perspective, they should not be seen as requital for some flaw or shortcoming so much as a call to the parents, family, friends and other members of the community to make supreme efforts in prayer, acts of kindness and charity, Torah study and the like. When a child's life is in the balance, God forbid, it is a most sombre reminder of the preciousness of life. "Generation to generation will praise Your works" (Psalms 145:4): each and every Jewish soul comes into the world to know and recognize God in a new way. Each soul is itself a unique revelation of God. It is this revelation that the *sitra achra* fights so hard to prevent — and this can only be countered by maximizing the revelation of God's sovereignty through prayer, Torah and mitzvot (see *Tefilin* pp. 81ff.).

Prayer

In the case of Rebbe Nachman's Shlomo Ephraim, even the many prayers did not bring him physical healing. But when the young son of the Rebbe's follower, Reb Shimon, was ill, although the decree seemed to have been sealed, his mother's prayers not only saved him but secured him a very long life (p. 70). The Rabbis taught that "God craves the prayers of Israel" (*Chullin* 60b). It is as if in certain cases God may send affliction in order to squeeze the most passionate prayers from the very depths of the heart in order to bestow life. For it is prayer that gives birth to the soul and brings it to life. The prayers of Abraham and Sarah actually brought into being the souls of the converts they made in Charan (Genesis 12:5, and see *Likutey Moharan* I, 31:6). And so too the earnest prayers of parents, family, friends and members of the community for sick babies and children can actually win them life.

As we have seen, in cases of children's sickness in Reb Noson's family, he relied on prayer alone, refusing to call in doctors (pp. 210ff.). Given the enormous advances in medicine since Reb Noson's time, it would today be the height of irresponsibility not to have a sick child treated medically when necessary. This does not mean that every minor headache, tummy-ache or temperature should be smothered with medications. Growing numbers of orthodox practitioners recognize that indiscriminate use of antibiotics and other medicines may be harmful, and many treatments that were routine less than a generation ago have been abandoned because of the long-term damage they caused. The Rambam's sage advice to minimize the use of medicines as far as possible (see pp. 40-1 and p.321) applies to children just as it does to adults.

Nevertheless, even apparently mild problems in children must be evaluated with the utmost care, as neglect can sometimes cause irreparable damage. As we have seen, Rebbe Nachman himself gave his endorsement to preventive medicine by insisting that his followers have their children vaccinated (pp. 203ff.). The Rebbe's caveat when going to doctors to be sure to seek out the very best most certainly applies to medical treatment for children. Having a child treated when necessary shows no lack of faith as long as we keep in mind at every step that it is not the doctor who gives life or health, but only God. We must put our faith in Him, not in a particular doctor, medicine or treatment.

Education

Deeper faith and increased efforts in prayer and mitzvot are without doubt the proper response to children's illness for the parents and other adults. But what about for the child? Obviously this depends very much on the age and maturity of the child. As in the case of adults, there is no wisdom in waiting for illness to strike before giving attention to the spiritual dimensions of healthcare. As part of children's Torah education parents and teachers should make every effort to inculcate in them the preciousness of God's gift of good health by pointing out the wonders of human bodily functioning and teaching them to take proper care of themselves. The emphasis should be on protecting health so as to be able to keep the Torah and serve God.

All this can be conveyed in simple ways even to children three or four years old. Example is the best of all teachers, and parents who live sensibly and moderately, avoiding smoking and other forms of abuse, are doing their children a lifelong service. Accustoming children to a wholesome diet from an early age will help them be content with a minimum of cookies, candies, etc., which should be given as special treats rather than being allowed to become a regular component of their diets. Children should be provided with every possible opportunity to enjoy fresh air and exercise.

As a child matures it is right and proper to talk to him seriously about the *takhlit* — the purpose of life. We have seen how Rebbe Nachman spoke to a nine-year-old boy about life and death (p. 68). This goes contrary to the widespread present-day tendency to "protect" children from knowledge of death and dying and other realities of our existence, even though most children are exposed to a constant diet of violence and murder through the media. This may be part of the reason for the widespread irresponsibility and often callous disregard for human life and dignity among many segments of contemporary youth. "Train a child in the way he should go" (Proverbs 22:6). With due sensitivity it is possible to imbue children and adolescents with a sense of responsibility and a strong feeling for the purpose of life, which can only help them appreciate life's preciousness, and encourage them to take full advantage of the opportunities they are given to fulfil themselves through Torah and mitzvot.

The Torah educational establishment fully understands the importance of teaching youth the basics of prayer, blessings, Shabbat observance, festivals and other regular mitzvot. It is therefore surprising that the mitzvah to "take care of yourself" (Deuteronomy 4:9) is widely ignored in religious educational institutions — this despite the fact that "bodily health and well-being are part of the path to God... and one must therefore avoid anything that may harm the body, and cultivate healthy habits" (*Mishneh Torah, Hilkhot De'ot* 4:1). Parents and teachers who make a serious effort to teach children and adolescents the basic principles of healthcare, hygiene, diet and exercise are obviously providing them with a sound basis for a lifetime of health, especially if they also make sure to teach them the principles of spiritual healthcare — faith, simchah and the vital embrace of Torah and mitzvot.

The best way for parents to convey to their children that illness and healing are from God is through the way they conduct themselves in practice. Even in the case of minor problems, one should make a point to say to a child, "Let's pray to HaShem for *refuah shelemah*." This can be done even while putting on a bandaid or before giving the child a spoonful of cough syrup. It leaves a lifelong impression on a child when he sees that in cases of fever or other problems the parent does not merely run to the medicine cabinet or rush off to the doctor but also takes a moment to give charity, say some words of prayer, recite a few psalms and ask "What mitzvah should we be paying more attention to?" When taking a child to a doctor, a parent should emphasize that the doctor is only God's agent, and that even when using medicine as a means of healing we must have faith in God and put our main efforts into teshuvah, Torah and mitzvot.

When caring for a sick child, raising the child's spirits in whatever way appropriate is just as important as it is in the case of adults. The key to healing is simchah, especially the joy of Torah and mitzvot. Sick children of sufficient maturity should be encouraged to pray and carry out other mitzvot as far as possible, because "they are our life and length of days," and children's prayers and mitzvot are very precious. In conversation with the child one should tell stories about the tzaddikim and discuss other Torah topics in accordance with the age of the child. Children who are faced with a life-threatening illness, God forbid, often have a deeper awareness of their situation than some of the adults around them imagine. Where the child wishes to speak about life and death matters in his or her own way, it is proper to respond and do everything possible to enhance the child's awareness of God's protective presence and kindness.

May God send health and healing, spiritual and physical, to all the sick children of Israel. And just as Elisha placed the staff of faith on the face of the son of the Shunamite and breathed life into him (Kings II, 4:31-4), so may the Tzaddikim breathe new life and strength into all the souls of Israel and bring about the fulfilment of the prophecy of Zechariah (8:4): "Old men and old women will again sit in the streets of Jerusalem, every man with his *staff* in his hand because of the many days of his life." Amen.

Prayers

Prayers

1. Simchah

Likutey Tefilot II, 21, based on Likutey Moharan II, 24 (see p. 123f.)

Ruler of the Universe, loving God, Master of happiness and joy: in Your presence there's only joy and no sorrow. "Glory and majesty are before Him, might and delight are in His place" (Chronicles I, 16:27). Kind and loving God, help me to be happy at all times. Your Tzaddikim have taught us that joy is the key to holiness, while gloom and depression are bound up with unholiness, which is the opposite of what You desire. A Jew comes to holiness through joy, and the basic reason why people are far from You and succumb to material cravings is because of sadness and depression.

But You know how far from true joy I am after everything that's happened in my life. I have therefore come before You, loving God, to appeal to You to help me find happiness. Show me the path to follow. Teach me a way to turn my very sadness and depression into joy. Don't let anything throw me into depression. Let me always keep to this path of joy and make every effort to turn my sadness into happiness. Don't let depression have any hold over me at all.

The good points

If at any time I begin to become depressed over the wrong I've done in my life, let me rejoice over the fact that You still love me. You've kept me alive, and You've not let me slip completely. You made me a Jew. I have the merit of carrying out many great mitzvot every single day. I wear tzitzit and put on tefilin. I recite the *Shema* and celebrate Shabbat and Yom Tov. I listen to the shofar on Rosh HaShanah, I fast on Yom Kippur. On Sukkot I sit in the sukkah and take the lulav and etrog. On Pesach I eat matzah... besides all the other holy mitzvot that we, Your holy People — even the very least of us — are constantly performing. You've shown us such goodness and kindness in

415

crowning us with these holy crowns. Despite our deep exile and the separation caused by our sins, Your love is still bound to us.

Even someone on my level has the privilege of carrying out numerous mitzvot every day, and this is certainly a good reason to be happy and turn depression into joy. Maybe I'm distant from God and suffer from all kinds of deficiencies. Even so, the fact is that I still have some connection with these awesomely holy mitzvot. Every day I unify Your Name. I crown myself with the "diadem of glory" — the tefilin — and clothe myself in the tzitzit, and carry out the other precepts of the King. No matter how hard that voice inside me tries to depress me with negative thoughts about my sins, I'll tell myself that, on the contrary, this is precisely why I should be happy, considering that someone as distant as I am has the privilege of touching such great holiness. "I've woken up, and I'm still with You" (Psalms 139:18). "You've crushed us in a place of jackals, and covered us with the shadow of death. But we have not forgotten the Name of our God or stretched out our hands to a strange god..." (Psalms 44:20-21). "I am my Beloved's and my Beloved is mine" (Song of Songs 6:3).

Ruler of the entire Universe, Joy of Israel: "Bring joy to the soul of Your servant, for to You, God, I lift my soul" (Psalms 86:4). Bring me to follow the path of true joy until I take hold of my very sadness and depression and turn them into happiness. Let me make every effort to keep happy at all times and fill myself with the holiness of the Ten Kinds of Melody, which encompass all holy joy. Let me make it a habit to put myself in a joyous mood at all times by singing happy songs. I'll sing out and rejoice in God with songs, praises, gladness and melody, and always be happy. And through this, put a spirit of holy vitality into the ten pulses that beat within me, so as to guard and protect me from any kind of pain and illness, physical or spiritual, because the root cause of all of them is sadness and depression.

Send us healing

Heal me and give me life by always sending me joy and happiness, for they are the key to healing all the illnesses in the world. Joy is the foundation of life. Heal us, God, and we will be healed, save us and we will be saved, for You are our praise! Heal all our illnesses and cure all our pains and sores. Heal our souls and our bodies. Give me the strength to keep happy at all times. Let me use every possible means to bring joy into my heart, whether by thinking about my good points, through playfulness and joking, or even by putting on a *show* of being lighthearted when necessary. For joy is the foundation of holiness and the root of man's vitality.

Loving God, Creator of all cures and remedies, Master of wonders: put joy into my heart. You know the hidden recesses of the heart, and You know the many different tricks the evil inclination and its troops use to try to throw us down into depression. One of their ways of deceiving us is by sending us seemingly righteous thoughts about the enormity of our sins. But this is nothing but a trap, because You've already taught us that for this we should set aside time each day to speak to You in our own words and express our regret over the past. Then, for the rest of the day, we should make every effort to be happy, even if we have to force ourselves, since joy is the gateway to holiness. For Your Name's sake, teach us the path of life. Help us see how to attain joy at all times. Bring me to carry out Your statutes and commandments joyously, with a heart flowing with appreciation of Your abundant goodness.

The dance of the tzaddikim

Let me experience the future joy and see the dance-circle You will make for the tzaddikim in time to come, when each one will point with his finger saying, "This is God!" as it is written, "And he'll say on that day, 'See, this is our God, we hoped in Him and He has saved us; this is God, we hoped in Him: let us delight and rejoice in His salvation'" (Isaiah 25:9). "And God's redeemed will return and come to Zion with glad song, with eternal joy on their heads. They will attain joy and gladness, and misery and sorrow will flee" (*ibid.* 35:10). "For you'll go out in joy and arrive in peace. The mountains and hills will break out before you in glad song, and all the trees of the field will clap hands" (*ibid.* 55:12). "And you'll draw water in joy from the fountains of salvation" (*ibid.* 12:3). "For God has comforted Zion, He has comforted all her ruins and made her wilderness like Eden and her desert like God's garden. Joy and gladness will be found there, thanksgiving and the sound of song" (*ibid.* 51:3). "Rejoice in God and exult, you righteous, and shout for joy, all you who are upright in heart" (Psalms 32:11).

*

2. Healing through prayer

from *Likutey Tefilot* II, 1
based on "*Sound the Shofar — Dominion*"
(LikuteyMoharan II, 1, see pp. 237-78)*

Compassionate God, don't let my days and years go to waste. Be kind to me and bring me to perfect prayer. Let me put my whole heart and soul into all my prayers. Prayer stands on the very summit of the universe: don't let me ever think of it as unimportant. Don't let me pray out of habit. Let my every prayer be an appeal for Your love and kindness. Don't let me feel my prayers to be a burden. Let me make every possible effort to concentrate all my thoughts and feelings on the prayers in the proper way. Heavenly Father, You know how hard it is for me to open my mouth to pray. My prayers are full of flaws. Kind and loving God, help me free and redeem prayer from the long, bitter exile we are suffering because of our sins. Have pity! Have mercy! Send help quickly — not for my sake but for the glory of Your Name. I'm like a dumb person: open Your mouth to me. "God, open my lips and my mouth will declare Your praise" (Psalms 51:17). Make my heart ready, and turn Your ear to me.

Loving God, Who is enthroned upon the praises of Israel: let my prayers always flow from my mouth, and fulfil the verse, "'Peace! peace to the one who is far off and the one who is near,' says God, who creates the fruit of the lips, 'and I will heal him'" (Isaiah 57:19). Send me healing through the strength of my prayers alone. All healing comes about only through the "Word of God" — through the prayers and supplications of the tzaddikim, the Masters of Prayer, who pray for the Jewish People and conciliate You in order to channel healing into the world. For all the healing herbs and plants in the world and all the planets and stars appointed over them receive their power from the angels above them. And they in turn receive their power from angels above *them*. The angels on each level receive and borrow from those above, and so it is from level to level, until they all receive their power from the great "Lender," the Master of Prayer who has attained the Word of God, which is the root of the entire creation from beginning to end, as it is written, "With the word of God the heavens were made and with the breath of His mouth all their hosts" (Psalms 33:6).

It is therefore impossible to receive any kind of healing except through prayer and supplication. Grant that I should know this with complete truth and perfect faith. Compassionate God, let us channel healing to ourselves and the whole Jewish People through the Word of God — through prayer alone.

Healing power in everyday food

Help us draw all kinds of healing powers into everything in the world — into bread and water and all the different kinds of food and drink You send to our mouths for us to eat and drink. No matter what they are, channel into them the healing powers of all the various curative herbs and plants, so that we will have complete healing any time we need it through bread and water alone. Carry out Your promise — "And He will bless your bread and water, and I will remove sickness from among you" (Exodus 23:25). Lovingly send us complete healing, physically and spiritually. Heal all of our two hundred and forty-eight limbs and three hundred and sixty-five arteries and veins. For You alone know all our pains and illnesses — those we know about and those that are hidden from us....

Help us totally cleanse ourselves of all forms of idolatry, immorality and bloodshed (despising other people), in order to attain perfect prayer. Help us pray in a way that is fitting, until our prayers become a channel for complete healing for ourselves, our children and all the Jewish People [and especially (...) the son/daughter of (...)]. For You are God, the King, the faithful and compassionate Healer. Grant that through our prayers all the herbs and plants of the field will with one accord put all their powers back into the words of our prayers, which are the "Word of God," their supreme Source. Put the healing powers of all the different herbs and plants into our prayers, fill them with goodness, and let us offer them to You as a sweet savor so that all the different herbs and plants will return their healing powers to their supreme Source. Let us thereby channel all the healing powers in the world into bread and water and all our other regular food and drink. Let all our pains and ailments be completely healed by ordinary means without our having to resort to healers or doctors at all. You Yourself in Your glory send us perfect healing, as it is written, "For I, God, am your Healer" (Exodus 15:26).

Send healing before illness strikes

Send us complete healing long before our illnesses manifest themselves, when they're still in their earliest stages and concealed within us without anyone knowing about them. For You alone know everything hidden within us. Kind and loving God: have pity on us and send the remedy before the blow.

As soon as an illness starts developing, send us healing before it spreads. You alone have the power to heal us, for we have no way of healing our wounds and illnesses — not when they're still concealed, and not when they start manifesting themselves.... We depend on You alone, and we are waiting and hoping for You to heal us. For You are the faithful Healer, the true Healer, the free Healer....

Grant that we should receive all forms of healing only through prayer. Show the world the truth, that there is no healing in the world except through prayer. Let us fulfil the verse, "And He said, If you will listen carefully to the voice of HaShem your God and do what is right in His eyes and give ear to His commandments and keep all His statutes, I will put none of the diseases upon you that I have put on the Egyptians, for I, God, am your Healer" (Exodus 15:26).

*

3. Sweeten the bitterness

from *Likutey Tefilot* I, 27, based on *Likutey Moharan* I, 27

Master of the World! Master of the entire Universe! "Heal me, God, and I will be healed, save me and I will be saved, for You are my praise!" You know the bitterness of my heart, the bitterness of my terrible wounds, and the bitterness of my crushed soul. My soul is very bitter! What is there to compare with my bitterness? Bitterer than death; bitterer than wormwood and gall; bitterer than all the bitterness in the world.

Master of the World: You know how weak my soul is as a result of the terrible damage I've done through my evil deeds and the wounds and diseases I have caused it. My soul is so weak that there isn't a single remedy in the world that can help me. And even if in Your compassion You can find some remedy that will help me, it will be impossible for me to bear the bitterness of the remedy needed to heal my wounds. I can't even bear the bitter purgatory involved in making amends for the damage caused by a single bad thought, let alone for such a multitude of evil thoughts and sins. If I tried to give an account of even the tiniest portion of my misdeeds in the space of a single day, I'd run out of time. Even the days that for me would be considered "good" are marked by a constant succession of lapses every single moment, not to speak of the bad days I've had. *Oy! Oy! Oy!* What can I say? The bitterness of my soul reaches the very heavens! Who can imagine the pain of my soul?

Master of the World! You know that even if You deal with me with the same compassion that You deal with all Your creatures, and throw all my sins "behind Your back," and send me only the slightest amount of bitterness as a remedy, it will still be impossible for me to bear it. For my soul is so sick, and the bitterness necessary to heal it so great, that I cannot bear even the tiniest fraction of it owing to my innumerable sins and transgressions. "You desired to lift my soul out of the pit of destruction and decay," and You have thrown all my sins "behind Your back." You have sent me the remedy needed to bring peace to my soul with only the barest minimum of bitterness, according to my capacity. Even so, even this little amount of bitterness is very hard for me to bear, because I am so weak, sick, spiritually hurt and confused that I cannot bear any bitterness at all.

Bring me to the Tree of Life

For this reason I've come to submit my request to You, my God and God of my fathers, "Great in counsel and mighty in action... Who performs great deeds that cannot be fathomed, miracles and wonders without number." For You nothing is impossible. "You can do everything, and no purpose is withheld from You." You are the true, faithful and compassionate Healer, and everything is in Your hand. "In Your hand is power and strength, and it is in Your hand to make great and to give strength to all." Who can tell You what to do? Therefore "I will stand at my post" and cry and shout to You incessantly, until You show me favor and sweeten the bitterness of my cure and show me the Tree of Life with which to sweeten the bitterness of the evil waters.

Compassionate God: remove every kind of bitterness from me, and give me strength, power and courage to bear with love the little bitterness that I must inevitably suffer in order to be healed. Merciful God, minimize the bitterness needed to cure me as far as possible, and quickly send me complete healing spiritually and physically. From afar I can see the infinite mercy with which You treat me at every moment. That is why I am casting my burden upon You alone. Have mercy on me. Protect me and spread Your tabernacle of peace over me. Send perfect healing to all the wounds and diseases of my soul and body. Fulfil in me the verse: "'Peace! peace, to the one who is far off and the one who is near,' says HaShem, who creates the fruit of the lips, and I will heal him."

*

4. Heal our wounds

from *Likutey Tefilot* II, 4. Based on *Likutey Moharan* II, 4
(see Chapter 9, pp. 93ff. and Supplementary Readings p. 433f)

Kind, loving God: Heal us completely from all illness and from all our pains and injuries. Send perfect healing to all the wounds of Your People Israel, physically and spiritually. In the merit of our charity, have compassion on all sick Jews who are suffering because of our many sins. Open their wounds and draw out all the infected fluids and impure blood from them — in the merit of the true Tzaddikim, the holy elders and true Sages, and in the merit of the holiness of the three festivals, "God's appointed seasons, the holy assemblies," which declare and reveal Your supreme Will. Cleanse and purify all the blood in our bodies, so that the blood will circulate in an orderly manner at the proper rate through all our two hundred and forty-eight limbs and three hundred and sixty-five arteries and veins. Shine on us with Your great kindness and close and heal all the wounds and plagues of Your People Israel, so that all Jews will have perfect healing from heaven for all their wounds and injuries. For we put our faith not in human remedies but in You alone. We are waiting and hoping for You to heal us, because You "heal the broken-hearted and bind up their wounds" (Psalms 147:3). Please heal all our wounds, physically and spiritually, for you, mighty God, are the faithful and loving Healer.

*

5. A good sweat

Likutey Tefilot II, 6, based on *Likutey Moharan* II, 6 (see p. 317)

O God and God of our fathers: Let me always be happy. Help me carry out all the mitzvot and other holy actions with all my strength, until I literally sweat while busy with the mitzvah, and so cleanse my blood of all poisons and impurities. Let me thereby overcome the turbidity in the blood caused by the spleen, which is the source of negativity and depression. Let me always be happy, and drive out sadness and depression. Let them have no hold over me at all. Let me only be joyous at all times. Have mercy on me and all the Jewish People. Guard and protect us from all kinds of disease, pain and weakness. Have pity on all Jews who have fallen sick. Cause them to sweat in a healthy way so as to cleanse them of all the poisons and impurities in their blood, and thereby send them perfect healing and bring them to great joy....

*

6. Faith

from *Likutey Tefilot* II, 5, based on *Likutey Moharan* II, 5 (pp. 284-9)

Master of the Universe: Help me elevate my fallen faith and repair all the flaws in my faith. Let me strengthen my faith to the utmost, and believe in You and Your true tzaddikim with strong, firm, clear, pure faith without any doubts or questions at all. Help me channel complete healing to all Jews suffering from sickness [and especially (...) the son/daughter of (...)]. God, please heal him/her spiritually and physically, and heal all our illnesses, pains and wounds. Remove all the terrible plagues "and evil and faithful diseases" (Deuteronomy 28:59) from us and from all the Jewish People for all time. Send complete healing from heaven to all those Jewish souls now suffering from those "terrible plagues" caused by inadequate faith — plagues that cannot be helped by any medicine in the world, not by prayer, ancestral merit, cries or sighs. God, have pity on them and us for Your sake. Do it for Your sake alone, and not for us. You alone know the tragic state we and they are in. You have the power to work awesome miracles. Send them and us complete healing from heaven and remove sickness from our midst. For You are God, the King, the faithful and loving Healer. Our only power is the power of the mouth. Healer of the sick, free Healer: heal us, O God and we will be healed, save us and we will be saved, for You are our praise.

Send the rains in their proper time for life, blessing and abundance. Mercifully cause plants and herbs to grow that will have the power to heal the sicknesses of the Jewish People. Let order reign among the various seeds and plants so that they will grow at the right time and place. Don't let us pick any fruit or herb at the wrong time. Loving God, send a chain of events that will enable everyone to receive whatever he or she needs for genuine healing easily and without effort through everyday food and drink. Send us our food at the correct time and season so that it will contain all the physical and spiritual healing powers each of us needs. For no doctor in the world has clear knowledge of all this except You. You are the Cause of all causes, and You know all that is hidden. "Then your light will break through like dawn and Your healing will quickly spring forth" (Isaiah 58:8).

*

Supplementary Readings

Supplementary Readings

1. The medicine of Torah must be administered softly

Likutey Moharan **I, 164**

Why does the Tzaddik tell stories? It's like when a doctor becomes sick and is forced to put himself in the hands of an outstanding specialist. The sick doctor wants to be given the kind of simple treatment he understands.... But the specialist knows very special remedies which he has to give him. Similarly it may happen that a person comes to the outstanding Sage and Tzaddik of the generation, who is the doctor of the ailments of the soul. The person wants the Tzaddik to give him medicines, i.e. spiritual pathways, in accordance with what he understands. But the Tzaddik has far more exalted medicines which he has to give him.

Sometimes it is necessary to give the patient a certain drug, but if the patient receives it just as it is he will undoubtedly die. Therefore the drug in question must be mixed with other things. Similarly, there are people to whom it is impossible to reveal the inner face of the Torah teachings they need for their healing. For the Torah brings healing, as it is written, "It will be health to your navel" (Proverbs 3:8). But the Torah has two powers: it can be either an elixir of life or a fatal poison, as our Rabbis said: "If a person is deserving, it becomes an elixir of life; if not, it becomes a fatal poison" (Yoma 72b). For this reason, if the person is given the teaching the way it is, he will certainly die, because for him, as someone who is as yet unworthy, it is a fatal poison. It is thus essential to clothe the inner face of the teaching within other Torah teachings. Sometimes this also is too much for the person to bear. The Tzaddik must then clothe his Torah teachings in apparently mundane stories or conversations in order that the person will be able to receive the medicine hidden beneath the surface. For the Torah teaching itself is now clothed within stories and conversations, because it was impossible to give it the way it really is.

*

2. Fever from overeating

Likutey Moharan I, 263

Know that fever can be brought on by overeating. For a person who eats more than he needs is like an animal. One of the marks of human dignity is to eat only what one needs. To eat more than that is to act like an animal, who eats and chews the whole day. This can bring on fever, God forbid. Another thing that can cause fever is when a person accidentally eats food containing sparks that have not yet been sufficiently refined for human consumption and are still fit only for animal consumption (unless the person in question is someone very great, who can skip a complete level and elevate such food to the level of human food).

Fire and Water

For when a person eats like an animal he descends from the level of a man to that of an animal. It is written, "You have caused men to ride over our heads; we've been through fire and water" (Psalms 66:12). "You have caused men to ride over our heads" — i.e. the human level is now *above* this person, because he has fallen below the human level and descended to that of an animal. As a result, "we've been through fire and water." This is the fever, with its alternating heat and cold.

We can now explain the saying of our Rabbis that "when the Holy One, blessed be He, said to the first man, 'And you will eat the grass of the field' (Genesis 3:18), Adam started shaking all over. He said, 'Will I be eating from the same trough as a donkey?' But when he was told, 'By the sweat of your brow you will eat bread' (ibid. v.19), he was relieved and his mind became settled again" (Tanna devei Eliyahu 31). His "shaking all over" is the fever that comes from eating the "grass of the field," which is animal food. "His mind (da'at) became settled again" — because fever signifies a flaw in one's knowledge and awareness of God, da'at. For a person with da'at is able to understand that divine mercy and severity, although apparent opposites, both stem from God's unity, and thus da'at makes harmony between fire and water, whereas in a fever the body temperature is out of balance. The reason why Adam became settled again when he was told, "with the sweat of your brow, etc." is that the remedy for fever is to sweat. That is why "his mind became settled again" — because a settled mind indicates that the fever, which signifies a flaw in da'at, has been cured

*

3. Epidemics

Tzaddik #459

Sometimes an epidemic breaks out, and the way it spreads is that one person catches it from another. There are differences in the way such an illness starts. Sometimes a person becomes afflicted directly because of a heavenly decree, without catching the illness from someone who already has it. In other cases, people become sick indirectly — in the sense that they catch the illness from somebody else. The difference is that in the case of the person who is afflicted directly, the illness manifests itself with its full array of symptoms. Thus, in the case of catarrh, the main symptom is headache, but there are also other symptoms, such as nasal congestion, sneezing, etc. Each of the different symptoms is a sickness in its own right. Whoever is sent the illness directly, as opposed to catching it from others, exhibits all the symptoms in their entirety. However, those who catch the illness from others do not exhibit all the symptoms.

*

4. Faith in God, not in the means

Likutey Moharan I, 62:6

The most serious error of those who are distant from true faith in God stems from the fact that in the main our knowledge of His Godliness is based on inferences we make about levels that are concealed from us on the basis of what we can see in the visible world. As far as they can see, the universe appears to be governed by the stars and galaxies, and as a result they have fallen into errors of various kinds. Some think that everything in the world is governed only by the laws of nature. Others believe it necessary to worship the intermediary. This was the mistake of those who worshiped the Golden Calf: they wanted to make the calf an intermediary between themselves and God, which is why they wanted to make a god "that will go before us" (Exodus 32:1), i.e. an intermediary.

Very many people fall into errors of this kind, making the means through which something comes about into an intermediary between themselves and

God. That is, they believe in God, but they also believe in the intermediary, saying that we have no option but to depend upon a particular means in order to bring something about. For example, they put their faith in their business activities as the *cause* of their livelihood, putting all the emphasis on their work, as if God would somehow not be able to give them a livelihood without their engaging in business. Similarly people put all the emphasis on the means through which healing comes about — the medicine — as if without medicine God does not have the power to heal. This is not so. The Holy One, blessed be He, is the Cause of all causes, and there is no absolute need for any one particular means. Even while resorting to a given means of trying to bring something about, we must believe only in God, and not put our faith in the means.

And when the prayer of the Tzaddik alters the course of events, negating the apparent inevitability of nature, this is visible evidence that God exists and listens to the prayer of the Tzaddik, reshaping the entire natural order. But all this will be in the future, as our Sages said: "The Tzaddikim will bring the dead back to life" and other wonders (*Pesachim* 68a).

*

5. The hands of the angels

Likutey Moharan I, 57:1

Know that from every single word that came from the mouth of the Holy One, blessed be He, an angel was created (*Chagigah* 14a). And every single word was divided into many sparks "as a hammer smashes a rock" (Jeremiah 23:29 and see *Shabbat* 88b), and many, many angels were created corresponding to the multitude of sparks. A word consisting of many sparks created a ruling angel who is chief over all the angels created from the sparks, and these secondary angels make up his camp.

Each individual angel is in charge of something. Even the trees and herbs all have captains over them, as our Sages said: "There isn't a single blade of grass down below that does not have an angel in the world above overseeing it" (*Bereshit Rabbah* 10). Each angel receives vitality from the Word of God (i.e. the Torah) that brought it into being, and in turn sends vitality into the thing it is in charge of, be it a blade of grass or something else. The two powers of the angel—to receive and to dispense—are called "hands." With the "right hand" the angel receives vitality, and with the "left hand" it gives it over, "striking [the blade of grass] and saying 'Grow!'" (*Bereshit Rabbah ibid.*) The blow is in the category of the left hand.

Faith in the Sages

Thus all remedies depend on the Torah, which is "health to all one's flesh" (Proverbs 4:22). For the Torah gives power to the angels, which in turn hand it over to the herbs and plants, whose power to cure comes from the Torah. But when a person lacks faith in the Sages and breaks the enactments they instituted as a protective fence around the Torah, there is no cure for his illness. As the Rabbis commented in one such case, "Perhaps a 'snake of the Rabbis' bit him and there's no cure" (*Shabbat* 110a). For someone who breaks a rabbinic "fence" disempowers the hands of the angels to the exact degree that he veers from the path laid down by the Rabbis. In commanding us to adhere to the teachings of the rabbis, the Torah says, "You must not turn aside from the thing they tell you *either to the right hand or to the left*" (Deuteronomy 17:11). If a person veers from the path of rabbinic teachings to the right, he disempowers the right hand of the angel, and it has no power to receive. If he veers to the left, this disempowers the left hand of the angel, which is then unable to give. When one or other of the hands of the angel is harmed, this person has no cure: the herb he needs for his cure has no healing power, because it has nothing to give it power.

"Every sickness and every plague which is not written in the book of this law" (Deuteronomy 28:61) — this refers to the "death of a Torah scholar," i.e. the death caused to a person by the Torah scholars, in the sense that the illness that strikes a person for contravening the teachings of the Rabbis has no cure, and he dies of the illness. This is the death that comes through "a plague which is not written in the book of this law," because the teachings of the Oral Law, which are not written in the Torah scroll, were entrusted to the Sages, and we are commanded to listen to them. There are cases of people who despise the words of the Sages and do not believe in them, because it seems to them that what the Sages say does not conform with the letter of the Torah. As a result, these people are afflicted with an illness which has no cure, and die from it....

Rectifying the angel's hands

"He draws the mighty with his power; he rises up, and he does not believe in his life" (Job 24:22). The Sages are called "alive," as the Rabbis said (*Berakhot* 18a-b): "'Benayah the son of Yehoyada, the son of a *living man*' (Samuel II, 23:20) — even after death the tzaddikim are called alive." However, when a person does not have faith in the Sages, he falls prey to a sickness so serious that "he does not believe in his life," i.e. nobody believes he will recover from this illness and live, because there is no cure for his wound. The remedy is for him to elevate his fallen faith and believe in the Sages. This is alluded to in the words of the verse in Job: "he rises up, and he does not believe in his life" — i.e. whereas before, he did not believe "in his life," i.e. in the Sages, who are called alive, he now raises up this fallen faith, and through this "he rises up," i.e. he rises out of this illness which was so severe that until now nobody could believe that there could be any remedy for his wound.

And through his very faith he is healed, because through faith in the Sages he repairs the hands of the angels, which are now able to receive power and channel it to the plants and herbs he needs for his cure. This is alluded to in the first words of the above-quoted verse from Job, "He draws the mighty with his power (*kocho*)": the "mighty" are the angels. Now each one has his power (*Ko'aCh*) restored, i.e. the twenty-eight phalanges of the two hands (the numerical value of the letters *Kaph Chet* is 28), and is thus able to send power to everything which is under its command. This person can then be cured, because the words of the Sages rectify the hands.

*

6. Healing from matzah

Likutey Moharan I, 56:8-9

"Matzah brings healing" (*Zohar* II, 183b). The reason is that matzah signifies conflict for the sake of Heaven [the Aramaic root *matza* denotes struggle]. Such conflict eventully leads to enhanced awareness and understanding of God and to greater harmony. This is why matzah brings healing, because harmony and peace bring healing, as it is written, "Peace! Peace to the one who is far off and the one who is close, says God... and I will *heal* him" (Isaiah 57:19). For the main cause of illness, God forbid, is a lack of harmony. The four basic elements making up the body are in conflict, with one element rising up against another. Therefore peace brings healing. And this explains why matzah is called "the bread of the poor" (Deuteronomy 16:3) — because "a person is only poor if he has no awareness of God" (Nedarim 41a). This is the root of illness. Thus Yonadav asked the sick Amnon, "Why, son of the king, are you so *poor*?" (Samuel II, 13:4). Matzah — Godly awareness — is the remedy, and this is why it is called the "bread of the poor" — because it is the remedy for "poverty."

*

7. Healing a wound

Likutey Moharan II, 4:12
(See Chapter 9, pp.93ff. For Reb Noson's prayer based on this discourse, see p. 422)

The Torah contains the remedy for all maladies, and all the ideas discussed earlier in the main body of this discourse (not translated here) are bound up with healing. **Charity** brings healing, as it is written, "To you who fear My name the sun of *charity* will rise, with healing in its wings" (Malachi 3:20). **The holy elder** (*ZaKeN*) — "this one has acquired (*Zeh KaNah*) wisdom" (Kiddushin 32b) — brings healing, as it is written, "The tongue of the *wise* is health" (Proverbs 12:18). **Divine favor** brings healing, as it is written, "God has sent me to bind up the broken hearted... to proclaim a year of *favor*" (Isaiah 61:1-2). And **the act of creation** brings healing, as it is written, "Healing came to the *work* in their hands" (Chronicles II, 24:13).

For the healing of a wound comes about in stages. In the first instance the wound must be opened. Next it is necessary to apply a drawing agency in order to draw out the infected blood and fluids from inside the wound. After this, all the blood must be cleansed until no impurities are left, so that the blood can circulate normally without obstruction. For when the blood circulates normally around the body, when it reaches a spot that is injured, i.e. the place of the wound, the blood is held up there, and all the impurities in the blood collect in that place. That is what normally happens: all the various different kinds of impurities in the blood collect in the place of the injury, and then the blood is obstructed there and is unable to circulate freely. For the blood circulates around the entire body in a fixed manner so many times an hour.

But when there are impurities in the blood, the blood is held up at the injured spot and is unable to circulate properly. This is why it is necessary to cleanse and purify the blood. Finally, the mouth of the wound must be closed.

Each of these stages of healing is accomplished by means of the concepts discussed in the lesson. **Charity** causes the wound to open, as it is written, "Do not close your hand to your needy brother. You must *open up your hand...*" (Deuteronomy 15:7-8). The drawing power is **wisdom**, as it is written, "The power to *draw wisdom* is more precious than pearls (*PeNiNim*)" (Job 28:18) — wisdom draws out that which is hidden from deep, deep inside (*miliPhNey umiliPhNim*) (see *Yerushalmi Shabbat* 10 on Proverbs 3:15). That is, wisdom draws out and removes the damage from deep inside, from all the innermost places.

The three **pilgrim festivals** are when God's **will and favor** are revealed, and it is through this that the blood is cleansed and purified so that it can then circulate normally. The concept of the pilgrim or "foot" festival (*ReGeL*) is bound up with that of the spring known as *Ayn RoGeL* (Kings I, 1:9), which was so called because the launderers used to tread the garments with their *feet* under the water in order to remove the dirt (see *Rashi ad loc.*). That is, through the foot festival, when God's favor is revealed, the blood is cleansed and purified and can then circulate normally. This is why the festival is also called *ChaG*, which has the connotation of circulation, as in "He sits above the circle (*ChuG*) of the earth" (Isaiah 40:22).

The act of creation involves the concept of mercy, for "the world was built with mercy" (Psalms 89:3). All the above stages bring about the flow of God's mercy, which then sustains the world, freeing the Jewish People for their spiritual mission: "and you will be called the priests of God" (Isaiah 61:6). Through the priest, who is the embodiment of mercy, the mouth of the wound is closed, as it is written, "And *the priest will close up the wound*" (Leviticus 13:4). For through mercy (i.e. the priest), the wound is totally closed and healed completely.

*

8. The month of Iyar: A time to heal

Likutey Moharan I, 277

All medicines come from the earth. Therefore during the season when the earth gives forth her bounty and puts strength into all the trees and plants, i.e. during the month of Iyar when the fruits ripen, all medicinal plants have greater power, because the earth then puts strength into them. However at other times, even if one were to take exactly the same medicines, they would not have the same power. This is why people take medicines in the month of Iyar — May.

The principal location is the Land of Israel, because all the different countries receive from the residue of the Land of Israel (*Ta'anit* 10a). The Land of Israel has two aspects: sometimes it is called the Land of Canaan, at other times it is simply called the Land. At times of conflict it is called the Land of Canaan. The name Canaan implies *KaN 'ANI*, "here is a poor person," as the Rabbis commented on the verse (Zechariah 14:21): "And on that day there will no longer be any Canaanite in the house of God" — "there is no one poor here." Canaan thus implies "here is a poor person." The reason is because of conflict, for "one controversy destroys a hundred livelihoods (see *Sh'ney Luchot HaBrit* 142a). Thus the Torah tells us that "there was strife between the shepherds of Abram's cattle and the shepherds of Lot's cattle," and immediately afterwards it is written: "the Canaanite... then lived in the land" (Genesis 13:7). It was because of the strife and conflict that the "Canaanite" was present, and the land is then called the Land of Canaan.

But when there is peace it is simply called the Land, and then "the land gives her bounty" (Psalms 67:7), i.e. the earth gives her power to all the fruits of the land, and all the medicinal plants and herbs have strength. For this reason the Hebrew letters making up the name of the month of Iyar (אייר) are the initial letters of the words א'יבי י'שבו י'בשו ר'גע (*Oyvai Yoshuvu Yeivoshu Roga*), "my enemies will turn back, they will be ashamed suddenly" (*ibid.* 6:11). For this is the season for all the medicines, which are bound up with the concept of peace — "the land gives her bounty" — the opposite of conflict, which is the concept of the Land of Canaan.

The letters making up the name of אייר, Iyar, are also the initial letters in the verse א'ני י' ר'ופאך (*Ani YHVH Rof'ekha*), "I am HaShem your healer" (Exodus 15:26).

*

9. Sweetening pain with divine awareness

Likutey Moharan I, 250

Know that the only reason why we feel pain and suffering is because of a lack of *da'at*, awareness of and connection with God. Someone who possesses *da'at* knows that everything is sent by God, and feels no pain or suffering, because "God gave and God took" (Job 1:21). It is true that there is a certain kind of suffering that is inevitable. This is the pain felt when the soul leaves the body, the pain of illness that comes when the soul begins to separate itself from the body. The soul is so tightly bound to the body in this life that one inevitably feels pain at the moment of separation.

Nevertheless, this suffering is very easy to bear if one knows clearly that everything is under God's providence. And this applies all the more to other forms of pain and suffering, which a person who possesses *da'at* does not feel at all. The main reason why a person feels pain and suffering is because his *da'at* is taken from him so that he will feel the pain.

Exile and the law of nature

The main reason for the suffering of the Jewish People in exile is that they have fallen from *da'at* and attribute everything to nature, chance and fate. This is why they experience pain and suffering. It has come upon them because they live amidst the non-Jews and have learned from them. They see the gentiles in their hour of ascendancy, while the Jews are lowly and despised. As a result the Jews have been influenced by the non-Jews and attribute everything to nature or chance.

This is the only reason for their suffering, because if they had the *da'at* to understand that everything is under God's providence they would feel no pain at all. The truth is that the Jewish People are beyond nature. It is only when they sin that they fall under the law of nature, just like the nations of the world, who are governed by nature and are subject to the stellar influences. The Jews then experience exile and suffering. The main reason for their exile and pain is that they lack *da'at* and attribute everything to nature....

Providence and prayer

In time to come, at the end of history in its present form, "nature" as we think of it will disappear, and the world will be governed only by providence, "For the heavens will vanish away like smoke and the earth will be worn out like a garment" (Isaiah 51:6). What this means is that the natural order as governed by the system of stars and planets will no longer operate as such. The expression "vanish away" in the verse signifies that all the constellations will be thrown into confusion and mixed up. Stellar influences and "fate" will no longer dominate; everything will be governed only by God's providence. The Jewish People will then be in the ascendant....

Through prayer we have the power to channel God's providence in a way that goes beyond nature. Nature may dictate one thing, but prayer has the power to change nature. This is "greatness" — "For what *great* nation is there that has God so near to them as HaShem our God whenever we call on Him?" (Deuteronomy 4:7) This is our greatness — that God hears our prayers and alters the course of nature through His providence. Thus Yehoram, King of Israel, said to Gehazi, "Please tell me the *great* things that Elisha did" (Kings II, 8:4), for "Whatever Elisha did, he accomplished through prayer" (*Megilah* 27a). Thus prayer, which gives us access to the realm of miracles and providence, the very opposite of nature, is "great."

Why do we cry when in pain?

Why do people shed tears when in pain? Tears draw down God's providence. This we learn from the rabbinic interpretation of the verse, "And the clouds return after the rain" (Ecclesiastes 12:2) — "This refers to a person's eyesight, which becomes weaker through crying [literally, the vision *goes* after the tears]" (*Shabbat* 151a). From this we learn that tears take away part of one's vision. The fact that tears weaken a person's eyesight and take part of it away means that the vision is drawn *into* the tears. And this is why people shed tears when in pain. When a person feels pain and suffering, it means he needs God's providence to be saved. This is why people cry — so as to thereby bring down and reveal God's watchful providence. For the providence and vision are drawn *into* the tears. This is why "Hezekiah wept sorely [literally, a *great* weeping]" (Isaiah 38:3) when he fell sick. Through his tears he drew down God's watchful providence, which is the concept of "greatness" and prayer.

*   *   *

Sources and Further Reading

Sources and Further Reading

Advice translated by Avraham Greenbaum, Breslov Research Institute. The classic compendium of Rebbe Nachman's teachings, arranged by subject.

Aleph-Bet Book by Rebbe Nachman, translated by Moshe Mykoff. Rebbe Nachman's collected epigrams containing distilled Torah wisdom on all areas of life.

Alim LiTerufah Collected letters of Reb Noson of Breslov, translated as *Eternally Yours* Vols. 1-4, by Yaakov Gabel, Breslov Research Institute.

Anatomy of the Soul by R. Chaim Kramer, Breslov Research Institute 1995. Study of the spiritual significance of the various body parts and organs.

Ari, Rabbi Yitzchak Luria (1534-72) Leader of the Safed school of Kabbalah and considered by many to be the greatest of all post-talmudic kabbalists.

Avanehah Barzel A miscellany of anecdotes, stories and teachings of Rebbe Nachman collected by Rabbi Shmuel Horowitz (1903-73).

Avi Ezer by Rabbi Shlomo HaKohen of Lissa. Supercommentary on the Bible commentary of Rabbi Avraham Ibn Ezra.

Ayeh? translated by Avraham Greenbaum. Rebbe Nachman's teaching on *"Ayeh?* Where is the place of His glory?" showing how to find hope in even the darkest, most desperate situations and turn them to our own advantage.

Azamra — I will sing! translated by Avraham Greenbaum, Breslov Research Institute. Rebbe Nachman's teaching on searching for the good points, together with selected explanatory material.

Bender, Rabbi Levy Yitzchak (1897-1989) A prominent Breslov elder, he was a student of Reb Avraham Chazan (*q.v.*) and resided in Uman for over twenty-five years before settling in Israel in 1949.

Biblical and Talmudic Medicine by Julius Preuss, translated and edited by Fred Rosner M.D., Hebrew Publishing Company, New York, 1978.

Birkey Yosef by Rabbi Chaim Yosef David Azulai (the *ChIDaH* 1724-1806). Halakhic work.

Biur HaLikutim by Reb Avraham b'Reb Nachman Chazan (1849-1917). Major commentary on *Likutey Moharan*.

Burnstein, Rabbi Avraham of Sokhatchov (1839-1910) Important halakhic authority. Author of *Avney Nezer*.

Burstein, Reb Nachman (b.1934) One of the leading Breslover Chassidim in Jerusalem.

Chafetz Chaim Rabbi Yisrael Meir Kagan of Radin (1839-1933). Outstanding halakhic authority of this century. Author of the classic *Mishneh Berurah* on *Shulchan Arukh, Orach Chaim*.

Chazan, Reb Avraham b'Reb Nachman (1849-1917) Son of Reb Nachman Chazan of Tulchin (*q.v.*). Outstanding leader and scholar of the fourth generation of Breslover Chassidim. Author of *Biur HaLikutim*, a major commentary on *Likutey Moharan*.

Chazan, Reb Nachman of Tulchin (1814-84) Principle disciple of Reb Noson of Breslov (*q.v.*), he was the major leader of the third generation of Breslover Chassidim.

Chinese Medicine by Manfred Porkert, Henry Holt, New York, 1982.

Crossing the Narrow Bridge: A Practical Guide to Rebbe Nachman's Teachings by R. Chaim Kramer, Breslov Research Institute. Detailed guidance on how to apply Rebbe Nachman's teachings in everyday life, covering faith, truth, joy, prayer, meditation, earning a living, bringing up children and many other subjects.

Derekh HaShem, ("The Way of God") by Rabbi Moshe Chaim Luzzatto (1707-46), translated by Rabbi Aryeh Kaplan, Feldheim, Jerusalem/New York 1988. Classic exposition of the fundamentals of Jewish belief by one of the most outstanding kabbalists of all time.

Dessler, Rabbi Eliahu Eliezer (1891-1954) One of the leading teachers of *mussar* in the last generation. Author of *Michtav MeEliahu* (*q.v.*).

Eight Steps to a Healthy Heart by Robert E. Kowalski, Warner Books, New York, 1992.

Eliahu, Rabbi, Gaon of Vilna (1720-1797) Towering Torah scholar of the 18th century.

Etz Chaim ("The Tree of Life") The major classic of Kabbalah, based on the teachings of the Ari (*q.v.*) and written by Rabbi Chaim Vital (*q.v.*).

Eybeshetz, R. Yonatan (1696-1764) Rav of Altona, Hamburg, Vengshel and later of Prague. Author of *Kraiti uFlaiti* and other works.

Feinstein, Rabbi Moshe (1895-1986) Outstanding 20th century halakhic authority.

Fiftieth Gate, Vols 1 & 2 by Avraham Greenbaum. Ongoing translation of Reb Noson's *Likutey Tefilot* (*q.v.*).

Gaon of Vilna see *Eliahu, Rabbi*.

Garden of the Souls: Rebbe Nachman on Suffering by Avraham Greenbaum, Breslov Research Institute. Rebbe Nachman's discourse on the "Master of the Field" and other teachings on the meaning of suffering.

Goldstein, Rabbi Nachman (b'Reb Zvi Aryeh) of Tcherin (1825-94) Outstanding leader and scholar of the third generation of Breslover Chassidim. Author of *Parpara'ot LeChokhmah*, a major commentary on *Likutey Moharan*.

Hanhagat HaBri'ut ("Guide to Good Health") see *Rambam*.

Healing Heart, The by Norman Cousins, Avon Books, New York, 1984.

Hishtapkhut HaNefesh see *Outpouring of the Soul*.

Ibn Ezra, Rabbi Avraham ben Meir (1089-1164) Classic Bible commentator.

Jewish Meditation by Rabbi Aryeh Kaplan, Shocken Books, New York. An introduction to some of the main techniques.

Kagan, Rabbi Yisrael Meir see *Chafetz Chaim*.

Keter Shem Tov by Rabbi Aharon b'reb Zvi HaKohen of Apta, Otzar Chassidim (Lubavitch), 5747 (1987). Anthology of teachings and sayings of the Baal Shem Tov, collected from the works of Rabbi Yaakov Yosef of Polonnoye.

Kitzur Shulchan Arukh ("Concise Code of Jewish Law") by Rabbi Shlomo Ganzfried (1804-86). Classic compilation of the basic laws of Jewish life. Available in several translations.

Kli Yakar by R. Shlomo Ephraim ben Aharon (d.1614). Classic commentary on the Torah.

Kokhvey Or by Rabbi Avraham b'Reb Nachman (*q.v.*). A collection of anecdotes, stories and teachings of Rebbe Nachman and his disciples.

Koenig, Rabbi Gedaliah Aharon (1921-80). A leading disciple of Rabbi Avraham Sternhartz (*q.v.*).

Likutey Halakhot by Reb Noson of Breslov. Reb Noson's collected discourses following the order of the *Shulchan Arukh* (*q.v.*), illumining the spiritual meaning of Jewish law in the light of Rebbe Nachman's discourses and other teachings. A monumental work on Breslov thought and Kabbalah.

Likutey Moharan by Rebbe Nachman. The seminal work of Breslover chassidut, consisting of Rebbe Nachman's collected Torah discourses, transcribed by his leading disciple, Reb Noson of Breslov. Several volumes of an authoritative translation with facing punctuated Hebrew text and full explanatory notes is now available from the Breslov Research Institute.

Likutey Tefilot by Reb Noson of Breslov. Collection of Reb Noson's prayers based on Rebbe Nachman's discourses in *Likutey Moharan*. The first forty prayers have been translated in *The Fiftieth Gate* Volumes 1 & 2, by Avraham Greenbaum, Breslov Research Institute.

Likutey Torah, Taamey HaMitzvot Part of the corpus of the teachings of the Ari (*q.v.*) written by Rabbi Chaim Vital (*q.v.*), consisting of a kabbalistic commentary on the Bible and discussions on esoteric aspects of the commandments.

Love, Medicine & Miracles by Bernie S. Siegel, M.D., Arrow, London, 1988.

Magid of Mezritch by R.Y. Klapholtz. Hebrew work about Rabbi Dov Ber, the Mezritcher Magid (1704-72), main leader of the Chassidic movement after the death of the Baal Shem Tov.

Maharsha Rabbi Shmuel Eliezer Aideles of Ostrog (1555-1632). Author of an important commentary on the Talmud.

Medicine in the Crisis of our Time by Arthur Jores, Berne, 1961.

Me'iri, R. Menachem ben Shlomo (1249-1316) Important Talmudic commentator.

Mekhilta The earliest commentary on the Book of Exodus, from the school of Rabbi Yishmael (c. 120 C.E.), often quoted in the Talmud.

Michtav MeEliahu by Rabbi Eliahu Eliezer Dessler (1891-1954). A *mussar* (moralistic) work discussing fundamental Jewish principles. Translated as *Strive for Truth*, Feldheim Publishers, Jerusalem/New York.

Midrash Rabbah The most important collection of midrashim, ranging from pure commentary to homilies, assembled during the earlier gaonic period.

Midrash Shmuel by Rabbi Shmuel ben Yitzchak Uceda (1538-1602). Commentary on *Avot*.

Mishneh Torah see *Rambam*.

Natural Healing through Macrobiotics by Michio Kushi, Japan Publications Inc., Tokyo & New York, 1992.

Noson, Reb, of Breslov (1780-1844) Leading disciple of Rebbe Nachman, he transcribed almost all of his works, and after the Rebbe's death laid the foundations of the Breslov Chassidic movement. His own major works are *Likutey Halakhot, Likutey Tefilot, Alim LiTerufah* and *Yemey Moharnat.* For a full biography, see *Through Fire and Water* by Rabbi Chaim Kramer, Breslov Research Institute.

Outpouring of the Soul (*Hishtapkhut HaNefesh*) translated by Rabbi Aryeh Kaplan, Breslov Research Institute. Collected teachings of Rebbe Nachman on hisbodedus.

Papo, Rabbi Eliezer (1785-1828) Author of the famous mussar (moralistic) work, *Pele Yo'etz (q.v.).*

Parpara'ot LeChokhmah by Rabbi Nachman b'Reb Zvi Aryeh Goldstein of Tcherin (*q.v.*). Major commentary on *Likutey Moharan.*

Peace, Love & Healing by Bernie S. Siegel, M.D., Arrow, London, 1991.

Pele Yo'etz Famous mussar work arranged alphabetically by subject, written by Rabbi Eliezer Papo, 1785-1828.

Praise of Rabbi Nachman translated by Rabbi Aryeh Kaplan. Highlights of Rebbe Nachman's life focussing on his spiritual attainments. Printed in *Rabbi Nachman's Wisdom (q.v.).*

Rabbenu Bachya ben Asher Ibn Halava (d.1340) Rabbi of Saragossa and author of the famous commentary on the Torah bearing his name.

Rabbi Nachman's Stories translated by Rabbi Aryeh Kaplan, Breslov Research Institute. Translation of the stories with masterful in-depth commentary.

Rabbi Nachman's Tikkun translated by Avraham Greenbaum, Breslov Research Institute. The Ten Psalms of Rebbe Nachman's "General Remedy" with translation and full introduction on the significance of the covenant and the ten kinds of melody.

Rabbi Nachman's Wisdom translated by Rabbi Aryeh Kaplan, edited by Rabbi Zvi Aryeh Rosenfeld. Rebbe Nachman's conversations on joy, faith, prayer, meditation and a wealth of other subjects.

Rambam Acronym of Rabbi Moshe ben Maimon, Maimonides (1135-1204). Towering Jewish legal codifier and philosopher, and an outstanding medical authority. Among his major works are his *Commentary on the Mishnah* and the *Mishneh Torah: Yad HaChazakah,* a codification of Torah law. His *Shemonah Perakim* ("Eight Chapters") is on Jewish faith and ethics. Among his extensive medical writings, one of the most important works is *Hanhagat HaBri'ut* ("Guide to Good

Health"), translated as *Treatise on the Regimen of Health* in *Maimonides' Medical Writings* Vol. 4 by Fred Rosner, M.D. published by the Maimonides Research Institute, Haifa, Israel. This volume also includes an annotated translation of the Rambam's *Hilkhot De'ot*, "The Laws of Human Temperaments," Chapter 4 of which explains the basic rules of healthcare.

Ramban Acronym of Rabbi Moshe ben Nachman of Girondi, Nachmanides (1194-1270). An outstanding talmudist, kabbalist and spiritual leader in Gerona, Spain. He wrote a classic commentary on the Torah as well as over fifty other works.

Rashba Acronym of Rabbi Shlomo ben Avraham Aderet (1235-1310). A student of the Ramban (*q.v.*) and an important halakhic authority, he authored commentaries on the aggadot of the Talmud and was one of the major Jewish leaders of his time.

Rashi Acronym of Rabbi Shlomo Yitzchaki (1040-1105).. Author of the most important commentaries on the Bible and Talmud, printed in almost all major editions.

Refuah Shelemah by Rabbi Menachem Mendel Shneerson, the Lubavitcher Rebbe (1902-94), Or Yaakov/Or Zarua Publishing, Kfar Chabad, 1991. Advice and guidance on spiritual and physical health collected from the Rebbe's letters.

Reishit Chokhmah by R. Eliahu de Vidas (1518-92). Encyclopedic work on morality drawing heavily from the *Zohar*.

Restore my Soul translated by Avraham Greenbaum. A highly inspiring collection of extracts from classic Breslov texts on conquering depression and deepening one's faith.

Sefer Charedim by Rabbi Elazar ben Mordechai Azkari (1531-1600). A classic *mussar* work discussing the mitzvot dependent upon the various limbs and organs of the body.

Sefer HaBrit by R. Pinchas Eliahu of Vilna, first printed in 1797. New printing by S. Kraus, Jerusalem, 1990. A compendium of the scientific knowledge of the time (astronomy, geography, physics, chemistry, biology, etc.) together with a presentation of the kabbalistic worldview.

Sefer HaNisraf ("The Burned Book") by Rebbe Nachman. A mystical work that Rebbe Nachman ordered to be burned while he lay sick in Lemberg.

Sefer Yetzirah: The Book of Creation translated by Rabbi Aryeh Kaplan, Samuel Weiser Inc., York Beach, Maine, 1990. One of the earliest and most important mystical works, attributed by some to Abraham and thought to have been written down in Talmudic times or earlier.

Shaar HaMitzvot ("Gate of the Commandments") Fifth of the *Shemonah She'arim* ("Eight Gates") by Rabbi Chaim Vital (*q.v.*) devoted to teachings of the Ari (*q.v.*) on the kabbalistic meaning of the commandments.

Shaar Ruach HaKodesh ("Gate of Holy Spirit") Seventh of the *Shemonah She'arim* ("Eight Gates") by Rabbi Chaim Vital (*q.v.*) devoted to the Ari's kabbalistic meditations relating to the prayer services and rituals.

Shaarey Kedushah ("The Gates of Holiness") by Rabbi Chaim Vital (1542-1620). A kabbalistic moralistic work explaining the purpose of the soul in this world and how to attain *ruach hakodesh* (holy spirit).

Shemirat Haguf veHanefesh Vols. I & II by Y. Y. Lerner, Jerusalem, 1988. A comprehensive study of rabbinic teachings on practices deemed hazardous to the soul and/or the body.

Shevachey HaAri Stories about the birth and life of the Ari, Rabbi Yitzchak Luria (*q.v.*) and his disciples, based on the Introduction to *Emek HaMelekh* by Rabbi Shlomo Shimmel b'Reb Chayim Meinstril.

Shevachey HaBaal Shem Tov ("Praises of the Baal Shem Tov") by Rabbi Dov Baer b'Reb Shmuel Shubb of Linetz. A collection of stories about the Baal Shem Tov and some of his closest followers. The work circulated in manuscript form during Rebbe Nachman's lifetime, and was first printed in Berdichov in 1815.

Shneerson, Rabbi Menachem Mendel (1902-94) The Lubavitcher Rebbe, leader of the Lubavitch (Chabad) Chassidic movement.

Sheney Luchot HaBrit ("The Two Tablets of the Covenant") by Rabbi Isaiah Horowitz (the *SheLaH*) of Prague (1556-1632). One of the great classics of Torah thought, Kabbalah and moralistic teaching.

Shulchan Arukh by Rabbi Yosef ben Ephraim Karo (1488-1575). The standard code of Jewish Law. Divided into four parts: *Orach Chaim* on prayers, blessings, Shabbat and festivals; *Yoreh Deah* on kashrut and other aspects of ritual law; *Even HaEzer* on marriage and divorce; *Choshen Mishpat* on judicial procedure and business law.

Siach Sarfey Kodesh Vols I-VI by Agudat Meshekh HaNachal. Collection of oral traditions about Rebbe Nachman and his followers, including many sayings, stories and anecdotes.

Sternhartz, Rabbi Avraham b'Reb Naftali Hertz (1862-1955) A great-grandson of Reb Noson of Breslov (*q.v.*) and outstanding leader of the fourth generation of Breslover Chassidim. He moved to the Holy Land in 1936. His disciples include many of the major Breslover leaders of the past decades.

Sweetest Hour, The by Avraham Greenbaum. Explains the meaning and purpose of *Tikkun Chatzot*, with complete English translation of the service and guidance as to when and how to say it.

Talmud Compilation of the Oral Torah as taught by the great masters from approximately 50 B.C.E. until circa 500 C.E., redacted by Rav Ashi and Ravina in Babylonia around 505 C.E. It is therefore often referred to as the Babylonian Talmud. (See also *Yerushalmi*.) After the Bible, the most important work on Jewish law and tradition.

Tanna devei Eliahu An early Midrash containing teachings attributed to the prophet Elijah.

Tav Yehoshua ("Joshua's Note") by Rabbi Yehoshua Briskin, Eshkol, Jerusalem, 1978. A compendium of rabbinic lore and teachings on diet, healthcare and *derekh eretz* (good manners), including an alphabetical guide to various foods and their nutritional qualities.

TaZ Acronym of *Turey Zahav* ("Rows of Gold") by Rabbi David ben Shmuel HaLevy (1586-1667). One of the most important commentaries on the *Shulchan Arukh*.

Tikkuney Zohar Part of the Zoharic literature, consisting of seventy chapters discussing the first word of the Torah. From the school of Rabbi Shimon bar Yochai (circa 120 C.E.).

Tikkun HaKlali see *Rabbi Nachman's Tikkun*.

Torat Nathan Edited by Rabbi Nathan Zvi Koenig, Bnei Brak. A digest of commentary material on *Likutey Moharan* derived from the discourses of Reb Noson in *Likutey Halakhot*.

Tzaddik: A Portrait of Rabbi Nachman by Reb Noson of Breslov, translated by Avraham Greenbaum, Breslov Research Institute. Intimate biographical portrait of Rebbe Nachman by his closest disciple, including numerous conversations, information relating to Rebbe Nachman's lessons, and a variety of his sayings, stories, dreams and visions.

Tzemach Tzedek Rabbi Menachem Mendel b'Rabbi Shalom Shachna Shneerson (1789-1866), the third Lubavitcher Rebbe.

Under the Table and How to Get Up: Jewish Pathways of Spiritual Growth by Avraham Greenbaum, Tsohar Publications, 1991. A practical handbook of Jewish spiritual practices.

Vital, Rabbi Chaim (1542-1620) Closest disciple of the Ari (*q.v.*) and leader after him of the Safed school of Kabbalah.

Yalkut Lekach Tov by Rabbi Tovia ben Eliezer HaGadol (1036-1108). Midrashic work incorporating many earlier midrashim. Also known as *Pesikta Zutratha*.

Yalkut Shimoni, or Yalkut compiled by Rabbi Shimon Ashkenazi HaDarshan of Frankfurt (c. 1260). One of the most popular early midrashic collections on the Bible.

Yemey Moharnat by Reb Noson of Breslov. An autobiographical account of his pilgrimage to the Holy Land and other important events in his life. English translation to be published by Breslov Research Institute.

Yerushalmi or Talmud Yerushalmi An earlier version of the Talmud, thought to have been redacted around 240 C.E. by Rabbi Yochanan (182-279) and his disciples in Tiberias. A work of major importance, although considered secondary to the Babylonian Talmud.

Zohar The primary classic of Kabbalah from the school of Rabbi Shimon bar Yochai (circa 120 C.E.), compiled by his disciple, Rabbi Abba.

Indices

Index of teachings discussed in the book

Likutey Moharan Part II

Rabbi Nachman's Stories

Rabbi Nachman's Wisdom

Tzaddik

General Index

We dedicate this book to the memory of our beloved child

הילד ר' יהודה יוסף אליהו חיים ז"ל

בשילחטו"א ר' נחמן ירחמיאל ומרים שרה

Yehudah Yoseph Eliahu Chaim Futterman ז"ל

נלב"ע כ"ח באייר תשנ"ה

.ת.נ.צ.ב.ה.

He brought so much joy into the world in his short life
and his very suffering inspired so many to
greater heights of Torah, prayer, acts of kindness
and ahavas Yisrael

Nachman and Miriam Futterman

In loving memory of my dear father

ר׳ ישראל לייב בן מנחם מענדל הלוי ז״ל

Louis Israel Rosen ז״ל

נלב״ע י״ג בחשון תשנ״ד

d. 28th October 1993

.ת.נ.צ.ב.ה.

who inspired me to follow the ways of HaShem
and to pursue the path of healing

Riphael Avraham Rosen